Books on the events of the early months of 1940 are dominated by the desperate fighting undertaken by the British Expeditionary Force in Northern France and Belgium following the German invasion of May 10th and it is often overlooked that prior to this another British expeditionary force was involved in fierce fighting in Norway. Indeed, the invasion on April 9th saw the first use of airborne troops in the war and was also one of the very few amphibious operations undertaken by the Germans during the Second World War.

It is hoped that Niall Cherry's new two-volume work covering the Allied intervention in Norway 1940 will fill this significant gap. The author provides a detailed account of the German invasion and the Allied reaction, including the land, sea and air battles. This includes such actions as the sinking of HMS *Glowworm* and HMS *Glorious*, the Gladiators on the frozen lakes and Maurice Force, the sacrifice of the Territorial Battalions at Tretten and the Independent Companies, to name but a few.

Volume 2 focuses on the evacuation and further Naval operations including the sinking of HMS *Glorious*. response. As in Niall's previous books, detailed research has been carried out using official reports, war diaries and veterans' accounts, supported by photographs and maps.

Niall Cherry was born in London in 1959 and recalls becoming interested in military history as a schoolboy from watching such classic war films as *'The Battle of Britain'* and *'A Bridge Too Far'*. He later found out that one of his Grandfathers fought in the Great War, serving as a chemical corporal at Loos in 1915 and ended up as a Captain. His father served in the REME in the 1950s and Niall continued in the family tradition by serving in the RAMC. During his time he qualified as a Combat Medical Technician Class 1 and an instructor in First Aid and Nuclear, Biological and Chemical Warfare, ending up as a Senior NCO.

Deeply interested in the major conflicts of the 20th Century, he has visited numerous battlefields including the Western Front, Arnhem, Gallipoli, Normandy and North Africa. He is a long standing member of the Western Front Association, the Military Heraldry Society and 23 Parachute Field Ambulance Old Comrades Association. He also has the honour to be the UK representative for the Society of Friends of the Airborne Museum Oosterbeek, secretary of the Arnhem 1944 Veterans' Club and secretary and a trustee of the Arnhem 1944 Fellowship.

He has now written ten books - *Red Berets and Red Crosses, I Shall Not Find His Equal, Most Unfavourable Ground, With Nothing Bigger than a Bren Gun, Striking Back, Arnhem Surgeon, Tunisian Tales, A Few Vital Hours, Four Days at Arnhem* and *Desert Rise Arnhem Descent.* Since 2000 he has led various groups around battlefields, contributed articles to After the Battle and Battlefields Review and has helped with around 30 books on the airborne forces and the Great War. Niall currently lives in Lancashire and works for BAE Systems in the aerospace industry.

DOOMED BEFORE THE START

THE ALLIED INTERVENTION IN NORWAY 1940

Volume 2
Evacuation and Further Naval Operations

Niall Cherry

Helion & Company

Helion & Company Limited
Unit 8 Amherst Business Centre
Budbrooke Road
Warwick
CV34 5WE
England
Tel. 01926 499 619
Email: info@helion.co.uk
Website: www.helion.co.uk
Twitter: @helionbooks
Visit our blog at blog.helion.co.uk

Published by Helion & Company 2017 Reprinted in paperback 2021
Designed and typeset by Mary Woolley, Battlefield Design (www.battlefield-design.co.uk)
Cover designed by Paul Hewitt, Battlefield Design (www.battlefield-design.co.uk)

ISBN 978-1-914059-09-4

British Library Cataloguing-in-Publication Data.
A catalogue record for this book is available from the British Library.

For details of other military history titles published by Helion & Company Limited contact the above address, or visit our website: http://www.helion.co.uk.

We always welcome receiving book proposals from prospective authors.

Contents

List of Photos

List of Maps

Introduction

This brief introduction is intended to give an overview of the events covered in Volume I of *Doomed Before The Start: The Allied Intervention in Norway 1940 – The Road To Invasion and Early Moves*. Those who have just read my first volume may wish to stop here and move to the main body of the text. However, those who are coming to the campaign 'fresh' may find this short introduction helpful in explaining what had gone before.

Norway had remained neutral in the Great War, but in the 1930s, Germany recognised its strategic location with regard to North Atlantic shipping routes; additionally, Germany relied to a great extent on iron ore imported from Sweden via Norway for its vital heavy industries. Germany realised that if Norway was to enter the war on the side of the Allies, it would potentially be in great trouble for the future production of iron and steel. Britain also realised that Germany was largely dependent on this iron ore leaving the Norwegian port of Narvik. Winston Churchill, who in the early part of 1940 was First Lord of the Admiralty, came up with a plan to land troops in the Narvik area and stop the flow of iron ore to Germany. This scheme also involved laying mines in Norwegian territorial waters, even though Norway was neutral. While Britain was contemplating her options, in March 1940, Germany opted to get its retaliation in first, and decided to invade and occupy Norway. A plan was developed and the first German troops landed in Norway on 9 April. The port of Narvik was quickly occupied, as was the capital, Oslo, and other strategic points.

Norway appealed for help, and Britain and France came to her aid. A tri-service force was assembled; but with the benefit of hindsight not all of the units selected were of the best quality. It is clear that most of the senior commanders' eyes – both militarily and politically – in London were focusing on France, where the BEF was stationed, waiting for the 'real' fighting to start.

Volume I covers the early part of the Norway campaign, from both a German and Allied viewpoint, with actions on land, sea and in the air.

After the initial wave of Allied troops were sent to Norway, the War Office realised more soldiers were needed, so a number of units from the 49th Division – a Territorial division – were sent to Norway, but it was a 'second front' that they fought on around the area of Lillehammer. Volume II covers this action, together with further naval operations, including the sinking of HMS *Glorious* – an incident which was still being debated 60 years later. The final part of this volume covers the Allied withdrawal from Norway, with several reports and conclusions from this ill-fated campaign.

1

Narvik – The Final Assault

As you may recall from the first part of this story, the port of Narvik was the focal point for all Allied operations, but by the middle of May 1940, apart from some shelling, no efforts had been made to actually assault the town. All of this was to change, with the original date for an attack being set for 21 May. It was postponed on a daily basis for a number of reasons, including waiting for landing craft to have completed moving guns, stores and personnel for airfield construction and defence and the arrival of the fighter aircraft. In any event, Admiral Lord Cork (the overall commander-in-chief of Allied forces in Norway), Lieutenant-General Claude Auchinleck (commander of the North Western Expeditionary Force, or NWEF) and Group Captain M. Moore (the senior RAF officer) felt it necessary on 24 May to issue a special order of the day to the troops:

> We have now well-established bases in northern Norway and the enemy is operating either at the end of a long line of difficult land communications or without any land or sea communications at all.
>
> It is our firm intention to stop the further advance northwards of the enemy and to round up their forces in the Narvik area. We then intend to turn the tables on them and to do to them what they have been trying to do to us. Our brave allies, the French, have already carried out a brilliant landing operation from boats near Narvik and bundled the enemy out of his forward positions; they are pressing forward steadily in the most difficult country and have the upper hand. We ask every one of you to give of his best and make up his mind that the enemy has got to be beaten and beaten thoroughly.
>
> We can only give of our best if every officer and man is determined, day in and day out, to use every bit of the brains, forethought, loyalty and determination which he possesses to make his own ship, unit, establishment or depot the best disciplined and most efficient in the Force.
>
> You all know how our men are fighting on the sea and in the air and in France and Belgium against much heavier odds than we are faced with. It is up to us all here to fight to win so that we too may claim that we have done our part in saving our country from the Hun. Every German killed here is one less to fight in France.
>
> Man for man you are more than a match for the Germans so give them what they deserve.

This is an interesting document, as orders had reached the senior command from London that Norway was to be basically abandoned to her fate. Problems with relations between the Allies had started almost from day one. With four nationalities on the Allied side – British, French, Norwegians and Poles – it was difficult to find a common language. Indeed, the French commander, General Antoine Béthouart, very soon after arrival at Harstad, sent the following message to Paris: "The lack of interpreters for both English and Norwegian is causing us great difficulties. I am urgently requesting interpreters, including officers. I have only one interpreter and he speaks Russian." It did not get much better, as when the French authorities did get their act together they sent a number of officers who were fluent in Finnish but did not speak a word of Norwegian. From 10 May, and the massive German attack on the Western Front, things were obviously going to be difficult in this 'sideshow', as Norway was now becoming.

The French as usual wondered at the seemingly nonchalant attitude displayed by the British. A French officer wrote about visits to the harbour at Harstad: "I never failed to meet British dockworkers disguised as soldiers, taking the umpteenth cup of tea of the day's umpteenth tea break, as a tank or truck dangled forlornly in the air, precariously suspended from a crane cable." This attitude was also starting to grow in the minds of some of the senior Norwegian commanders. General Otto Ruge, Inspector-General of the Army, commented: "We gradually acquired the impression that the Allies hesitated to involve themselves too deeply in new undertakings." His suspicion was soon to come to fruition, but from London came comforting words. On 13 May, the new Minister of War, Anthony Eden, was telling the Norwegian Minister in London that "the Allied action in Norway would be pursued with the utmost energy". But within a few days, the Allies began seriously to consider, and reconsider, the cost of being engaged in northern Norway. There was of course a perfectly valid reason for this, which was the worsening situation on the Western Front, with the Germans making huge inroads into France and Belgium.

In spite of there being a change in the political leadership in Britain, with Winston Churchill replacing Neville Chamberlain as Prime Minister, the French seemed in even more disarray. French President Paul Reynaud, on the morning of 15 May, received a call from Edouard Daladier, the Prime Minister, stating that "our Army is dissolving, the battle is lost". A couple of hours later, Churchill received a call from Reynaud stating the same; Churchill was sceptical but agreed to travel over for talks.

So at 1500 on 16 May, Churchill flew to Paris for an urgent meeting of the Supreme War Council, accompanied by Generals Sir John Dill (Vice-Chief of the Imperial General Staff) and Hastings Ismay (Churchill's chief of staff). Landing at Le Bourget airfield near Paris, Churchill and Ismay were immediately struck by the atmosphere of defeat and depression that seemed everywhere to be in the air. Ismay was advised that the Germans were expected in Paris in a few days at the most. The party moved to the centre of Paris, to the government offices on the Quai d'Orsay, where staff could be seen burning files and papers. After a meeting with the senior politicians and the French Commander-in-Chief, General Maurice Gamelin, Churchill commented that he "noted utter dejection was written on every face". Churchill did his best to improve morale, but was himself astounded when he heard Gamelin say that the French Army was unable to counter-attack, having no strategic reserves. Churchill later stated: "I admit this was one of the greatest surprises I have had in my life." Gamelin and Reynaud repeatedly requested more fighter squadrons from the RAF, and in spite of his own reservations, Churchill promised and obtained from his War Cabinet the movement of a further 10 fighter squadrons to France.

Perhaps buoyed up by this news, Reynaud decided on the 17th to remove Daladier from his post as Minister of War and take the job himself, also removing Gamelin and replacing him with General Maxime Weygand. Weygand was 73 and no one regarded him as a 'military genius', but he had been Chief of Staff to Marshal Foch in the Great War and it was hoped this might encourage the French troops a little. It was also felt there was no-one else available for the job. He was hurriedly recalled from Syria to take charge. In the interim, the French also asked if it would be possible to have their Chasseurs Alpins back from Scotland, where they were waiting for virtually non-existent transport to Norway. On the following day, back in London, Churchill advised the War Cabinet of the extreme seriousness of the position in France and wondered whether "we should consider whether Narvik was eating up what we needed for our own defence, particularly in destroyers, anti-aircraft guns and fighters". For several days this question was left unanswered as, ever the supreme optimist, Churchill was buoyed by relatively good news from Norway with the capture of Bjerkvik, and he felt "it seemed likely that Narvik would be captured at any moment".

But over the coming days the Germans advanced further and further into France, and the commander of the British Expeditionary Force (BEF), Lord Gort, feared that an evacuation from France may be necessary. On 20 May, Churchill felt at a meeting of the War Cabinet that the policy for northern Norway was unclear. He was again disappointed with the lack of progress, and "it was causing a heavy drain on our resources in equipment and shipping". An even more damming comment was that, "the Chief of Staffs should now consider carefully whether we were likely to get a dividend out of our occupation of Narvik, even after we had succeeded in capturing it. It was clear that the troops, ships and equipment occupied in the operation were urgently needed elsewhere."

Churchill had of course invested a lot of political capital in the Norwegian expedition, and would be reluctant to abandon another of his pet schemes without some sort of success, and kept stressing the political value of the capture of Narvik. Yet ever the realist, he had to admit that if things got worse in France (as they seemed to be getting), then the prospect of an evacuation of the BEF, the surrender of France and a German invasion of Britain now all seemed highly likely. On 23 May, the War Cabinet received a report from the Chiefs of Staff that strangely recommended the capture of Narvik followed by the complete evacuation of Allied forces from Norway. Perhaps the Chiefs of Staff merely wanted to prove that the Germans could be defeated, but felt that in light of the precarious position in France, it would be impossible to supply troops and material to hold northern Norway indefinitely, as had been the original plan. Whilst this was a logical decision, Churchill did not appear happy, as he "depreciated asking troops to incur heavy losses in assaulting a town which it was proposed to evacuate immediately afterwards". The Chief of the Air Staff apparently said, "the Chiefs of Staff fully appreciated the political advantages of being able to say that we had captured Narvik", but Churchill countered by saying that "these advantages had been considerably minimised by the situation on the Western Front".

In spite of this, the prospect of abandoning Norway was a difficult pill to swallow, and the First Lord of the Admiralty, A.V. Alexander, expressed the hope that "no decision be taken at that meeting to abandon Norway. There were grave political considerations which needed full consideration." Churchill replied that he did not seek an immediate decision: "Plans for evacuating Norway should, however, be worked out at once. I have no doubt that this country would shortly be subjected to a very heavy attack. The guns, destroyers, aircraft carriers, shipping and troops at present devoted to the Norwegian project were urgently needed for our own defence." Some of the War Cabinet agreed, but it seemed there was a consensus of opinion that it was politically important to capture Narvik. In any case, Churchill felt that "it would be some weeks before withdrawal could be effected", and he expressed the sentiment that "in the interval we should take every advantage of our position in northern Norway to mine the approaches to Lulea to the maximum possible extent". He added: "We should on no account mention withdrawal to the Norwegians until it had actually begun. We should then offer the King of Norway and his entourage asylum in this country."

On 24 May, Lord Cork was informed that Norway was to be abandoned to its fate was sent, receiving instructions from the Defence Committee "to evacuate Narvik as soon as possible", this order endorsed the following day by the War Cabinet. Plans had first to be put in place to attack Narvik. Then came the sting in the tail for the senior British commanders; they were not allowed to inform the Norwegians of the evacuation plan, and also had to keep it from the French. On 27 May, Lord Cork sent a telegram to the Chiefs of Staff:

> In view of active operations being carried out by French forces in close contact with the Norwegians, I have felt bound to communicate decision to General Béthouart, which I did yesterday 26th May. General Béthouart represented to General Auchinleck who entirely agrees, that there may be extreme difficulty in withdrawing British and French troops now fighting side by side with Norwegians in contact with enemy without betraying them.

After weeks of going through the motions of attempting an attack on Narvik, the day was approaching where something would finally happen. The attack was to go in on the night of 27/28 May.

At NWEF HQ, contact was kept with Colonel Pollock, who was in charge of the British Mission with the Norwegian Government, then based in the Tromsö area. He had much valuable information regarding the state of political feeling and views amongst Norway's high command. After the evacuation of Bodø at the end of May, relations with Colonel Finne, the Chief Norwegian Liaison Officer at NWEF HQ, became very difficult owing to the necessity of keeping from him and other Norwegian officers that plans were being formulated to leave Norway.

Following the successful landings neat Bjerkvik and the subsequent operations which led to the clearing of the Oijord peninsula and the north shore of the Rombaks Fjord as

General Béthouart doing his best to direct operations at Narvik, pictured on board HMS *Cairo*. (Imperial War Museum HU93730)

far east as Lilleberget, plans had to be formulated for the capture of Narvik. Lieutenant-General Auchinleck instructed General Béthouart to take the port. However, until the area north of the eastern entrance to the Rombaks Fjord had been cleared, it looked as though an assault on Narvik would have to be launched on "difficult beaches which were believed to be strongly defended by machine guns". Such an operation would not have much element of surprise, since the ships and landing craft would have to be assembled in the Ofotfjord in daylight in full view of the Germans.

The plan that General Béthouart came up with was for an attack to come in from three different directions. In the north-east, the 13th Demi-Brigade of the Foreign Legion, supported by some Norwegians, would set out from Oijord, cross the Rombaks Fjord in landing craft and land on Orneset close to the railway line. A second wave would then land slightly west of here at Taraldsvik. Then the Polish Brigade would land at Ankenes and cross the Beisfjord with the intention of taking the southern part of Narvik. The final piece of the jigsaw was a battalion of Chasseurs Alpins, again supported by Norwegian troops, landing on the north shore of the Rombaks Fjord and attacking eastwards towards Hundalen. It should be noted that there were no British troops taking part in this assault. Yet the only real British troops in the area were the depleted numbers of 24 Guards Brigade, who were probably in no fit state to take part, as they had taken many casualties over the previous days and weeks. The landings would be covered by gun-fire from Royal Navy ships.

At about midnight on 27 May, the invasion fleet was in place with Lord Cork and General Béthouart on board HMS *Cairo*. Béthouart was initially to command the fire from the ships, and then go ashore to lead the attack. Behind the ships lay a small number of landing craft carrying the 1st Battalion of the French Foreign Legion, and as they approached Orneset, Béthouart gave the signal for the Navy to open fire. On the shore was a mixed bag of Germans from the 139th Mountain Regiment supported by some 'land-locked' sailors, one of whom recalled later:

> A red flare shot up into the sky and after that all the cannons spewed out a devastating fire. Hundreds of shells crashed without interruption on the railway, exploded with a thunderous roar in front of tunnel entrances, rained down with a terrific whine on the cliffs on Framnes, detonated among the houses of Vassvik, as huge boulders came hurtling down the slopes of Fagernesfjell with an earth-shaking roar. In the town as in the harbour, at Fagernes and on the shores of Ankenes, wooden houses burned like torches. Each detonation sent thousands of iron and rock fragments whistling in all directions. The whole coastline from Orneset to Taraldsvik was blotted out by a thick cloud of powder and dust, which was constantly pierced by the flashes of new explosions.

Just after midnight on 28 May, the first wave from the 1st Battalion of the Foreign Legion hit the beach without encountering serious opposition from the 50 or so German sailors who were guarding it. However, a number of these Germans fell back to a position along the railway line behind the beach. This gave them a better field of fire, and the Legionnaires now had to scale the cliffs at Orneset under fire. Meanwhile, aware that potentially an attack was under way, the Germans used some of their artillery to fire shells on the harbour at Oijord and delayed operations somewhat. Auchinleck commented:

> The initial landing was hardly opposed and was accomplished with little loss, the first contingent of troops quickly being successfully established on shore. The subsequent movement of troops across the Rombaks Fjord was hampered for short periods by a small gun firing from further to the east on the south shore. This gun caused some casualties, but was soon silenced by Naval gun fire and by 0330 one battalion of the Foreign Legion and the Narvik battalion of the Norwegian Army were ashore on the peninsula.

A particular thorn in the side of the Allies at this early stage was Hill 457, where the Germans were firmly entrenched with commanding views from the heights. After a bout of hard fighting, the Legionnaires managed to take the hill and for a while things were quie,t but the Germans soon put in a determined counter-attack from the east. The French had to fight hard to maintain their hold on the hill, but the forward movement by the Germans also allowed them to fire on the beach. It was during this period that Commandant Paris, Chief of Staff to General Béthouart, was killed by shrapnel in a landing craft.

One soldier who took part in this action recalled: "Then came the counter-attack; two German companies rushed on us. A Legionnaire leapt forward, but was almost immediately cut down, his legs torn off by a burst of machine gun fire." An officer said: "Some of our men had almost reached the top of the first slope when down below, along the railway line and the pass leading to Orneset, the Germans were driving a wedge in our flanks and setting up their heavy machine guns. Soon, they would cut off our companies fighting on the slope from the landing beach of Orneset." An NCO belonging to one of these companies added:

> The intensity of the shooting half a mile behind us seemed to indicate that a very strong attack was being brought to bear mainly on the Norwegian unit that had just taken over from us. We were cut off from the battalion, which must also have been cut off from the rest of the brigade, since the fighting now raged halfway up the slope and the Norwegians fell back on the eastern side of Orneset beach, which the crossfire of mountain cannons, mortars and machine guns was fast rendering untenable. That fire also swept the fjord, blocking the arrival of landing craft loaded with reinforcements, supplies and ammunition.

Nevertheless, the counter-attack was beaten off and the advance inland continued. Two tanks were ferried across in MLCs but got bogged down on the beach and took no part in operations. Fortunately the Luftwaffe had probably been caught napping and none of its aircraft appeared in the early stage of the landings. It then seems that a bank of fog rolled across Bardufoss and effectively stopped aircraft taking off. This gave a window of opportunity for the Luftwaffe between about 0500 and 0700 to send large numbers of aircraft to the area and attempt to bomb the fleet. General Béthouart later commented:

> The whole artillery of *Cairo* fired in vain at the assailants, who dropped a hail of bombs. Everyone ducked instinctively. Two bombs exploded on the ship, one on the fo'c'sle in front of us, the other between the two funnels. Splinters rained upon us. We got up. All the crew of the cannons had been mown down: 20, 30 mangled corpses and blood spattered everywhere. Replacement crews emerged from the hatchways, pushed the corpses aside and resumed the fire. Behind us a heavy machine gun had been hit and its ammunition was burning.

It is said that seven men were killed and 25 wounded in this attack. The ships tried to make a smokescreen and withdraw a little. As well as HMS *Cairo*, the ships consisted of the cruisers HMS *Southampton* and HMS *Coventry*, supported by the destroyers HMS *Fame*, HMS *Firedrake*, HMS *Havelock*, HMS *Walker* and HMS *Whirlwind*.

Meanwhile, the Poles had landed at Ankenes, but after establishing themselves the Germans took advantage of the lack of naval fire support to launch a counter-attack and succeeded in pushing back the left flank of the Poles. The weather at Bardufoss then cleared and some Hurricanes were able to take off, and arrived over Narvik around 0600, meaning the 2nd Battalion of the Foreign Legion was able to land at Taraldsvik. On the

Polish troops waiting to disembark at Ankenes. (Imperial War Museum HU93734)

slopes of Hill 457, the situation was about to enter a critical phase; the Legionnaires felt that the Germans were starting to waiver. A Legionnaire present later wrote:

> On the slopes in the midst of all the disorder, confusion and wavering a cry suddenly rang out: 'A moi! La Légion!' Despite a mortal head wound, Captain de Guittaud rallied his Company and launched it against the enemy; the wounded rose, a lieutenant, pistol in hand, led the way for his section; 20 Legionnaires out of 35 were killed. The Company lost 60 men. Legionnaires and Norwegians, side by side, now held fast, and the Norwegians progressively overtaking the men of the Foreign Legion, inched their way to the top.

Auchinleck later commented:

> The landing operation was rendered particularly hazardous by the scarcity of landing craft which, owing to enemy action and mechanical breakdown, had been reduced to three ALCs (Assault Landing Craft) and two MLCs (Motor Landing Craft). This meant that the number of men in the first landing party had to be reduced to 290, the numerical weakness of which caused considerable anxiety both to General Béthouart and myself. The operation was originally intended to take place on the night 24th/25th May, but at a conference with General Béthouart on 23rd May (the gist of which is recorded in Appendix B), I came to the conclusion that unless the weather was very propitious it

> would be an unjustifiable risk to undertake it with the support of only one fighter squadron of aircraft, in view of the strength and efficiency of the enemy bombers. I decided that it should be postponed until after the arrival of the Hurricane fighter squadron which was due on 27th May. Lord Cork agreed with this decision.
>
> After taking this decision the news of the intention of HMG (His Majesty's Government) to evacuate northern Norway was received and it became necessary to consider whether the operation was to be proceeded with or not. After consulting General Béthouart I recommended to Lord Cork that it should be carried out as intended on the night of 27th/28th May. In doing so I considered that, apart from the desirability of making sure whether the facilities for shipping ore from Narvik had in fact been destroyed as thoroughly as had been reported, the chances that a successful attack would do much to conceal our intention to evacuate the country in the immediate future would outweigh the possible disadvantages involved in extending our commitments by establishing troops in close contact with the enemy on the Narvik peninsula, where his main force was thought to be located.

Meanwhile, slowly but surely the French and Norwegians were gaining the upper hand, isolating and mopping up German positions. The 2nd Battalion of the Foreign Legion was advancing along the railway line towards Narvik and meeting weaker opposition. It is worth adding here that there were about 2,000 Germans in the area, a mixture of Army and Naval personnel. However, they were relatively thinly spread out as they had a large area to garrison. South-west of Narvik, men from the 2nd Polish Battalion reached Nybord, which was a relatively important strategic point as from here it was possible to bombard Ankenes. To the north-west, the Chasseurs Alpins, supported by Norwegian ski troops, were forcing the Germans back in the Haugfjell and along the Rombaks Fjord.

The local German commander, a Major Haussel, was faced with a worsening situation. Communication with the HQ of General Eduard Dietl, commander of the 3rd Mountain Division at Narvik, was patchy, there were little or no reserves and he only had about 400 men to counter around 5,000 Allied soldiers. Haussel decided that discretion was the better part of valour, and around 0700 he ordered those men who could to evacuate Narvik, taking with them as many weapons and ammunition as possible. This order did not reach all of his men, so isolated groups fought on, mainly at Hill 457 and Fagernes. But by around 1700, advance elements of the Allied invasion force entered the eastern part of Narvik, to be told by jubilant locals that the Germans had fled. Some Legionnaires made a right flanking move westwards and entered the harbour area. Within hours, General Béthouart entered the town to joyous scenes. On the following day, part two of the plan was put into operation, which involved trying to push the remnants of General Dietl's force back towards the Swedish border.

Meanwhile, in northern France, on 28 May the Belgian Army surrendered; on the previous day, Lord Gort had been told that his mission was "to evacuate the maximum force possible" and his troops were falling back doggedly towards the Channel ports, mainly to Dunkirk.

Summing up the operation to capture Narvik, Auchinleck later said:

> Once the initial landing had succeeded the progress of General Béthouart's troops was steady and continuous. From reports subsequently received it appears that the enemy withdrew in considerable haste eastwards along the Beisfjord and by 2200 the whole peninsula west of a line from Fagernes to Forsneset was in French hands, together with some 200 prisoners. After an initial set-back [sic] the Polish troops also pressed forward along the Arkenes peninsula and established themselves on high ground overlooking Beisfjord. Thus ended an operation which, in my opinion reflects great credit on the judgement and pertinacity of General Béthouart and on the fighting qualities of his troops. Reconnaissance after the capture of the town revealed the full difficulties of landing on the beaches close to the town and the wisdom of the plan finally adopted. Though he knew of the decision to evacuate Norway before the operation started, General Béthouart persevered with his plan and the vigour with which the advance eastwards was pressed after the capture of the town drove the enemy back on to his main position covering Sildvik and Hundalen, thus making it difficult for him to attempt a counter-attack against Narvik at short notice; this enabled the subsequent evacuation to be carried out under more favourable tactical conditions than at one time seemed likely.
>
> Nevertheless, it is my considered opinion that the operation was carried out with the barest margin of safety and for this reason might well have resulted in failure. Not only had the strength of the first echelon to be put ashore to be limited to 290 men, but this small force had to maintain itself unsupported for 45 minutes. Had the enemy been able to launch an immediate counter-attack the result might have been disastrous. It must always, in my opinion, be unwise to embark on operations of this character unless landing craft are available to land a first flight of adequate strength, and, in addition, provide an adequate floating reserve to meet unforeseen contingencies. Moreover, the absence of bomber aircraft deprived the attack of one of the most effective means of repulsing an enemy counter-attack; as has already been mentioned the broken and intricate nature of the ground prevented accurate observation by the supporting ships and artillery. The risk, however, was, in my opinion, worth taking and as things turned out, was justified.

Of course there was still the plan that Narvik was to be evacuated, and so on 1 June, operations east of Narvik were suspended, but still the Norwegians had not been informed of the decision taken in London and Paris. The decision to evacuate had been taken some days earlier, and at a War Cabinet meeting on 27 May an agreement was made that "the question should be brought before the War Cabinet again in two or three days". Even at this late hour, no-one felt able to trust the Norwegians. The politicians feared a backlash from any bad news and perhaps an immediate capitulation, which would make evacuating the troops a desperate affair.

Against this backdrop the evacuation of Bodø was carried out, which effectively left the road to Narvik open for the Germans. The British Ambassador to Norway, Sir Cecil Dormer, was holding regular meetings with the Norwegian Government, and after one of these reported back to London:

> Mr Koht and the Prime Minister were visibly suffering under some great strain when I was received by them this morning and I soon learned that this was caused by the news that the British troops were on the point of evacuating the whole Bodø area. Mr Koht stated that the decision had apparently been reached without consulting General Fleischer the Norwegian commander, that it was contrary to the explicit assurances which had been given to him in London, and, moreover, that it would bring the Germans considerably nearer to Tromsö, where the Government were hoping that they would be able to establish themselves firmly.

2

The Evacuation of Narvik

Orders to evacuate Norway had arrived from London with Lord Cork on 25 May, and he told Lieutenant-General Auchinleck the same day, along with a few key senior staff officers. General Béthouart was advised the following day, but this news was not given to the heads of services or to the junior staff officers until 29 May. In the interim, many steps were taken in preparation for the evacuation, such as the loading of stores and equipment in various ships and the removal of certain personnel. But those in the know were doing their best to foster deception ruses, and it seems that thed decision to evacuate was relatively well hidden, with the rank and file to a large extent unaware of it.

Three Polish battalions were at this time in contact with the Germans in the Ankenes-Beisfjord area, while east of Narvik the French Foreign Legion had advanced towards Sildvik. A Norwegian infantry battalion was acting as the Narvik guard force, with a battalion of Chasseurs Alpins located on the north shore of the Rombaks Fjord and in contact with German positions opposite Stromnes. General Fleischer's 6th Norwegian Division, consisting of five battalions, was holding a position on the left of the Chasseurs towards the Swedish frontier north of Bjornefjell.

Auchinleck was in close contact with Béthouart, and later commented:

> General Béthouart was particularly anxious that the withdrawal of his troops should not compromise or endanger the Norwegian troops in his sector. I shared his anxiety which was all the more acute because HMG did not communicate its intention to evacuate to the Norwegian Government until 1st June, when Sir Cecil Dormer came to Harstad and was informed by Lord Cork of the decision to withdraw from Norway. Sir Cecil Dormer then told the Norwegian Government.

It had been a difficult time, especially for Auchinleck trying to keep the Norwegians out of the loop, and on 30 May he had written to General Edmund Ironside, Commander-in-Chief Home Forces: "The worst of it all is the need for lying to all and sundry in order to preserve secrecy. Situation vis-à-vis the Norwegians is particularly difficult and one feels a most despicable creature in pretending that we are going on fighting when we are going to quit at once." Against this background, on 31 May the War Cabinet in London again decided again to postpone whether or not to tell the Norwegians. However, on 31 May, Lord Cork decided to take matters into his own hands: "General Auchinleck and myself were invited to Tromsö to discuss future operations. The position was obviously impossible. It was decided that the information must be imparted."

King Haakon and Crown Prince Olav, taken just before their departure for England. (Imperial War Museum HU128791)

It cannot have been an easy meeting for Sir Cecil Dormer, the British Ambassador to Norway, who travelled back to Tromsö by flying boat and arrived on the afternoon of 1 June. The minutes of a Norwegian Cabinet meeting held before his arrival on the morning of 1 June, and in the presence of King Haakon VII of Norway, are illuminating:

> We all agreed that if the Allies were to evacuate their troops entirely – and there are indications that this is a distinct possibility – our situation would become practically desperate. Indeed, apart from the fact that we lack anti-aircraft guns and planes, we have almost entirely run out of ammunition. More than a month has now passed since Great Britain promised to send us rifles and ammunition.

When Sir Cecil arrived at Tromsö, he first spoke with the Defence Minister, Ljungberg. It was a difficult meeting and Sir Cecil chose his words carefully: "I said, speaking personally and in strict secrecy, that the Allies would, I thought, decide to evacuate and if so, His Majesty's Government would be prepared to bring away at the same time the King and the Government." Ljungberg, reading between the lines, apparently asked if the Allies would leave behind enough weapons and stores to at least temporarily continue the struggle, but Sir Cecil felt everything would be taken away. However, there was still time for a diplomatic initiative, and although the original plan of evacuation was for it to start on the night of 2/3 June, it was postponed for 24 hours due to an urgent request from Sir Cecil, in order to allow the Norwegian Government to try to implement the Mowinckel Plan.

Shortly before the Allies' withdrawal, the Norwegian and Swedish governments, and eventually the German government, became involved in what came to be called the Mowinckel Plan, named after its author, Johan Ludwig Mowinckel, a former Prime Minister of Norway. According to this plan, an area of northern Norway would be a neutral zone with all foreign troops to be withdrawn from here to a line south of Mosjöen, and the Germans leaving Norway free north of this line. Narvik would be occupied by the Norwegians, or temporarily by Sweden, with the port remaining open for shipping. But this plan came to naught, and amongst the military permission to delay the evacuation was given with great reluctance in the likelihood of continuing German air raids. In the interim, upon hearing of the failure of this plan, General Ruge was summoned to Tromsö, and as he later recalled: "The decision had been taken, the King, the Government and the President of the Storting were to leave for England in order to continue the struggle. I expressed complete agreement." But an evacuation still had to be carried out.

Auchinleck said the Norwegian High Command, informed by its government of the evacuation, "after a very natural display of some anger and scorn", co-operated loyally until the end, rather than surrendering at once and gravely prejudicing the Allied withdrawal. He continued:

> It was a trying period for all concerned, throughout which Colonel Pollock, head of the Military Mission at Tromsö was of the greatest assistance to Lord Cork and myself; in spite of everything he managed to maintain cordial relations with the Norwegian authorities to the last. Bodø having been evacuated there was a distinct though not perhaps grave danger that the enemy working up the coast, might appear on the south coast of the Ofotfjord and Vestfjord and embarrass our withdrawal from there; all craft carrying French troops from the Narvik-Ankenes area had to pass through the Tjelsundet Fjord past Harstad and beyond before re-embarkation into transports could take place. There was also a risk that enemy detachments, sea or airborne, might effect a landing on the long indented coastline of Hanoy Island in which Harstad stands and directly interfere with our main embarkation centre. To counter these possible dangers, patrols by warships and aircraft of the Fleet Air Arm and by motorised troops on the island were organised and maintained throughout the evacuation period.

Whilst the plans for the evacuation were being worked up and some men and equipment were being evacuated, further problems developed. At the beginning of June, General Ruge advised his political leaders that he was unwilling to leave Norway with the Allies. As he had already abandoned his men in central Norway, he said he could not do so again without completely losing the respect of his troops. Despite several attempts by his high command, he was adamant that he would surrender with his troops once the king and government had left Norway and were out of the reach of the Germans. Perhaps even more seriously, King Haakon was also having second thoughts about the plan. Sir Cecil Dormer recorded an unexpected visit on 5 June from a friend of the king: "About 10 p.m. I had a visit from Mr Johan Anker, a personal friend of King Haakon, who brought me a letter from HM, written in pencil and marked private, to the effect that on further reflection, he felt it his duty to remain behind in Norway."

Sir Cecil immediately relayed the news to the Foreign Office in London, and on the following day they sent a strongly worded note suggesting that this course of action would be unwise. Before the arrival of the note from London, Sir Cecil travelled to the king's retreat and found that e was still undecided. Sir Cecil pointed out that if he stayed in Norway after the Allies had left, he would become a virtual prisoner, unable to help his people in any way, and the Germans could issue orders in his name; in short, he would play into the Germans' hands. If he went to London he would be a free agent and Norway could carry on with the struggle against the Germans. King Haakon finally agreed with this strategy.

Meanwhile, the Allies had cut communication with the south, much to the annoyance of the Norwegian authorities, but it was a sensible precaution with regard to the need for secrecy. The Germans moved up the coast in small steps, hindered as much as they could by the efforts of the Royal Navy, and by 7 June they had reached the area of Ballangen. However, the Allies were lucky in that over the evacuation period (3–8 June) the weather was generally overcast, which to a large extent stopped the Luftwaffe interfering with the evacuation plans. The Allied high command was certainly worried about the air threat, with around 27,000 men needing evacuating, but as it turned there was practically no danger from the air.

The orders for the evacuation, issued on 31 May, alluded to the need for secrecy:

> To all recipients of NWEF Movement Order No.1.
> The 'story' to which all persons in the secret of Alphabet will adhere will be as follows:-
>
> 1. Now that Narvik has been captured it is possible to reduce the forces in that area and redistribute them to better advantage.
> 2. In view of the danger of air attack on Harstad the base is to be moved to Tromsö.
> 3. This move will make possible a reinforcement of north eastern Norway if a German threat should develop, with Russian connivance, from that direction.
> 4. The true object will NOT be disclosed to any person other than those on the Alphabet List, and paras. 1–3 are intended to guide you in answering questions, or meeting any situation which may arise with persons not on the Alphabet List.

The Movement Order can be found in Appendix D. Whilst these were the orders for the evacuation, Auchinleck had been advised by the new CIGS in London, Sir John Dill,

Major Haussels, the Narvik garrison commander, with General Dietl and General Feuerstein after the reoccupation. (Bob Gerntsen collection)

that his primary objective was to save and bring away personnel, with the salvage of arms, equipment and stores being a secondary objective. With this in mind, Auchinleck issued orders that if necessary all anti-aircraft artillery was to be kept in action until the last moment and all fighter aircraft in operation until the last man was evacuated, and then destroyed. As it turned out, owing to the relative inactivity of the Luftwaffe, it was found possible to save most of the anti-aircraft guns, and the fighter aircraft were flown to aircraft carriers off the coast. The main danger from a tactical point of view was the disengagement, withdrawal and embarkation of the troops in contact with the Germans around Narvik. There was also a danger when the troops had to undertake transfer from ship to ship: the plan was to move first by puffers from the shore to destroyers, and from them into transports out at sea. These transfers would realistically require the ships to be stationary, and therefore virtual sitting ducks for any German aircraft.

Nine anti-aircraft guns (four heavy and five light) were eventually handed over to the Norwegians, and the evacuation went smoothly. It is recorded that the morale and cheerfulness of the troops remained high throughout, although their destination was not known to them until they were at sea, so well was the secret kept. Narvik was evacuated with virtually no casualties; it is probably fair to say that if the Germans did have any idea that the Allies were being evacuated, they might have been tempted to just let them get on with it as they had just been pushed back and did not have many troops in the area. If the Allies were going to give the area up, why bother fighting for it?

The Chasseurs Alpins provided the final rearguard around Harstad, but the actual rear party around the quays came from Royal Engineers and Military Police.

A "sufficient number of large liners" had been despatched from Britain for the evacuation, together with three stores ships and one horse ship. For the evacuation from Harstad, in many cases the troops were able to board destroyers directly, but at Skaanland and in the Narvik and Sorreisa areas, the puffers had to be used in a shuttle service out to the destroyers. They then had to sail about 70 miles out to sea to meet up with the troop ships, which were filled three at a time. These in turn moved to anchorages in fjords awaiting orders for the forming of a main convoy, which was carried out during the night of 7/8 June. At each embarkation point, alternative spots for embarkation were selected in case of enemy air attack, whilst a reserve of puffer boats was held at each locality in case of any difficulties. The puffers were formed into small fleets, with an army officer in charge and two British ORs on board each puffer. The last troops to leave the Narvik area – around 2,500 Frenchmen – would be embarked on the last day direct into six destroyers, thus ending the short Allied occupation of Narvik. As 7 June came to an end, around Narvik the remaining French and Polish troops silently pulled back from their positions, some leaving dummies in a bid to fool the Germans. The men forming the rearguard pulled back and the last of the troops boarded destroyers around midnight, with General Béthouart and his staff being some of the last to leave. With the Germans deciding not to interfere, it was almost a text book evacuation.

One of the members of the French Foreign Legion in Norway was Jaime Homs, a Spaniard who had fought against the Germans in the Civil War there and escaped to France in 1938. He then volunteered for service with the Foreign Legion, and after training was posted to Morocco. In early 1940 his unit was moved first to France and then to Liverpool, before sailing to Norway on the *Monarch of Bermuda*. He took part in the landings at Narvik. On his first landing they assaulted in small boats and they got stuck some distance off shore on rocks and were under light German fire. But they got ashore not too wet, and with the help of a French light tank, managed to overcome the German resistance and took most of them prisoner. For the following days their time was largely spent guarding the railway line before taking part in the second landing, although this time proper landing craft had been found. He recalled: "The Germans put up a spirited defence and we suffered a lot of casualties but we got ashore and eventually advanced to a frozen lake with some German aircraft on it. We did not do a lot here and within a few days we got the order to evacuate and that was that. We went back to France just in time to get involved in the fighting there."

Large amounts of material were left behind – hopefully rendered useless – and it is said that a number of mules were left to wander around the almost deserted streets. Right to the last there had been confusion and counter-order. A day or so before the final evacuation, Auchinleck received a message from the War Office telling him not to hand over any small arms or ammunition to the Norwegians. But in the early hours of 8 June, whilst in the North Atlantic, Lord Cork was advised to hand over 3,000 rifles and a corresponding amount of ammunition to the Norwegians. On the following day, one of the last Norwegian formations still active, the 6th Division, was disbanded, and on 10 June an armistice was declared in northern Norway, leaving the whole country under German rule. So it would remain for nearly a further five years.

A few days earlier, on 6 June, Sir Cecil Dormer had advised his superiors that the Royal Navy would be picking up King Haakon, whom he had persuaded to leave his homeland for the safety of Britain, the following night. As he was leaving the house that the king was staying in, Crown Prince Olav (the next in line to the throne) suggested to Sir Cecil that although he thought it correct that the king was leaving to go into self-imposed exile, he ought to stay behind. Sir Cecil argued that this would almost be as bad as the king staying behind, with the potential for the Germans to play one off against the other. Crown Prince Olav saw sense and agreed that he should also go, so Sir Cecil returned to Tromsö and telegraphed London that all was well and to confirm that a Royal Navy ship would be ready the following evening for an evacuation.

The ship that was provided was the heavy cruiser HMS *Devonshire*, which would sail at the latest at 2000 from Tromsö on the evening of 7 June. On that afternoon, towards the end of a final meeting of the Council of Ministers, the Prime Minister, Johan Nygaardsvold, put forward a proposal that "the King, the Crown Prince and the Government depart for an Allied country and that this decision be announced by proclamation to the Norwegian people". This was agreed and the wording sorted out, after which King Haakon said: "Having duly weighed the situation, I am come to the firm conclusion that in the present situation, my Government and myself have no other alternative than to leave the country in order to pursue from aboard our work for the benefit of Norway."

With these few words, King Haakon, no doubt with a heavy heart and many unanswered questions flashing round his head, announced his decision. Later that evening, as the British Mission to Norway boarded the *Devonshire*, followed by many Government ministers and officials, there was no sign of the king. Then at last the king, Crown Prince Olav and their entourage arrived on the quayside. One of the Norwegian officials later wrote: "From where we stood at the railing, we could see the King and the Crown Prince climbing the ship's ladder. The King seemed extremely depressed. It was certainly one of the most painful hours of his life." Just after 2000, HMS *Devonshire* left the harbour at Tromsö and slipped out to sea.

3

German Navy actions, Operation Juno and HMS *Glorious*

The German Navy had certainly taken a bit of a beating at the hands of the Royal Navy in Norwegian waters, particularly in the Narvik area, in April 1940, losing a battle cruiser, two cruisers and 10 destroyers sunk, along with several other vessels and U-boats, and numerous other ships badly damaged. However, undeterred, the German Naval High Command prepared an operation in May against the supply lines of the British Army centred around the seas off northern Norway.

The operation, codenamed Juno, was to be a major undertaking, with two of the biggest ships in the *Kriegsmarine*, the battleships *Gneisenau* and *Scharnhorst*, taking part, supported by the heavy cruiser *Admiral Hipper* and four destroyers, *Karl Galster*, *Hans Lody*, *Erich Steinbrinck* and *Hermann Schoemann*. There were also support and resupply ships the *Adria*, *Samland*, *Nordmark* and *Dithmarschen*, together with repair ship *Huascaran*, providing logistic support. The squadron's commander, Admiral Wilhelm Marschall, was on the *Gneisenau*.

The operation started on 4 June at 0800, when this German squadron sailed from Kiel, escorted by a small number of torpedo boats and a minesweeper. Steady progress was made, and Skagen, the northern tip of Denmark, was passed at 0630 on 5 June, and soon after noon the escort ships returned to Wilhelmshaven. By the early hours of 6 June, the fleet was doing 24 knots and in Norwegian waters off Bergen. That evening, they rendezvoused with the tanker *Dithmarschen* and topped up their tanks. Then on the evening of 7 June, Admiral Marschall gathered together all his captains for a conference and revealed that later that evening they would be heading for the Harstad area.

The *Admiral Hipper* spotted two Allied ships, the *Oil Pioneer* and *Juniper*. The former was hit by *Gneisenau* and finished off by a torpedo from the *Hermann Schoemann*, whilst the Juniper was sunk by the *Admiral Hipper*. At 0940 the following day, the *Admiral Hipper* intercepted and sunk the *Orama*, but allowed the hospital ship *Atlantis* to sail away.

At 1330, the *Admiral Hipper* and the four destroyers were sent to Trondheim to refuel, while the *Scharnhorst* and *Gneisenau* continued to Harstad. Whilst the two capital ships were steaming towards Harstad, one of the look-outs in *Scharnhorst* reported smoke on the horizon to the east at 60° at 1646.

As we have seen, the evacuation of Allied forces from the Narvik area had gone well, and it was decided to send these troops back to the UK in convoys. These were split into two – the first (Group I) sailed on 7 June, and the second (Group II) left the next day. Both convoys reached the UK safely. There were a number of Royal Navy ships in the area, including two aircraft carriers, the *Ark Royal* and *Glorious*, both of whom were operating north of Andenes Point in the Lofoten Islands. *Glorious* had flown on 'salvaged' RAF fighters for transport back to Britain, and also had on board 10 fighters and five torpedo bombers from the Fleet Air Arm.

Ark Royal and *Glorious* were to have formed part of the escort of the Group II convoy, but in the early hours of 8 June, the commander of the *Glorious*, Captain Guy D'Oyly-Hughes, sent a signal to Vice Admiral Aircraft Carriers (VAA) Lionel Wells on *Ark Royal*, asking for permission to proceed independently to Scapa Flow, via a route which took him some 300 miles to the west of the German airfield at Trondheim and then ran south-west to pass between the Faeroe Islands and the Shetlands.

The request was approved, and *Glorious* and her escort of two destroyers, HMS *Ardent* and HMS *Acasta*, parted company with *Ark Royal* at 0353 at the position 70°17'N, 14°10'E. Detailed accounts are available from British and German sources of what happened on 8 June, and the time line and selected details are as follows:

1646:
The German battleships, while at 69°00'N, 03°10'E steaming north at 18 knots on course 345°, spotted smoke on the horizon to the east.

Midshipmen Goos and Schulte from *Scharnhorst* foretop control identified smoke on the horizon with bearing 60° to the east on the German ship's starboard side. A report was immediately sent to the *Gneisenau* for Admiral Marschall.

1658:
Another communication was immediately forwarded from *Scharnhorst* to the *Gneisenau* saying that a British force had been spotted to the south-east at a distance of 40 kilometres.

1700:
The German battleships turned to course 330°; speed was now 19 knots. Wind was WNW 4 (approximately 6½ knots), sea was calm (state 2), temperature 1° Celsius (34°F) with very good unlimited visibility.

The order was given back to *Scharnhorst* from the Fleet Commander on board *Gneisenau* to increase to maximum speed.

1701:
On board HMS *Glorious*, two unidentified ships were spotted. At the time, *Glorious* and her escorts were sailing on a rough course of 205° at 17 knots and using zig-zag tactics to avoid potential U-boat torpedo attack. The aircraft carrier was at the 'fourth degree of readiness', which means steaming with 12 out of her 18 boilers on line. No aircraft were ranged on the deck, nor were any in the air, patrolling.

Glorious was carrying in her hangars 10 Hurricanes and 10 Gladiators from the RAF, which had been employed in Norway, plus her own nine Sea Gladiators and five Swordfish.

The destroyers *Ardent* and *Acasta* were disposed two cables ahead on either bow, *Ardent* to starboard and *Acasta* the port side of *Glorious*. None of these ships had radar fitted, and the *Glorious* had no look-out in her crow's nest.

HMS *Ardent*, under the command of Lieutenant-Commander John Barker, was ordered to close and identify them, being the closer destroyer to the approaching ships. Meanwhile, HMS *Acasta*, under Commander Charles Glasfurd, was ordered to remain close to *Glorious*, moving from the port side of the aircraft carrier to her starboard side. Additional orders were issued for the five Swordfish of 823 Squadron to be got ready and brought up to the flight deck.

1702:

Action stations was called on board German units, with the order to clear the ships and get ready for battle.

1706:

A turn to starboard was executed by the Germans; their course was now 30°. The *Scharnhorst* was leading with *Gneisenau* following close on her port side; the German battleships were now on a collision course with the British ships.

1707:

The speed of the German battleships was 24 knots and their radars were switched on to assist with estimating the range.

Glorious was doing her best to increase speed, while the *Ardent* and *Acasta* were steaming on her quarter position.

1710:

One of the *Scharnhorst* gunnery officers located in her foretop control reported a thick funnel and mast with battle centre made out, probably also a flight deck.

1712:

Scharnhorst and *Gneisenau* altered course, turning to starboard on course 70°; *Scharnhorst* leading with *Gneisenau* positioned on her port side aft.

1713:

Scharnhorst reported it had sighted an aircraft carrier, believing it to be the HMS *Ark Royal*, escorted by two destroyers. One destroyer was to the north and one destroyer to the south of the aircraft carrier.

1715:

Ardent was closing in on the German ships making challenges by signal lamp. *Glorious* was increasing speed and *Acasta* was moving across from the port side of *Glorious* to the starboard side.

1718:

Ardent reported to *Glorious* that she was unable to positively identify the approaching ships, and was preparing to attack them to provide *Glorious* and *Acasta* with more time to sail away if possible.

1720:

Action stations was sounded on board *Glorious*, which transmitted a contact report: "Two battle cruisers bearing 308° distance 15 miles on course 030°. My position 154° from 69'N 04°E."

1721:

The German battleships made a last turn to starboard on course 150°. Now the enemy was on their port side, suitable for broadside shooting.

Ardent made a turn to port to avoid getting closer and started a parallel run to the German ships, she being around eight nautical miles south-east of the German ships, hoping in time to be able to launch a torpedo attack.

1723:

Glorious turned to port while *Acasta* started laying a smokescreen. On board *Glorious*, efforts were continuing to bring the Swordfish aircraft up to the flight deck and make them ready to take off.

1726:

Glorious was now steaming at 26 knots, while on the *Scharnhorst*, orders were given to the main armament to engage the aircraft carrier and the smaller weapons to engage the destroyer to the north.

1727:

Gneisenau opened fire against *Ardent* and hit her in Number 1 Boiler room with her first salvo, causing a reduction in her speed. *Ardent* started to lay down a smokescreen and zig-zag whilst firing her 4.7in guns.

1728:

The speed of the *Scharnhorst* was 29 knots. *Ardent* kept on zig-zagging and fired her first salvo of torpedoes against the German ships, one of which was seen to pass close ahead of the *Scharnhorst*.

1730:

Permission was given for the *Scharnhorst* to open fire on *Ardent* at a range of 14,500 metres. *Ardent*, after having fired several torpedoes, turned away back into her own smokescreen.

1732:

Gneisenau sent a message to *Scharnhorst* to open fire with main armament at the aircraft carrier. The range is recorded as 26,000 metres (approx. 16 miles).

Ardent had already opened fire on the German ships, and kept on zig-zagging to try to avoid being hit from such close range.

1733:

Scharnhorst's secondary armament ceased fire due to interference from her main armament firing at *Glorious*. *Gneisenau* continued to engage *Ardent* with secondary armament on her port side. *Scharnhorst*'s first salvo fired at *Glorious* dropped short.

Both British destroyers were making dark smokescreens very effectively, using both smoke from their funnels and their smoke generator equipment.

1734:

On board *Glorious*, the first group of Swordfish were now on the main deck and getting ready to be launched, armed with torpedoes. *Scharnhorst*'s second salvo went over *Glorious*.

1736:

The *Scharnhorst* was doing 29 knots, with *Gneisenau* 30 knots. Fire was continuing with main and secondary armament against the British ships.

When the range was found and the first hit on *Glorious* was registered from *Scharnhorst*, it was at a distance of around 24,000 metres (15 miles). A 280mm shell penetrated the flight deck and burst in the upper hangar, starting a big fire, and a large crater was left on the upper deck, which made it impossible to launch any aircraft. Aircraft (believed to be two Swordfishes) were seen falling off the deck. Shell splinters pierced a boiler casing and smoke entered the air intakes. This caused a temporary drop in steam pressure from two boilers, but steam was built up again as the smoke cleared.

Acasta opened fire with her 4.7in guns at the German ships.

1740:

Scharnhorst's secondary armament restarted firing at *Ardent*. In spite of aggressive manoeuvring by her commander, she received hits due to extremely accurate fire from the German ships.

1741:

Acasta's smokescreen was becoming very effective, hiding *Glorious*. *Ardent* was moving into her own smokescreen.

Scharnhorst fired at *Glorious* from 23,000 metres (14½ miles).

1742:

Gneisenau ceased firing on *Ardent*, leaving *Scharnhorst* to continue to engage the destroyer. *Gneisenau* turned to starboard at full speed. *Ardent* was getting ready to fire another salvo of four torpedoes

1743:

Gneisenau was moving fast across *Scharnhorst*'s wake. Admiral Marschall sent a message to *Scharnhorst*, advising that he could deploy shipboard aircraft as needed. However, Captain Kurt-Caesar Hoffmann did not find this necessary.

Ardent launched her second set of torpedoes against *Scharnhorst*.

1744:

Gneisenau was now sailing on *Scharnhorst*'s starboard side and opened fire at *Glorious* with her 280mm guns.

1745:

On *Scharnhorst*, torpedo tracks were spotted coming from the direction of *Ardent*; the course was quickly changed with a fast turn to port and later back on course 170° to avoid them.

1747:

Ardent kept popping in and out of her own smokescreen to fire at Scharnhorst. The Germans commented that "the British destroyer's black smokescreen generated via the funnel seemed exceptionally effective."

Ardent hit *Scharnhorst* with a 4.7in shell and fired her third set of torpedoes.

1749:

There was another alert on board *Scharnhorst* due to further torpedo tracks. Again, a fast turn to port was made and *Scharnhorst* was back on course 170°.

1751:

Glorious was on fire and listing heavily to starboard.

1752:

Both German battleships were on course 170°.

1753:
Anorder was given from *Gneisenau* to *Scharnhorst*, to alter course to 130°.
1755:
Ardent fired her fourth torpedo salvo at *Scharnhorst*. Torpedo tracks spotted from bearing 110° on board *Scharnhorst*.
1756:
Glorious received another 280mm shell direct on the bridge, killing Captain D'Oyly-Hughes and almost all of the bridge personnel.
1758:
Glorious was still under fire and listing heavily, doing her best to hide behind various smoke screens. *Scharnhorst*'s main guns ceased fire while *Gneisenau* kept on firing at *Glorious*. *Scharnhorst*'s Chief Engineer reported an engine room out of service, and speed was decreasing.
1800:
Gneisenau ceased fire due to *Glorious* being hidden in a smokescreen. Firing continued with secondary guns at the destroyers, while Admiral Marschall ordered both ships' gunnery officers not to waste too much ammunition.
1802:
Scharnhorst was now making 27 knots due to the engine problems. Boiler 1.1 was out, probably due to a split tube.

Gneisenau engaged *Glorious* and *Acasta*, having passed *Scharnhorst* and now sailing on her starboard side. *Ardent* was engaged from *Scharnhorst* and was on the German battleship's port side. *Acasta* and *Glorious* were located on *Gneisenau*'s starboard side.
1803:
Ardent fired the fifth salvo of torpedoes at *Scharnhorst*.
1804:
Scharnhorst scored another hit on *Ardent* with her secondary guns. *Ardent*, after being hit, was now moving at 15 knots and listing heavily to port.
1805:
Another torpedo alert sounded on *Scharnhorst*, with three torpedoes approaching from bearing 330°.

Acasta started to lay a smoke curtain in front of *Glorious* from west to east.
1808:
The following communication was sent from the German ships to Naval Command in Germany: "Engaging aircraft carrier on Quadrant 2160 while sailing south-east."
1810:
Another torpedo alert – direction 320° – on board the German battleships.
1811:
Scharnhorst's heavy anti-aircraft guns (105mm) opened fire at *Ardent* and hits were recorded. *Ardent* fired her sixth salvo of torpedoes at *Scharnhorst*.
1812:
Acasta had just completed another smoke curtain for *Glorious*, then turned

to the south, steaming at 35 knots, to try to make another one ahead of the aircraft carrier.

1813:

A further torpedo alert on board *Scharnhorst* showed that *Ardent* was fighting very hard.

Glorious started being visible again through the smokescreen.

1815:

Orders were sent from *Gneisenau* to *Scharnhorst,* not to waste any more ammunition. Heavy anti-aircraft guns ceased firing at *Ardent.*

1817:

Glorious was burning fiercely astern. *Ardent* fired her seventh set of torpedoes at *Scharnhorst,* in spite of being hit many times by the German ship's secondary armament.

1818:

Glorious became clearly visible again, the smoke clearing away. Consequently, the order was given from Admiral Marschall for both German ships to reopen fire at the aircraft carrier with main weaponry.

Ardent was increasingly listing but still firing.

1819:

Scharnhorst sent the following communication to *Gneisenau*: "Admiral Marschall, *Scharnhorst* having engine problems, not able to sail faster than 28.5 knots at the moment."

Gneisenau was now the hunter of the *Glorious* and *Acasta* at full speed; Scharnhorst was taking care of *Ardent,* which was already in great difficulties.

1820:

Scharnhorst was steering on course 150°.

Gneisenau kept on firing at *Glorious* from approx. 20,000 metres (12 miles). *Glorious* received another 280mm hit that entered the centre engine room, causing much damage. *Glorious* began to lose speed, develop a starboard list and commenced a slow circle to port. *Acasta* was starting to lay another smoke curtain for *Glorious.*

1822:

Ardent finally capsized and sunk. *Scharnhorst* ordered secondary armament to cease firing on *Ardent* and resumed main armament fire at *Glorious* from 23,450 metres.

1823:

Torpedo alert from direction 10° on board *Scharnhorst,* the last ones fired from *Ardent. Gneisenau*'s main guns kept on scoring hits on *Glorious,* who was losing speed and became progressively easier to be hit.

Ardent was not visible any more. Carley floats were all around where she sank.

1824:

Scharnhorst's secondary armament switched target to *Acasta.* The last torpedoes fired from *Ardent* were passing ahead of *Scharnhorst. Glorious* was burning even more fiercely.

1825:
A message was sent from Admiral Marschall on board *Gneisenau* to *Scharnhorst*: "Congratulations for having sunk the destroyer north."
1826:
Scharnhorst's secondary armament recommenced firing at *Acasta*, but the distance was too great (18,520 metres – nearly 12 miles) and fire was ceased. Meanwhile, it kept firing at *Glorious* from 22,000 metres (14 miles) with her main guns.

Acasta's Commander Glasfurd decided to attack the German ships with torpedoes. He turned to a westerly course away from *Glorious*, and getting ready his torpedo tubes, instructions were passed to get ready to attack from 8,000 yards, which was about the limit for effective torpedo firing.
1829:
Admiral Marschall sent a message to *Scharnhorst*: "I will not tolerate any more waste of ammunition." *Gneisenau* was 4,000 metrdes closer than *Scharnhorst* to *Glorious* at that point.
1830:
Gneisenau's main armament was scoring hits on the *Glorious*, which was sailing very slowly. The distance between *Gneisenau* and the heavily damaged and listed *Glorious* was around 18,500 meters (nearly 12 miles), but it was rapidly decreasing and fire from *Gneisenau* was more accurate and intense.
1831:
Acasta was making smoke and firing her guns whilst sailing a westerly course. It is noted she was being very skilfully handled, similar to *Ardent*. *Acasta*'s shells were falling 50 metres ahead of *Scharnhorst*. *Glorious* was clearly visible again, and now under very intense fire from *Gneisenau*'s main guns.
1832:
Acasta seemed to be making ready for an attack on the German ships. *Scharnhorst*'s secondary guns received permission to fire, and reopened fire on *Acasta*.
1833:
Acasta turned and fired from her portside tubes a salvo of four torpedoes. *Scharnhorst* foretop control signalled three torpedoes fired from *Acasta*.
1834:
Scharnhorst resumed course to 150°. Its ultra short-wave set was unserviceable, but it was still firing at *Acasta* from 13,300 metres (8 miles). *Acasta*, after having completed a 180° turn to the east, was zig-zagging and kept on firing until she re-entered her own smokescreen.
1835:
Acasta was sailing east on course 90°, crossing *Scharnhorst*'s bow from starboard to port. *Acasta* received a hit that damaged her pom-pom platform, but still managed to fire a second salvo of four torpedoes at *Scharnhorst* from her portside tubes.
1836:
Gneisenau's main guns were finishing off *Glorious* from short range (less than 10,000 metres – 6 miles).

1839:
Scharnhorst reported a severe tremor astern, apparently a torpedo hit. The main guns ceased fire and the radar was unserviceable. On *Acasta,* the crew saw the flash and the huge water column on the *Scharnhorst* aft starboard side. They knew they had hit the German ship.

Gneisenau was firing a last broadside at *Glorious.*

1840:
Acasta was still making a thick dark smokescreen trying to protect the aircraft carrier from German fire, and sailed back again between the German ships and the *Glorious* while firing her 4.7in guns.

1841:
Scharnhorst reduced speed and a turn to starboard of 90° was made on course 240° with the intention to close up with the *Gneisenau. Gneisenau* ceased fire on *Glorious* and switched target to *Acasta.*

Acasta was now sailing east, having passed close to *Glorious* to be ready to turn and come back again, making a smokescreen to protect *Glorious.*

1842:
Scharnhorst gave permission again to the secondary armament to fire at *Acasta.*

1843:
Scharnhorst turned to port on course 190°. *Gneisenau* also opened fire on *Acasta,* the only ship fighting back as the *Glorious* seemed a dead duck.

1844:
On board *Scharnhorst,* reports were coming in of damage, such as "evacuation of turret with heavy explosion and flooding, thick smoke belching out. Report from command centre declared torpedo probably hit at level of C turret on the starboard side, magazines being flooded." The engine room said the starboard engine was out of action. Its speed was still 26 knots.

1846:
Scharnhorst on course 260°. C turret magazines were all flooded. *Gneisenau* still fired at *Acasta* with secondary armament from around 11,000 metres.

1847:
Gneisenau fire on *Acasta* was now very intense, with many hits being recorded. To avoid getting torpedoed, *Gneisenau* circled around *Acasta,* remaining by and large out of torpedo range.

1848:
Scharnhorst was increasingly listing to starboard. The Chief Engineer was checking the engine rooms. *Acasta* turned to port in order to come back again to try to help *Glorious* and get away from the fire of *Gneisenau.*

1849:
Scharnhorst sent a signal message to *Gneisenau*: "Torpedo hit astern." Engine Room reported knocking noises in HP bearing starboard engine. Ship control reported hits in compartments III and IV. Secondary armament was silent, but the ultra short-wave link resumed.

Gneisenau was still firing at *Acasta* with her secondary guns. *Acasta,* laying a smokescreen while coming back on course 300° to WNW, was still firing her guns against *Gneisenau*.

1851:

Scharnhorst communicated to *Gneisenau*: "*Scharnhorst* hit by torpedo on the starboard in compartments III and IV. Turret C unserviceable."

1852:

On board *Scharnhorst*, damage reports were coming into the Control Room: "Turret C magazine, water being pumped out." Foretop reported *Acasta* out of torpedo launching range. Request coming from *Gneisenau* asking what speed *Scharnhorst* could maintain. *Acasta* was seen coming back in the German ships' direction.

1853:

Acasta in sight again. Permission given for *Scharnhorst*'s secondary armament to open fire again on *Acasta*. *Gneisenau* secondary guns also firing at *Acasta*.

1855:

Gneisenau signalled to *Scharnhorst* to assume formation in line astern of the flagship. *Scharnhorst* turned on course 160°. *Gneisenau* secondary guns score several hits on *Acasta*. Destroyer damaged and undertaking a slow turn to the south.

1857:

Scharnhorst reports torpedo hit would not interfere with running of the ship.

1859:

Request from *Gneisenau* to *Scharnhorst*: could *Scharnhorst* maintain 28 knots? *Scharnhorst* reports Chief Engineer confirmed T1 and T2 was running clear, T3 running but with knocking noises.

1900:

Scharnhorst to *Gneisenau*: maximum speed likely to be 27 knots. *Scharnhorst* listing to starboard; stern deck was 3 metres down compared to the normal level.

1904:

Gneisenau ceased firing on *Acasta*, now heavily damaged and listing to port.

1905:

Scharnhorst reported revolutions on centre engine were dropping fast.

1906:

Scharnhorst centre engine stopped. Report from engine room declared apparent major water inrush in T1. One propeller was knocking very heavily. Message sent to *Gneisenau*: "Centre engine out of service."

1908:

Glorious sinking and slowly disappeared from view. *Acasta* was on fire astern and heavily listing to port. To save ammunition, *Scharnhorst*'s secondary armament was ordered to cease fire.

1909:

Scharnhorst speed now 25 knots.

1910:

Acasta was still firing and hit the *Scharnhorst* on the B turret right gun barrel.

Fire resumed by *Scharnhorst*'s secondary armament. *Scharnhorst*'s Chief Engineer reported need to reduce speed because T3 was knocking badly. *Acasta* was still burning, heavily listing and now unable to manoeuvre.
1912:
Glorious was completely gone and a lot of Carley floats were all around her sinking place. Captain of *Acasta* orders "abandon ship".
1915:
Scharnhorst ceased firing at *Acasta*. *Acasta* was still burning and Carley floats were all around her.
1917:
Scharnhorst received message from *Gneisenau* to turn to course 70° at 24 knots. First Officer reports starboard propellers heavily knocking. Aft platform deck starboard side 1 metre under water. Pumping under way. Fuel oil being transferred to compensate for list.
1920:
Gneisenau orders the war flag to fly at half mast and crew to stand to attention to honour the brave crew of the British destroyer that was sinking.
1922:
Scharnhorst suggests speed of 21 knots.
1924:
The battle was declared over.
1925:
All three British ships have been sunk and only Carley floats and rafts with around 900 survivors were on the sea. *Gneisenau* and *Scharnhorst* sailing towards Trondheim in Norway on course 70°.
1928:
Scharnhorst temporarily not answering helm and steering to port.
1930:
Scharnhorst now confirms no difficulties as regards steering.

The German ships decided not to pick up any of the Royal Navy survivors from the water, which was probably a correct decision, even though there did at times in 1940 seem to still be a small amount of chivalry between both navies. It was thought there were about 900 men in or on the water, and picking them up would have been a long and slow job, potentially leaving both German ships open to submarine attack.

Scharnhorst had suffered serious damage, and 48 members of her crew had been killed.

The *Scharnhorst*'s C turret and magazines were filled with smoke, gun crews were evacuated and magazine flooding was ordered, but cancelled when no danger of fire was reported. The torpedo fired by HMS *Acasta* blew out a section of hull roughly 14x6 metres. The explosion of the torpedo's warhead tore the torpedo bulkhead from the armour deck and bent its top edge inboard 1.7 metres. That bulkhead was damaged from the level of the side armour to a platform above the shaft alley for 10 metres. Two transverse bulkheads, the battery deck and the first platform deck were damaged. The armour shelf and some adjacent structure were also slightly damaged.

The torpedo struck at a point where the propeller shafts passed through the torpedo bulkhead, a really crucial part of the hull to hit. As a result of this damage, four of the 22 main watertight compartments had some flooding; around 2,500 tons of water was taken on board. The Scharnhorst had a list of about five degrees to starboard and was down three metres by the stern.

The propulsion plant of the *Scharnhorst* was also seriously affected by flooding and damage. The starboard shaft, which passed through the lower part of the underwater side-protection system abreast of turret C, was destroyed, and the shaft alley began to flood immediately. A seaman was trapped there, and when another man opened a watertight door in a rescue attempt, the after engine room, which supplied power to the centre line shaft, began flooding so rapidly that it was impossible to properly secure the plant. One of the turbines, under maximum load, cooled so quickly that the housing came in contact with the turbine blades, and it had to be stopped. All steam connections were shut off in this space. With the starboard engine room also secured, the ship had only one shaft in operation.

Turret C was out of action. Some compartments below the magazine were flooded, and electrical and other equipment in the magazine was damaged. Some cartridges and a few powder cases burned; many were damaged. The cartridge magazine contained 283 projectiles and cartridges combined, ready to be fed to the turret above.

The starboard aft 150mm twin turret was put out of action by flooding of sub-turret compartments and damage to the electrical system. The fire control system for the after group of 105mm guns was also damaged.

The ship was limited to a maximum speed of 20 knots en route to Trondheim. Collision mats were rigged in an attempt to prevent further structural damage, but could not be secured, and the attempt was abandoned. However, the *Scharnhorst* was still basically seaworthy and, accompanied by the *Gneisenau*, sailed towards Trondheim, where they arrived around noon on 9 June. That afternoon, divers inspected the hull and reported that the hole was 14x6 metres. Emergency repairs were carried out by the repair ship *Huascaran* and the salvage ship *Parat*, the damage being temporarily patched over. Both ships stocked up on ammunition from the supply ship *Alstertor*.

On 10 June, an RAF Coastal Command aircraft spotted the *Scharnhorst* in the harbour at Trondheim, so as a security measure, Admiral Marschall ordered the *Gneisenau*, accompanied by the heavy cruiser *Admiral Hipper* and four destroyers, to sail, but returned the following day. This was just about in time for an air raid from 12 Hudsons of Coastal Command, who dropped a number of bombs on the moored ships, but all missed their targets. Sensing there were a number of valuable targets at Trondheim, the battleship HMS *Nelson* and aircraft carrier HMS *Ark Royal* were then dispatched, remaining within 300 miles. By midnight on 13 June, *Ark Royal* was around 170 miles from Trondheim – also covering the passage of troop transports – and launched fifteen Skua bombers from 800 and 803 Squadrons on a raid. The attack was made in daylight without adequate supporting cover. They were intercepted by German fighters, and eight of them were shot down. The others attacked the *Scharnhorst*, but only one bomb hit, and although it penetrated the upper deck, it failed to explode. Only two Skuas of 800 Squadron and five of 803 Squadron returned. This was the last attempt to try and attack the *Scharnhorst* in Trondheim harbour, and the propulsion turbine for the centreline shaft was repaired in 10 days. The damage to the starboard shaft was believed to be serious and could only be surveyed in a dry dock; since it was feared that the shaft had been severed by the explosion, the propeller was lashed to the hull.

One of the many Skuas from *Ark Royal* shot down was the CO of 800 Squadron, Major Richard Thomas Partridge, Royal Marines, who later commented:

> After we crash landed we made our way to some wooden huts visible in the distance. We broke into the huts and found them to be full of sacks of oatmeal and so we lost no time in getting a fire started and making some porridge.
>
> After a while we heard a whistle outside the hut and expecting it to be a Norwegian ski patrol we left the hut. However it turned out to be the crew – 3 NCOs – of the German Heinkel bomber which we had earlier shot down! We were not armed whereas the Germans where, however the Germans were very friendly and joined us in the hut for some porridge. I then informed the Germans that we were going to walk to the large house we could see in the distance to hopefully find help. The Germans allowed us to leave and when we got to the house we found it to be a very recently abandoned hotel. So we helped ourselves to the drinks cabinet and slept in the two finest rooms in the hotel. There was still food in the hotel and after a good night's sleep made a breakfast of bacon and eggs.
>
> Soon after we had finished breakfast the Germans from the hut came over to the hotel and were not nearly as friendly as before. The Germans had clearly not enjoyed their night in the hut and appeared unhappy that they had allowed us to leave. I had before the war holidayed in Switzerland and knew the rudiments of skiing and I had found a pair of skis in the hotel. I suggested to the Germans that I wanted to ski to the distant houses to try to make contact with the locals. One of the Germans insisted on coming with me but he could not ski and soon started trailing. As we approached the ridge of the hill before the houses we were surrounded by a Norwegian ski patrol. The Norwegians were very hostile and clearly thought we were both German. Both myself and the German informed the Norwegians that we were British and during the remonstrations the Norwegians shot the German dead. I only managed to convince the Norwegians that I was British when I produced English notes and coins from my pockets bearing the profile of George VI.

On 18 June, *Scharnhorst* was running engine trials in the fjord, and on 19 June the ship was declared ready to sail, with a top speed limited to 24 knots. On the following day, she sailed for Kiel, escorted by three boats of the 1st Minesweeping Flotilla, the destroyers *Hans Lody*, *Hermann Schoemann*, *Karl Galster* and *Erich Steinbrinck*, and the torpedo boats *Greif* and *Kondor*. At midday on 21 June, the torpedo boats *Falke* and *Jaguar* were also attached. As an additional screen, the *Gneisenau* group set sail to try to attack patrolling British cruisers. Instead of surface ships, the danger came from submarines – the silent service – and at 2209 on 20 June, Captain Ingram, commander of HMS *Clyde*, spotted the German ships. Within 30 minutes he had manoeuvred his submarine into an attack position and fired a salvo of six torpedoes against *Gneisenau*.

One of the six torpedoes launched hit *Gneisenau* on the bow on the starboard side, creating a big hole but not causing critical damage. *Gneisenau* limped back to Trondheim at around 19 knots, arrived on the morning of 21 June.

Work started almost immediately with the German repair ship *Huascaran*, continuing until 19 July.

On 21 June, RAF Coastal Command reconnaissance aircraft spotted the *Scharnhorst* group off the Isle of Utsire, and around 1500, six Swordfish torpedo planes attacked, but were easily repulsed by anti-aircraft fire. At 1630, nine Beauforts attacked with 500lb armour-piercing bombs, but were also driven off by anti-aircraft fire and German fighters. In these attacks, the ship expended 900 rounds of 105mm, 1,200 rounds of 37mm and 2,400 rounds of 20mm ammunition.

When German radio intercepts revealed that much of the British Home Fleet was at sea, the *Scharnhorst* was ordered into Stavanger. At this time, some British ships had closed to within 35 miles of her position. On the evening of 21 June, the group put into Skudenes Fjord near Stavanger, moving round to an anchorage in Dusavik Bay at 0400 the next morning. At 0530 on 22 June, *Scharnhorst* left Stavanger, heading for Kiel, arriving there in the late afternoon of 23 June. She entered dry dock C at Kiel on the afternoon of 24 June. That night, the bodies of the dead crewmen were removed from the flooded stern rooms. The funerals were held on 27 June. The next five months were spent making repairs, until 21 November, when she went to Gotenhafen to undertake trials in the Baltic, before returning to Kiel on 19 December.

Meanwhile, the *Gneisenau* was at Trondheim for most of July undergoing repairs, and on 25 July she left Trondheim escorted by the *Admiral Hipper* and four destroyers, *Hans Lody*, *Karl Galster*, *Paul Jacobi* and *Friedrich Ihn*. She also safely made it to Kiel, arriving on 28 July. *Gneisenau* remained in Kiel until 21 October, then she went to the Baltic for trials, returning to Kiel on 19 December.

The controversy over the sinking of the *Glorious*

There were certain questions raised in the coming weeks, months and indeed years about why the Glorious and her two escorts had to leave Norway 'early', and the lack of 'contact' reports that were or were not sent.

Operation Alphabet, the evacuation of all British and Allied forces from Norway, had beencarried out from 5–8 June. Two troop convoys had sailed on 7 and 8 June, reaching the UK safely. *Ark Royal* and *Glorious* were to have formed part of the escort of the second convoy, but *Glorious* commander Guy D'Oyly-Hughes was granted permission to proceed independently to Scapa Flow. *Glorious* and her two destroyers then proceeded on course 250° at 22 knots. Later that morning, *Glorious* reduced speed to 17 knots and, in an attempt to confuse enemy submarines, commenced zig-zagging.

D'Oyly-Hughes had served as a submariner in the Great War and it is fair to say that he was not a great fan of air power, and so was probably not overjoyed to be given command of an aircraft carrier. He is rumoured to have said earlier in 1940 that "as far

HMS *Glorious* in the background with some of her escorts. (Imperial War Museum HU128793)

as anti-submarine operations were concerned, no aircraft had ever sunk a submarine or ever would".

The fact that HMS *Glorious* was undertaking zig-zag manoeuvres and her failure to have aircraft in the air indicates that he was probably more concerned with the threat of submarines than with surface raiders. This may explain to some extent why no aircraft from *Glorious* were airborne to carry out reconnaissance missions during the trip back to the UK. However, it appears that the main reason for *Glorious* to return independently to Scapa Flow was to hold a court-martial of his Commander (Air), J.B. Heath, who had refused an order to carry out an attack on shore targets on the grounds that the targets were at best ill-defined and his Swordfish aircraft were unsuited to the task, and who had been left behind in Scapa to await trial.

There are other questions that need to be raised. Firstly, how, on a day of calm sea and unlimited visibility, and with only a slight advantage in speed, did the German battleships overwhelm the carrier and her escort in so short a time? And why did no British warship or shore station receive an enemy report from the British force during the first part of the action?

In 1940, all Royal Navy radio communication between ships and shore stations was normally by Morse Code. In the Royal Navy, radio was known as 'Wireless Telegraphy', or W/T. Large cruisers of the older classes, such as HMS *Devonshire*, were usually equipped with two long-range transmitters, a Type 36 main transmitter of 5kw output and a Type 37 secondary transmitter of 1kw output. Both of these could transmit between 100–550 kHz and between 3–12 MHz. Frequency shifts could be accomplished very quickly, probably in less than a minute. *Glorious* probably carried similar or identical equipment.

Most large ships were also equipped with several 100w auxiliary General Purpose (GP) transmitters. Destroyers were usually equipped with 1kw transmitters. In order to reduce the possibility of a single hit disabling all of the ship's W/T equipment at once, most warships located the main and secondary transmitters in different parts of the ship. In *Glorious*, however, the main and secondary transmitters were in adjacent compartments, one deck below the flight deck and forward of the island.

When larger ships were at action stations or in a high state of readiness, a Remote Control W/T Office (RCO) would be manned from which any transmitter could be keyed directly. This Remote Office was located in the bridge superstructure (or the island in carriers), and was in direct voice-pipe communication with the bridge. At other times, signals were passed between the bridge and the Main W/T Office by pneumatic tube. Aerial arrays in aircraft carriers were carried on light steel masts along the sides of the flight deck. These were hinged so they could be lowered outboard to the horizontal position when flight operations were in progress.

It was also standard practice for any contact with the enemy to be reported immediately.

The unexpected presence of enemy surface ships represented a great danger to the Group II convoy (8,000 troops escorted by the *Ark Royal*, two cruisers and six destroyers), and to broadcast a warning should have been the highest priority for *Glorious*. Yet only one brief transmission was heard by Royal Navy units, and its significance was not immediately appreciated. The Admiralty was very concerned that no useful enemy reports had been received, and later asked all UK shore W/T stations if anyone had heard any sort of signal from *Glorious* or her two destroyers. None had.

Glorious commenced transmitting her enemy contact report shortly after 1620 with the main set on 253 kHz and the secondary set on one of the Home Station HF frequencies, 8.29 MHz. The correct frequency for an enemy report was 7.3 MHz, the Narvik area wave, but this was not used until later in the action when the GP set in the Main Office started up on this frequency. It was one of these 7.3 MHz transmissions that was heard by HMS *Devonshire* and *Gneisenau* at 1720. Evidence available indicates that *Glorious* continued to keep the main set on 253 kHz until it was disabled at about 1720.

Glorious also transmitted her enemy contact report on the reconnaissance wave (probably 230 MHz) from a GP set in the RCO, but this was an uncertain means of communicating over 200 miles, given the bad atmospheric conditions reported by the Germans. Ships in the Narvik area had been directed to shift from Narvik area frequencies to Home Station frequencies upon crossing 65°N. This should normally have occurred about 0740 on 9 June but, for reasons which have never been established, *Glorious* changed over at 1300 on 8 June, while still some 300 miles north of this line.

On 8 June, carriers and cruisers in the Narvik area were keeping watch on 230 kHz (Fleet Air Arm wave) and 3.7 MHz (Area wave). Destroyers were on 3.7 MHz from 0400 on 8 June. In the Narvik area, Fleet Air Arm wave 230 kHz was being used instead of Fleet wave 253 kHz because of 'intolerable interference' on the latter. It is evident that *Glorious* had not received the information that the use of 253 kHz had been discontinued and that ships were to shift to Home Frequencies upon crossing 65°N. There was considerable traffic on 3.7 MHz on the afternoon of 8 June. *Ark Royal*, three cruisers and at least a dozen destroyers were within 200 miles of *Glorious* at the time of the action. Many of these ships were in relatively close company, and operators may have cut back their RF (radio frequency) use to avoid strong signals blocking their receivers. This, combined with the large amount of traffic and the bad conditions reported by the Germans, would have reduced the probability of a distant signal being heard on the area frequency.

At the time of the action, HMS *Devonshire*'s W/T department was in two watches, with both her Main W/T and Remote Office listening on the high and low frequencies of both Home and Narvik areas. At 1700, *Devonshire*, then about 70 miles west of *Glorious*, heard a weak signal on 3.7 Mhz, "reception very doubtful", addressed to VAA Wells on *Ark Royal* from *Glorious*: " … My 1615 2PB 1640." There were some unreadable fragments of Morse before "My 1615". The warbling note of the signal was identified by the Admiralty as coming from a Type 53 auxiliary transmitter.

At 1652, *Gneisenau* heard *Glorious* transmit the following message on 8.29 Mhz, addressed to Scapa W/T: "Two battle cruisers bearing 308° 15 miles course 030°. My position 154°69'N 04°E. 11 miles = 1615." The Germans reported that the message was sent with "badly fluctuating signal strength possibly due to interruptions in the power supply". At 1719, *Gneisenau* heard *Glorious* calling VAA Wells on 3.7 Mhz and attempted, unsuccessfully, to jam the signal. This was undoubtedly the signal received by *Devonshire* at 1720.

There is no record of the two destroyers sending any enemy contact reports at all. This is very difficult to explain. The W/T specialist in the Signal Department of the Admiralty made the following comments in the enquiry file dated 18 June 1940, and now in the National Archives:

> It is believed that the escorting destroyers attacked the enemy and no explanation can be given for their failure to make an enemy report. Any suggestion that they assumed that *Glorious* had made the necessary reports can hardly be accepted. *Glorious* must have remained afloat for at least 30 minutes after 'open fire'. If her W/T was out of action it is reasonable to expect that she would have told the destroyers to make enemy reports.'

Officially only one brief transmission was heard by a Royal Navy unit (HMS *Devonshire*), and its significance was not immediately appreciated nor forwarded.

However, following investigations by the GLARAC (Glorious, Ardent, Acasta) Association for a Channel 4 documentary in the 1990s,it would appear that the fact that a message from *Glorious* was not received or was almost unintelligible was not the story told by six members of HMS *Devonshire*'s crew. They differ in some recollected details, but all are adamant that what was heard at 1720 that day was, at the least, sufficiently intelligible to cause considerable consternation on *Devonshire*'s bridge because the ship was kept sailing away from *Glorious*, which was in clear danger.

According to PO Senior Telegraphist T. Jenkins, who was in charge of the W/T Remote Control Office, the message was clear and contained all details, and was received by one of his operators, who called his attention to it, while in the main wireless office another operator also received and confirmed it.

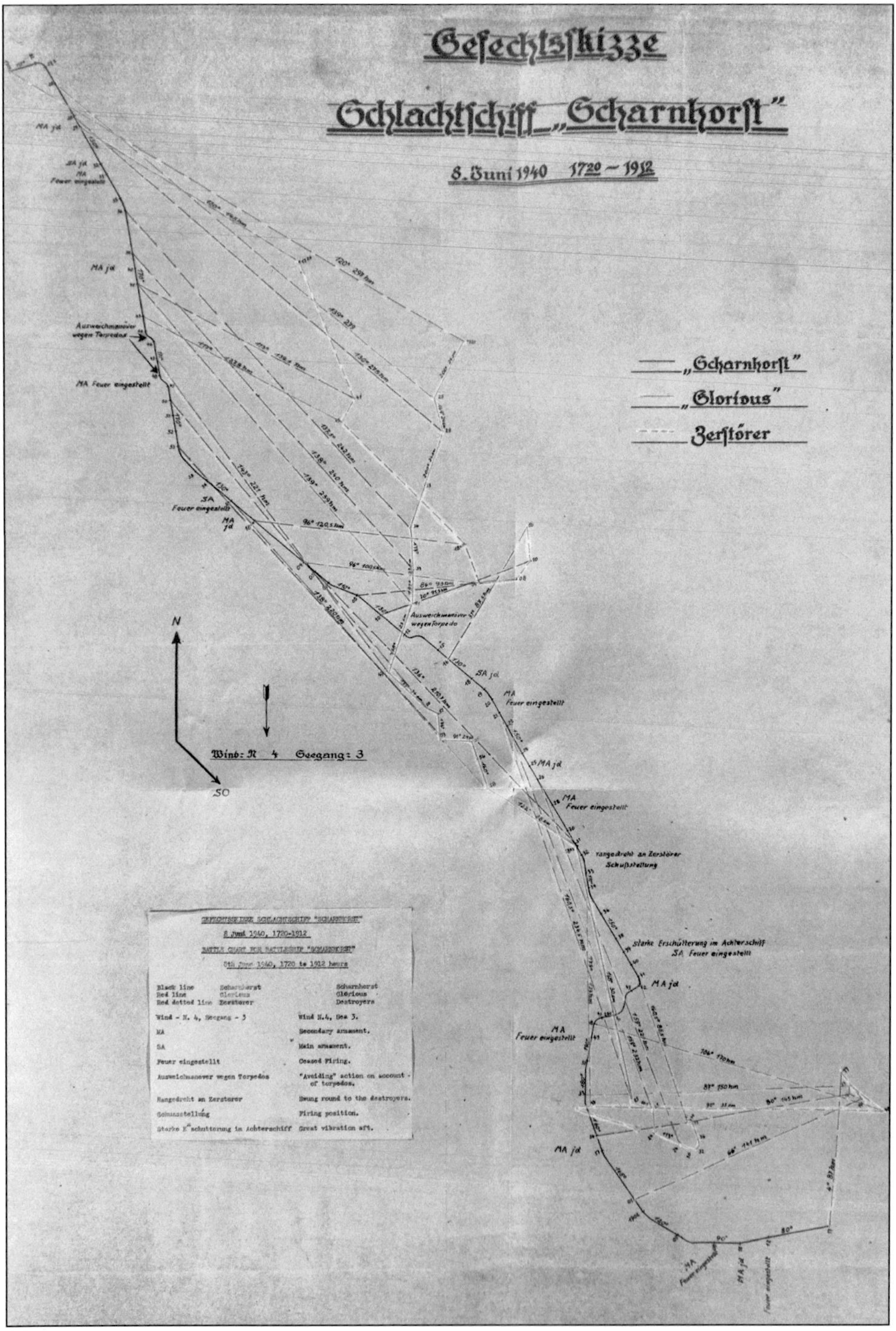

Chart showing German view of the action against HMS *Glorious.*

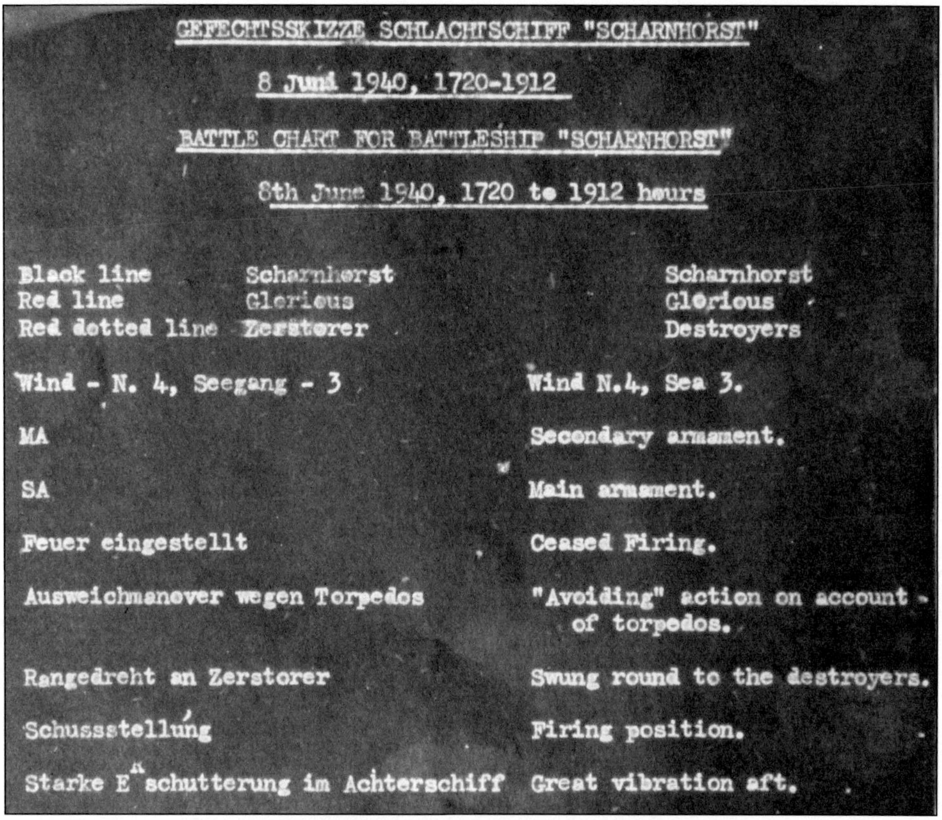

GEFECHTSSKIZZE SCHLACHTSCHIFF "SCHARNHORST"

8 Juni 1940, 1720-1912

BATTLE CHART FOR BATTLESHIP "SCHARNHORST"

8th June 1940, 1720 to 1912 hours

Black line	Scharnhorst	Scharnhorst
Red line	Glorious	Glorious
Red dotted line	Zerstorer	Destroyers

Wind - N. 4, Seegang - 3	Wind N.4, Sea 3.
MA	Secondary armament.
SA	Main armament.
Feuer eingestellt	Ceased Firing.
Ausweichmanover wegen Torpedos	"Avoiding" action on account of torpedos.
Rangedreht an Zerstorer	Swung round to the destroyers.
Schussstellung	Firing position.
Starke Erschutterung im Achterschiff	Great vibration aft.

Key to chart in map on previous page.

Midshipman D. Corkhill confirmed that when plotted, it clearly showed to the *Devonshire* senior officers how close they were was to *Glorious.*

It would appear that this message immediately went on a 'restricted circulation' on the orders of Vice Admiral John Cunningham (who was on board), and all copies were handed to his staff Flag Lieutenant, including the operators log.

So this message was 'officially' never received on board HMS *Devonshire*, according to the Admiralty and the latter day Ministry of Defence; they only declare *Devonshire* having received garbled and unintelligible signals at 1820.

At this time, *Devonshire* was 30 miles to the west of the German ships and around 40 miles from the *Glorious. Devonshire* did not change course, but actually increased speed and kept heading towards the UK. It is worth adding here that the King of Norway and most of the Norwegian Government were on board, and perhaps Cunningham had orders that no matter what he was to get them to the UK.

The complete message from *Glorious* as recorded on *Gneisenau* would have been transmitted in the 'self-evident' code used for enemy reports, and would have been transmitted in Morse as follows:

VE MTA V OW2 O-U 2BC 308 15 030 154GQOX 11 BT 1615 IMI

Breaking this down, we have:

VE = Prefix for all RN messages
MTA = Call sign for Scapa W/T
V = From
OW2 = Call sign for Glorious
O-U = Prefix for most immediate, the dash or 'short break' being transmitted as 'ii' in Morse.
2BC = Two Battle Cruisers
308 = Bearing 308°
15 = 15 miles
030 = Course 030°

The transmitting ship's position was coded as:

154 = Bearing to reference grid point (in this case GQOX)
GQOX = Reference grid point (GQOX = 69°N 04°E)
11 = Distances to reference grid point in miles
BT = Long break, transmitted as 'BT' in Morse.
1615 = Time of origin (GMT Time)
IMI = Please repeat message if received.

At 1800, *Devonshire*, then about 50 miles west of *Glorious*, heard a further weak signal on 3.7 Mhz, again "reception very doubtful", addressed to VAA from Glorious: "My 1615 2PB 16:40." There were some unreadable fragments of Morse before "My 16:15". The signal was once more identified by the Admiralty as coming from a Type 53 auxiliary transmitter. Probably the missing Morse fragments were the single word 'amend', making the whole message "VE 1NR (call sign of VAA) VOW20-U AMEND MY 1615 2PB = 16:40".

Why *Glorious* wanted to alter the first, and correct, identification of the enemy must remain a mystery. The B Dienst operator on *Gneisenau* recorded this as "the very same message" as the enemy report heard at 1752.The Germans reported that the message was sent with a "badly fluctuating signal strength possibly due to interruptions in the power supply". This was undoubtedly the signal received (officially) by *Devonshire* at 1820.

The Germans were fully expecting *Glorious* to transmit on 7.3 MHz, and had a transmitter on *Gneisenau*, pre-tuned to that frequency in order to jam any outgoing signal. The Germans used a rather subtle jamming technique; instead of generating a lot of noisy interference, they attempted to drown out the legitimate signal by simultaneously generating a series of false signals which would overwhelm it, using standard RN call signs and procedures. No ship or shore station reported receiving *Gneisenau*'s bogus messages, and in fact *Devonshire* was unaware that the Germans were attempting to jam *Glorious* signals.

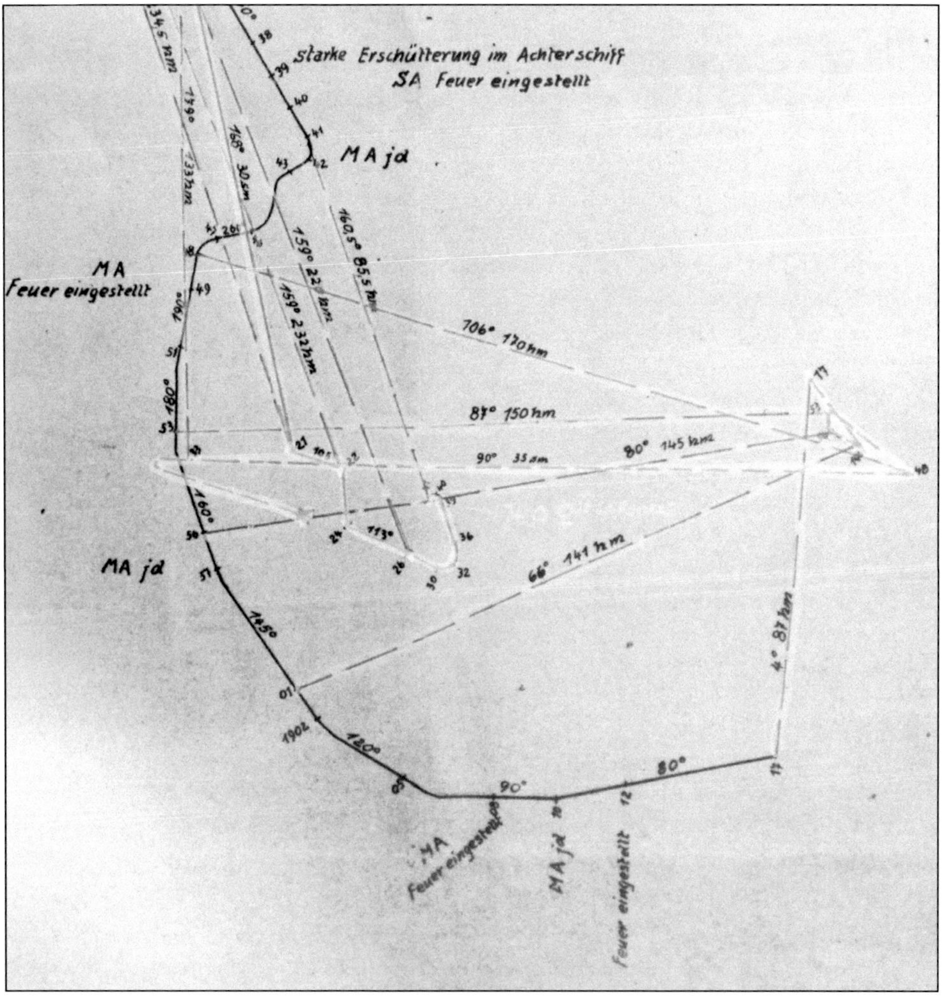

Detailed view of German chart showing the end of the action against HMS *Glorious*.

The part played by HMS *Devonshire*

HMS *Devonshire* was on passage from Norway to the UK on 8 June with 461 passengers, among whom were the King of Norway, his family and the Norwegian Cabinet and their families. Orders were to keep radio silence (broken the day after at 0200 to ask for an escort). It has been established by naval specialist re-plot that at 1720 she was less than 30 miles from the German ships, when *Glorious* first sighting signal originated, and around 40 miles from *Glorious*. Similarly, it has been estimated that *Devonshire*, which kept sailing away, increasing speed, was around 60 miles from *Glorious* when she first received the second signal at 1820.

Devonshire crew members Midshipman D. Corkhill and Petty Officer Telegraphist T. Jenkins reported consternation on the *Devonshire* bridge because of the ship keeping course and sailing away from *Glorious* after Vice Admiral Cunningham had ordered the *Glorious* position to be plotted; how could they have plotted the position of *Glorious* without having received the signal with her position clearly stated?

Furthermore, one of the passengers, a Major Owen, reported that from *Devonshire*'s lookout top, two mast-heads were seen to the east (probably *Scharnhorst* and *Gneisenau*), and this was also confirmed by Signalman Slocombe.

At 1720, *Devonshire* started exercising her 8in main, guns and at 1823, she increased her speed to 30 knots and started zig-zagging, just when *Glorious* was transmitting her last report. *Devonshire* maintained 30 knots for more than two hours until well after 2000, and eventually landed her important royal cargo on British soil.

The 1,000 or so survivors from the *Glorious*, *Acasta* and *Ardent* were now facing an uncertain future in the cold waters off Norway. The Germans likely did not pause to rescue them as they were concerned about the possibility of Royal Navy ships reaching the area, because of the *Glorious* radio transmission potentially having been intercepted by other British ships known to be at sea, and due to the damage that had been suffered by the *Scharnhorst.* It is reported that by 1930 the sea was calm, and the survivors were floating on rafts waiting to be rescued, with a very limited availability of water and food on the Carley floats or the rafts – on some of them nothing at all.

No help came from Royal Navy ships in the area, even though two destroyers, HMS *Vanoc* and HMS *Veteran*, had been ordered to leave the convoy they were escorting to look for the *Glorious.* They sailed through the area without noticing anything untoward, and ended up docking in the Faroe Islands. A sailor later commented:

> As the troop convoy cleared the Norwegian coast, *Veteran* and *Vanoc* were suddenly detached from the convoy escort and ordered northward to intercept *Glorious* and supplement her destroyer screen … When we reached our rendezvous we were in midnight sun latitudes, calm sea, maximum visibility but no *Glorious.* We searched unsuccessfully until the old fuel problem loomed, then headed for the Faroe Islands … where we found thirty exhausted, frostbitten survivors of Glorious.

On the morning of 9 June, the hospital ship *Atlantis* met the British battleship HMS *Valiant* and reported the presence of the two German battleships she had seen the previous morning It is probably only at this point that London became aware of two German capital ships in the area, and connected this with the messages – garbled or otherwise – from HMS *Devonshire.*

Another cruiser in the area, HMS *Southampton,* records for 9 June: "12:55 body sighted in the water, altered course to investigate. 3 bodies seen in the water. 13:05 proceeded at 20 knots to re-join convoy." The position of HMS *Southampton* at noon was 68°46'N, 03°40'E, and these bodies were almost certainly casualties from the previous day's engagement. Then at about 1600 on 10 June, the Norwegian ship SS *Marita,* en route from Tromsö to Thorshavn in the Faroes, sighted empty rafts, rafts with dead bodies and heavy oil at 68°39'N, 04°05'E.

Between 2345 on 10 June and 0555 on 11 June, the Norwegian merchant ship SS *Borgund*, also sailing from Tromsö to Thorshavn, sighted 21 rafts at 68°15'N, 02°20'E and 67°59'N, 03°42'E, rescuing three officers and 35 sailors from *Glorious* and one survivor from *Acasta*.

These men were landed at Thorshavn at 1930 on 13 June, and were subsequently returned to the Firth of Forth in Scotland by HMS *Veteran*, where they arrived at Rosyth on 18 June.

Five *Glorious* sailors rescued by another Norwegian ship were taken to Norway and became prisoners of war, and two sailors from *Ardent* were rescued by a German seaplane and also became POWs. This gave a total of just 46 men plucked to safety from the sea. Because of the extra passengers from the Norway expedition probably on board all three ships, the actual number of casualties will probably never be known. However, three sources give the number of as either 1,561, 1,530 or 1,519. It was a serious maritime disaster, and questions would be asked for many years to come.

It had probably been wrong for Admiral Wells to approve *Glorious* request to proceed independently to Scapa Flow, regardless of the reason, as aircraft carriers were becoming crucial assets. Wells probably chose to ignore the fact that *Glorious* sister ship, *Courageous*, also escorted by a pair of destroyers, had been torpedoed and sunk by U29 off the coast of Ireland the previous September with the loss of over 500 men.

The lack of a German reaction to British operations in the Norwegian Sea lulled the Admiralty and the Fleet into a dangerous sense of complacency. The carriers *Ark Royal*, *Furious* and *Glorious* had, in the weeks preceding the action, repeatedly made the 2,000-mile return trip to the Narvik area with only a destroyer escort. This was *Glorious* fifth trip. The Admiralty appears to have taken the safety of these valuable and vulnerable ships for granted.

The Admiralty did not pass on its knowledge of German movements to operational forces at sea. Bletchley Park – the W/T interception and codebreaking centre – had warned the Admiralty that analysis of wireless intercepts indicated that German heavy units had left the Baltic and might be moving north into the Norwegian Sea. The Admiralty did not pass this information on to the fleet or RAF Coastal Command. Receipt of this information might have led Wells to refuse *Glorious* request to proceed independently.

Glorious did not exercise adequate measures to protect herself and her escorts from unexpected attack. *Glorious* should have had at least one aircraft aloft during the day. This would have given the ship visibility of at least 40 miles, allowing her to avoid interception and warn the fleet by W/T long before the Germans could have threatened her. At the very least, *Glorious* should have been prepared to launch aircraft at short notice once German forces were detected.

Glorious was slow in reacting to the presence of the German ships. Although she was just about within the range of the German big guns when she was sighted, a quick turn away to the south-east while working up to full speed would have greatly improved her chances of survival. There were potentially two options that would have given *Glorious* a better chance to escape. One was to steam directly downwind and away from the German ships, i.e. on a course of 130°, at 30 knots. This would have made launching aircraft more difficult, though by no means impossible, and would have made the smokescreen more effective. A second option was to put the German units directly astern and steam almost directly south. Although *Glorious* had no speed advantage over the *Scharnhorst* and *Gneisenau*, if the enemy had been pocket battleships she could have run away from them. The decision to remain on course 200° until 1647 was both imprudent and tactically inept.

The Narvik W/T organisation must bear a good deal of blame for *Glorious* failure to get off an effective enemy contact report. *Glorious* should not have been permitted to sail before Narvik W/T was sure she was aware that the use of 253 kHz had been discontinued for the Narvik area, and that ships were to change frequencies upon crossing 65°N. Also, the defensive tactics used were questionable. *Ardent's* solo torpedo attack at 1642 seems strange, as it would appear that a co-ordinated assault by two destroyers would have been more effective than individual attacks by single ships.

The failure of the destroyers to send enemy reports is inexplicable. The destroyer *Glowworm*, sunk after an unexpected encounter with the German heavy cruiser *Hipper* the previous April, had followed the initial sighting report with further transmissions until her W/T equipment was disabled.

But there were also recriminations on the German side. Upon his return to Trondheim, Admiral Marschall was relieved of his command for disobeying orders to attack shipping at Harstad, endangering his ships by attacking an old aircraft carrier and expending too much ammunition.

Here is the Scharnhorst's gunnery summary of the encounter:

Main armament in action against *Glorious*:

Time	Bearing (Deg True)	Range (hm)*	Range(yards)
1620	120	297	32,480
1625	139	279	30,512
1628	130	275	30,074
1636	137.5	242	26,465
1639	138	240	26,465
1641	139	230	26,137
1647	143	221	24,169
1653	138	220	24,059
1705	136	210	22,966
1722	160.5	234.5	25,645
1723	159	232	25,372
1726	159	220	24,059
Average		242.5	26,515

Secondary Armament in action against *Ardent*:

Time	Bearing (Deg True)	Range (hm*)	Range (yards)
1620	120	145	15,857
1641	113	139.5	15,256
1643	117	128	13,998
1700	096	120.5	13,178
1704	084	104.5	11,428
1710	070	91.5	10,006
1716	031	87.5	9,569

Secondary Armament in action against *Acasta*:

Time	Bearing (Deg True)	Range (hm*)	Range (yards)
1734	179	133	14,450
1748	106	170	18,591
1753	087	150	16,404
1756	080	145	15,857
1801	066	141	15,420

Ammunition expended:
Main armament – 212 rounds (69 salvos)
160 armour piercing
45 HE base fused
7 HE nose fused

Secondary armament – 842 rounds
489 HE nose fused
353 HE base fused

Heavy Anti-Aircraft – 136 HE time-fused**

* 1 hectometre (hm) = 100 metres

** This ammunition was expended, primarily against *Acasta*, in order to maintain and improve the morale of the German gun crews.

Admiral Marschall made the following comments in his gunnery report of the action:

> The ammunition expenditure of 212 rounds in *Scharnhorst* and 175 rounds in *Gneisenau*, is slight – it shows the effectiveness of both forward heavy turrets on the target. Regarding choice of projectiles, it should be stated that a sufficient penetration was effected against the armour of *Glorious* with the HE base fused, and therefore the high expenditure of armour piercing shells employed by *Scharnhorst* was not absolutely necessary. However, I approve the decision of the First Gunnery Officer of *Scharnhorst* to employ armour piercing shells in order to impair the speed of the enemy.

The *Glorious* disaster and the failure to mount an effective rescue was clearly an embarrassment for the Royal Navy. All ships encountering the enemy should routinely broadcast a sighting report, and so the lack of one from *Glorious* was eventually raised in the House of Commons. It later became known that the heavy cruiser HMS *Devonshire* had passed within 30–50 miles of the battle, flying the flag of Vice Admiral John Cunningham, who was carrying out orders to evacuate the Norwegian Royal Family to the UK and maintain radio silence. Some surviving eyewitnesses from *Glorious* and *Devonshire* later testified that the sighting report had been correctly sent, and received in *Devonshire*, but that it had been suppressed by Cunningham, who departed at high speed in accordance with his orders.

The 22,500-ton carriers *Glorious* and *Courageous* had been converted in the 1920s from being heavy cruisers into an aircraft carrier, armed with only 4.7in guns. The light armament was justified by the Admiralty in order to save weight and the belief that such ships should rely on their screening ships in order to protect them.

Many questions were raised at the time in Parliament Labour MP by Richard Stokes, and have continued to be asked until the present day. Did Admiral Forbes really know of the movements of *Glorious* and her destroyer escort, and if not, was he in a position to give assistance if they encountered trouble? Were two small destroyers really enough to protect a valuable asset such as an aircraft carrier, when HMS *Courageous* had been torpedoed by U29 with the loss of 500 men? Why did the Admiralty leave nearly 1,000 men to drift for three nights and two days before a mere handful were picked up by chance? Why had *Glorious* separated from *Ark Royal* and her group only thirteen hours before? Why were no lookouts posted? Why had she not been warned that enemy ships might be along the route? Why were her urgent signals never heard, or if they were, not acted upon? Why didn't the destroyers send a report of enemy sightings?

The answers that have been given, first by the Admiralty and then by the Ministry of Defence, have been questioned right from the start. The official reason given for *Glorious* independent departure from Norway was that she was short of fuel and could not wait another 24 hours to come back with *Ark Royal*. Both Winston Churchill and Captain S. Roskill (the latter in 1980 after conducting extensive research), who had written the official history of the Royal Navy in the Second World War, poured scorn on this explanation.

There are three reasons why such an explanation is open to question. The first is that there are no corroborating signals, logs, reports or witnesses. The second lies with the fuel position. Was it more economical to return at 17 or 18 knots (the speed at which she was travelling when she encountered the *Scharnhorst* and *Gneisenau*) by herself or return at 13 or 14 knots with the convoy? Of course *Glorious* would have used more fuel in waiting for the convoy to assemble, but overall, she would have used less fuel by waiting and returning with the other ships. In addition, if a ship is short of fuel and has a number of her boilers shut down, it is more difficult for her to reach full speed and thus outrun the pursuers, which is what happened in *Glorious* case. If such a situation arises, isn't it therefore obvious that the ship will be safer in company?

Why was *Glorious* in such a hurry that she ignored these considerations? A handwritten note in an Admiralty file provides a clue. The note was from the CO of one of the destroyers in the Ark Royal group, Commander Le Geyt, who noted a signal flashed from *Glorious* to *Ark Royal* requesting permission to depart immediately, the purpose of which was to make preparations for courts martial. The ship departed 30 minutes later. It was no secret that the captain of *Glorious* had been in a state of conflict with his FAA staff. Things had come to a head on a previous trip to Norway, when the FAA officers had expressed doubts over a plan that involved, in their view, a futile and nearly suicidal ground attack. When *Glorious* returned to refuel, the Commander (A) was put ashore pending court martial. While the Admiralty and more recently the MoD have argued that a court martial would have been an extremely trivial reason to risk a carrier, two destroyers and 1,500 lives, when the story was being researched by Stephen Roskill, he contacted a number of retired naval officers who had served under the CO of *Glorious*, and none of them tried to dissuade him that "the fuel story is bunkum … the problem was the Captain's impatience for a court martial".

Following on from this, why did Vice Admiral Wells in *Ark Royal* allow the *Glorious* to return independently? Unfortunately, Wells was never interviewed, and so we shall never know for sure. Why didn't the Admiralty pass on the intelligence from Bletchley Park, that German surface forces were likely to leave Kiel for the North Sea, to the ships out at sea? That the intelligence had reached the Admiralty was indicated in the official history of British Intelligence during the Second World War and supported by Sir Harry Hinsley, who had passed the intelligence onto the Admiralty (and written the official history), but contradicted in a 1997 paper entitled 'HMS *Glorious* – Points of Controversy', published by the Ministry of Defence's Naval Historical Branch. It was argued that only one faint and garbled message was heard by the one ship, the *Devonshire*, which could not take any action, and was carrying the King of Norway and his Cabinet in any case. However, five members of the *Devonshire*'s crew maintain that enough of the message was heard that to realise that *Glorious* had sighted two German warships and was in trouble. If this was the case, why didn't Vice Admiral Cunningham pass on a warning to the troop convoys, as thousands of troops were at risk? The question is made even more difficult as the *Devonshire*'s logs are missing. Why did the *Devonshire* exercise all four main turrets within minutes of the *Glorious* sending her first enemy report? Why did the *Devonshire* increase to 30 knots and start zig-zagging a few minutes after *Glorious* final signal was sent, according to German signals? Finally, why was *Glorious* flying no air patrols, despite a week earlier flying 'safe circle' air patrols through the very same waters?

Despite all these questions over the incident and the available evidence to the contrary, the sad fact remains that the MoD remains tied to the excuse that it was the lack of fuel that forced HMS *Glorious* to leave for Scapa Flow, even though the sinking of the ship occurred over 70 years ago.

A TV programme was made on the sinking of HMS *Glorious* in 1999 and it was the subject of a debate in the House of Commons on 28 January 1999, raised by the MP for Berwick-upon-Tweed, Alan Beith. The report of this taken from Hansard can be found in Appendix U.The closing of the debate appeared to be the end of the matter, and the sinking of the *Glorious*, *Acasta* and *Ardent* was just one of a number of tragedies that occurred between 1939 and 1945. There is now a small memorial at Trondenes churchyard in Norway to the men who lost their lives on that fateful day in June 1940.

There was, as referred to earlier, a Board of Enquiry into these sinkings. It was held in August 1940, and some comments from surviving documents are as follows:

> It is clear, as the Commander-in-Chief, Rosyth, says, that the *Glorious* was unprepared for action and to have been unsuspecting of enemy forces in her vicinity. The Board of Enquiry has elicited the following facts:-
>
> 1. There were five TSRs (Torpedo-Spotter-Reconnaissance) on board which might have been used for reconnaissance, but none was in the air for twelve hours, prior to, or during, the action.
> 2. There was a lack of a proper look-out on board and of precautions generally against a possible surface attack.
> 3. Before the action began the only shell at the guns was for anti-aircraft attack.
> 4. All the boilers were not connected up.
>
> Then there is the external aspect, which is referred to in paragraph 2 (b) of the Board of Enquiry's finding, namely the apparent absence of any surface cover to protect the ship from the attack which she met or what enemy intelligence, if any, was given to the Commanding Officer of *Glorious*.
>
> A Court Martial in a case such as this might be held either for the trial of someone on a specific charge, e.g. negligence or to investigate the loss and try the survivors under Section 92 of the Naval Discipline Act. We do not feel that any of the survivors can be held responsible for the state of preparedness of the ship and the only value of a trial of the survivors would be officially to exonerate them from blame.

Perhaps it is fitting to virtually let the last word come from Vernon Day, a naval air mechanic whose normal role was looking after the Swordfish aircraft on HMS *Glorious*. He later recalled;

> Some Hurricanes landed but two of them were damaged from the landing and so I together with others was working on them in the hangar. Then action stations was sounded and it seems almost immediately a shell came through the flight deck which hit one of the Hurricanes and set it on fire. This set others on fire and so the flames were soon getting out of control. Then we got the order to

> abandon ship and I was lucky enough to get into the water and swam to a Carley float. There wasn't enough room for more than about 24 people on the raft and so we had to wait for people to die to bring others on board. Somehow I lasted the night but there was [sic] only four of us left alive. Then thankfully we were picked up by a Norwegian trawler.

You may recall mention of the German tanker *Samland* and that revenge of a sort for the loss of the *Glorious* was extracted by the submarine HMS *Tetrarch*. The *Tetrarch*'s commander, Lieutenant Commander R. Mills, said later:

> We were again patrolling south of the Lister and on 16th June I sighted a fairly large merchantman escorted by a number of E-boats coming my way. I waited until she was in range and fired a salvo of four torpedoes and we heard two explosions. After the second explosion we could hear sounds of the ship breaking up. I dived down to 300 feet and we then counted twelve depth charges going off but we suffered no damage. We later found out we had sunk the *Samland*. This was the only real highlight of our third patrol in Norwegian waters.

4

Other operations – Maurice, Sickle and Hammer

Narvik had always been the main prize for the Allied forces sent to Norway, and whilst this remained foremost in the planners' eyes, attention was also being focused elsewhere. In London, after receiving the news in early April that Narvik would "fall within a matter of hours", other plans came to fruition. After the naval battle at Narvik on 13 April, the first idea was Operation Henry, involving a party of around 300 sailors and marines from various ships, who would land at Namsos the following day. Next came Operation Primrose, intended to be a diversionary landing by 600 sailors and marines at Alesund on the morning of 16 April. Finally, Operation Maurice was intended to be the main landing of around 5,000 men at Namsos on 16 April, with the capture of Trondheim being their main aim. Cobbled together quickly, it was suggested on the morning of 14 April to strike while the iron was hot, with one of the two brigades then on the way to Narvik to be diverted to Namsos. The infantry unit selected was 146 Brigade. General Ironside, the CIGS, protested, but Churchill brushed aside his objections; after speaking with the French, Churchill secured the services of their 5 Demi-Brigade of Chasseurs to be sent to Trondheim. The War Office in London ordered 146 Brigade to be sent to Namsos. When the new instructions were received, the men of 146 Brigade were on board two transport ships – the *Chrobry* and *Empress of Australia* – about 100 miles off their original destination of Narvik. They then sailed south for Namsos, halving the infantry available for the Narvik expedition.

In the original plan, called R4, one battalion from 146 Brigade (the Hallamshires) was to be sent to Bergen, but with the German invasion on 9 April their destination was changed to Trondheim. Then the two battalions from 148 Brigade were originally planned to go to Stavanger. However, there was a lack of reliable intelligence on what was happening in southern and central Norway. What was certain was that the Germans were ensconced in the Oslo region and other key centres, and after 14 April further intelligence came in courtesy of Lieutenant Colonel Edward King-Salter, the newly appointed British Military Attaché to Norway.

By the evening of 9 April, the Military Coordination Committee in London had in mind the seizure of footholds around Namsos and Åndalsnes. Next morning, the Chiefs of Staff recorded the intention of attempting this if the Narvik operation did not require the whole of the Allied forces available. On 11 April, however, the Chief of the Air Staff, Cyril Newall, at the meeting of the Military Coordination Committee, raised the possibility of an operation against Trondheim or Bergen, which would follow up the intended successful landing at Narvik, and permission was given to investigate these schemes. This later became known as Operation Maurice, and would be an additional landing to those planned under Operation Rupert, the assault on Narvik. On 12 April, the War Cabinet heard requests from the Norwegian Government for the recapture of Trondheim, as it was felt that if something was not done in this region it would lead to the total collapse of Norway, and possibly Sweden. The War Cabinet therefore agreed that landings on the Norwegian coast, even in limited numbers and locations, would have an important political and morale effect on the Norwegians, and so should be undertaken. The Military Coordination Committee ordered a plan to be prepared for landings using such forces that could be scraped together.

It was decided that the troops already allocated for the Narvik area would be left to carry on, with five battalions, plus four anti-aircraft guns taken from Britain's air defences, spared for Operation Maurice. Again, intelligence on what might be found on landing was sketchy, so much reliance was placed on what could be found out from the landings by the naval parties. The intended date for Operation Henry (the landing at Namsos) was put back 24 hours due to a submarine scare, and eventually took place on 14 April. A small number of cruisers and destroyers, led by Captain Frank Pegram in HMS *Glasgow*, formed one of two groups which were now searching the Leads (the waters off Narvik) from Alesund to the north. At about dusk, 350 seamen and Royal Marines under Captain W. Edds of the Royal Marines from the *Glasgow* group were landed by destroyers. Men from the cruiser HMS *Sheffield* were landed east of Namsos, while those from the *Glasgow* were south of the village of Bangsund. The landing parties met with no opposition, although Captain Pegram was certain that their presence had been spotted from the air. It was later revealed that the Germans had intercepted and been able to crack a naval signal on 12 April which mentioned Namsos, with Mosjöen as an alternative spot suitable for a landing and reconnaissance. The sailors and marines were accompanied by a small military advance party who sent a report back to London on the following morning, after consultation with Norwegian officers. This report stated that the Germans made a daily air reconnaissance of the area; that there was only a very small chance of concealment for any considerable force at Namsos or Bangsund; that movement was very difficult or impossible owing to the snow; and that a move southward at anything above battalion strength would be slow, and conspicuous from the air.

In the late evening of 13 April, the Military Coordination Committee believed that "the landing of the Rupert force might possibly be made in the town itself" and, subject to confirmation of the view that serious opposition at Narvik was unlikely, authorised the diversion of 146 Brigade from Narvik to Namsos. The naval authorities had pressed for this, informally, as early as the night of 11 April, and had to some extent arranged the convoy accordingly. Its arrival would follow that of the cruiser parties and would coincide with the landing of another small naval force at Alesund, south of Trondheim. On the afternoon of 14 April, after further consideration by the Chiefs of Staff, this diversion was ordered, and it was followed almost at once by the transfer – with French permission – of the first Demi-brigade of Chasseurs Alpins (three battalions) to reinforce Maurice instead of Rupert. Optimism regarding the situation at Narvik now reached its peak: the Military Coordination Committee passed a resolution which apparently anticipated a speedy resumption of ore exports to the United Kingdom, and some authorities in London even began to contemplate the transfer to the south of 24 Brigade – the only brigade now left for Major-General Pierse Mackesy, commander of ground forces at Narvik – as its task in the north would soon be completed.

Meanwhile, the landing south of Trondheim was expanded to form an integral part of the general Norwegian plan. Its main weight was transferred from the islands at Alesund to the mainland at Åndalsnes, and the naval landing parties would be used to secure a base for 148 Brigade, which had previously been earmarked for Namsos. It was hoped that a relatively small advance inland would invest Trondheim from the south, a manoeuvre in which the French saw great possibilities. Further reinforcement was contemplated for the new Sickle force, coming down towards Trondheim from the north.

However, the naval success at Narvik on 13 April perhaps influenced the planners' minds and it was suggested at a meeting of the Military Coordination Committee that evening, after HMS *Warspite* had successfully penetrated the entire length of the Ofotfjord, that part of the Maurice Force might be landed straight at Trondheim. This was the start of what was known as Operation Boots, which soon evolved into Operation Hammer, a direct attack on Trondheim which would hopefully meet the increasingly urgent demands of the Norwegian Government and Commander-in-Chief for immediate help. From a Norwegian point of view, it was clear that the prompt recapture of Trondheim would be an almost ideal counter to the German thrusts. Politically, the city is of great importance as the medieval capital of the country, the crowning place of Norwegian kings and the traditional centre of the second richest agricultural area. Economically, it was the third largest town in Norway (with a 1940 population of around 56,000), having considerable industries, especially in timber, and an extensive harbour with outlying accommodation for vessels of deep draught. Strategically, it can almost be described as the key to Scandinavia. Looking south, Trondheim is at the head of two alternative routes through the mountains to Oslo; to the north, it is the starting point of the only road or rail link with northern Norway; and eastwards, it guards the approach to two valleys which throughout history have afforded a main route from Norway to Sweden. It follows automatically that, once the modern capital of Oslo was effectively in German hands, Trondheim assumed supreme importance as the natural alternative centre on which to base the re-establishment of the government's authority and the movement for the expulsion of the Germans.

Accordingly, on 12 April at 1425, the British Government had received a telegram from its Ambasador in Norway, Sir Cecil Dormer, informing them that the Norwegian Government urgently desired the recapture of Trondheim to maintain their authority in the country. This was also the policy of the Norwegian Commander-in-Chief, General Ruge, who asked for a British division to be sent and held two or more of his own battalions in readiness for an attack on the city from the south. This fitted in well with the first stage of the plan given to Maurice Force, which was to make a rapid push forward from the north, so as to secure at once as much of the area between Namsos and Trondheim. On 16 April, the Ruge sent another telegram through King-Salter, the British Military Attaché, requesting a decision about the recapture of Trondheim. Lieutenant Colonel King-Salter then pressed the matter further by reporting certain details furnished by the Director of

Military Intelligence at General Ruge's Headquarters. This officer recommended a direct attack past the Agdenes forts or, if the Agdenes defences proved too strong, an attack towards Vinje and Surna, 60 miles to the south-west of the town. This intelligence was based on the officer's local knowledge, as he had previously acted as Chief of Staff to the division based around Trondheim. In peacetime, their role had been geared towards defence of the area based on an attack coming from Agdenes, and additionally of landings around Kyrksaeteröra, Vinje, and Surna with the intention of taking Trondheim.

Initially, 10 battalions had been suggested for the Trondheim expedition, half of them British (Regulars) and half French. But the troops finally allotted to the task were 15 and 147 Infantry Brigades and two Canadian battalions. Commanded by Brigadier Herbert Smyth, 15 Brigade was a Regular formation and consisted of:

1st Battalion The Green Howards (Lieutenant Colonel A. Robinson)
1st Battalion The King's Own Yorkshire Light Infantry (Acting Lieutenant Colonel E. Cass)
1st Battalion The York and Lancaster Regiment (Lieutenant Colonel A. Kent-Lemon)
168th Light Anti-Aircraft Artillery Battery, Royal Artillery
260th Heavy Anti-Aircraft Artillery Battery, Royal Artillery
55th Field Company Royal Engineers (less one section)

The Territorial 147 Brigade consisted of:

5th Battalion West Yorkshire Regiment
6th Battalion Duke of Wellington's Regiment
7th Battalion Duke of Wellington's Regiment

The other formations intended for Norway as part of the Maurice and Sickle Forces respectively were 146 and 148 Brigades.

Another Territorial unit, 146 Brigade was commanded by Brigadier Charles Phillips and consisted of:
4th Battalion The Royal Lincolnshire Regiment (Lieutenant Colonel R. Newton)
4th Battalion The King's Own Yorkshire Light Infantry (Lieutenant Colonel W. Hibbert)
The Hallamshire Battalion, The York and Lancaster Regiment (Lieutenant Colonel C. Robbins)

Also Territorials, 148 Brigade was commanded by Brigadier Harold Morgan. It only consisted of two battalions instead of the usual three:

5th Battalion The Royal Leicestershire Regiment (Lieutenant Colonel G. German)
8th Battalion The Sherwood Foresters (Lieutenant Colonel T. Ford)

Of these, 147 Brigade was to be embarked separately as a reserve; the remainder, including Divisional and Brigade Headquarters, constituted the assault force, to which the Navy contributed a Royal Marine battery of 3.7in howitzers. The expedition was to be commanded by Major-General Frederick Hotblack, who received his instructions on 17 April but suffered a stroke the same evening. His successor was Acting Major-General Horatio Berney-Ficklin, from 15 Brigade, but his command was terminated when he was injured in an air accident on the morning of 19 April. Major-General Bernard Paget then received orders to take over command of the expedition.

The instructions originally given to Major-General Hotblack can be found in Appendix A. As it turned out, 147 Brigade and the Canadians never got anywhere near Norway in 1940. It will probably come as no surprise to read that given all the previous orders and counter-orders issued over the Norwegian campaign, that by the morning of 19 April, the Chiefs of Staff had got cold feet about a direct attack on Trondheim. The order for General Paget to go north had already been withdrawn by the War Office, about one hour after it was issued. An Admiralty telegram to the Commander-in-Chief formally announced the cancellation of Operation Hammer at 1140 on the next day, but it was still "keen" on the ideas of landings north and south of Trondheim.

The Navy would of course be instrumental in any planned operations. On the evening of 13 April, the Naval Staff announced that they anticipated no difficulty in silencing the shore batteries outside Trondheim, and the Service Staffs were instructed to prepare their plans accordingly. On the afternoon of 15 April, the Committee was told that the Navy would be ready for the direct attack in about a week. On the 16th, the First Lord of the Admiralty, A.V. Alexander, said that another seven or eight days would be required to mount the operation, in which it was assumed that the Germans would receive not more than two hours' warning, so that they could not make much call upon their air strength in Denmark or Germany. Two carriers would put up 80 aircraft to deal with the Luftwaffe based in Norway, and the ships could in theory deal with any shore-based artillery. On 17 April the Committee determined the date of the operation as the 22nd, but on the 18th, after the news of the collapse of General Hotblack, a postponement to 24 April was contemplated as having the additional advantage of providing the troops with time for disembarkation practice. On the morning of 19 April, agreement as to the naval preparations was completed, when the Committee decided that the *Warspite* must be withdrawn from the Narvik operations in order to take part. It had been resolved, however, to avoid the bombardment of the city itself, if at all possible; the initial landing points would be beyond, in the bay near Vaernes and at Levanger.

The commander of the naval force, Admiral Sir Charles Forbes, was informed of Operation Hammer in the early hours of 14 April, while he was still at sea off the Lofoten Islands in HMS *Rodney*, with a request for his opinion as to the possibility of destroying or dominating the shore batteries so that transports could enter, and for particulars of the ships required. In his answer, at midday on the 14th, he said that the operation was not feasible unless the Government was prepared to face very heavy losses in troops and transports, because German bombers would have sufficient warning to provide continuous air attack. Forbes also pointed out that no ships of the Home Fleet had on board the high explosive shells which would be needed for their main armament. But the Admiralty answered, "Pray consider this important project further." It said large troopships would have to be brought into the danger zone somewhere, and for this operation they should be in a position to put both Stavanger and Trondheim airfields out of action – the first by RAF bombing followed up by bombardment from the cruiser HMS *Suffolk*, the latter by the attacks of naval aircraft and bombardment from ships. The Admiralty also said that high explosive shell for the 15in guns had been despatched to Rosyth and that the aircraft carrier *Furious* and the 1st Cruiser Squadron would be employed.

Sir Charles Forbes, having received details of the defences and confirmation of the fact that the Germans had seized the batteries at the entrance of the fjord, replied to the Admiralty on 15 April, complaining about the withdrawal of the 1st Cruiser Squadron from Kirkenes and that of the *Furious* from Narvik, and proposing a force to consist of the aircraft carrier *Glorious*; the three capital ships *Valiant*, *Renown* and *Warspite*, of which the last named was to carry out shore bombardments; at least four anti-aircraft cruisers; about 20 destroyers; and "numerous landing craft". The admiral added that his previous reply had been misunderstood: he did not "anticipate any great difficulty from the naval side", provided the troops were conveyed in men of war instead of transports. The Admiralty went ahead with its preparations, and on the 19th the *Valiant* sailed for Rosyth to transport the HE shells for the bombardment. Meanwhile, the plan had been received by the Commander-in-Chief on his arrival with the Home Fleet at Scapa, and arrangements were made for the whole of the military assault force to be embarked according to his wishes in cruisers, destroyers and sloops, which would also carry the stores, howitzer battery and six landing craft. Embarkation was fixed for 21 April at Rosyth, whence the expedition would proceed to Scapa to pick up the reserve brigade and rendezvous with the aircraft carriers *Ark Royal* and *Glorious*. These last were not available until the 23rd, so the attack was put back to 26 April at the earliest.

The new strategy, however, still envisaged the capture of Trondheim, though more slowly, by a pincer movement, with landings at Namsos and Åndalsnes. After the upheavals in the chain of command, Lieutenant-General Hugh Massy, who was Deputy Chief of the Imperial General Staff, was appointed as 'Commander of Allied Forces in Norway except in the Narvik area'; while Major-General Adrian Carton de Wiart was appointed as the commander of Operation Maurice.

Carton de Wiart, who received the Victoria Cross during the First World War for his actions during the Somme offensive in July 1916, had a colourful career before his appointment in Norway. After the Great War he served in Poland as second-in-command and then head of the British Military Mission, seeing action against the Bolsheviks and Lithuania, with a brief period in Lithuanian captivity and having to fight off Red Army cavalry with his revolver. When Poland was victorious in its war with the Soviets in 1921, Carton de Wiart resigned his commission and spent the remainder of the interwar years living in Poland.

His peaceful Polish life was interrupted by the oncoming war in July 1939, when he was recalled and appointed to his old job as head of the British Military Mission to Poland. When Hitler invaded Poland, Carton de Wiart escaped back to Britain via Romania on a false passport, having survived a *Luftwaffe* attack on a convoy he was travelling in. For the rest of 1939 and early 1940 he was in command of the 61st Division based in the Midlands, before joining the forces in Norway.

As commander of Operation Maurice, he received the following instructions from the CIGS, General Ironside:

> Instructions to Major-General Carton de Wiart Commanding Force Scheduled for 'Maurice Operation'.
>
> 1. His Majesty's Government and the Government of the French Republic have decided to land an expedition in Central Norway with the object of:
>   (a) Providing encouragement for the Norwegian Government.
>   (b) Forming a rallying point for the Norwegian Government and armed forces.
>   (c) Securing a base for any subsequent operations in Scandinavia.
>   This operation will be carried out concurrently with but independent of the operations already initiated in northern Norway.
> 2. You are appointed to command the Allied forces which are being despatched to Central Norway.
> 3. Your role will be to secure the Trondheim area. Subsequently you should take such steps as are possible to secure the use to the Allies of the road and rail communications leading from Trondheim, especially to the east.
> 4. Points of Landing.
>   (i) It is suggested, but of this you, together with the Senior Naval Officer, must be the final judges, that the initial landing should be in the Namsos area, and should be carried out by Morgan's and Phillips' Brigades.
>   (ii) A second landing should be carried out about Trondheim preferably to the east of the town, and after the Navy has cleared the fjord of German vessels, by 147th Infantry Brigade and Chasseurs Alpins.
>   (iii) Administrative facilities should initially be developed about Namsos until Trondheim has been secured.
> 5. A forecast of the dates of arrival in the Trondheim-Namsos area of the elements of your force is as follows:-
>   (a) 146th Infantry Brigade, Brigadier Phillips, available on 15th April.
>   (b) One infantry brigade (less one battalion), under Brigadier Morgan, should be available about dawn 17th April.
>   (c) 147th Infantry Brigade, with artillery and ancillary troops, should be available on 20th or 21st April.
>   (d) Two battalions Chasseurs Alpins available (in the same area) 18th April.
> 6. Should you become a casualty or otherwise be prevented from exercising command of the force, command will pass to the next senior British officer, who will exercise command, and in the event of a French General officer being with the force, assume the acting rank of Major-General until another British officer can be appointed.
> 7. As soon as you are established ashore you will get in touch with any Norwegian forces in your vicinity, inform them of the impending arrival of further Allied forces and secure their co-operation in action against any German forces.

8. The Royal Navy are making preliminary landings in the Namsos area with landing parties about 300 strong in all and it is their intention to seize and hold any point in the Namsos area at which your disembarkation might take place.
9. Your force is not organised for landing in face of opposition, and it is not intended that you should undertake such an operation.
10. During the voyage and during landing operations, the Senior Naval Officer will be in command, and he will decide, in co-operation with you, where and when to land.
11. A note as to the strength of the Norwegian forces in the area, and of the strength of any German forces operating in the vicinity, is being given to you separately.
12. Your force will constitute an independent command directly under the War Office. You will keep a constant communication with the War Office and report as regularly as is practicable as to the situation.

Meanwhile Lieutenant-General Massy had been told that he was in command of all troops outside Narvik, yet he was expected to undertake this role from the UK. He commented:

> When the original plan for operations in southern Norway was made, the landings at Åndalsnes and Namsos were intended as diversions to a main attack to be made on Trondheim. When our troops advanced inland from these bases, it was decided that Trondheim might be captured by a converging movement instead of a hazardous direct attack from seaward. It was hoped too that sufficient troops could be put into Åndalsnes to stiffen Norwegian resistance in the south and thus put a limit to the German advance from Oslo. It was against this background that I was instructed on 19th April to assume the appointment of Commander of the North Western Expeditionary Force and to form my Headquarters with a view to taking command as soon as possible of the operations in progress north and south of Trondheim.

Carton de Wiart, soon after his appointment as Commander of Allied Forces in central Norway, arrived at Namsos with a junior staff officer, Captain Elliott, in a Sunderland flying boat. The initial aim was to confer with the navy landing parties, but the expedition did not get off to a good start. With the flying boat and a destroyer, HMS *Somali*, moored in the Namsen fjord, they were spotted by German aircraft and repeatedly attacked with bombs and machine gun fire. Captain Elliott, who is said to have been airsick nearly all the way across to Norway, was wounded, thus ending his brief Norwegian adventure. As the landing of troops direct from their transports was thought impractical, it was decided that they would have to be cross-decked to destroyers at Lillesjona and then moved to Namsos on two successive days. Carton de Wiart felt that Namsos had inadequate quays and unloading facilities, and the long fjord leading to it was narrow and believed to be virtually impassable to the large ships. It was hoped that the cross-decking could be carried out without any intervention from the Luftwaffe.

However, it was 'leaked' to the press and radio in London on 14 April that "landings at several points in Norway had taken place". The Norwegian Government also announced to the world that "assistance was assuming great proportions", which was not strictly true as the forces involved numbered less than 10,000.

Most of these forces heading for action in Norway were Territorial bolstered by the Regulars of 15 Brigade, who in April 1940 were based in France as part of the BEF. The CO of the 1st King's Own Yorkshire Light Infantry (KOYLI) was told at 2150 on 16 April, together with his Adjutant at Brigade HQ, and in less than 24 hours they were leaving for Quesnoy station in northern France. By 0300 on 18tApril, they had arrived at Boulogne and started loading their kit onto the *Mona's Queen*, and by 1015 were in Dover. Brigadier Berney-Ficklin had taken over command due to the illness to Major-General Hotblack, so Lieutenant Colonel Smyth took over command of the brigade, moving from the KOYLI, and Major Cass took over command; both of them left for London to receive orders. The rest of the battalion left Dover in two trains, routing through Guildford, Manchester and Carlisle before arriving in Dunfermline around 1000 on 19 April. As their war diary records: "Marched to Camp, 1½ miles from town. Day spent in settling down in Camp, receiving Arctic clothing and bundling all equipment into one man loads."

The first troops in theory to arrive were those diverted from Narvik, namely the three battalions of 146 Brigade: 4th Battalion The Royal Lincolnshire Regiment, 4th Battalion KOYLI and The Hallamshire Battalion, The York and Lancaster Regiment.

The 4th Lincolns of 146 Brigade were based like the rest of the 49th Division in the north of England around Yorkshire, and on 2 April received orders at their Ripon base to despatch an advance party to HQ Scottish Command at Edinburgh under a general warning order received for movement of the unit to an unknown destination. The small advance party, under the command of Captain Round-Turner, left at 0800 on 3 April. The rest of the battalion were advised at 1200 they would not be moving until 8 April at the earliest, then five hours later at 1700 the move date was brought forward to the 7th. Leather jerkins were issued to the battalion on 6 April, with much packing of stores. At 0735 on 7 April, the 4th Lincolns left Ripon station, heading north for what for most of them was an unknown destination. It is recorded that on leaving Ripon, the battalion strength was 29 officers and 603 men. In keeping with their sister units, the final destination was Rosyth, and the 4th Lincolns embarked at 1600 on 7 April on HMS *Berwick*. The Navy then advised on 8 April that as the ship was felt to be under threat of attack by German diver bombers, the Lincolns would need to disembark as soon as possible, the order arriving around 1130. The move was duly carried out, *Berwick* sailing within two hours, but many of the Lincolns' stores were left on board. The battalion then marched to Camp 4 outside Dunfermline, where they found their advance party. They spent a couple of days here before moving by train on 11 April to Gourock, where they arrived around noon and heard they would be embarking later that day on the SS *Empress of Australia*. They left at 2200 to be told they were heading for Narvik. Eventually, off Scapa Flow, they formed up into a small convoy of troop ships also comprising the *Monarch of Bermuda*, *Rio de Pacifico*, *Chrobry* and *Batory*, together with an accompanying naval escort. On the 14th, the Lincolns' war diary records that "personnel issued with immense store of Arctic equipment, requiring two large kit bags to carry it. The issue included two pairs of large boots, socks, leather jerkin, arctic coat, gloves, fur helmet, dark goggles and two sleeping bags."

Whilst at sea on 15 April, news came that 146 Brigade would now be diverted to Namsos. Some documents that survive from the Hallamshires give an insight into life on the voyage to Norway for the soldiers, and can be found in Appendix F.

One of the staff officers sent to accompany Major-General Carton de Wiart was a certain Captain P. Fleming, who had been selected by Colonel Gubbins to assist him in the Norwegian campaign but had ended up with Carton de Wiart. His brother Ian was also in military service and would later become famous for writing the *James Bond* books. The following are a couple of signals sent, the first from Captain Fleming on 15 April at 0240, giving some details of what might be expected ashore:

> Norwegian 5th Division HQ at Kvam report at 2300/14 no enemy north of Hell. They estimate total enemy strength 1600. Norwegian strength uncertain. Trains south from Namsos running to Verdal today. Naval landing party will be in position south of Bangsund and east of Namsos by dawn 15th April. Locals co-operating. Area reconnoitred daily by enemy aircraft. Both Namsos and Bangsund being snow covered, partially evacuated and offer very small chance of concealment for considerable force. Local deployment impossible owing to four feet of snow. Some MT available no details yet rolling stock on track railway. Southward move any force much larger than battalion must be both slow and conspicuous from the air. Namsos at present short of fresh water. Expect Wiart dawn 15th April.

The following signal was from Major-General Carton de Wiart to Brigadier Phillips, timed at 2359 on 15 April:

> I propose to land two battalions in Namsos area tomorrow night 16th/17th April. I will arrive in *Somali* a.m. tomorrow 16th April and will confer on arrival. Destroyers should be ready to sail with two battalions on board at noon. Two companies will be landed at Bangsund and are to be embarked in one destroyer. Remaining destroyers will go to Namsos quay. It will be necessary for *Somali* to lead the force as Captain (D) has the local knowledge. Battalion and company commanders should all embark in *Somali* in addition to her quota of troops.

The Hallamshires were to be the first of 146 Brigade to land, with the intention of securing the town and to act as a guard force for the rest of the brigade. The 4th KOYLI was to follow them, with the task of blocking the road and railway north-east of Namsos. Bringing up the rear would be the 4th Lincolns, who were to secure and block the road south of Namsos.

The 4th KOYLI had left Thirsk by train at 0630 and 0730 on 7 April, arriving at Rosyth later that day and boarding HMS *York*. The battalion strength was 30 officers,

Men from 147 Brigade on their way to Norway. (Imperial War Museum N30)

eight warrant officers and 590 other ranks. Like the rest of the brigade, on 8 April they were bundled off the ship, leaving some of their equipment on board and marching to a camp in Dunfermline. On the 11th they moved by train to Gourock and embarked with the 4th Lincolns in the SS *Empress of Australia*. By 16 April the *Empress of Australia* had anchored off Ranfjord and the ship was bombed on and off for about three hours; it is reported that eight bombs were dropped, with two near misses, but no real damage being caused. Around 1830, the 4th KOYLI cross-decked to the *Chrobry* via the destroyers HMS *Afridi* and *Vance*. This was completed by 0330 the following morning, and it is dryly recorded that "more equipment and stores [were] lost".

On 17 April, the 4th KOYLI arrived at Namsos at 2130. It was an unopposed landing for all units. Upon the arrival of 146 Brigade, the naval landing parties were withdrawn but the KOYLI reported that around 130 tons of their equipment had either not been landed, was lost or never left the UK. The disembarkation order for the 4th KOYLI can be found in Appendix G.

The Hallamshire Battalion had received orders on 1 April that they would be proceeding overseas and that all MT vehicles together with two officers and 80 ORs were to remain behind at their base in Thirsk and join up at a later date. On 6 April, the Hallamshires left Thirsk in two special trains at 0755 and 0910. Their war diary records the travelling strength as being 28 officers and 733 ORs, together with another seven officers and 26 ORs attached for duty from other technical units. On 12 April, the MT with the two officers and 80 ORs drove from Thirsk to Musselburgh, just outside Edinburgh. The Hallamshires were treated the same as the other units in the brigade, being embarked and disembarked, and didn't get under way towards Norway until leaving Scapa Flow on 12 April.

The main problem for the British forces was still German air superiority. Captain Donald McIntyre in his 1959 book *Narvik* wrote the following:

> Enemy aircraft found them even so far north. The destroyers left in a flurry of frothing stern wash, curving bow waves and the tall thudding splashes of bomb burst for their high-speed run down the coast to Namsos where they arrived during the night of the 16th April. By daylight the Hallamshires had all been landed, the men dispersed from the quay sides and all traces of their arrival obliterated.

However, the speed of the embarkation and the constant harassment by the Luftwaffe meant that the KOYLIs of 146 Brigade were still aboard the *Empress of Australia*. The air raids at Lillesjona had been almost continuous. Near misses constantly shook the converted liners, and Captain McIntyre wrote that the bombardment "shook also the morale of the young inexperienced soldiers, receiving their baptism of fire cooped up helplessly aboard". Unfortunately, after the KOYLIs disembarked, the *Empress of Australia* was sent home still carrying 170 tons of stores. The *Chrobry* left with 130 tons of supplies and stores still aboard.

By the late evening of 17 April, Maurice Force was ashore but struggling to cope with conditions. Snow was around 2ft deep on average, but much deeper in the drifts and piled at the sides of the roads. Once ashore it became clear that frequent ploughing would be required to keep the roads open, and that potentially skis and snow shoes would be needed to aid mobility – but of course none had been provided. Another problem was the amount of kit each man was meant to carry. For example, most had three kitbags, while the lambskin-lined Arctic coat alone weighed 15lb. Another problem was that no motor transport had accompanied the expedition, so the three battalion quartermasters had initially been instructed to try to hire or commandeer local transport. That was not easily done in a small isolated community, and great reliance was placed on the single-track railway to move men around. There were no guns of any sort for air defence or support purposes, and a lack of 3" mortars and their bombs. There was also no real GHQ set up, so logistics was going to be a problem.

However, in the mind of the War Office in London, things were going to get better as they still envisaged a three-pronged attack against Trondheim (to include Operation Hammer) and placing the Chasseurs Alpins, who would be landed in two tranches of three battalions each, under Carton de Wiart's command. The prospect of their early arrival meant that the units of 146 Brigade could be pushed forward to their locations as planned. The only feasible way of getting them to these locations was to use the railway, so local trains were commandeered, moving the 4th KOYLI forward to the Steinkjer area. Their war diary records:

> Arrived Namsos 2130. Disembarked at once and entrained at 0300 for Steinkjer. Whole night spent in moving kit and baggage. Still more kit and equipment lost in violent hurry to get off before dawn and arrival of bombers. Before entraining CO received orders from Brigade to move south and occupy Verdal, Röra, Sparbu areas.
>
> Arrived Steinkjer 0700 18th April. Entrained for forward dispositions at 2200. Strength 30 Officers, 8 Warrant Officers, 589 Other Ranks (1 OR admitted to hospital at Steinkjer). Battalion still in possession of Arctic clothing, three kit bags per man, which took all night shifting under cover. Men by now very exhausted from constant fatigues on baggage moving. No transport of any sort.'

On the following morning, the KOYLI was positioned as follows: B Company at Maere; Battalion HQ, HQ Company and C Company at Sparbu; D Company at Röra; and A Company at Strommen

The main problem for the KOYLI still seemed to be transport, and they had to commandeer four cars and eight lorries from local sources. The Luftwaffe appeared to know exactly where the KOYLI were, and their attacks necessitated most of the unit remaining under cover during daylight.

Meanwhile, the 4th Lincolns had landed at Namsos around 2100 on 16 April, and within about three hours 300 men under the command of Major K. Black left for Grong. On the 17th, an HQ was established at the railway station, with the other troops being billeted in barns and a local school. The rest of the Lincolns arrived from Namsos at around 2315 on 18 April, the reunited group moving within an hour to Steinkjer. Their war diary records: "Authorities were unable to move any of our kit bags or stores, arrangements made for them to follow next day." As with many other British units in Norway, the old Army saying 'never get separated from your kit' was not being adhered to.

Captain Dick Newsum from the 4th Lincolns commented:

> We travelled by train to Steinkjer at the head of the Trondheim fjord. On arrival we discovered how short of equipment we were, as much of it had been left behind in the UK due to our rather hurried and mismanaged departure. We had mortars and bombs but no sights, telephones but no exchanges, and absolutely no transport, not the best way to start a war.

The last unit of the brigade, the Hallamshires, were the first arrivals at Namsos around 2130 and secured the town with ease, A Company taking up position around the road bridge. C and D Companies were offloaded from destroyers at Bangsund. On the following day, D Company was ordered to move to Steinkjer, this being carried out by road in locally commandeered transport, and other elements of the Hallamshires went to the Beitstadfjord area to secure both sides of the fjord. This fjord is the innermost part of the long Trondheimsfjord; any positions on its western bank at Follafoss would act as a blocking point against any German advances from the shore opposite Trondheim. This appeared to be a key position on the road from Steinkjer to Trondheim. By the afternoon of the 17th, Steinkjer and Follafoss had both been reached. The general policy was to build up forward as quickly as possible: by the evening of 19 April, Brigade Advanced Headquarters was in the northern outskirts of Steinkjer and detachments were posted at Röra and Stiklestad, up to 17 miles further south. Having passed right across the base of the Inderöy peninsula, Maurice Force had now reached the main Trondheimsfjord at a point which was only about 60 miles from Trondheim. The snow did not seriously interfere with the advance, which was along the line of road and railway, the use of the rail route east to Grong and thence in a big loop south to Steinkjer being supplemented by the employment of local transport.

Meanwhile, efforts were being made to involve the Norwegian Army, with local troops from the 5th Division, normally based in the Trondheim area. They were out of contact with General Ruge, the Norwegian Commander-in-Chief, but were in contact with the 6th Division north of Narvik. The commander of the 5th Division, General Laurantzon, was contacted at his headquarters by a British advance party on 15 April, and decided to make liaison with the British base at Namsos his personal responsibility. He did not, however, favour any advance beyond Steinkjer until Agdenes had been taken, and had, before the British arrived, adopted a rather passive attitude towards the German invasion. He was also not a well man – towards the end of the month he went on sick leave – and on 17 April a Colonel Getz was put in command of all Norwegian troops in the area as commander of 5 Brigade. On paper this formation had a strength of four battalions, but on the 18th, when 146 Brigade's Brigadier Phillips first met with Colonel Getz, he found that it actually only had two battalions, with one from each of the two locally recruited regiments. These had, after completing their mobilisation, been withdrawn north of Steinkjer, acting as a blocking force in a strategic position on the seven-mile wide isthmus between the head of the fjord and Lake Snaasavatn. They were supported by a machine gun squadron of dismounted dragoons at Verdalsöra, west of Stiklestad.

Another problem was the lack of experience and resources that Colonel Getz had under his command. He described his troops as inexperienced militia, and emphasised that stocks of ammunition amounted to only one day's battle issue (around 100 rounds per rifle and 2,500 per machine gun). When these limited stocks had been used, the Norwegians would need to be re-equipped with British weapons, since ammunition of the right calibre for their own weapons was unavailable outside Norway. Phillips felt that due to this logistical problem, it might be best to use the Norwegians in a reconnaissance role, using their local knowledge and ability to ski.

Colonel Getz urged the seizure of the Fetten defile beyond Aasen, where the road from Levanger again touched the fjord, about 30 miles short of Trondheim. The valley had the potential to be a key location both defensively and offensively, with an inland route into Stjördal, the valley by which the railway from Trondheim climbs eastwards into Sweden. There was also a small Norwegian position in a hilltop fort at Hegra with less than 300 men. This fort was under the command of Major Holtermann; but Colonel

Getz, though he had recently been in touch with the garrison, does not appear to have made clear to the British the help that Hegra, with its four 105mm, two 75 mm and two old field guns, might provide along that line of advance.

Whilst the British started to advance, reinforcements for Carton de Wiart's force arrived in the shape of three battalions of Chasseurs Alpins from the French 5 Demi-Brigade who landed at Namsos on the night of 19/20 April. In theory this was a major boost as these troops were trained in Arctic warfare. However, like 146 Brigade, they had been diverted from Narvik and much of their equipment – including such vital elements as skis, transport, mules and anti-aircraft guns – failed to materialise. The French liner *Ville d'Alger* did later turn up with some of this equipment, but when it was unloaded it was found that the straps for the skis were missing, making them virtually useless. Some French troops managed to get hold of Norwegian skis, so were eventually able to assist in the fighting. The Germans had spotted all this activity around Namsos and had bombarded the town, virtually turning it into a smoking ruin and blowing up most of the French reserve ammunition.

Meanwhile, the men of 146 Brigade finally came into contact with the Germans on 21 April. The snow was starting to melt and the fjords becoming free of ice, which meant the danger from German landings was increased. The report of the CO of the 4th Lincolns for period 19-23 April can be found in Appendix H.

23 April was a black day for Maurice Force, as the attack was running out of steam and the German landings were a grave threat. One report gives the losses for Maurice Force up to this day as 19 dead, 42 wounded and 96 missing. Carton de Wiart later commented:

> Still I waited for news of our naval attack, which was to be my signal to take Trondheim, but still it did not come. Hourly it became more and more obvious to me that with my lack of equipment I was quite incapable of advancing on Trondheim, and could see very little point in remaining in that part of Norway sitting out like rabbits in the snow. I wired to the War Office to tell them my conclusions, only to get back the reply that for political reasons they would be glad if I would maintain my positions. I agreed, but said it was about all I could do. They were so relieved that they actually wired me their thanks.

With the chances of taking Trondheim disappearing, Carton de Wiart sent one of his staff officers, Captain P. Fleming, back to the UK by flying boat to find out what the War Office wanted to do now. Fleming apparently came back a couple of days later with the news the War Office in London appeared to be in complete chaos and told Carton de Wiart, "You can really do what you like, for they don't know what they want done."

After these trials and tribulations there was some good news on 25 April as 15 vehicles arrived from England, and these were put under the command of Brigade HQ.

The report of the 4th KOYLI for this period can be found in Appendix I. This signalled the end of the fighting carried out by the 4th KOYLI, and on 28 April they briefly came under the command of the French before reverting to the command of 146 Brigade.

British troops from 146 Brigade, part of Maurice Force, entering Namsos harbour on board SS *Oronsay*, with HMS *Fury* (H76) in the background. (Imperial War Museum N42)

The war diary of the Hallamshires also recorded their change in destination from Narvik to Namsos, with the aim of securing Trondheim:

> 15.4.40 0518 Following message received; To *Chrobry*, *Empress of Australia* from Cruiser Squadron 18 For OC Troops. Reduced opposition faced Narvik and securing of Trondheim urgent. 146th Infantry Brigade now diverted to Namsos area where it comes under command of Major-General Carton de Wiart who should arrive Namsos by air early today Monday. If no orders are received from him Brigade Commander will endeavour to establish his force ashore as early as possible in Namsos area so as to cover the disembarkation of further Allied troops. Decision regarding locality for landing to be made with Senior Naval Officer. Suggest landing 1 Bangsund 2 Namsos. Arrival of transports will be timed as late in the day as possible consistent with safety of navigation and every effort will be made to disembark troops during dark hours using every available craft. Troops will probably transfer to destroyers for this purpose.

With Brigadier Phillips still being in limbo at Scapa Flow, the CO of the Hallamshires was acting Brigade Commander. So whilst still at sea, Lieutenant Colonel Robins issued orders at 1400 on 15 April that his battalion would land first and stressed the need for a foothold to be gained at any cost. On the 16th, Carton de Wiart arrived in HMS *Somali* and by around 2100 the Hallamshires were ashore in Namsos. Over the next few days the Hallamshires moved forward, taking up positions around Steinkjer, Vist and Namdalseid, but it was not going well. They were continually harried by the Germans, mainly from the air, with the war diary recording on 20 April, “This was a day of intense aerial activity here, bombers passing over all day. Namsos was heavily bombed and our rear party suffered casualties.”

Commander R.W. Ravenhill, on the destroyer HMS *Nubian* off Namsos on 20 April, commented, “The whole place was a mass of flames from end to end and the glare on the snows of the surrounding mountains produced an unforgettable spectacle.” So it was somewhat fortunate that 146 Brigade had mainly been moved out of Namsos, as within 24 hours of embarkation the Luftwaffe descended on the town, completely unopposed, reducing the place to rubble and setting it ablaze. The base for Maurice Force was now largely obliterated, making reinforcement and supply almost impossible.

On 21 April, whilst the KOYLIs and Lincolns were doing their best to stop the German forces who had landed on the shores of the Trondheimsfjord, the Hallamshires were moved into a defensive position on the line Hjellebotn-Snaasavand to hopefully cover the withdrawal of their sister units, with all companies being in their allocated positions by the following morning. The move to these positions was not without incident, however, as the C Company convoy was spotted and machine gunned by aircraft – fortunately no casualties being caused – whilst Steinkjer was also bombed and a quantity of stores and equipment destroyed.

On the 22nd, the Hallamshires war diary records, “Many posts of all companies were machine gunned from the air as were several recce parties of officers, but there were only two minor casualties. It was a day of continual rumours of which the worst were the surrender of the 4th KOYLI and the annihilation of the 4th Lincolns.” Fortunately these rumours were false and the units were still functioning.

On the next day, it was decided that the brigade would withdraw northwards via Beistad and Bangsund, and during the night about 50 percent of the Lincolns withdrew through the Hallamshires after withdrawing from Steinkjer, where they had been heavily shelled from the sea and also attacked by German landing parties. The Hallamshire’ war diary also notes:

> A day of anxiety for the safety of the 4th KOYLI who it was hoped would be able to reach our position. There were many rumours of enemy advance on the front and flanks. The Battalion had been ordered to withdraw in the evening when the 4th KOYLI came through, but in view of these reports and the apparent uncertainty of the whereabouts of the 4th KOYLI, Colonel Robins applied to the Brigadier for permission to withdraw from our present exposed position to a much stronger position at the head of the Hjellebotn. Whilst the advisability of this move was being debated B Company reported over the Battalion signals that the 4th KOYLI were then passing their position.

Germans picking their way across a blown bridge near Steinkjer. (Imperial War Museum HU128794)

Over the next couple of days the Hallamshires gradually fell back on the Namsos area, complaining in their war diary that they seemed to be constantly on the move by night, and on each withdrawal more stores were being lost or left behind. It comments for 24 April:

> During the last six days at least two companies and large quantities of Battalion and Brigade stores have been moved each night. Great difficulty has been experienced in the obtaining of transport and the Transport Section have been busily engaged in rescue work in ditches or broken down lorries. Snow in the fields is up to 4 foot in depth and road conditions are very bad. This work has often been carried out in blinding snowstorms. These moves and the frequent moving of Battalion HQ has also necessitated a great deal of work in keeping in communication and the Battalion Signal Section have dealt very ably with the situation under most adverse conditions. The frequent changes of pan have caused a great deal of work and organisation and sleep has been short and seldom.

On the afternoon of 26 April, a German patrol – whether by accident or design – literally walked into one of the Hallamshires forward positions, and two of them were taken prisoner, the rest escaping by bicycle. Even a few bicycles would have given the men of 146 Brigade some sort of mobility, at least on the roads, but no surviving documents mention bicycles being shipped as part of the stores taken to Norway.

On 27 April, a patrol consisting of officers was sent to Kvam to hand over the remaining supplies of 146 Brigade's supply dump to the Norwegian Army, in theory to be held in safe custody on behalf of the British Army. It was intended and indeed hoped that the Norwegians would be able to move these stores further northwards to stop them falling into German hands, as seemed likely in the near future. Then on the night of 28/29 April, the Hallamshires moved to the Bangsund area, their positions being taken over by the French, although it was clearly noted that they would not move until at least some of the French troops were in position. As from noon on 28 April, the Hallamshires came under command of the local French commander until they moved through Namdalseid, when they would revert to the command of 146 Brigade.

By the morning of 30 April, the Hallamshires were concentrated in and around Bangsund, the actual locations being as follows: A Company at Strommen bridge, B Company at Fjor, C Company at Reitin, and D Company and HQ at Bangsund itself. The day was spent reorganising themselves, and although the Luftwaffe was again very active, the Hallamshires were not greatly troubled by them, aided no doubt by being located near a number of anti-aircraft guns.

On 1 May, orders were received stating that there was to be a general evacuation of the area by the Allies, and in the evening of 2 May, the CO of the Hallamshires attended a brigade conference at which detailed orders were given for the evacuation. For the Hallamshires, this involved ordering all the companies to set out on foot immediately as they were leaving that night.

General plan for the evacuation

It is necessary to go back a few days to explain the reasoning behind the sudden decision to abandon Maurice. It became clear that within days of landing that the proposed attack on Trondheim had changed into a precarious defensive operation. Carton de Wiart sent a telegram to the War Office on the afternoon of 23 April, before the process of extrating 146 Brigade had been completed, which described this unit as having been "very roughly handled", stressed the danger of increasing enemy air activity and discussed how the evacuation could proceed. As was often the case, the War Office in London believed the position to be better than those on the ground were stating. Before news of the defeat in front of Steinkjer had reached London and been assessed, the earlier disaster of the destruction of the base at Namsos had already been acted upon. Before midday on 22 April, an Admiralty message was sent to advise Carton de Wiart that anti-aircraft guns were on the way, an aircraft carrier with fighters would arrive on the 24th and that shore fighters would "probably" be established on the 25th. Accordingly, the new policy as expressed in the orders to Carton de Wiart in the field, and in more detail in a memorandum drawn up by Lieutenant-General Massy in London, was to keep Maurice

Major-General Carton de Wiart at his Headquarters. (Imperial War Museum N67)

Force in being and in position as "a standing threat to the Germans at Trondheim".

Some air cover for the exposed British troops appeared for the first time on 25 April when some aircraft from the Fleet Air Arm appeared, but three of them were forced to land due to lack of petrol. However, since this cover could not be maintained, the Luftwaffe realistically retained air superiority. On 26 April, an advance party of the RAF arrived to search for landing grounds, which came to naught, and as an Army report puts it, "should have been undertaken as soon as the leading troops arrived".

On the following day, the advance party of Carton de Wiart's staff arrived – up to this point he had basically been relying on the services of captains Fleming and Lindsay (of the Military Intelligence Directorate) and one other officer who had arrived on 23 April. He received a boost as on the same ship as the staff came a Royal Marine howitzer battery, a field ambulance, a dock labour company, representatives of a 'base sub-area organisation', rifles and ammunition for the Norwegians and many other stores and equipment. However, due to the fact that the quay was already piled high with French stores and that a French ship was alongside the one useable jetty unloading transport and equipment, only the HQ Staff, some of the howitzer battery (but with no ammunition) and some dock labourers could be got ashore.

Carlton de Wiart also learned on the 26th that the second Demi-Brigade of Chasseurs Alpins was to be sent to Narvik, and General Béthouart left by destroyer the next day to take command there. Carlton de Wiart had already telegraphed on the 23rd that, even with air superiority, he would require more troops – "say a brigade" – before he could advance again south of Bangsund. But generals Audet and Béthouart, who were perhaps encouraged by the lull in the air attack to minimise the significance of the reverse which the British troops had sustained, had been planning a counter-attack with the Norwegians on the left flank under Colonel Getz. The Norwegians were in good heart because their position on either shore of Snaasavatn had not been seriously attacked by the Germans, who had taken longer than they had expected to enter Steinkjer and did not propose to advance past Sunnan, the occupation of which on the evening of 24 April gave them full control of what they called the Steinkjer Pass. In such skirmishing of patrols as had occurred, the Norwegians, helped by conditions of terrain and climate, had given a fair account of themselves. The French had not been in action at all.

The 13th Chasseurs Alpins went forward to Namdalseid to the positions held by the Hallamshires, whom they would relieve, and also began to send ski patrols up the valley of the Bongaa east of the main road on to the heights. French and Norwegian patrols were there to join forces, the immediate object being to assert control of the isthmus east of Hjelle and reconnoitre further towards Steinkjer. The KOYLI and the 67th Chasseurs Alpins would be in the rear area and at the disposal of the French general for the operation. This arrangement, which had the Force Commander's approval, left two British battalions and one French battalion under Brigadier Phillips to hold the base and line of communications east from Namsos towards the Norwegian base area round Grong.

A Norwegian intelligence report of 27 April, which put the number of Germans in and around Steinkjer at 300, was highly optimistic; three battalions was nearer the mark. The Germans remained strictly on the defensive and did not consider themselves capable of any forward movement without a further reinforcement of two battalions of mountain infantry. Early on 28 April, when the French anti-aircraft batteries had at last been landed with their stores and equipment – an activity which monopolised the quay so completely that 7,000 rifles and 250 Bren guns with ammunition for the Norwegians had not left the *Chrobry* – Carton de Wiart received his expected orders to evacuate the Allied forces. For security reasons, the Norwegians were not to be told; the delay in obtaining the weapons which they needed and had been promised for the counter-attack was used to explain away its indefinite postponement.

Carton de Wiart held a meeting on 28 April with Admiral John Vivian (Flag Officer 20th Cruiser Squadron), General Audet (commanding French forces) and Brigadier Phillips, at which it was decided to plan for the evacuation on two successive nights. In the interim, however, it was possible to get away the French 53rd Chasseurs Alpins battalion on the night of 28/29 April in a returning transport ship.

The plan for the main embarkation was to be in two phases, on 1/2 and 2/3 May. A general withdrawal had now to be organised as unobtrusively as possible. Namsos was heavily attacked from the air on 28 April and again with dive-bombers on the 30th. The sloop *Bittern* was disabled and had to be abandoned, as were three out of eight anti-submarine trawlers, though the trawler *Arab* (whose commander, Lieutenant Richard Stannard, received the Victoria Cross) crowned a series of exploits in fire fighting and rescue work during these attacks by downing a German bomber single-handed on her way home. Stannard's citation was gazetted on 16 August 1940:

> The King has been graciously pleased to approve the grant of the Victoria Cross to Lieutenant Richard Been Stannard, RNR, HMS *Arab*, for outstanding valour and signal devotion to duty at Namsos. When enemy bombing attacks had set on fire many tons of hand grenades on Namsos wharf, with no shore water supply available, Lieutenant Stannard ran *Arab*'s bows against the wharf and held her there. Sending all but two of his crew aft, he then endeavoured for two hours to extinguish the fire with hoses from the forecastle. He persisted in this work till he had to give up the attempt as hopeless.
>
> After helping other ships against air attacks, he placed his own damaged vessel under shelter of a cliff, landed his crew and those of two other trawlers, and established an armed camp. Here those off duty could rest while he attacked enemy aircraft which approached by day, and kept anti-submarine watch during the night.
>
> When another trawler near-by was hit and set on fire by a bomb, he, with two others, boarded *Arab* and moved her 100 yards before the other vessel blew up. Finally, when leaving the fjord, he was attacked by a German bomber which ordered him to steer east or be sunk. He held on his course, reserved his fire till the enemy was within 800 yards, and then brought the aircraft down.
>
> Throughout a period of five days *Arab* was subjected to 31 bombing attacks and the camp and Lewis gun positions ashore were repeatedly machine gunned and bombed; yet the defensive position was so well planned that only one man was wounded.
>
> Lieutenant Stannard ultimately brought his damaged ship back to an English port. His continuous gallantry in the presence of the enemy was magnificent, and his enterprise and resource not only caused losses to the Germans but saved his ship and many lives.

Carton de Wiart had decided that it was best to get the French away first. He therefore decided to bring both the British and French troops back by a series of leapfrog movements. The 13th Chasseurs Alpins lay nearest to the enemy, a little more than halfway from Namsos to Steinkjer. Much closer to Namsos were the positions held in succession by the KOYLI, the Hallamshires and the 67th Chasseurs Alpins; the Lincolns were nine miles up the railway to the east. The first stage of evacuation was to be the withdrawal of the 13th Chasseurs Alpins in small groups, which might escape enemy attention, leaving their sections of skiers as a rearguard. The KOYLI would withdraw after them. It was intended that these two battalions should go round by sea from Bangsund to Namsos, but they eventually moved back by road, so that the Hallamshires in their turn provided the rearguard, with orders to hold the bridge at Bangsund at least until 2130 on 2 May. This would give time for the two battalions previously mentioned to get back to Namsos. In the same way, the 67th Chasseurs Alpins withdrew into Namsos, followed by the 4th Lincolns who covered the road from the east, along which a German advance was less likely. The Lincolns' rearguard would eventually be relieved at the south end of the large bridge into Namsos by the rearguard of the Hallamshires, who would move back into the town itself at the very last moment, accompanied by the French skiing sections. By the late evening of 1 May, the plan was in full operation and the two battalions of Chasseurs Alpins were in the neighbourhood of the quay.

Vice Admiral Cunningham had sailed from Scapa on 29 April, planning to bring off half the expedition in three big French transports on the first night, and the other half in the British cruisers HMS *Devonshire* and *York* and the French cruiser *Montcalm* on the second night. There was an aerial attack on the afternoon of 1 May, when the *Devonshire* and a transport received near misses. Then in the evening, Cunningham ran into thick and widespread fog 40 miles short of his rendezvous, the Kya Light, which in turn was 40 miles from Namsos. The operation for that night (1/2 May) was therefore cancelled by a message which reached Force Headquarters at 2130. This meant the re-dispersal of the assembled troops, who just got back into position by daybreak. To make the situation more disheartening, there was clear sky over Namsos itself, as was found by four destroyers which groped their way in through the fog. They were forced to put to sea again without embarking any troops, the good weather facilitating the renewal of German air attacks; one destroyer suffered 23 casualties from a near miss as she hid in a fog-bank which was just too low to cover the masthead.

The attitude of the Norwegians, from whom the Allied intentions could not be concealed indefinitely, might also create serious complications, and the smoothness of any co-operation with the French might be impaired inasmuch as they would regard the re-embarkation as a British responsibility. Two other factors, unknown to Force Headquarters, made the situation still more precarious. The two aircraft carriers had left Norwegian waters earlier that evening, while the political situation prevented the Prime Minister from any further postponement of a statement on the progress of the war in Norway, which would virtually announce to the Germans that southern and central Norway was being given up by the Allies. The Prime Minister's statement was broadcast on the afternoon of 2 May, much to the discomfiture of Maurice Force. It was Carton de Wiart's opinion that the shortness of the hours of darkness made the completion of the evacuation in one night as impracticable as it was clearly desirable. But Admiral Cunningham had been warned at the outset by the Commander-in-Chief, Home Fleet, Admiral Sir Charles Forbes, that the work might have to be done in one lift, and he had prepared and announced an alternative plan on 30 April, when he knew that one battalion of French had been got away in the store ships on the 29th. There were about 5,400 men to be provided for: three transports could embark 1,700 men each at the stone pier, and the balance could be taken by the cruiser HMS *York*, receiving them from trawlers a couple of miles off the town. Admiral Vivian, who had been in the port with the anti-aircraft cruiser HMS *Carlisle*, shared Carton deWiart's view, but Admiral Cunningham's transports were running short of fuel and he finally decided to make the attempt.

On the second night (2/3 May) the cruiser squadron emerged from the fog bank about 40 miles from the Namsenfjord, where it divided. The admiral with two cruisers and four destroyers waited off the Kya Light, while the three French transports, HMS *York* and five destroyers went straight in, arriving off Namsos itself about 2230. Two transports were loaded at the stone quay; the other two big ships were loaded from destroyers and trawlers, and the destroyer *Afridi* took the last parties on board at 0220. It was touch and go at the end, as the Bangsund bridge was not exploded by the rearguard until after

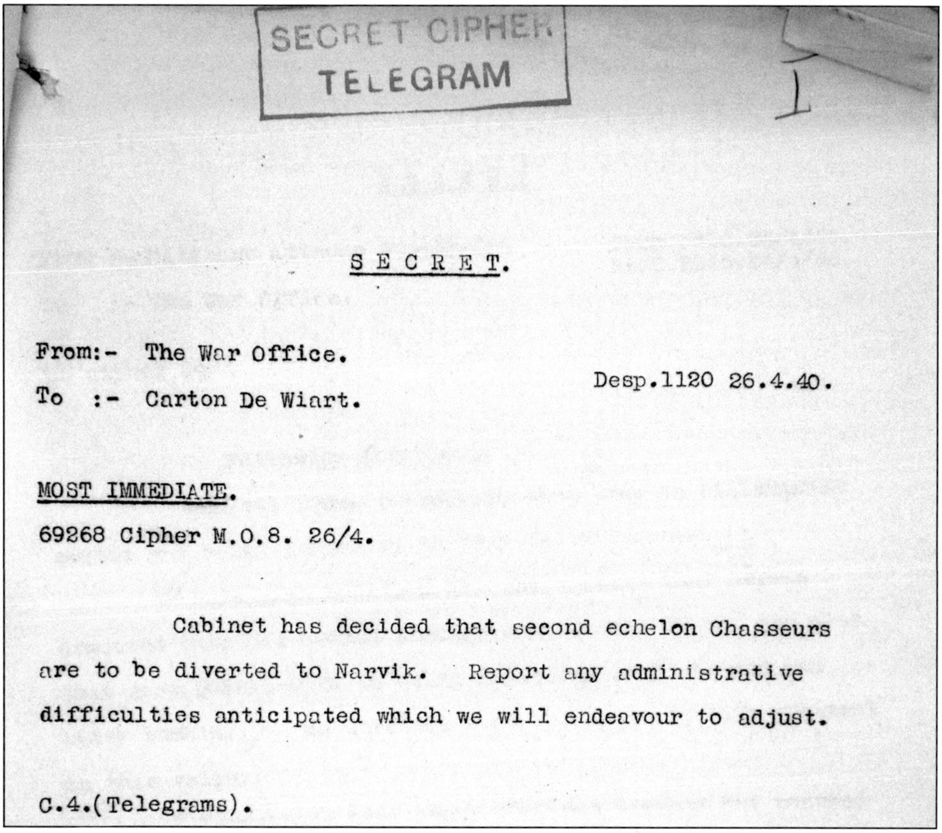

SECRET CIPHER
TELEGRAM

S E C R E T.

From:- The War Office.
To :- Carton De Wiart.

Desp.1120 26.4.40.

MOST IMMEDIATE.

69268 Cipher M.O.8. 26/4.

Cabinet has decided that second echelon Chasseurs are to be diverted to Narvik. Report any administrative difficulties anticipated which we will endeavour to adjust.

C.4.(Telegrams).

Information sent to Carton de Wiart advising that the Chasseurs were diverting to Narvik. (National Archives)

midnight, leaving them with 10 miles to cover to the embarkation area. At around 0130, as Carton de Wiart reported, "the translucent twilight over the hills round the harbour became brighter, full daylight was fast approaching", but the trucks arrived soon after. The shelling of the massed motor transport on the quay by the *Afridi* on her departure emphasised the haste of the escape.

As it was, the Germans had received enough notice to make this voyage, which began at a point far beyond the range of British fighter escorts, much more hazardous than that from Åndalsnes on the previous two nights. The sun cleared the fog early enough for the regular enemy air reconnaissance at around 0430 to spot the later groups in the convoy – two big French transports, each escorted by one of Admiral Cunningham's cruisers and destroyers. They were attacked on five occasions between 0845 and 1530, by which time the first air escort of one Sunderland was approaching the head of the convoy, at distances ranging from 140–220 miles from the German-occupied airfield of Vaernes. It is said that anti-aircraft fire from the warships and from the French transports under Rear Admiral Cadart destroyed two or three aircraft out of the 50 or so that came in against the convoy, and the ships eventually formed a single line, hoping to give mutual support, with the anti-aircraft cruiser HMS *Carlisle* last ship in the line. The third attack set on fire the French destroyer *Bison*, which was sunk by British destroyers after they had taken aboard the survivors of its crew. This caused some delay to the destroyers concerned, one of which, HMS *Afridi*, was hit by two bombs at 1400 while trying to return to the convoy. She eventually capsized with the loss of about 100 killed, including thirteen men of the Hallamshire battalion which had formed the rearguard.

The following is from the Hallamshires war diary about this period:

> 03.05.40 0100 Embarkation was carried out by the Battalion at Namsos quay from this time onwards. HMS *Afridi* being the last to leave at 0430. Embarkation was carried out at immense speed and much equipment that had reached the quay had to be abandoned.
> 0430 Before leaving HMS *Afridi* shelled and destroyed the stone quay.
> 0900 Enemy aircraft began to raid the convoy and continued until about 1200 starting again about 1330 and finishing about 1600. About 0930 a salvo of bombs hit the French destroyer *Bison* setting her on fire. HMS *Afridi* went to her assistance and collected what survivors they could, finally sinking her by shell fire.
> 1330 About this time just as HMS *Afridi* was catching up the convoy again she was hit on the bows by a bomb and sank within 20 minutes. 13 ORs of our battalion lost their lives, the survivors being taken off by HMS *Griffin* and HMS *Imperial* which were able to come alongside. Conditions in the three French ships were very bad, the men being hopelessly overcrowded and there being a great shortage of food and fresh water.
> 04.05.40 A quiet day, considerable comfort being given by the presence of a British aircraft.
> 05.05.40 0500 The convoy arrived in Scapa Flow. The day was spent in sorting out the various units, the battalion being collected on SS *Duchess of Athol*. The last party arriving aboard at about 1900. Sailed at 2000.
> 06.05.40 A calm day with no excitement or events passing down the Minch and up the Clyde anchoring off Gourock about 2400.
> 07.05.40 The whole day was spent lying in the Clyde anchorage off Gourock.
> 08.05.40 1230 Started up river for King George V dock where we arrived at 1630. The Brigade landed almost immediately and was addressed by the CIGS General Sir Edmund Ironside.

The following day, the Hallamshires moved to a camp near Hawick in the Scottish Borders, and their war diary records: "This was the end of the Battalion's Norwegian campaign which started on April 6th, 13 Other Ranks were killed and one Officer and about 13 Other Ranks wounded, only two of the latter happening on land and all the former and the remainder of the latter being due to aerial activity at sea. The Battalion was granted 10 days leave from 13.05.40."

The 4th Lincolns had a similar experience after their departure from Norway. Their war diary contains the following entry for 5 May: "Personnel of unit were transferred from the various ships and embarked on SS *Reina del Pacifico* with 4th KOYLI and HQ 146th Infantry Brigade. It was a great relief to get some good food and water again after three days of nothing but French Army biscuits, *vin ordinaire* and French tinned meat (said to be monkey)."

There is not a lot to add here from the 4th KOYLI, except that their war diary does record the strength of the unit on 2 May, which was 29 officers, eight warrant officers and 541 other ranks. When the battalion left Gourock on 11 April, this figure was 30 officers, eight warrant officers and 591 other ranks.

The evacuation from Namsos had been an operation that could only be done during the hours of darkness, which at this time of the year were short. The operation was dogged by fog. Captain Lord Louis Mountbatten in the destroyer HMS *Kelly* was part of the naval task force under Admiral Cunningham, who stressed the importance of speed and the minimum of equipment being taken by the men.

But the Hallamshires 780 or so men were still some way from Namsos. Their job had been to hold the retreat in good order, to deny the Germans transport and protect the embarkation. Admiral Vivian, who was ashore at Namsos to superintend the operation, called for volunteers from anyone who could drive a car to take any available lorry to fetch them.

A convoy of vehicles was assembled and the bulk of the regiment reached the pier by 0220. But the British destroyer HMS *Afridi* had to remain. Lieutenant Colonel Robins and 33 men of the Hallamshires who had been detailed to blow away the last rearguard bridge at around midnight, and had ten miles of atrocious, snowbound road to cover, had not yet arrived.

As hilltops were in view against the morning twilight, lorries clattered onto the pier at 0315 and disgorged the rearguard. They quickly boarded HMS *Afridi* and she sailed out of Namsos.

The York and Lancaster Regiment's official history of the Norwegian campaign sums up their operations in Norway by stating that although the Hallamshire Battalion "had only met the enemy on land in two minor actions the success of these and the whole experience gained in the campaign definitely raise the morale of all ranks". The history continues:

> The extreme climatic and other difficulties imposed very heavy tasks upon some of the officers and other ranks with specialist duties. Nevertheless, in spite of everything, they succeeded in carrying them out. In this connection particular mention must be made of the Assistant Transport Officer Second Lieutenant J. Randall, and his twenty drivers, who had to work entirely with local lorries and cars: the Signals Officer, Second Lieutenant S. de Bartoleme and his signallers; and last but by no means least, of the Adjutant, Captain H. Marsh.
>
> The names of the other ranks killed in HMS *Afridi* on 3rd May 1940, were: Corporal Goddard; Lance-Corporal Starkey; Privates Barker, Bell, Bruce, Crookes, Lee, Lockwood, Martin, Peacock, Shaw, Shepherd and Wade.

Perhaps a more poignant summing-up of the campaign come from an ordinary soldier:

> Part of my horror of the Norwegian campaign comes from the sinking of the *Afridi* which I survived but hearing as we pulled away that at least one of our soldiers could be heard crying for help. They had been trapped beneath the buckled steel and could not be rescued, but were aware of their fate as the destroyer slowly took water and slipped beneath the waves.

Surviving Hallamshires could also hear the loud metallic crashes of U-boat torpedoes against the hull of their transport ships. Fortunately for the British, a technical fault in torpedo fuses meant that although some reached their target, they failed to detonate.

The deaths of the thirteen Hallamshires on the *Afridi* was a terrible blow to the battalion and their families. They were poor working-class men from Sheffield and adjacent towns, and had been the only breadwinner of their families. In November 1941, one of the widows wrote to the Commanding Officer at their headquarters in Iceland describing the difficulties faced by the bereaved families. The Hallamshires set up an '*Afridi* Christmas Fund' to bring a little happiness at Christmas for the widows and children of the men killed. The appeal raised £44 and 10 shillings, and Christmas gifts equivalent to £3 for each widow and £1 for each child were sent to the relatives.

In recent years, the Norwegians have also erected a memorial for the Hallamshires who died in the *Afridi* bombing in Namsos.

The following extract is from a post-operation report by Lieutenant-General Massy, who commanded all troops in Norway but those at Narvik:

> On the 25th April, I was directed by the Chiefs of Staffs to submit an appreciation on the situation in Norway. As it appeared to me then, the possibility of landing further troops or of maintaining the troops then ashore depended entirely on our being able to obtain control of the situation in the air. In my appreciation I stated this fact and gave it as my opinion that should adequate air support be available I had no reason to suppose that we could not hold our existing positions against the Germans, and at a later date eject them from Trondheim. Without it I had little doubt that any further operations would become impossible and that we should be compelled to evacuate our forces from southern and central Norway. I further stated that should evacuation be decided upon it would have to be done at short notice and that all necessary plans for this operation must therefore be made without delay.
>
> During the 28th, plans for the evacuation were concerted with Admiralty representatives and orders were issued to both General Carton de Wiart and General Paget as to how the evacuation was to be carried out.
>
> It was decided that the French contingent should re-embark before the British, but that the French would leave some ski troops to operate with the British rear guard. The probable dates for evacuation were the nights of 1st/2nd and 2nd/3rd May. On the night 28th/29th April a battery of Bofors guns was landed

> at Namsos. These guns were unfortunately without predictors. On the following day General de Wiart received a message instructing him to send a detachment to Mosjöen by sea and to post a rear guard at Grong which would delay the enemy for as long as possible and then withdraw northwards overland to Mosjöen.
>
> At first he appears to have been in some doubt as to whether the rear guard at Grong was intended to compromise his whole force and he referred the matter to this Headquarters. The reply made it clear that the strength of the rear guard to remain at Grong was entirely at his discretion.
>
> It had been planned when the force was evacuated from Namsos that a rear guard should fall back by land to Mosjöen retiring in the face of the enemy, and that in the meantime a party should be sent by sea to ensure holding the latter port against enemy troops landed by parachute from the air, and orders to this effect were issued. General Carton de Wiart opposed this plan on the grounds that owing to lack of petrol and transport and more importantly still, the fact that the road during the thaw was practically impossible, the operation would be likely to end in disaster.

Fortunately sense was seen and this plan was put into the pending file. Massy's report continued:

> The evacuation of the French was commenced on the night 28th/29th and arrangements were made for the evacuation of the remaining troops from Namsos to be completed on the nights of the 1st/2nd and 2nd/3rd May, but the plan was made sufficiently elastic so that if necessary the process of evacuation from this latter port could be put forward 24 hours.
>
> In the early hours of 30th April, a party of 340 personnel, mostly wounded, were embarked on HMS *Fleetwood* from Åndalsnes and at 1900 HMS *Janus* embarked 100 men and two Bofors guns at Namsos and conveyed them during the night to Mosjöen where they arrived on 2nd May having been delayed by dense fog. On 1st May thick fog off Namsos prevented the ships entering the harbour. The whole evacuation of Namsos was however successfully carried out on the night of 2nd/3rd, the last ship leaving at 0220 and a total of 5,400 having been embarked during that night, an operation for which the greatest credit is due to the Naval forces employed.

Perhaps the final word should be left to a senior officer, Lieutenant Colonel Hingston, who fought with the KOYLI at Namsos and recorded:

> The retreat of 146th Infantry Brigade to Namdalseid is not a bright story in the history of the British Army. Indeed it is doubtful whether British troops have ever been forced to retire with so little effort on the part of the enemy. On the other hand it is also doubtful if a British force have ever been asked to do so much with so little.

5

148 Brigade

The second wave of British troops to arrive in the central/southern area of this part of Norway consisted of the 5th Leicesters and the 8th Sherwood Foresters of 148 Brigade. On 6 April, the 5th Leicesters boarded two trains around midnight at Cockfield Station in Durham, with A and D Companies, part of Battalion HQ and Brigade HQ in the first train, and B and C Companies on the second. Both trains arrived at Rosyth around midday and soon boarded the cruiser HMS *Devonshire*. That evening, cross decking was practised with the *Afridi*, but on the following day the battalion received orders to leave the *Devonshire* at great speed and marched to a transit camp about seven miles away near Dunfermline. The following few days until the 13th were spent here, and then on 14 April they marched back to Rosyth and boarded the SS *Orion*. The 15th was spent sorting out kit and doing lifeboat drills, before on the 16 April A and D Companies and part of Battalion HQ left the *Orion* and cross-decked to various cruisers and destroyers, including HMS *Arethusa*, HMS *Carlisle*, HMS *Curacao* and HMS *Galatea* for the passage to Norway. The rest of the battalion remained on the *Orion*.

Five graves of men from the Sherwood Foresters in the churchyard at the small village of Biri, which lies a short distance off the main route from Oslo to Trondheim about 15km south of Lillehammer. (Steve Foster)

The 5th Leicesters' war diary for 17 April records: "In the early hours of the morning the leading party of the Battalion sailed for Norway. There was a heavy swell and few of the troops were on their feet after the first few hours. There were repeated alarms and the crew were at action stations a great deal of the time." For the 18th it continues:

> A similar day to the 17th. A Company landed at Molde and were taken to Åndalsnes. The remaining ships sailed straight on to Åndalsnes. Before daylight the whole of the leading party of the Battalion had landed at Åndalsnes and D Company were left on the quay as a guard. The remainder marched about four miles to a Norwegian rest camp. At about 1600 orders were received to leave the camp and the Battalion entrained the same evening and headed south.

This is the strength of the 5th Leicesters as they left their camp for Norway by train:

		By Main Train	By Special Train	With Transport	Billeting Party	Total
HQ Company	Company HQ	6				6
	1 Pl	33				33
	2 Pl	16				16
	3 Pl	16			1	17
	4 Pl	10	19			29
	5 Pl	20				20
	6 Pl	25		11		36
	Bn HQ	46				46
Attached	Fitters		1	1		2
	Armourers	2				2
	Shoemaker	1				1
	From Bde				1	1
A Company		92		1		93
B Company		92		1		93
C Company		95		1	1	97
D Company		91		1		92
Officers		26	1	1	1	29
Total		571	21	17	4	613

The following are excerpts from the Operational Orders on the amount of equipment the men were expected to carry:

> Dress:
> Field Service Marching Order.
> a. Either greatcoats worn and one blanket in pack or greatcoat in pack and one blanket folded and carried under supporting straps.
> b. Gas capes rolled.
> c. FS cape.
> d. Steel helmet on left shoulder.
>
> Stores and equipment and weapons.
> i. All rifles will be carried.
> ii. Anti-tank rifles carried in boxes in heavy baggage.
> iii. Four Bren guns per rifle company carried loose and ready for action. Tripods for these also carried loose. Remainder in boxes in heavy baggage.
> iv. One pair of wire cutters per section to be carried.
> v. One magazine filler per section to be carried.
> vi. One Dixie per 25 men will be carried with personnel and will always be kept easily accessible.
> vii. All other tents and equipment in heavy baggage.
>
> Clothing:
> In pack
> Either one blanket or greatcoat and blanket
> Vest and pants
> Two pairs socks
> Housewife
> Cap comforter
> Leather jerkin
> Haversack
> Towel
> Holdall (containing knife, fork, spoon, washing and shaving kit, laces, comb)
> Cleaning kit
> Mug
> Mess tin and cover
> Ration bag
> Ground sheet
> Sea Kitbag
> Second suit
> Spare underclothing
> One pair boots
> PT kit
> Sports kit
> Canvas if in possession
> Hair brush

Ammunition:

1. 50 rounds SAA per rifle to be carried.
2. 672 rounds (24 magazines of 28 rounds) per Bren gun carried loose to be carried in pouches.
3. 672 rounds (24 magazines of 28 rounds) per Bren gun in boxes to be carried in steel boxes in heavy baggage.
4. 12 rounds .38 pistol SAA to be carried in pouches per Officer, WO and OR who carry pistols.
5. Remainder SAA, mortar ammunition, grenades and anti-tank ammunition to be taken in bulk by Companies and QM.

For the 8th Sherwood Foresters, a similar tale can be told except that on 16 April, orders were received to split the unit into two parts, which occurred during the night of 16/17 April. One of the surviving officers later referred to these two parts as the left and right wings. The battalion split so that each wing would be able to operate independently. The Right Wing was under the command of Battalion CO, Lieutenant Colonel T. Ford, with the Adjutant, Intelligence Officer, Medical Officer and the RSM. It also had about half of HQ and Support Companies comprising: ½ Signals, ½ Mortars, ½ Carriers, ½ AA Platoon, ½ Pioneers and ½ Admin Platoon, together with the QM and RQMS, plus two of the four rifle companies, B and C. The Left Wing was under the command of the unit's second-in-command, Major J. Roberts, assisted by the Assistant Adjutant and the Signals Officer. It comprised ½ Signals, ½ Mortars, ½ Carriers, ½ AA Platoon, ½ Pioneers and ½ Admin Platoon, together with the Assistant QM and the other two of the four rifle companies, A and D.

Lieutenant Colonel Dudley Clarke, who had accompanied Brigadier Harold Morgan, the brigade commander, as one of his chief advisers – and became known as a pioneer of military deception during the war – commented on their early hours in Norway and the first meeting with the Norwegians: "After midnight, on the morning of the 20th we found ourselves face to face with General Ruge (the Norwegian C-in-C) and any doubts we may have had before of Norway's determination to fight on disappeared for good, leaving behind some shame that we should ever have voiced them at all." The meeting was kept short and to the point, with Ruge making it clear that he felt he was staking everything on help from Britain. He asked Brigadier Morgan about his orders and, according to Clarke, added dryly that "for some reason he had never been informed of the strength of the British troops nor of their intended plan of campaign". Morgan advised Ruge of his intentions, which were basically an attack towards Trondheim. It is said that Ruge tactfully but firmly stressed that he "expected all troops in the country, of whatever nationality, to conform to his own strategy". As far as Ruge was concerned, this meant "concentrating every available man on the decisive front below Lillehammer until British reinforcements could redress the inferiority in numbers".

For his part, Brigadier Morgan agreed that "as he had been sent to help Norway, he would give General Ruge maximum assistance wherever he needed it the most". Morgan decided to 'ignore' his orders and send his troops south towards Lillehammer. Within an hour of the meeting, at around 0300 on the morning of the 20th, Ruge and his staff

This sangar is believed to be one of the locations of the Sherwood Foresters' Battalion HQ near Tretten, overlooking the main road. (Steve Foster)

had their first sight of Morgan's men. One of Ruge's staff officers later recorded: "The disappointment upon seeing the British troops that marched past was easy to read on his face. They were not regular troops and we were alarmed to see that they were only armed with rifles and light machine guns, no anti-aircraft guns, no heavy anti-tank weapons, no artillery and no vehicles."

In spite of this, the men of the 5th Leicesters and 8th Sherwood Foresters were despatched towards Lillehammer. According to the war diary of the 5th Leicesters for 19 April:

> The train reached Dombaas and Lieutenant Colonel Guy German received orders to leave the train to fill some other position. The remainder proceeded south with no definite instructions nor knowing where they were going or to whom they were to report.
>
> At Otta Major German received a message that Brigadier Morgan wished to speak to him on the telephone. He was told to return to Dombaas but the railway authorities refused to carry out the instructions. After many further telephone calls, orders were finally received to continue the journey south. About midday the train was stopped at Tretten and a Norwegian officer informed Major German that the troops must detrain. The next part of the journey to the south of Lillehammer was made in buses and lorries and on reaching a point about four miles south of Lillehammer, the convoy was attacked by low flying aircraft and machine gunned for a considerable time without suffering any casualties. It was learned afterwards that they were taken too far south owing to a mistake in a Norwegian order.

There were two 'Germans' in the 5th Leicesters; one was the CO and the other a company commander; hence the mention of a Lieutenant Colonel German and a Major German in the war diary entry.

Here was yet another area of operations in which British forces suffered with confusion and conflicting ideas: 148 Brigade struggled with a lack of numbers and their almost total lack of support weapons. The main aim of the operation was of course to get to Trondheim, and at the meeting with General Ruge the overall strategy was discussed together with some tactical manoeuvres. Ruge reacted rather coolly to the Allies' plan, although it had partly originated in Norwegian official circles, and he did not conceal his regret that the British authorities had so far kept him in the dark about their intentions. Incensed by rumours of a British scheme to blow up the railway through Gudbrandsdal (which would have blocked his own retreat as well as the German advance), he insisted in principle that, as he was Commander-in-Chief under the Norwegian Government, whose territory was to be defended, operations must conform to his strategy. This was that the recapture of Trondheim could wait, and bad weather might help by stopping the Germans flying in troops and supplies. But the front south of Lillehammer, he argued, was of paramount importance, since, so long as it held firm, Allied forces would be able some day to deploy into the more level districts of eastern Norway, in which manoeuvre was possible. He therefore insisted that British troops should at once be used to reinforce

General map from 8th Sherwood Foresters War Diary.

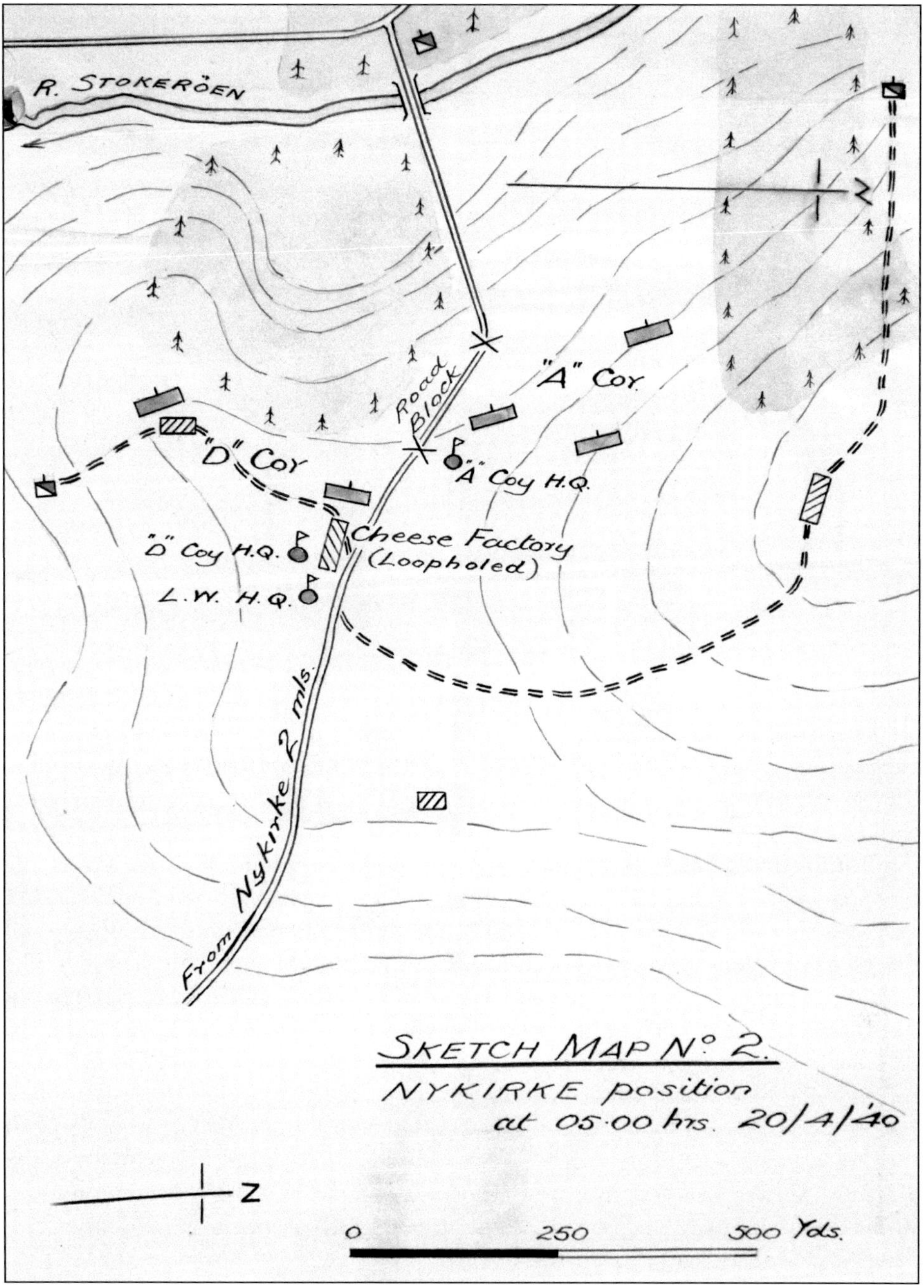

General map of Nykirke from 8th Sherwood Foresters War Diary.

The officers of the 8th Sherwood Foresters before they went to Norway. Photograph taken in March 1940. (Steve Foster)

the Norwegian 2nd Division, which had two infantry battalions and a battery of artillery on the east side of Lake Mjösa under the direct command of the Divisional Commander, General Haug, and another group on the west side under Colonel Dahl. Brigadier Morgan agreed, though with considerable misgivings, Ruge receiving his agreement with enthusiasm.

British troops were then hurried south by train from Dombaas down the Gudbrandsdal, so that by the time the earliest reinforcements reached Åndalsnes, not only had this base but even the advanced position at Dombaas been stripped of all troops, all of whom were now concentrated at or beyond the mouth of the valley. The lines of communication were now about 140 miles long. Meanwhile, at dawn on 20 April, General Ruge, whose responsibilities and disappointments in the preceding 10 days had been enormous, and whose lack of sleep was evident, was on the station to welcome the first British companies as they completed the journey down the valley. But Brigadier Morgan soon found that, instead of acting as a stiffening in one part of the line, his men were being widely dissipated. Rather than acting as a partial relief to a mainly Norwegian force, they were being left to hold hastily improvised positions without support of any kind, as has been illustrated by the comment above from the 5th Leicesters'war diary for 19 April.

On the morning of the 20th, Brigadier Morgan received a telegram from General Ironside, the CIGS, cancelling his original instructions to move north from Dombaas (which the abandonment of Operation Hammer had just rendered less urgent), and suggesting:

The Cheese Factory in Tretten as it was in 1940. (Steve Foster)

The Cheese Factory in Tretten as it was in 2010. (Steve Foster)

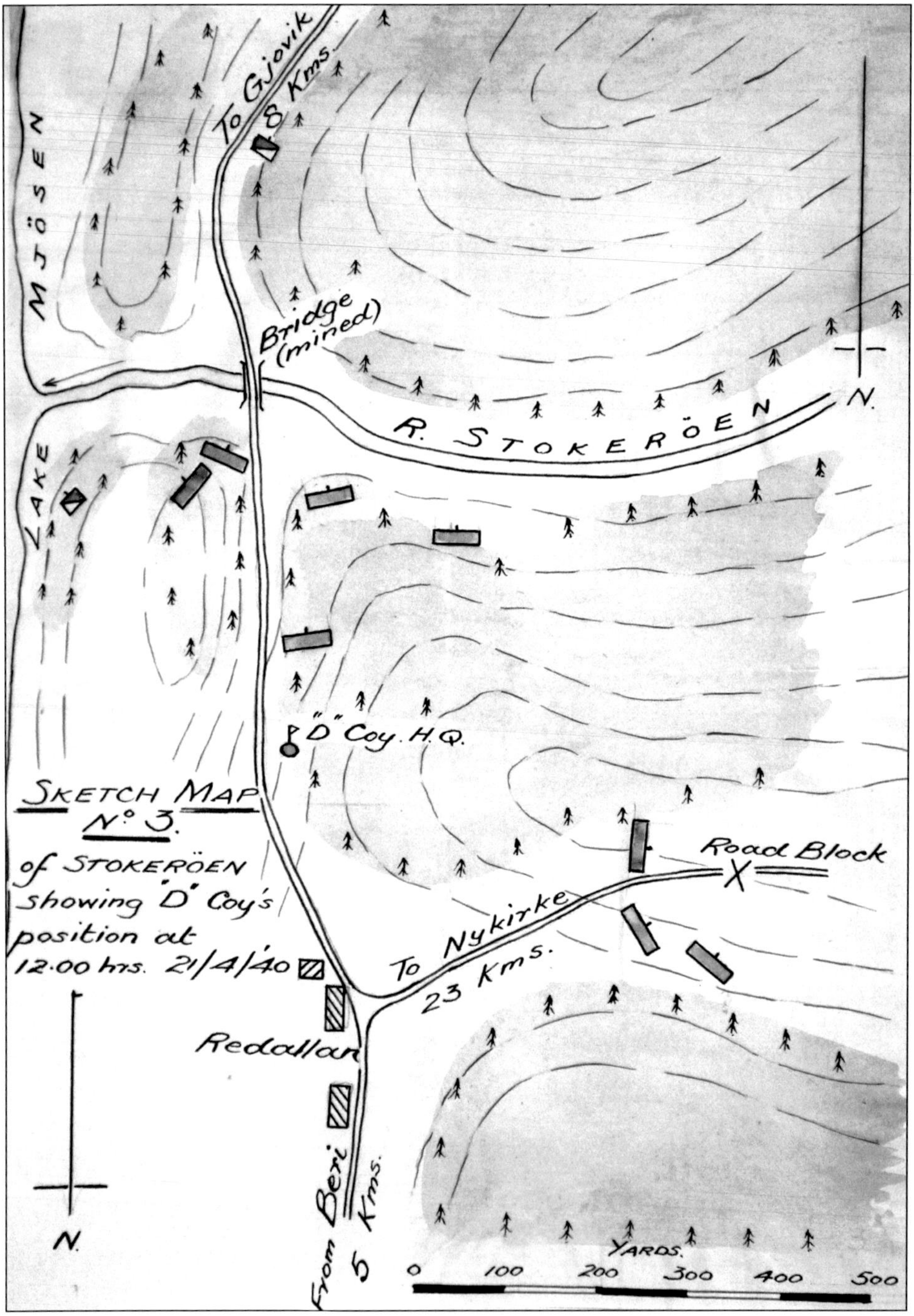

Map from the 8th Sherwood Foresters War Diary.

> You know situation of Norwegians in Lillehammer area. Clearly necessary to prevent German advance from south east in order to secure Dombaas. Although you remain independent command under the War Office, you should, if you can spare troops, co-operate with Norwegian Commander-in-Chief while making use of Dombaas. Now probable that you will be reinforced by another Brigade. Tell Norwegians.

Brigadier Morgan had also sent a message to the War Office asking for more support, and this had coincided with an independent suggestion from Winston Churchill, who as Chairman of the Military Co-ordination Committee had proposed to the Chiefs of Staff that half a battalion be sent south to enable General Ruge "to sell ground more dearly and more slowly".

Relations were not helped when General Ruge put forward a written declaration at a conference on 20 April, requesting that British forces must comply with his wishes or else he would resign. The atmosphere of the conference was also affected by the fact that Ruge bitterly resented a (mistaken) suggestion that there might be a leakage of information at his General Headquarters. In this difficult situation, the British Military Attaché – Lieutenant Colonel Edward King-Salter – took upon himself responsibility for delaying delivery of a message decoded at 1015 that day, in which Ironside explicitly informed General Ruge that Brigadier Morgan had instructions to co-operate with him but would not come under his orders. King-Salter's report of the conference also refrained from putting Ruge's ultimatum in its bluntest form, though, together with the French Military Attaché, he continued to press for Major-General Bernard Paget, the expedition commander, on his arrival, to be placed under Norwegian command. Morgan contrived a satisfactory ending to the conference. Ruge said he would endeavour to hold the Lillehammer front until Trondheim had fallen, but thought it involved risks. He added that he would feel confident with one British division at Trondheim and Morgan's force co-operating with his men on the Lillehammer front.

In the course of 20 April, British troops were deployed to positions under Norwegian command; 148 Brigade Headquarters was situated at Lillehammer but had no operational control. First to move were two companies and half the headquarters company of the Sherwood Foresters, who detrained at Faaberg and were sent along the west bank of Lake Mjösa to Biri, and thence up a side valley to the village of Nykirke, about 35 miles from Lillehammer. They arrived at 1400 and were quartered in the parish church, the only large building which could be heated sufficiently in the bitter cold, while a telegram was sent to the Norwegian High Command reporting that British soldiers had taken up their first position in Norway. The intention was to protect the right flank of the Norwegian forces operating west of Mjösa against a possible flank attack by the Germans, who had now come up against the Norwegian 4 Brigade in the region of the Randsfjord farther west. But in the afternoon of the same day, the Sherwood Foresters were brought back to the neighbourhood of Biri, in rear of the Norwegians' position at Braastad bridge on the lakeside just north of Gjövik, on which the Germans were converging from several directions.

Brigadier Morgan deserves much sympathy in the early days of April 1940, as he had received numerous and conflicting orders. On 6 April, it was intended for the two

A plaque for the Sherwood Foresters placed close to the sangar near Tretten. (Steve Foster)

battalions of 148 Brigade to sail to Norway in two cruisers and then land at Stavanger; the brigade had been at sea for about a day when these orders were cancelled and the troops and their equipment unceremoniously dumped ashore, with much loss and damage being caused. Then on 13 April, orders were received to be prepared to land at Namsos, but this was also cancelled three days later. With their sister unit, 146 Brigade, landing as we have seen at Namsos, they were diverted yet again, this time to Åndalsnes. This order arrived when they were aboard the Namsos-bound SS *Orion*, and again the men had to transfer to naval destroyers, once more losing and damaging stores in the process. Lieutenant Colonel Dudley Clarke, who had managed to wangle himself away from his War Office job to go as an observer to Norway, later commented:

> The hatches were now off and the scene below decks had become a sort of storeman's inferno, with shadowy figures burrowing in the semi-darkness of shaded lamps and torches. In the original haste to get off to a quick start, goods of every kind had been stowed in the holds in the order in which they arrived, with each following consignment piled in on top. Now reserves of food and ammunition were mixed with unit equipment and skis for the Norwegians, bicycles and sappers tools lay with medical provisions, while such things as the long-range wireless equipment as often as not was split between two holds. There

A German photograph of POWs from 148 Brigade after capture. (Steve Foster)

> was never a chance of sorting this out in the dark and getting it into the right ships in time, so the plan was being adopted of skimming the top layers from every hold and loading them in turn into each warship as she came alongside.

The enormity of what had happened probably only hit home when the troops were actually ashore in Norway, when it was realised that most of the brigade's communication equipment, range-finders and searchlights for the few anti-aircraft guns and nearly all the mortar ammunition had been left behind. The transport that they managed to take consisted of one lorry and three motorcycles. In spite of this, the War Office gave the troops the grand name of Sickle Force and issued orders to Brigadier Morgan as follows:

> The War Office,
> 14th April 1940.
> To Brigadier Morgan from The War Office.
> 1. Your instructions as follows.
> 2. Festing will have told you role of Carton de Wiart and of Hotblack's projected combined operation on Trondheim. Small force British guerrillas operating your right flank. About 600 sailors landing Åndalsnes night 17/18. Their role after landing will be communicated to you later.

The jetty at Åndalsnes, pictured in 2010. (Steve Foster)

Allied troops landing at Åndalsnes. Note the ruined buildings in the background. (Imperial War Museum HU93728)

3. Your role to land Åndalsnes area, secure Dombaas then operate northwards and take offensive action against Germans in Trondheim area. Not intended that you should land in face of opposition. Second echelon your force will follow you two days later. As you are without transport you should rely on Norwegian rolling stock and locally impressed transport. You will be kept informed of progress and timings of other British forces operating Trondheim area.
4. Your force independent command under War Office until receipt further orders. Intention later place you under Commander General Operations Trondheim area.
5. During the voyage and during landing operations Senior Naval Officer will be in command. He will decide in co-operation with you where and when to land.
6. Previous instructions re co-operation with Norwegians and reports to War Office unchanged.

These were the bare bones of Morgan's orders, with point 3 naming the key objective, and it is easy with hindsight to say that they were somewhat ambitious. Dombaas was around 60 miles from Åndalsnes, and once his depleted brigade had in theory struggled over this distance they were then have to go to Trondheim – about a further 100 miles away (as the crow flies, and the roads rarely followed the crows in Norway). However, whilst at sea further orders arrived from General Ironside in London, which read: "When you have secured Dombaas, you are to prevent the Germans from using the railway to reinforce Trondheim … You should make touch with Norwegian GHQ, believed to be in area Lillehammer and avoid isolating Norwegian forces operating towards Oslo." Looking at a map, these orders are clearly contradictory; after taking Dombaas, Morgan's men would be expected to assist Norwegian troops in the Oslo area, but at the same time demonstrate towards Trondheim – in a completely different direction. If he did try to do these, he would be handicapped by having to leave troops behind in order to "secure Dombaas" and "prevent the Germans from using the railway". While Morgan had been promised reinforcements, there was no intelligence as to when they might arrive and in what numbers. Other problems that no-one seemed to consider were the questions of air support and how close the co-operation should be with the Norwegian Army.

King-Salter, the newly appointed British Military Attaché to Norway, met Morgan at Dombaas on 19 April, when King-Salter forcefully pointed out his view that it would be suicide for the depleted brigade to march on Trondheim. King-Salter explained that his force would soon be attacked in the rear by Germans advancing northward from Oslo. He felt it would be better to listen to the advice from General Ruge and reinforce Norwegian forces trying to contain the Germans south of Lillehammer. It was agreed that Brigadier Morgan would travel down to Öyer and meet General Ruge. As the Post-War Official History put it, "this was to be the very first meeting between the commanders of two newly allied forces, in great danger of fighting two separate campaigns in the same country against the same enemy."

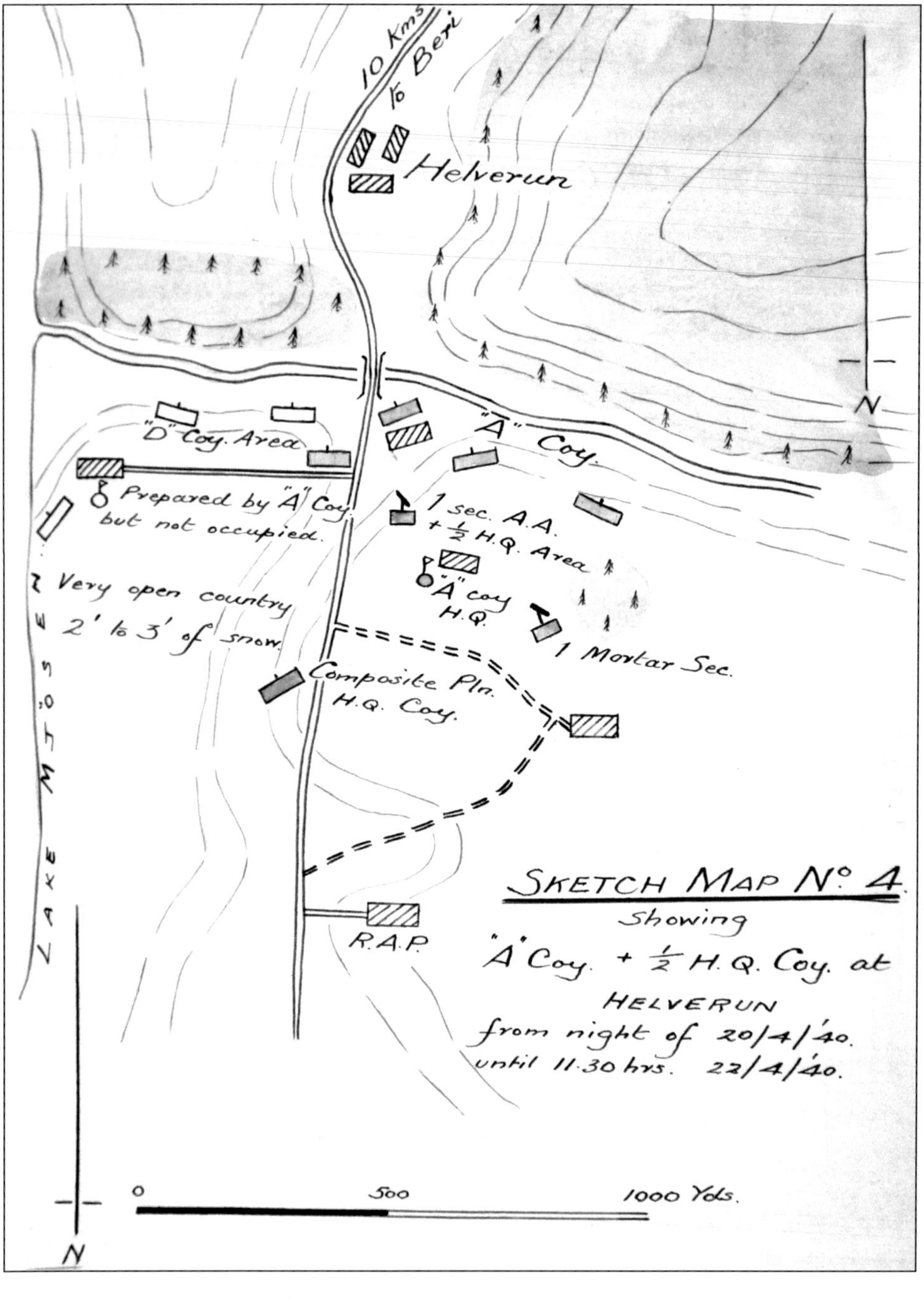

Map from the 8th Sherwood Foresters War Diary.

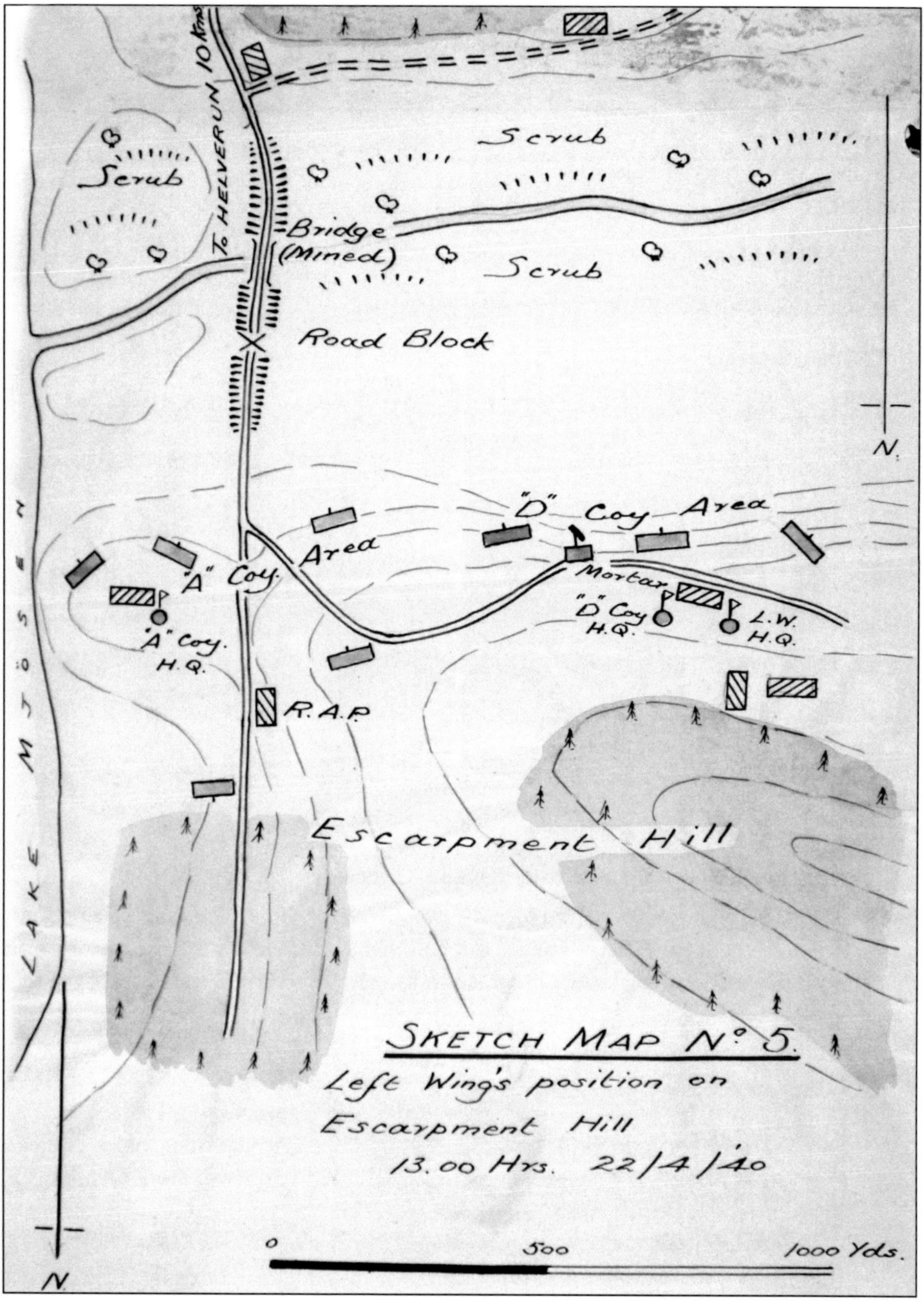

Map from the 8th Sherwood Foresters War Diary.

A view from a Sherwood Foresters sangar, waiting for the Germans to arrive, possibly belonging to B or C Company. (Steve Foster)

However, any local difficulties were overcome and the troops were moved south into a most compromising position. From this point on, things become a little blurred as many of the surviving records do not give the full picture of the struggles of the Leicesters and Sherwood Foresters. The following are comments from the war diary of the 5th Leicesters regarding events after the move south by train towards Lillehammer:

> 20/4/40 Lieutenant Colonel Guy German rejoined the Battalion and a few hours rest were obtained on the outskirts of Lillehammer.
> 21/4/1940 At 0700 a message was received that the Commanding Officer was required to go up into the front line and he and Major German went forward to the Advanced Norwegian Headquarters. It was pointed out that it was extremely urgent that some British troops should go forward. At 1100 A Company left Lillehammer and got up into the front line 15 miles south of Lillehammer at 1430. D Company was in a position behind them. When A Company arrived a fierce battle was raging and any attempt to organise a proper defensive position was impossible. In the evening A Company retired through D Company to Aasmark. On the way back Private Lawrence of A Company received injuries which proved fatal. (This was the first known casualty. His date of death is given by the Commonwealth War Graves Commission as 23 April 1940 and he now

Lieutenant Colonel T. Ford of the Sherwood Foresters being led away after being captured at Tretten. (Steve Foster)

lies in grave IB5 in Lillehammer Northern Civil Cemetery. He was aged 21.) The troops obtained an hour or two's rest.

22/4/40 About midnight a message was received that the troops were to retire to a position north of Lillehammer and that Norwegian transport would pick them up four miles away at 0100. In a very short space of time the Battalion was on the march, but the Norwegian transport failed to turn up. Every effort was made to march back before daylight, but the hours of darkness were so short that the Germans caught up [with] the Battalion and a great number of them were cut off. The following officers were missing from that time:- Cripps, Astbury, Savage, Scott, Gorrie (MO), Shields.

22/4/40 The 8th Foresters had retired before us and had taken up a position north of Lillehammer. They continued fighting during the whole of the day until the Germans came in on the flanks and 9 Platoon of A Company was sent in to help. Most of them got back, but Strachan, their Platoon Commander was not seen after this.

The same evening the whole force retired and on the way back were caught up by enemy aircraft which bombed and machine gunned them as they took cover in a wood. A composite Battalion was then formed of Leicesters and Foresters and a defensive position was taken up in front of Öyer. At about 1700 B and C Companies rejoined the Battalion and reinforced the position. It was hoped this position might be held until 2200 but the Germans broke through before this and another position had to taken up about six miles south of Tretten.

23/4/40 The Germans again attacked at daylight and the Battalion fought a rear guard action back towards Tretten. During the morning Ramsden was killed (Captain H. Ramsden, aged 41 now buried in grave IH1 in Lillehammer Northern Civil Cemetery). At midday the 8th Foresters took over the position and gradually fell back into the village. A stand was made by troops of all companies on Tretten bridge, which the Germans shelled incessantly for several hours. Ford-Smith was killed at this time (Captain J. Smith, aged 31, now lies in grave IA4 in Lillehammer Northern Civil Cemetery), many troops were missing after this and also the following officers:- Atkins, Symington, Barratt, Coleman, Phillips, Thompson, Kirk, Adcock and Lubbock.

After retiring through Tretten another position was taken up on both sides of the road about one mile north of the village and was held until approximately 2000 when the whole of the remainder again retired. After this Lieutenant Colonel Guy German, Jessop and Musson were missing and also a number of troops. Major Garner was wounded and was seen making his way back. By lorries and on foot the troops got back to a rest camp. Major Dowson and Major German set out to find the next line of defence, but there did not appear to be one.

24/4/40 The remainder of the Battalion rested.

25/4/40 The Battalion spent the day in a valley just south of Otta. By keeping absolutely concealed, enemy aircraft were unable to spot them and they had a quiet day.

26/4/40 In the evening the Battalion went by buses and trains back to Dombaas where they lay low in cellars while the Germans bombed and completely destroyed the place.

27/4/40 A similar day to the 26th. Air raid warnings were sounded every few minutes. Great difficulty was experienced in getting food over to the billets.

28/4/40 In the evening the remnants of the Battalion began to make their way back to the base. The bad narrow road and the single track railway had been bombed daily and any available transport was used. The hours of darkness were taken up by marching.

29/4/40 The gradual retirement to Åndalsnes continued.

30/4/40 By the early hours of the day all that was left of the Battalion had got back to a position just south of Åndalsnes. In the evening they all went on board, with the exception of 60 Other Ranks.

1/5/40 60 Other Ranks under Major R. German and Second Lieutenant A. Speak remained behind as rear guard and moved to a position about two miles further south.

2/5/40 About 0130 the order was received to retire and get on board ship at Åndalsnes. This was done and the whole of the remainder left Norway, during the hours of darkness, without a single shot being fired or a casualty suffered.

Scapa Flow was reached safely on 4th May and Glasgow on 6th May where in company with many other troops they were addressed by the CIGS, before going by train to Hawick and then later on leave.

The following is a list of the officers with the 5th Leicesters on their departure from the UK:

Battalion HQ
Lieutenant Colonel G. German, Commanding Officer
Major A. Atkins, Second-in-Command
Captain J. Ford-Smith, Adjutant
Captain R. Barratt, Assistant Adjutant
Captain R. Coleman, Intelligence Officer
Captain E. Duckworth, Padre
Lieutenant G. Gorrie, Medical Officer
Second Lieutenant D. Astbury, Messing Officer

HQ Company
Captain S. Symington, Officer Commanding
Captain J. Hobbins, No. 1 Platoon
Second Lieutenant A. Speak, No. 4 Platoon
Second Lieutenant Snelling, Motor Transport Officer
Lieutenant S. Morson, Quartermaster

A Company
Major R. German, Officer Commanding
Second Lieutenant J. Shields, Second-in-Command
Second Lieutenant W. Musson
Second Lieutenant T. Strachan

B Company
Major W. Garner, Officer Commanding
Captain H. Ramsden MC, Second-in-Command
Second Lieutenant J. Phillips
Second Lieutenant F. Thompson

C Company
Captain R. Lubbock, Officer Commanding
Second Lieutenant I. Jessop, Second-in-Command
Second Lieutenant J. Adcock
Second Lieutenant D. Kirk

D Company
Captain M. Cripps, Officer Commanding
Second Lieutenant J. Scott, Second-in-Command
Second Lieutenant R. Savage
Second Lieutenant J. Guy

The graves of men, mainly from the Leicesters and Sherwood Foresters, at Lillehammer Northern Civil Cemetery. (Steve Foster)

Out of these 29 officers, 19 are mentioned in the war diary as either being killed or missing, nearly a 66 percent casualty rate. Some companies lost three out of four officers. Regretably, there are no available records showing how many 5th Leicesters Other Ranks were killed and taken prisoner, but if the 66 percent casualty rate is also applied to the 584 OR that left camp in the UK in April, just under 200 would have made it back the following month.

The story of the 8th Sherwood Foresters' part in these events is difficult to follow, as they do not have a surviving war diary. Soon after their return to the UK there was much correspondence between the unit and the War Office about the 'loss' of their diary, but this achieved nothing, and all that is filed at the National Archives as their 'war diary' are some accounts by surviving officers. From these scanty sources, the following can be pieced together.

On 19 April, 148 Brigade made contact with German forces in an open valley south of Lillehammer, staging a fighting withdrawal north to allow the remnants of the Norwegian Army to pass through their positions and regroup. After four days of constant fighting in Arctic conditions, and with very little food or sleep, 148 Brigade made a stand about a mile south of the village of Tretten to prevent the road bridge falling into enemy hands and thus cutting off the Norwegian Dahl Force, which was retreating on the opposite side of the valley.

British POWs pictured near Lillehammer. (Imperial War Museum MH2619)

The Vardekampen Heights was chosen as a defensive position as it protruded into the valley at a farmhouse called Rindheim and descended steeply to the valley road, which in turn had a steep gorge dropping away from it to the valley below. It was hoped this narrow front would prevent Austrian ski troops from turning the brigade's left flank, which had been a feature of all previous engagements further south. British troops, with help from Norwegian civilians, hastily prepared rock defensive positions in the pine forests, as it was impossible to dig trenches in the frozen ground. The fighting at Tretten commenced early on 23 April and lasted all day. Subjected to continuous mortar and machine gun fire (the Foresters' mortar platoon only had smoke ammunition), the hungry and cold Territorial soldiers, armed only with rifles and limited ammunition, attempted to stem armoured and ski troops overrunning their positions and taking the strategically important bridge at Tretten. These forward positions were eventually overrun as tanks and supporting infantry passed through them and continued north to take the village of Tretten, where hand-to-hand street fighting took place between the Germans and brigade rear echelons/reserve companies. At about 2100, after a day of constant fighting, detached brigade staff volunteered to form a rearguard to the north of the village to allow the remnants of the brigade to withdraw. Pockets of Sherwood Foresters continued to fight on the slopes of the Vardekampen Heights until nightfall, but all were eventually silenced.

The brigade thus ceased to exist as a fighting unit, the majority being killed, wounded or captured at Tretten. The remnants (only three officers and about 200 men of the Foresters) continued to retire north, staging various rearguard actions to stem the German advance until they eventually passed through the British 15 Infantry Brigade, which had

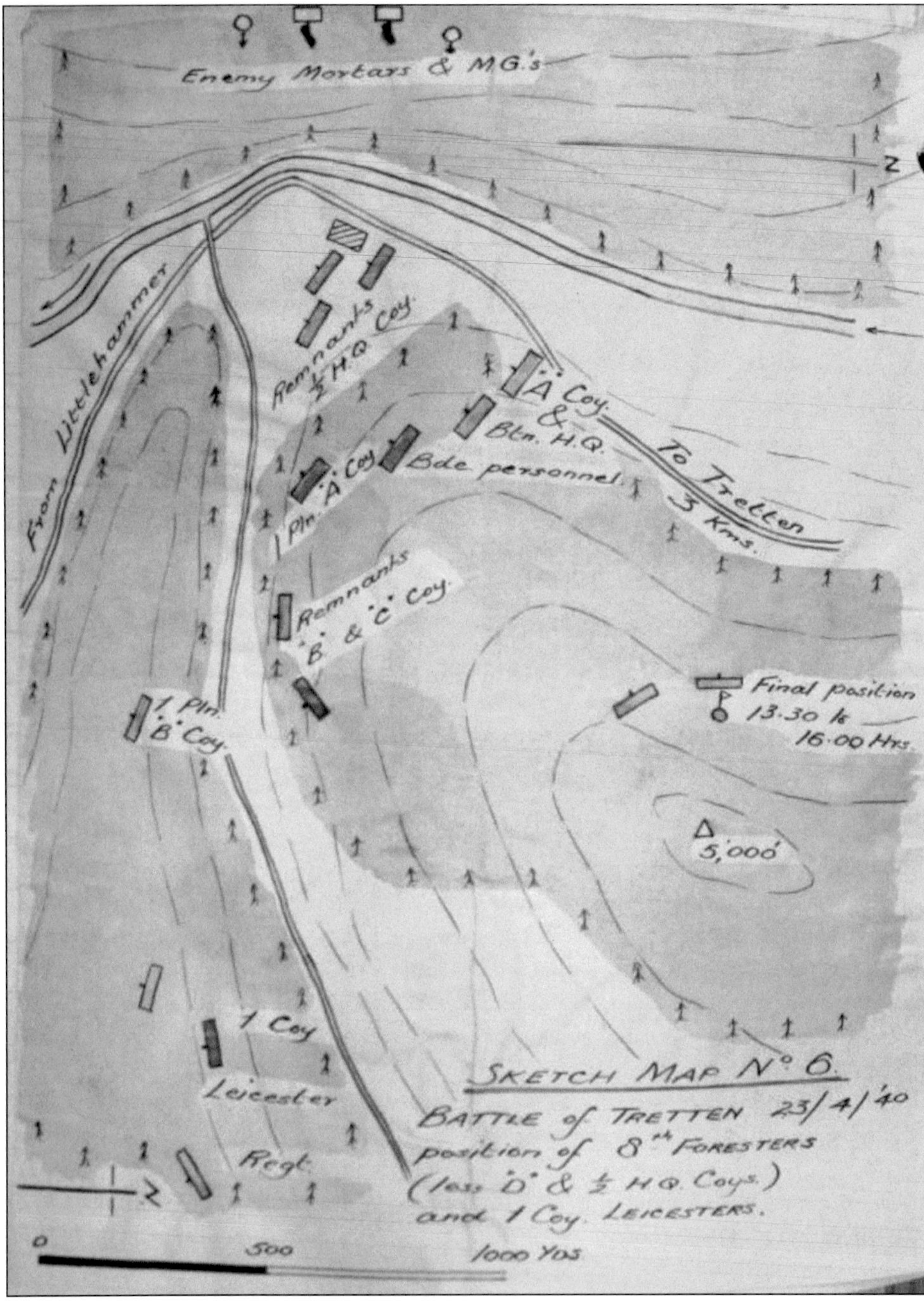

Map from the 8th Sherwood Foresters War Diary.

landed on 23 April, and which held the Germans at Kvam. Another account gives the brigade strength at the end of 23rd April as nine officers and 300 Other Ranks, with another party of around 40 managing to make it to neutral Sweden after an arduous trek across mountainous terrain.

Various accounts from the so-called 'war diary' of the 8th Sherwood Foresters can be found in Appendix L. The following records the personal observations of Major T. Roberts, Second-in-Command 8th Sherwood Foresters, on the Battle of Tretten on 25 April:

> After reporting to CO 8th Foresters on the morning of 23rd April, I made a complete reconnaissance of the position. This was on a wooded slope with small clearings, varying up to a 100 yards in length. The road passed through the position on the extreme right and made an almost right angle bend just within the position. The side of the road, nearest the river, fell abruptly to its bank, there being a drop of approximately 30 feet. CO 8th Foresters had the remnants of Right Wing; one company of 5th Leicesters and thirty personnel from Brigade HQ staff. The company of the Leicesters was occupying the extreme left flank of the position and a road block was ready to be let down at the road bend.
>
> In front, about two kilometres, OC 5th Leicesters was holding a position astride the road and at 0830 could be heard heavily engaged with the enemy. Dispositions were as shown in sketch map number 6 on page 110.
>
> On the way back to Brigade HQ after completion of reconnaissance I met the Military Attaché, Lieutenant Colonel King-Salter, who was now with Brigade HQ. On being acquainted of Left Wing's arrival, he asked for one of it's [sic] companies to be brought up here. CO 8th Foresters approved and A Company was sent for. D and ½ HQ Company were instructed to take up a reserve position at Tretten; one platoon of D Company to the west of the river, covering the bridge and the remainder of the company in position on the southern outskirts of the village. The ½ HQ Company (less mortar section and AA section) were to take up a position on the left of D Company, where they could overlook the east side of a ridge of hills, thereby guarding against a surprise attack by the enemy's ski troops who might attack round this feature. Lieutenant Bradley was sent back to place D Company and ½ HQ Company in their positions. Unfortunately this officer was killed on returning to the forward position, after he had arranged for D and ½ HQ Companies positions.
>
> A Company arrived up at 1100 and were placed in their positions by myself, as time was now of the first importance. The Leicesters, who had been holding the forward position, were already withdrawing through us. Heavy salvoes of artillery and mortar fire about this time began to descend on the Foresters' position. The enemy on the west bank of the river had by now advanced to a level with our position and could be seen getting machine guns and heavy mortars into position on the high wooded slopes to our immediate right. The road block of heavy trees was replaced after the Leicesters had passed through. There was, however, insufficient time to interlock the timbers satisfactorily before the enemy attacked the position with heavy tanks. This came in the nature of a

A typical view from one of the Sherwood Foresters' defensive positions near Tretten. (Steve Foster)

surprise, as it was the first intimation we had of the enemy being in possession of anything heavier than troop carrying tracked vehicles. The tank attack was launched at 1200, the leading tank striking the road block in the bend of the road at very high speed. This displaced some of the baulks of timber. The impact caused the tank to leave the road, where it narrowly missed falling into the river. It remained precariously hanging over the edge and was thereby out of further action. Oncoming tanks succeeded in battering a way through the obstacle and pushed through the forward posts along the road.

A short distance behind the first bend the road again took a sharp turn to the right and the tanks, reaching this second bend, were able to form a semi-circle along the road round the forward and reserve platoons in the vicinity of the road. Battalion HQ was also in this area.

Simultaneous with the tank attack, the left flank of the position was attacked and the company of the Leicesters was forced to give ground. The enemy next brought his heavy mortars and machine guns into action, which were on the opposite slope across the river and subjected our right flank to a very heavy bombardment. This fire, together with the fire of five heavy tanks, made the position of the forward and reserve platoons in the neighbourhood of and astride the road, untenable and by 1330 these platoons were forced to withdraw up into the wooded slopes to the left of the road. Here they took up positions facing the road (lengthwise). The enemy's infantry, by this manoeuvre was still prevented from advancing up the road and the centre of the position was still holding their ground.

At 1345 the enemy tanks commenced to advance up the road. The only effect of the continued fire from our own A/T rifles was to make the tanks remain closed down. One tank, using a ride leading back off the main road, tried to cut off Battalion HQ. The attempt was seen in time and HQ managed to cross the ride and reach some boulders above it, where the tank was unable to follow. A new position was reconnoitred and all available men were collected on it. This position was well up on the boulder strewn base of the high mountain at the back of the position. From here the road could still be covered and the enemy's infantry was held up until 1600, by which time ammunition had run out and casualties had been suffered due to the heavy and accurate mortar and machine gun fire from the high ground on the far side of the river. Every effort was now made to get away up the mountain side, with the object of getting behind the reserve position at Tretten, which could be heard engaged with the enemy tanks since 1430. All attempts to get back over the mountain proved impossible, as a sheer cliff face was found to be at our backs and which was unscaleable. The deep snow which was about two feet deep could not be traversed without skis. The only way possible and an extremely slender one at that, was to gain the road and make one's way north as best one could. On nearing the road, about 1800, we were seen and the CO, Captain Athorpe, two clerks and myself were taken prisoner by an enemy Battalion HQ.

It was learnt later that one of the centre platoons under Lieutenant Dolphin had held out in a well concealed position until 1800. They had then attempted to get back via the east side of the mountain track [and] suffered the same fate to be captured some days later, as they were never able to get in front of the enemy's advance along the road. The main difficulty was the soft snow. It also became known that D & ½ HQ Companies, after a stiff resistance on the southern outskirts of Tretten were withdrawn to its northern outskirts, where a final stand was made by them.

The following is a list of officers from the Left Wing:

Major J. Roberts, OC Left Wing
Major J. Kirkland, OC D Company
Captain E. Beckwith, OC A Company
Lieutenant F. Sketchley, A/Quartermaster
Lieutenant J. Esam, D Company
Lieutenant R. Bradley, A/Adjutant
Second Lieutenant W. Dowson, D Company
Second Lieutenant J. Wright, A Company
Second Lieutenant K. Laing, Signal Officer
Captain G. Stoker, Medical Officer

The Sherwood Foresters HQ sangar at the top of the mound, with the plaque erected later by locals clearly visible. (Steve Foster)

List of officers of the Left Wing killed and wounded:

Killed:
Lieutenant R. Bradley, 23 April
Lieutenant J. Esam, 23 April
Second Lieutenant J. Wright, 23 April

Wounded:
Major J. Kirkland, 23 April
Second Lieutenant W. Dowson, 22 April

List of Other Ranks of the Left Wing killed and wounded:

Killed:
Corporal H. Mastin, 22 April
L/Corporal A. Taylor, 22 April
Private Kendrick, 22 April
Private H. Brown, 22 April
Private Davis, 22 April

Wounded:
Private Radford, 22 April
Private Albans, 22 April

Most of the men are buried in Lillehammer. Here is a full list of men buried in this cemetery from the Leicesters and Sherwood Foresters:

Name	Date of Death	Age	Unit	Grave
Private R. Askew	28 April 1940	20	Foresters	I E 4
Lieutenant R. Bradley	26 April 1940	31	Foresters	I C 1
Private W. Brown	28 April 1940	17	Leicesters	I C 1
Private C. Bryan	25 April 1940	20	Foresters	I G 3
Private B. Coleman	25 April 1940	20	Leicesters	I F 3
Private F. Copson	23 April 1940	21	Leicesters	I C 3
Corporal G. Cordon	6 June 1940	NK	Foresters	I H 2
Private L. Cowdroy	21 April 1940	NK	Foresters	I G 2
Private W. Dickenson	23 April 1940	21	Foresters	I H 4
Lieutenant J. Esam	28 April 1940	26	Foresters	I D 3
Private P. Flint	25 April 1940	35	Foresters	I D 4
Private F. Godwin	22 April 1940	30	Foresters	I C 2
Private B. Lawrence	23 April 1940	21	Leicesters	I B 5
Private H. Marsh	23 April 1940	unknown	Leicesters	I B 4
Private L. Mellors	23 April 1940	26	Foresters	I D 1
Private N. Pritchard	21 April 1940	21	Foresters	I D 2
Captain H. Ramsden	23 April 1940	41	Leicesters	I H 1
Private R. Roberts	25 April 1940	21	Leicesters	I F 4
Private R. Scott	21 April 1940	unknown	Foresters	I A 5
Private H. Smith	23 April 1940	20	Leicesters	I E 1
Captain J. Smith	23 April 1940	31	Leicesters	I A 4
Private G. Till	23 April 1940	33	Foresters	I F 2
Private J. Turner	27 May 1940	unknown	Leicesters	I G 2
CQMS F. Wass	23 April 1940	31	Leicesters	I B 3
Private A. Woolf	20 April 1940	unknown	Foresters	I F 1
Second Lieutenant J. Wright	24 April 1940	25	Foresters	I H 3

Lieutenant Colonel T. Ford of the Sherwood Foresters, on the left, at the moment of his surrender. (Steve Foster)

An edited account from Major B. Dowson on the activities of the 8th Sherwood Foresters between leaving Shildon, County Durham, on 6 April and returning to Clydebank on 7 May 1940 can be found in Appendix M, and accounts from Lieutenant F. Sketchley and Second Lieutenant M. Kirk in Appendix N.

Private Frank North was a member of Captain Beckwith's A Company of the 8th Sherwood Foresters and relates his experiences after getting off the train at Dombaas and travelling forward in trucks before taking up a position on the eastern side of the valley:

> We saw a German armoured car supported by infantry coming up the road and we opened up on it with the Boyes A/T rifle and stopped it. A small victory for us and we suffered no casualties. For a while things quietened down but then started up again with more German infantry advancing along the western side of the lake. We were given the order to withdraw but the Germans had outflanked us and we felt we were marooned in No Man's Land. So towards nightfall we felt we ought to carry on and try and get ahead of the Germans – eventually we came to a building which I think was a hotel and we found Captain Beckwith, our OC here, we now numbered about 20 and we stayed overnight here. In the morning Captain Beckwith said we would now move north but we seemed to be still behind the Germans. Captain Beckwith decided that it would be best to move by night and hide up in the day and after a few days we reached Otta. Captain Beckwith stated "it was difficult to move in the day due to the melting snow and so we would move by night." To me this was easier said than done and

The battle of Rindheim – A sketch illustrating an episode at Tretten, with troops trying to stop tanks with grenades. (Steve Foster)

> it was hard going. We were now in the valley by Otta and we had to cross the valley, we were using a churchyard at Otta as cover but we walked right into a German patrol which greatly outnumbered us and we surrendered without a shot being fired. I think we were captured by a group of Austrian mountain troops and initially we were treated OK. We were taken to Dombaas where I was given the PoW number of 344. The Germans seemed far better equipped than us and eventually we ended up in Oslo and then Germany, where I remained a prisoner until I was liberated by the Americans at Nuremburg in April 1945.

Private Sydney Barthorpe of the Sherwood Foresters here tells of his experiences:

> It was rumoured that the British were to evacuate within 36 hours. Sergeants Rouse and Davies, Corporals Kirk and Houlton and I were separated from our

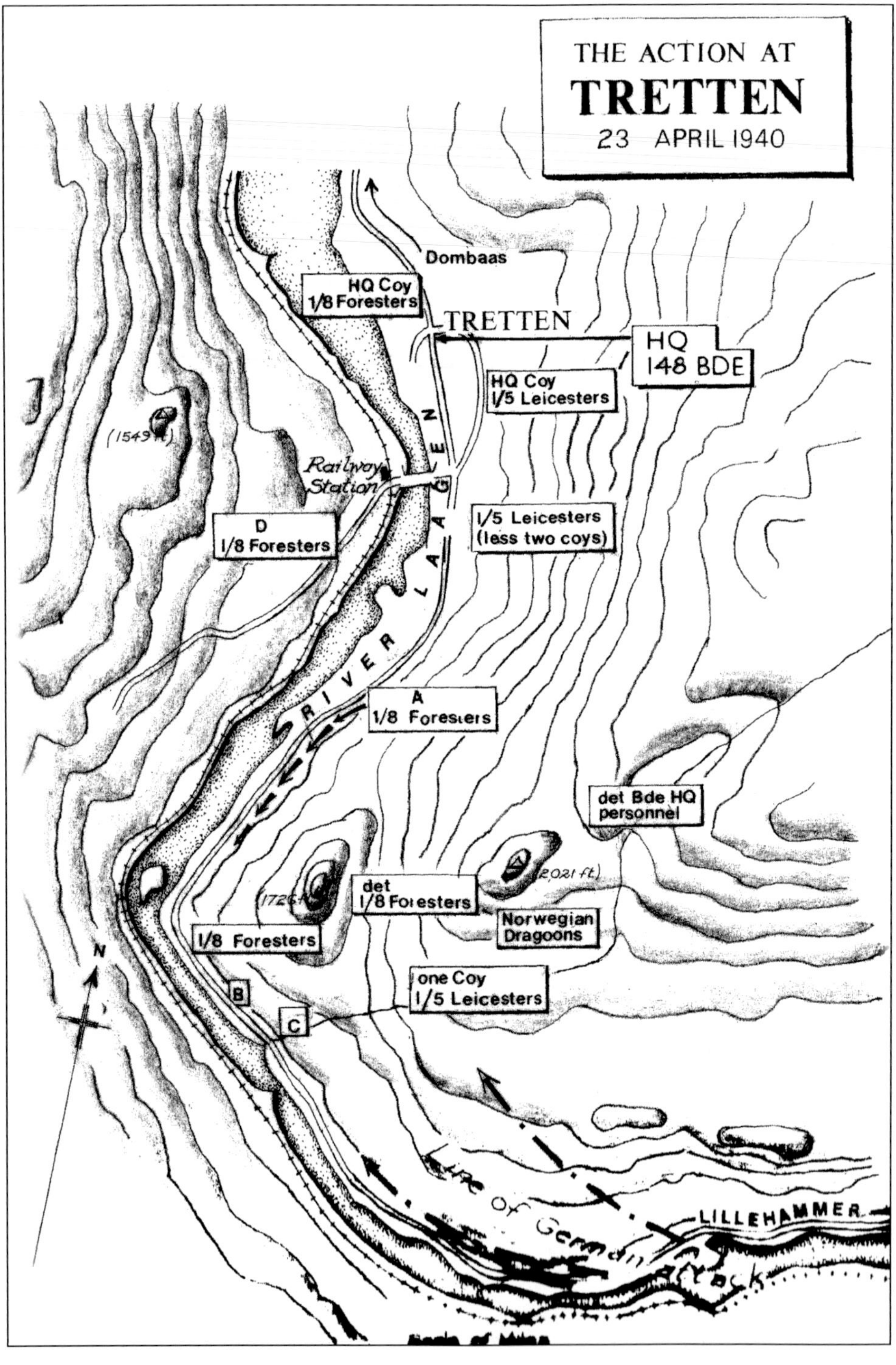

Sketch plan of the positions south of Tretten on 23 April. (Steve Foster)

A shot of Tretten, apparently taken in April 1940. Note that there is still a large amount of snow around. (Steve Foster)

The same view of Tretten in 2010, but without the snow. (Steve Foster)

A view from Tretten bridge looking along the valley road towards Vardekampen. (Steve Foster)

company at Tretten and trying to get to Åndalsnes when we met three Norwegian officers who were trying to catch up with their own regiment, heading the same way on the road to Otta. It appeared that the Germans had broadcast a message saying the Norwegian troops could lay down their arms and go home if they wished. This is what these officers were doing. Their names were Captain Ole Bergseth, Lieutenant Rypdal and Second Lieutenant Hofseth.

We left Punjen Seter about midnight, making our way north, walking easily on the deeply frozen snow crust. Every now and then one of the Lieutenants would go scouting ahead on skis to see if any patrols were about. If any were spotted we made detours but were still able to stick to the right direction. We spent the time walking and trying to get to know one another. In the early stages we got the impression that they thought the British had let them down, but we got on very well together.

At the end of this day we came to a large ski hostel named Peer Gynt. Here we found some venison tubs in the attic. There was no shortage of logs outside, so we were able to keep quite warm. When we left, there didn't seem to be any danger so we travelled in daylight, but were often going knee deep in snow. That night we stayed at a place near Vardhoj. On the next day we saw Fieseler Storch spotter planes patrolling the area. We arrived at Haugesietre and took a short rest before carrying on to Breidjoriet, where we spent the night.

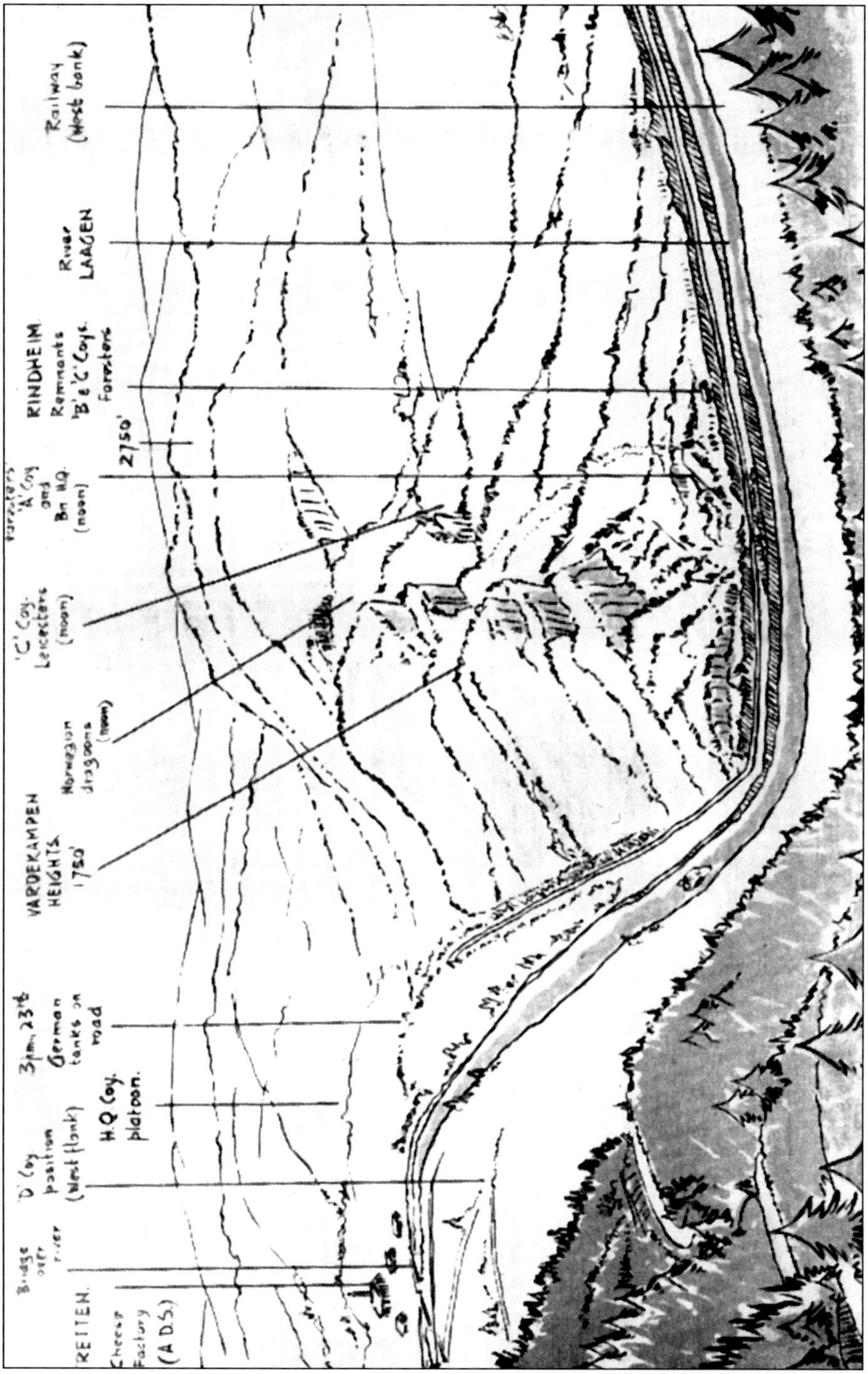

Sketch map of the Tretten area, with company positions annotated. (Steve Foster)

The Railway Station at Tretten in 2010. (Steve Foster)

On the following morning, the two Lieutenants were scouting around and it was quite some time before they returned. When they did return, the three Norwegian officers got together and had a serious discussion. We knew by the looks on their faces that all was not well. They came to us and said the situation was serious. We were surrounded by Germans and today they would have to say goodbye, for if they stayed and were caught with us, they would certainly have been shot for helping us to escape. We exchanged souvenirs and addresses, and set off once more. The Norwegians stayed with us for about one mile, then we stopped and shook hands, but before they left they said; "If any of you could have spoken Norwegian, we could have taken you as one of us." It was with sorrow that we waved them goodbye.

From now on we had to go back to doing our own thinking. Our position at this time was in the high Rondane mountain area around Dovre. The whole area was like a snow desert. We walked and walked with no food and nowhere to sleep for two days, then at 3 a.m. on the third morning, we saw the dim outline of three bungalows. Had we known they were in a dangerous position, I think we would have passed them by, but in our condition they were a welcome sight. We searched each building for food and then settled down in the one with most bedding. After cooking ourselves a meal we got down to some well needed sleep.

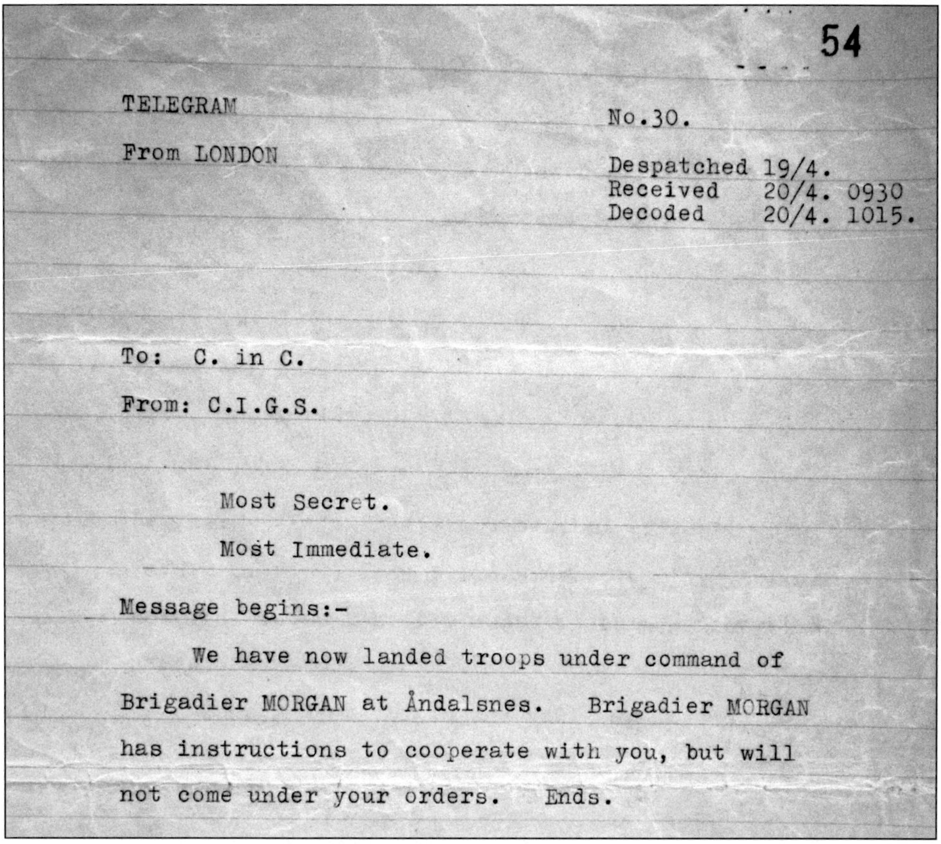

54

TELEGRAM

From LONDON

No.30.

Despatched 19/4.
Received 20/4. 0930
Decoded 20/4. 1015.

To: C. in C.

From: C.I.G.S.

Most Secret.

Most Immediate.

Message begins:-

We have now landed troops under command of Brigadier MORGAN at Åndalsnes. Brigadier MORGAN has instructions to cooperate with you, but will not come under your orders. Ends.

Telegram advising that 148 Brigade had landed.

We awoke at 11 a.m. the following morning and got a real shock. The Germans were only about two hundred yards away filling up shell holes in the road. This was a very unhealthy situation. Behind us was just bare snow-covered mountain with no cover whatsoever. There was a forest about half a mile beyond the Germans, but our only hope of getting there was if the Germans decided to go to their field kitchen for a meal, leaving the road clear for us.

We sat wondering what was to be our next move, when for some reason someone suggested that if we were going to be another three days without food we had better eat, while the enemy dispersed. Like fools we lit the fire to cook something, none of us thinking about the smoke. Sergeant Davies went out with the binoculars to keep a lookout in case they came across to our bungalow to see whether anyone was in hiding. Unknown to us, they were curious about the smoke, but instead of coming frontal wise, the Austrian mountain troops did a wide detour and came up behind us without being seen. One officer went up to Sergeant Davies, who was still looking through the glasses and tapped him on the shoulder.

A German burial party after the battle at Tretten. (Steve Foster)

"Don't bother about them," he said, "the war is over for you."

Four of us were sat round the fire. I was stirring the coffee and Bert Rouse was seeing to pearl barley. The door was in the far corner behind us; we heard nothing until a voice said, "Come on, get dressed."

I stood up and looked round and found myself looking down the barrel of a Luger. In all, five officers stood behind us, three of whom could speak English. They asked us to get dressed once more, then took us out onto the road.

Then the questions came. "What regiment are you. What ship did you come on. What day did you land?"

We gave them no answers. They demanded again an answer to these questions, saying; "If you don't tell us we'll shoot you."

The bridge at Tretten in 1940. (Steve Foster)

A similar view of Tretten's bridge taken in 2010. (Steve Foster)

We didn't give much for our chances anyway; however, at that moment a staff car pulled up and out jumped an Austrian Alpine Major. He came over to the Lieutenant in front of us and it was soon obvious that they were falling out. Not knowing any German we could not follow the conversation. The Major drew his pistol on the Lieutenant then called some of the troops and we were marched away.

These men were friendly and did their best to try and converse with us. Eventually we ended our journey at Dombaas Tourist Hotel. We were kept in the ballroom which was below ground level and were fairly well treated. Our time was spent cleaning the dining hall and loading lorries with captured materials. During the few days we were there, the Major asked us where we had come from and we said Tretten. He asked us how and we told him on foot the whole way, which seemed to surprise him and he also said: "You British fought well at Tretten, I was there too."

I had some Norwegian kroner and asked him if I could go to their canteen and buy some chocolate and he said "With pleasure". So I went round to the canteen window and was met by the Lieutenant who had captured us and he said, "Chocolate? Not for you, English swine."

I went back and told the Major and he said, "Give me the money and you can have mine."

A few more prisoners were brought to us, so they said they were sending us to Germany. We set off on open lorries and finished the journey by bus; some of the scenery especially round Tretten was familiar to us.

6

The Medical Services in Norway

As is usual in most campaigns, the Medical Services often get overlooked, but they have always been a vital part of any campaign by the British Army, with their key role of the 'maintenance and repair' of the fighting man, and therefore deserve mention here.

The British Army has always worked on a casualty evacuation chain, with casualties moved from the point of wounding rearwards through a number of different units where their condition is assessed, stabilised and their priority for treatment determined. Usually there were three types of casualties:

Priority 1: Casualties needing urgent resuscitation and/or surgery e.g. severe bleeding, respiratory obstruction, open chest wounds and penetrating abdominal wounds. The aim is to get these casualties on an operating table within six hours of wounding.
Priority 2: Casualties needing early surgery and possible resuscitation e.g. multiple wounds, compound fractures and large wounds of muscles. The aim is to get these casualties operated upon as soon as possible after six hours.
Priority 3: All other casualties.

The main principals of the evacuation chain are:

a. The collection of casualties from forward units by those further back.
b. Early first aid followed by rapid, smooth evacuation through a series of checkpoints where the casualty's condition is checked, and steps taken to ensure their fitness to continue along the evacuation route.
c. Ensuring that casualties reach a surgeon as soon as possible, certainly inside six hours for priority one cases. The table below shows the longest conventional chain. Some of the staging posts may be omitted according to the situation or the evacuation means available; for example, during the Normandy campaign in 1944 casualties were airlifted from dressing stations via forward landing strips direct to the UK.

At the top of the medical chain of command is the Director General Medical Services, with varying command appointments downwards to positions such as Deputy Director Medical Services (DDMS), normally at Corps level and with the rank of brigadier or colonel. Immediately below this at Division level is an Assistant Director Medical Services (ADMS), normally with the rank of colonel or lieutenant colonel. For the Norwegian

Casualty Evacuation Chain

Point of Wounding
FEBA/FLOT

↓

RAP

↓

Advanced Dressing Station

↓

Main Dressing Station

↓

Casualty Clearing Station

↓

Base/Stationary Hospital

↓

Hospital Care Blighty

Casualty Evacuation Chain diagram

campaign, a DDMS NWEF was appointed on 20 May 1940; he was Colonel P. Mitchiner, who in theory was the top man. Given the fractured nature of the fighting, four ADMSs were appointed as follows: for the Narvik area, Colonel J. Rusby; for the Namsos area, Colonel W. Bissett (from 27 April only) and Lieutenant Colonel A. Beveridge; and for the ill-fated Sickle Force based at Åndalsnes, Colonel G. Blake. The assets allocated to each area was as follows:

Narvik area:
137th Field Ambulance
147th Field Ambulance
21st Field Hygiene Section
25th Field Hygiene Section
No. 7 Casualty Clearing Station
No. 9 Ambulance Train
22nd General Hospital
Hospital ships *Atlantis* and *Aba*

Namsos area:
146th Field Ambulance (HQ only without transport from 27 April only)
158th Field Ambulance (did not disembark)

Åndalsnes area:
146th Field Ambulance (A Company without equipment or transport)
158th Field Ambulance (part of A Company without transport)
189th Field Ambulance (HQ only without transport)

Dealing with the medical services support at Narvik first, Harstad had been selected as the base for Force HQ, and given the nature of the geography in this area sea transport was going to play a major part in the movement of casualties. The importance of this can be gleaned from the following comments from one of the field ambulances:

> Before 10th May there was no road open because of snow and even when the roads were open they were very tortuous and rough. This made the main channel of evacuation by boat down the Ofoten Fjord. Land evacuation was very difficult. Before 10th May [there was] hand carriage through thick snow, hand-drawn stretcher sledges being used to the roads and horse-drawn sledges on the roads. The hand carriage was often long (up to three miles) and over mountainous country. Between 10th and 20th May it was possible to use wheeled stretchers on the tracks and horse-carts on the roads. After 20th May mechanical transport was available, three two-stretcher ambulances (British) and one four-stretcher ambulance (French) being used. It was found that the sledge bearers became very exhausted.
>
> The MT solved one great difficulty, that of conveying stores. Before 20th May each advance entailed moving stores by hand, often entailing three journeys, one

for kit, one for stores and one for rations, of which a week's supply for personnel and patients were held.

The evacuation by water after some practice became very easy. Stretchers were shortened by 4 inches to make loading easier and to enable them to be used in the French transport. Slings were used to lower the stretchers into the holds of the puffers and patients were slung from the jetty to the boat deck by means of a ship's donkey-engine. The holds were levelled off with loose boards and with careful loading 10 to 16 lying cases could be accommodated in the hold and the same number of walking wounded in the cabin. The ship's crew and the Field Ambulance crew (1 Officer and 10 Other Ranks) usually lived on the boat and did the loading and unloading. The journey by sea was normally from 6 to 10 hours and hot drinks and so on had to be served to patients. The patients were always comfortable and usually slept even when the sea was rough. The water evacuation was as follows:

(1) To MDS (Main Dressing Station) which was a 350 ton steamer, SS *Trondenes*, fitted to take 50 lying and 50 sitting cases, with the transfer done at sea.
(2) By puffer direct to 7 CCS (Casualty Clearing Station) at Taorstad or to 22 General Hospital at Harstad.
(3) By puffer to a destroyer when speed was essential.

Later it was found that one ship was not sufficient for the movement of casualties and another was added – the SS *Salten*, with men from 9 Ambulance Train being sent to man this ship. Another problem with the use of the puffers for evacuating casualties was that they were liable to be 'diverted' to other duties such as moving stores, equipment and men, and on occasions apt to either break down or disappear. It was noted that this mainly seemed to happen during air raids, in spite of there being some soldiers as board these vessels. However, senior commanders state that without the fleet of puffers the solution to the problem of casualty evacuation would have been almost impossible. In a post-operation report, the senior commanders also had remarks to make about the German air intervention:

> It should be borne in mind that the water evacuation was at all times liable to interference by bombing. The Germans took no notice whatever of the Red Cross with which the larger ships were marked and ultimately it was found necessary to substitute trained naval crews for the Norwegians, who deserted rather than face the fierce and frequent air attacks to which all the craft were subjected.

Any wounded or sick men who were lucky enough to have a 'Blighty one' would be sent back to Britain by sea, and this in the early stages of the campaign was carried out by the HS *Atlantis* and, after the Battle of Narvik, by the HS *Aba*. The *Atlantis* anchored in the vicinity of Harstad on 29 April, and it is reported that during her stay here she was repeatedly bombed, with several near misses, but thankfully the damage caused was minimal and no casualties were sustained. The arrival of HS *Atlantis* in the area eased the casualty care position greatly, as she could take 600 cases, and she was soon in action as she took on board 22 (20 stretcher) casualties from the Polish destroyer *Grom*, which had been sunk by German aircraft off Narvik. By 12 May, the *Atlantis* was looking after 126 casualties, including a number of wounded prisoners of war, but after this date it is stated that casualties started to arrive at the rate of 50 every two or three days. On 21 May she sailed for England with 432 patients from the four countries involved in the conflict. It is recorded in the medical services report on Norway at the National Archives:

> HS *Atlantis* returned to Harstad in time with HS *Aba* to assist with the general evacuation of Norway by the Allies that took place early in June. On this occasion she carried back to England 194 patients plus 52 unwounded; HS *Aba* carried 370 patients. A quotation from HS *Aba*'s voyage report is worth recording as evidence of good organisation to be set against a record of many failures of the expedition. "While the ship was making her way to her anchorage at Harstad two hospital carriers were circling round her, and as soon as the anchor was dropped they came alongside one to port and one to starboard. Within 25 minutes of anchoring the first patient was being hoisted on board by Mammy Chair for walking cases and stretcher carrier for lying cases. Two derricks did the hoisting, one working to each carrier. Loading was started at 2200 on 31st May and proceeded throughout the night – there being no darkness at all. When the two carriers were unloaded, they returned to the jetty and filled up again, and on their return to the ship loading recommenced. In addition a tender came alongside with several tons of medical stores for shipment back to home ports. Loading of both patients and stores was completed by 0720 on 1st June. Permission to proceed to home port was immediately asked for by signal and written orders arrived at 1000 by launch. The anchor was weighed and the ship sailed at 1015. The patients who numbered 369, were composed of British, French and Polish soldiers, Royal Navy, Royal Marines and Merchant Navy."
>
> The immense advantages of water transport were illustrated by the difficulties encountered by the medical units based on Namsos and Åndalsnes respectively. Here operations took place mostly away from the coastal districts, and evacuation was necessarily by land. It was possible to use the local railway, but not, apparently to any great extent.

At Åndalsnes, the situation was not easy for the medical units as basically they reached Norway short of all their transport, which had been sunk on the journey ashore – it is fortunate that the bulk of the unit's personnel were not travelling in the same ships. The evacuation of casualties was thereafter taken over by the Norwegians under the direction of Colonel Solst. He apparently had at his disposal a number of Red Cross cars and ambulances, and his plan was to move the injured first to small local cottage hospitals and later to larger hospitals at Åndalsnes and Molde. The somewhat static personnel of 189th Field Ambulance opened a 'hospital' at Hen, a few miles from Åndalsnes, and all serious cases were kept there until a ship was returning to the UK.

At the Namsos, it is clear that the medical cover was rather haphazard. The original plan according to the medics was that the force sent there was intended to act as a 'police force' for a larger and more aggressive field force coming later from England, so no field medical units accompanied them. The only instructions given by the War Office were to "make local arrangements". After some initial difficulties, co-operation was established with the local authorities, and some Norwegian doctors and stretcher bearers were employed. In Namsos, two single-stretcher ambulances were made available, but none in the surrounding district. The local Norwegian SMO offered two more 'ambulances', but these were found to be buses, stripped of their seats with mattresses on the floor. A report from an unnamed British Medical Officer said:

> I took the seven casualties by one motor ambulance to Snasa, a terrible journey as the road was in a shocking condition due to the combined effects of a thaw and military traffic. It was more like a farm track than a main road. The 40 kilometre journey took 3½ hours. The Quaker Ambulance Unit was reported in the mountain pass north of Grong with little prospect of getting through; also an American Ambulance Unit of 20 cars was also held up by snow. Our most pressing need was ambulance cars.

The medical services report also details the kit and equipment issued to medics heading for Norway with the expedition:

> Vests, light 2
> Vests, woollen, heavy 2
> Drawers, heavy 2
> Jerseys, heavy 2
> Jerkins, leather 2
> Pullover 1
> Overcoat, Tropal 1
> Socks, woollen, pairs 9
> Stockings, footless, pairs 2
> Gloves, woollen, pairs 2
> Gloves, leather, fur-lined, pairs 2
> Mittens, pairs 2
> Snow goggles, pairs 2
> Cap, fur 1
> Sleeping bag, kapol 1
> Boots, ankle special, pair 1
> Boots, ankle rubber, pair 1
> Kitbags 3

All this would have been very difficult for the medics to move about, three kit bags being issued to pack it all in, and then there was all the other regular kit to also look after. The report continued with the following comment:

Local Norwegians trying to help clear snow. This gives a clear indication of how difficult it was to move cross country. (Imperial War Museum HU128792)

Authoritative opinion – both military and medical – held that this was not a well selected kit. Its bulk and weight were certain to reduce the efficiency and especially the mobility of the man carrying it. Moreover fur of any kind is difficult to dry when wet. The use of windproof cloth, rendering heavy undergarments unnecessary, would have delayed and minimised exhaustion in a country where movement had constantly to be made through snow or icy slush. Furthermore excessive weight and bulk may lead – and here more than once did lead – to grave delays in embarkation and transhipment. Complaint was also made of the ill-fitting frames of the snow glasses and of the unduly large size – mostly 12 – of the boots provided. It should also be observed that cases of trench foot were caused by the wearing of rubber boots instead of the leather boots which had been lost.

Nevertheless, apart from the loss of mobility, the kit, particularly the footwear, did afford good protection from the rigours of the climate and the consistently high level of health maintained throughout the campaign was no doubt partly due to this. It may be added that criticism of excessive weight of kit stands side by side with criticism of the failure to provide skis. But it is difficult to see how, in the short time when conditions made their employment desirable, skis could have been used by men wholly untrained in their management.

As previously mentioned, many of the infantry units went into battle in Norway without their normal equipment: why should the medical units be any different?. As the medical servicesr report put it: "There was one outstanding lapse which was to prove universally detrimental – the absence of a proper organisation to deal with the whole problem of loading the equipment of the Expeditionary Force at its port of embarkation. Much of the loading was done by civilian dock labour which worked to no tactical – or indeed any other – method." The report went on to give reasons for the loss of equipment:

1. Diversion of units from their original destination owing to a last minute change of plan. When this happens as the result of orders transmitted to a convoy while at sea, it may well be that – in the absence of tactical loading – the unit goes to one place and its baggage to another. When it is remarked that such orders actually resulted in the separation for some days of a Brigadier from his Brigade, it is not surprising to learn that such an experience should have fallen to the humbler lot of the Medical Services.
2. Original order of loading altered to enforced transhipment and reloading.
3. Dispersion of Units. A Field Ambulance has only one Quartermaster; when its component parts are dispersed he obviously cannot organise the baggage of more than one detachment. For the rest the expert has vanished and his substitute cannot have an equal degree of experience, knowledge, skill and authority.
4. Enemy action.
    a. Sinking of transport ship *Cedarbank*. A large quantity of both military and medical equipment was lost when this ship was sunk en route to Norway.
    b. Destruction by bombing. The effect of air raids directed on harbours was often – in the absence of air defence on our part – disastrous in this respect. A quote from the war diary of a Field Ambulance demonstrates this: "Fire started by bombing on jetty and greater part of medical equipment destroyed during night. As a result medical stores now available only surgical haversacks, medical companions and shell dressings carried by personnel."
5. Loss of HMS *Effingham*. On 18th May HQ 137th Field Ambulance embarked on HMS *Effingham* and sailed for Bodø. Nearing Bodø the ship stuck a rock and sank. All the unit's equipment was lost.
6. Type of transport ship employed. Either through an error of judgement or through the exigencies of the situation the type of transports employed to convey the Expeditionary Force was not desirable. The use of ships of the Royal Navy, though obviously advantageous in respect of speed and defensibility, had equally serious drawbacks. One of these was seen when a large part of the Expeditionary Force, already embarked on cruisers, was forced to disembark and tranship with all possible speed when it was learned that the German Navy was operating in Norwegian waters. Apart from such a possibility it is clear that a warship, in which almost every inch of space is already allotted, cannot be a convenient form of transport. Nor are large, luxury lines much more to be commended since the use of these too

> much resembles the process known as 'putting all your eggs into one basket'. Transports of 3,000 to 4,000 tons with plenty of small landing craft are suggested by one of the leaders of the Force.
>
> Conclusion.
>
> Some, though, by no means all, of the difficulties encountered by the Medical Services in this highly important business of equipment have now been made plain. Nor is it easy to think that any of these troubles were of their own making. Rather were they due to that quality of improvisation, to which allusion has already been made and which clogged the activities of the Expeditionary Force from its agitated departure to its mournful and inglorious return. It was this that, in the end, accounted in a great measure for the shortage of equipment and for the loss of equipment and the destruction of equipment, and that, when equipment was present, frequently offered the singularly unpleasant alternative of unloading either in darkness or under rain of bombs.

In spite of such difficulties as these, the medical services continued to function with a fair amount of success.

A Field Ambulance is composed of around 180 officers and men commanded by a lieutenant colonel. Its role is to look after the treatment and evacuation of wounded soldiers from the front line. The Field Ambulance provides a transport service using whatever means are at hand, ranging from stretchers, railways or ambulances to the CCS, which is realistically the first place where surgery can be carried out. From the CCS, after the patient's condition has been stabilised, he will, if deemed necessary, be moved along the casualty evacuation chain to a hospital.

The Field Ambulance is therefore a fairly mobile unit, usually operating under canvas, but most medics will ry to set up in a suitable building such as a school, warehouse, hotel or even a hospital. For example, 7 CCS, when based at Tarstad, set up shop in a number of buildings, including a concert hall, school and some empty houses. For the Royal Army Medical Corps (RAMC), the Norwegian campaign also brought new locations for medical facilities into play, as they used floating MDSs in two ships, the SS *Trondenes* and SS *Salten*. The former was run by men from HQ 147th Field Ambulance and the latter by 9 Ambulance Train. Medics who were part of an Ambulance Train were in theory meant to act as the medical cover for patients travelling on special ambulance trains. Ambulance trains were much used in the Great War, moving large numbers of wounded from areas such as the Somme back to the coast of France, where a large number of hospitals were located. In Norway in 1940, the Base Medical Stores Department was established in a hall in Harstad, but due to a lack of space large quantities of stores had to be left outside the building. The ADMS for the Narvik area set up his office in a private house at Harstad, with the clerks living and sleeping on the upper floor while the ground floor was opened as an aid post. The position at Bodø was far better, as the locals had offered the use of their well-equipped, 200-bed hospital, and at Mo, B Company from 137th Field Ambulance were able to establish an Advanced Dressing Station (ADS) in an unused hospital about two miles north of the town.

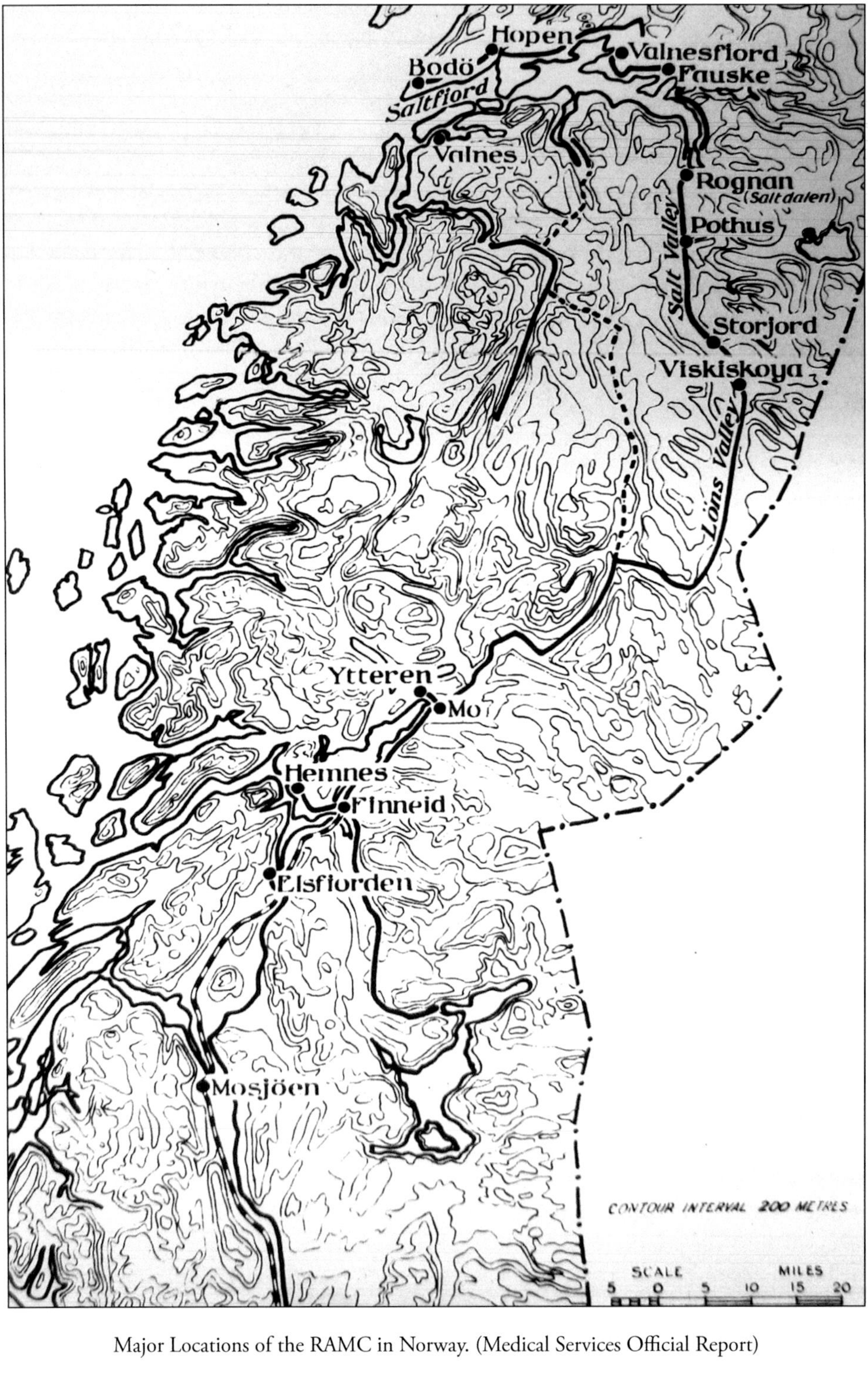

Major Locations of the RAMC in Norway. (Medical Services Official Report)

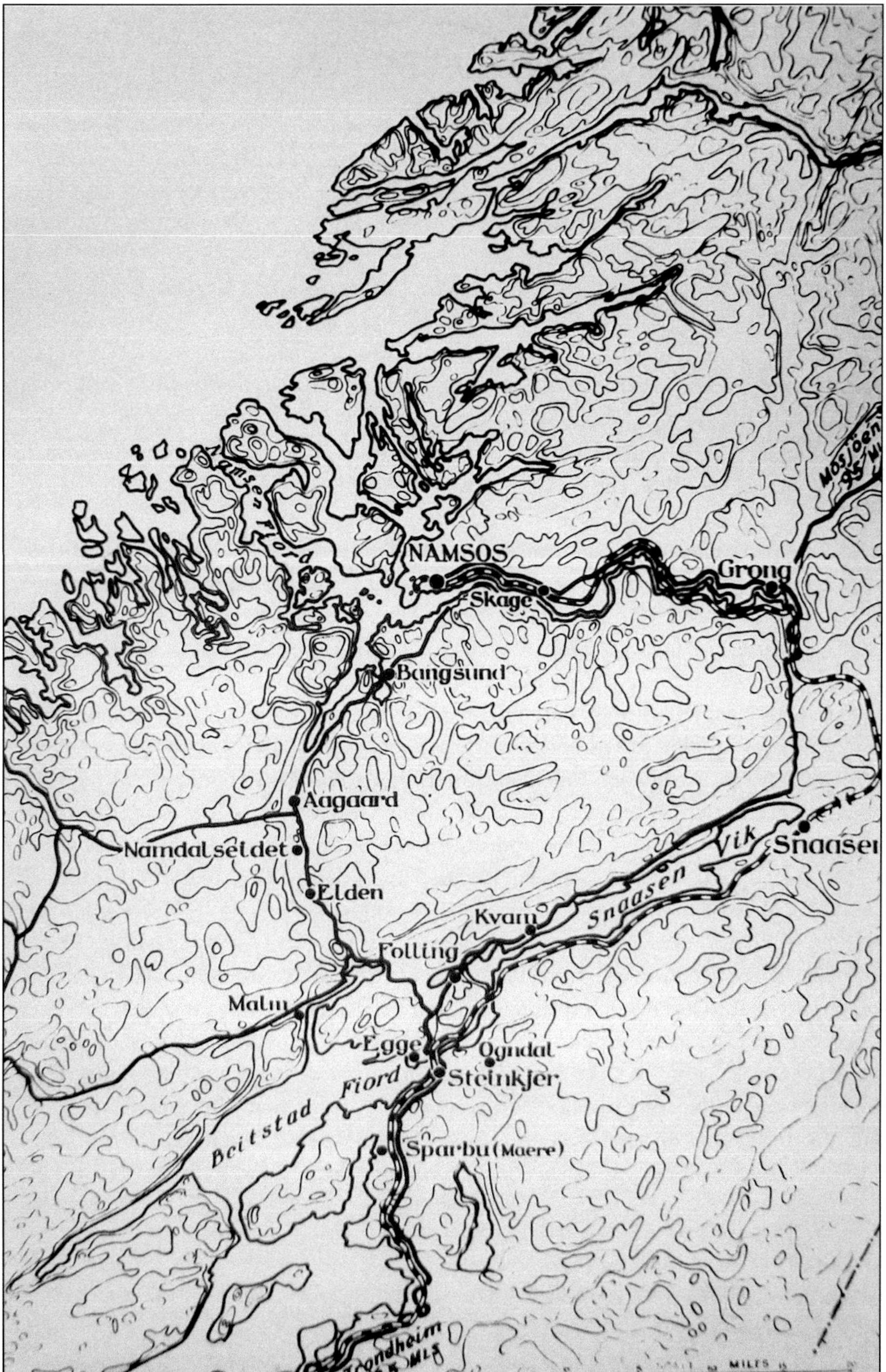

RAMC map of the Namsos area. (Medical Services Official Report)

For those medical units that pitched up at Namsos, they had to a great extent to rely on local goodwill. They were fairly lucky in that the local civilian hospital which was situated on the outskirts of the town, a wood and brick building, had 240 beds and facilities such as operating theatres and X-ray machines. A preliminary inspection had been carried out by a Naval Medical Officer before the Army arrived and declared it fit for purpose, although it is reported that the senior Norwegian doctor was initially difficult to deal with before relations slowly thawed. It is interesting to note that for each Allied soldier who was treated there, the hospital received a daily payment of 8 Kroner (in the British currency of the day, 10 shillings and 6 pence, or in today's money about 53p. A report at the time says: "The hospital changed hands many times during the stay of our troops, being Norwegian, French, Anglo-American and again Norwegian in turn. It was bombed and completely evacuated and re-staffed again, but it never really ceased to function as a hospital and did extremely good work."

Around Steinkjer, several houses and village halls were commandeered and turned into 20–40-bed facilities. The ADMS commented:

> Eventually we acquired two houses for use as hospitals, one of 20 beds and the other with 24, close to one another and situated about 2½ kilometres outside the town. They were within easy reach of each other and the intention was to use one for sick and one for wounded. To staff them I took the RMO from the Lincolns and his stretcher bearers and obtained the assistance of a lady doctor. There were sufficient hospital fittings and dressings in each to cope with an emergency. There was a qualified Norwegian nurse at each and a staff of lady helpers similar to our VADs (Voluntary Aid Detachments). Later, when Steinkjer was heavily bombed and partly evacuated, these Norwegian doctors, myself and some nurses, together with hospital utensils and dressings went to Evam and there took over the village hall, which was quickly cleaned and adapted for accommodation for 40 casualties.

For Sickle Force around Åndalsnes, 189th Field Ambulance initially opened a MDS in a school there, and after much of the town had been destroyed by air attack they moved to Hon. At Dombaas, a number of men from 158th Field Ambulance set up shop in a church, the plan being to keep in contact with the Norwegian medics in the area and also HQ of 15 Infantry Brigade. Things were very difficult in this area, as the medics were few in number, ill-equipped and short of transport. Another general problem was communication, and the ADMS at Harstad commented:

> The difficulties in communication by message, telephone, signal or wire were very great; much time had to be spent in getting calls through as wires were very often on civilian exchanges and delays of many hours were frequent. Moreover German spies were almost certainly present in the towns and there was by no means a negligible risk that telephoned information might reach the enemy almost as soon as its proper recipient.

At Harstad – essentially the main base – there were also difficulties with communication with the Navy. At the outset it was normal for the Navy to signal their requirements and casualties separately. This was the cause of a great deal of unnecessary work, as it was common in the early days that a request from one unit duly met by the Navy might be followed an hour or two later by a request from a second unit stationed close by, meaning two trips when one might have done. This problem was to some extent lessened when a Naval Liaison Officer was located ashore.

The medical services were relatively fortunate in that they were operating in a friendly country, and with one or two exceptions in the earliest stages of the campaign, co-operation with the Norwegian medical services was cordial and complete. It probably helped that both sides had things to offer the other, which aided the fostering of cordial co-operation. The Allies required suitable buildings where – partly for reasons of security from air attack and partly because of the nature of the terrain – the use of tents and huts was virtually impossible, and the Norwegians were quite happy to donate space in hospitals and houses. The Norwegians, meanwhile, on account of the cutting of their normal supply chains from Oslo, were soon in need of drugs and minor medical items, which the Allies, in spite of the loss of much of their own equipment, were able to supply. The chief demands from the Norwegian hospitals were X-ray films, anaesthetics and drugs. It is reported that when a list of demands was sent in, they were always met by the RAMC. At Harstad, permission to use hospital facilities (X-ray, theatre etc.) were readily granted, and in return Allied surgeons and other specialists were allowed to operate and advise on Norwegian casualties.

At both Namsos and Åndalsnes, the majority of the arrangements for both evacuation and treatment were undertaken by the Norwegians, either military or civilian. The problem here with the few medics ashore in these places was their lack of transport. Some help was obtained from an American Ambulance Unit operating in the area, but generally the medics attached to 146 Brigade had to struggle on as best they could using improvised and commandeered means. It was indeed fortunate that the number of casualties needing to be moved was low in number.

Help was obtained from the locals, and the medical services report states: "Of the numerous civilians who put their services at our disposal I cannot speak too highly. They willingly undertook long hours, travelled round the country at short notice and were lavish in gifts of food, bedding and dressings for the use of the sick and wounded."

As well as good relations with the locals, co-operation also had to be made and nurtured with the French. The Narvik ADMS wrote:

> Contact with the French Medicin-en-Chief, Merklan, was made on 29th April and from that date on daily consultations and conferences with him were held, changes of location, impending operations, questions of supplies were discussed and the closest touch kept between the two forces. The association was of the happiest and most valuable and his loyal co-operation in every project was much appreciated. Later when the Poles arrived the same co-operation was maintained.

The facilities at Harstad were used by the British and their allies, as were the hospital ships. It does appear, however, that the French and Poles evacuated their casualties from the front line by whatever means were available, normally by sledge. When the road surfaces improved, motor ambulances were used and the normal point of offloading was one of the British Field Ambulance posts and then by puffer to Tarstad or Harstad. During the Allied advance in the Bjorvik sector, the Field Ambulances moved forward and tried to keep in touch with the French and Polish troops, but in the early stages long carries over ground deeply covered by snow, and sometimes under bombardment, was extremely exhausting for the bearer parties. In preparation for the main attack, a small number of RAMC orderlies under the command of an NCO were attached to support the RAPs (Regimental Aid Posts) of the two attacking French battalions. For the Poles, as it was thought that they would not be facing serious opposition, just a small number of stretcher bearers was allocated. The RAMC provided stretchers, blankets, Thomas splints and dressings, and virtually a complete issue of kit to a French RMO whose kit had been destroyed by air attack.

It seems that the French appreciated the efforts of the RAMC, as General Béthouart, the French commander in Norway, wrote to the DDMS: "Your Government have given to the British Medical Services the task of ensuring the evacuation and hospitalisation of the 1st Division of Chasseurs Alpins. This task has been carried out without failure from our first action to the battle after the fall of Narvik. I thank you and ask that my congratulations may be conveyed to the British Medical Services." Meanwhile, Anglo-French co-operation in the Namsos area appears to have been on a smaller scale, for when the French took over the hospital there they offered to look after and treat any British casualties, an offer which was accepted. The evacuation of suitable casualties to the UK was along the lines of an informal agreement between the French and 158th Field Ambulance, under which suitable cases were put aboard any ship returning to the UK, provided that its captain could be persuaded to take them.

The 22nd General Hospital was a large unit that was meant to run a facility of 1,200 beds. It was sent to Harstad, which whilst convenient for evacuation by sea, was not well suited by way of accommodation, as they had to take over a number of buildings in varying degrees of suitability. The departments and wards were scattered around the town, and matters were not helped by the condition of the roads. One report from the unit says it was "damaged successively by frost and thaw and constantly by enemy action, [and] offered a slow and perilous means of communication. The administrative difficulties arising from this situation were aggravated by the difficulties of communication by telephone." In keeping with the rest of the NWEF, they were always battling against the elements and on arrival reported that there was on average 5ft of snow at Harstad; on 27 April, a blizzard which lasted the best part of 24 hours, deposited a further 18in. Another handicap in the early days was the absence of equipment, in spite of a comment that 22nd General Hospital was fairly unique in that it was able to assemble virtually all its equipment. However, it took about a week to achieve this: personnel arrived on 16 April, and when the transport bringing the equipment finally did arrive on 24 April, it was forced to discharge the loads using the local puffers, which basically dumped the stores wherever they felt appropriate and it took a while to collect everything together. Another problem was the threat of German air power; the following is taken from the unit's war diary for 20 May:

> At 1830 AA fire opened on an enemy plane which appeared to be making a reconnaissance flight. A short time later the naval vessels in the harbour and all land AA guns opened very heavy fire upon a number of planes which appeared suddenly. A very heavy bombardment lasting about three hours followed, causing much damage to the town. High explosive bombs were dropped, one within a few yards of the branch of the unit at the High School, Harstad, resulting in the death of 7364758, Private V.W. Ennis. Every window at the rear of the building was shattered. Private Ennis was killed in a ward on the first floor of the building whilst in the course of his duties and the twelve patients in the room miraculously escaped with minor scratches. The whole building was badly shaken and it was decided to evacuate all patients. The evacuation was carried out swiftly and without any further incident. Several incendiary bombs were dropped in the grounds of the Trondenes Hospital, but were extinguished without having caused any damage. One of the oil tanks, which were situated perhaps a mile away, burst into flames and on account of the danger of the fire spreading, by means of the trees, nearer the hospital, a number of cases were evacuated by means of the small Norwegian fishing boats and the remainder were moved to the basement ward. There were also a number of deaths among the civilian population and the manner in which the personnel behaved under their first heavy bombardment was very praiseworthy.

7364758 Private V.W. Ennis was killed on 21 May and now lies in grave D10 in the Allied plot at Harstad Cemetery.

The unit had sailed from Glasgow in two parties, a small advance group leaving on the 6 April, with the main body – including 40 personnel from the Territorial Army Nursing Service (TANS) – following on 11 April. The advance party landed at Harstad on 15 April, with the bulk of the unit arriving by destroyer after having cross-decked on 16 April. The use of tents was out of the question, so a rapid reconnaissance found accommodation in a number of schools, other buildings and private houses (the latter being used to accommodate the unit personnel), the aim being to get buildings in the town and along the periphery of the bay. However, four miles separated the furthest locations. The locations used by 22nd General Hospital were as follows:

1. Seljestad School – three kilometres south of the town. Equipped as a Norwegian ARP Emergency Hospital with 76 beds. It was later expanded by utilising other buildings to cope with up to 150 lightly wounded, although it is recorded the maximum number of patients at any one time was 120. There were also facilities for operations to be carried out.
2. 2 Military School in Harstad. This was equipped and run by 22 as an 80-bed facility. An operating theatre was also opened.

3. The gymnasium at the Military School. This was first used as a store for the G1098 stores, but after the evacuation of the High School (see below) was fitted out as a 70-bed facility.
4. The Civilian Hospital at Harstad. According to a report this was "a well-equipped, modern building occupied by Norwegian civil and military patients, this offered facilities for X-ray, theatre and laboratory work immediately on arrival until the unit equipment became available. The theatre was used throughout for serious cases from the Military School, some of whom were retained after operations in the civil hospital. The blood transfusion service was carried out from the laboratory and the X-ray equipment was at the disposal of the unit radiologist, who also undertook some of the civilian work." This facility at times was able to provide accommodation for 32 Allied wounded.
5. High School. This large stone building in the town was fitted out with 194 beds, but was evacuated on 20 May after a German air raid which damaged the structure.
6. Gymnasium near the High School. This wooden building was used as a depot for I1248 equipment and also as the central dispensary.
7. Barnkjemmet (children's home). This again was a wooden building outside the town and was used as a medical and isolation facility with 30 beds.
8. Trondenes Folkshogskule. This school building was 3km to the north of the town and used initially as accommodation for personnel from 22 [22nd General Hospital], 7 CCS and 9 Ambulance Train, but it was later changed to form a hospital of 100 beds with an operating theatre with two tables. Transport by road was at times difficult, but a nearby jetty provided an alternative means of transport by puffers and was used to move patients, rations and equipment.
9. Dental centre. This was established in the surgery of a local dentist on active service with the Norwegian Army.
10. Medical Inspection Rooms. This was established in an arms store of the Norwegian Army and was used for all base troops who had no unit medical officer. It was equipped and staffed by 22nd General Hospital.
11. Tromsö. After a reconnaissance by the CO, during which the potential for the town to be used a 'hospital base' was explored, it was decided by NWEF HQ to carry on with the equipping of buildings in Harstad as a temporary hospital and later establish a 1,200-bed unit in huts outside the town. Meanwhile, on 23 May, a small group from 22nd General Hospital consisting of three officers and 15 other ranks went to Tromsö and opened a 200-bed facility, but it only looked after a few locals before the NWEF evacuated.

So after a shaky start and despite a lack of equipment, within five days of their arrival at Harstad, 22nd General Hospital was doing its best to provide a high level of service, improvising where possible: for example, the blood donor team used locally purchased

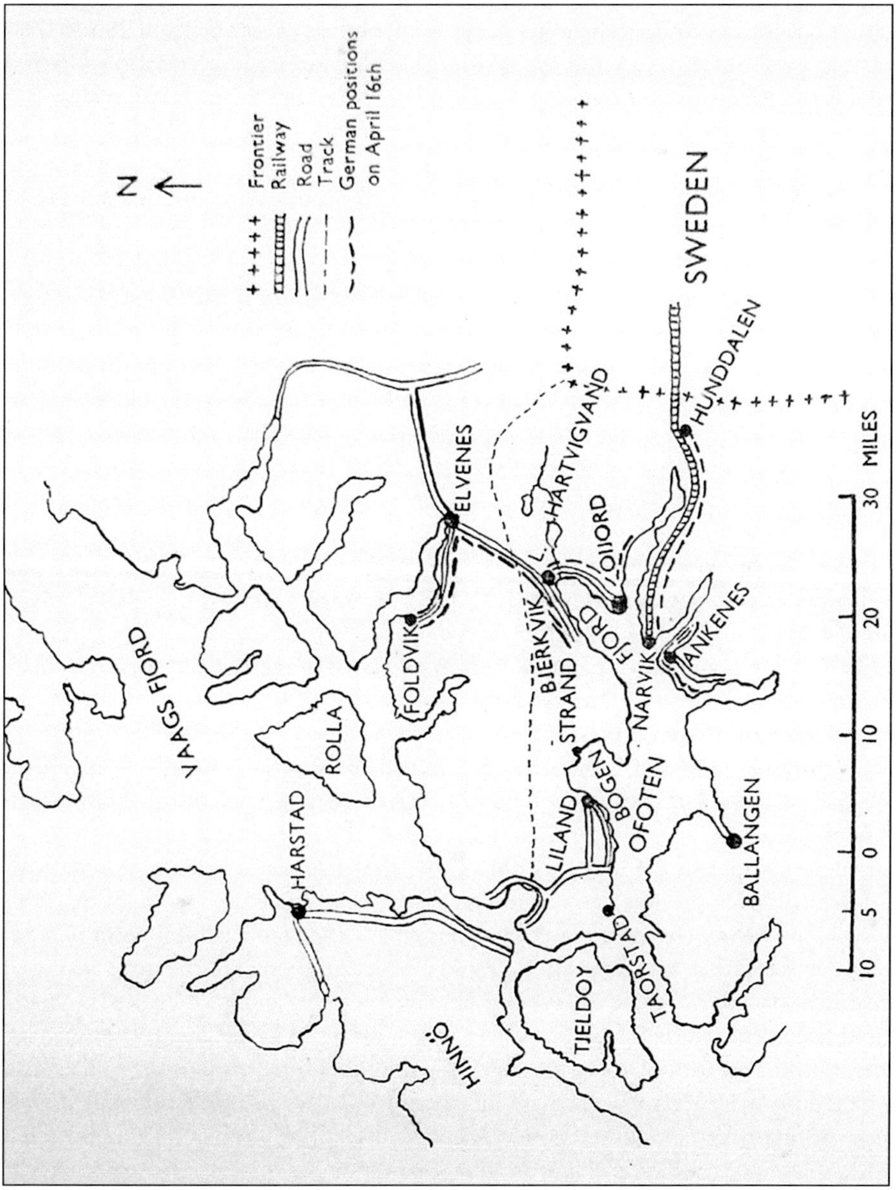

RAMC map of the Narvik area. (Medical Services Official Report)

soda water bottles as containers pending the location of the correct ones, and donors were found from locals, base troops and the personnel of the unit itself. Normally, a General Hospital is sub-divided into surgical and medical divisions, but in the Harstad area, due to the many locations, it became necessary to form smaller surgical teams that could be spread out amongst the locations. Another two teams were sent to 7 CCS, where the surgeon had contracted a septic hand during his first day's operating shift. Seven teams in all were formed, and when large convoys of severely wounded arrived they were quickly dealt with. The support functions such as Quartermaster, linen stewards, cooks, sanitary personnel and so on also had to be split up and spread out amongst the various locations. Other problems involved the disposal of rubbish and sewage, as the local facilities were not up to the influx of numbers into the area; sewage was discharged by boat in the harbour and rubbish was burnt in improvised incinerators. The unit was also made responsible for meeting all convoys at the quays and transporting any casualties in ambulances detached from mobile medical units to wherever they were going. The evacuation to hospital ships was also carried out by personnel from 22nd General Hospital, so realistically they were acting as a transport company, using whatever vehicles they could press into service. A convalescent depot was opened at Karsfjord, about eight miles from Harstad, but this had to be abandoned on the orders of NWEF HQ as it felt there was too much of a threat in this area from German parachute landings.

Other 'exercises' and moves came in the form of orders from above to prepare for mass casualty scenarios. There were five of these – before the planned action at Grattangen, Narvik (when 22nd General Hospital was warned to expect 1,000 casualties), Bjorvik, the evacuation of Bodø and finally the capture of Narvik – the unit being ordered to evacuate (i) all cases who would not be fit in fourteen days and (ii) all cases which were movable.

After the campaign, the unit mentioned that they felt that less than 20 percent of the total casualties in the area passed through the CCS, so the buffer action of that unit was lost. Many cases were therefore evacuated prematurely from a clinical point of view. They also reported that "the necessity for rapid evacuation prevented the undertaking of the treatment of many chronic cases – hernias, varicose veins and haemorrhoids – many of whom had been unfit before sending overseas". Compared to the later role of medical services in other theatres of the war, these seem almost minor, insignificant cases, but show that Norway was very low down on the pecking order for available front-line troops.

It seems many casualties were admitted to 22nd General Hospital having bypassed the normal casualty evacuation chain, arriving direct from the RAP. As one report puts it:

> Many had endured extreme hardship and exposure, waiting in deep snow and having been carried over rough ground before reaching water transport or being immersed in icy fjord water when they were victims of sea warfare. Finally, cases had to be evacuated by hospital ships whenever the opportunity arose, to provide against a sudden large influx of casualties. As a result many cases had to be evacuated earlier than they should normally have been and before even the immediate consequences of treatment could be observed.

It is worth adding a word or two about the dental team, who appear to have been in great demand and were helped by being able to take over a couple of dental surgeries which had a wealth of equipment. It is recorded that the dental staff saw 873 patients in their time in Norway, drawn from units of the Royal Navy, Army and RAF, the French Army and Foreign Legion, the Polish and Norwegian Army and the Merchant Navy. One dentist commented:

> Attention must be drawn to the large number of extractions necessary. No attempt appears to have been made in a great proportion of units to render the men dentally fit during the training period. In the 22nd General Hospital, where such an effort was made, only three minor cases have occurred on active service, thus conserving the time of the Dental Officer.

It also appears that a demand was made on the dental team for dentures – 252 separate items – particularly after the loss of kit following the sinking of HMS *Effingham* and SS *Chrobry*. The Dental Officer added: "Dentures appear to have been reposing anywhere but in the mouths of their owners."

Admissions to 22nd General Hospital, 21 April to 5 June 1940:

	Wounded	Frostbite	Accidentally injured	Sick	Total
Army	173	50	228451		
Royal Navy	100	10	43153		
RAF	8	3	5	16	
Total British	281	63	276	620	
Allies	368	85	28	92	573
POW	108	2	110		
Total	757	85	93	368	1,303

Discharges:

Duty	Sick convoy	Death	Other hospitals	
Army	196	249	6	
Royal Navy	37	113	3	
RAF	1	15		
Total British	234	377	9	
Allies	79	485	8	1
POW	17	64	3	26
Total	330	926	20	27

Total attendances at the outpatients clinics numbered 3,570, including the 873 attendances at the Dental Department.

The 22nd General Hospital was evacuated in three parties from Harstad between 4–6 June in destroyers which later transferred them to transports waiting out at sea, but a large amount of equipment had to be left behind. The attached nurses from the TANS left on the HS *Aba* on 1 June.

Commenting on the actions of the 22nd General Hospital in Norway, the CO said:

> The TANS sisters worked indefatigably and were not deflected from their duty either by falling snow or dropping bombs. Eight months training in England enabled the potentialities of the unit to be well summed-up with the result that on active service, in spite of difficulties inherent to the weather, the terrain, the uneconomic splitting-up of the personnel and equipment and to enemy action, the resources of the hospital were fully applied to the care of the sick and wounded. The unit showed itself capable of adapting itself to meet all that was required of it and the personnel was courageous, loyal, industrious and disciplined with a well-developed esprit-de-corps throughout the short campaign.

The actions of the Field Ambulances

The 147th Field Ambulance's first real action was on 27 April, when its A Company supported the 2nd South Wales Borderers in their landing at Skjomnes, while B Company aided the Chasseurs Alpins in their attack at Foldvik. The 147th Field Ambulance was formed in 1938 and expanded to its war establishment as part of the general expansion of the Territorial Army. It managed to complete an annual camp at full strength in the summer of 1939, only to be called up for real a few weeks later. In February 1940, as part of the 49th Division, it was warned for service overseas, embarked for Norway on 11 April and landed at Harstad on 16 April. It was allotted a billet area about a mile outside the town, which was reached by a steep road which was said to be knee-deep in soft snow. About 22 tons of stores had to be manhandled up the icy road. The unit remained for a short period in billets, much time being spent in checking and arranging stores, putting men through upgrade tests and making contact with other units with which it might be working in the future. On 30 April, the Field Ambulance HQ was established in a small coastal steamer called the *Trondenes*; one of the two puffers allocated was given to B Company and the other held by HQ until it could be handed over to A Company. The unit noted: "Aat this stage such roads as existed were impassable by any kind of wheeled traffic and collection of wounded was by hand carriage or sledge and evacuation by water."

The 7 CCS was established at Tarstad on the north side of the Ofoten Fjord over 20 miles from Skjomnes, where A Company had established an ADS and evacuated its casualties through the CCS. Evacuation from the CCS to Harstad was by either the SS *Trondenes* or SS *Salten*. Much time and effort was spent in fitting out the *Trondenes* as a hospital ship. The work was started by 137th Field Ambulance and completed by 147th Field Ambulance. Canvas awnings and screens were fixed up to enclose the decks from the elements, and Brechot gear mounted to carry ordinary stretchers, while Neil Robertson stretchers, borrowed from the Navy, were used for lowering casualties on board by means of the donkey engine (steam-powered winch) or for lifting them through the doors in the side of the vessel. The original passenger saloon was fitted out as a treatment room, with bunks arranged for patients. The Norwegian crew numbered three officers and 20 men, and with the medics on board the ship became somewhat crowded, yet it was still able to fit on board 150 stretcher cases and 100 sitting cases. The Red Cross insignia was painted on the ship, but as one medic recalls, "more solace was probably found in the fact that we had been given a number of lifebelts from the Royal Navy".

The records for 147th Field Ambulance break their account down into three phases, of which the first phase deals with the period 1–12 May for B and A Company and HQ.

B Company:

The ADS at Sandnes evacuated the wounded of the Chasseurs Alpins. It was dispersed in unoccupied houses with the stretcher bearers working eastwards towards the Elvenes-Bjerkvik road. Relay posts had been established along each route, but poor conditions made the carries very laborious and the work later became even more difficult as the snow melted. On one occasion a carry in the Labergdalen district took four hours, in 3–4ft of snow and under repeated air attacks. Fortunately battle casualties were not very heavy, but there was a considerable number of frostbite cases. B Company was meant to exist on composite rations, but was able to supplement these by bartering with the French and the few remaining Norwegians.

A Company:

The ADS was first at Skjomnes and later at Haakvik. Carries were generally long, but conditions were not as severe here as in the B Company area. Being nearer to Narvik, they were subject to more frequent and intense air raids. In addition, there was a constant threat from enemy ski patrols, which crossed the mountains from inland. At first activity was chiefly centred on the coastal road, but as ground conditions improved it became possible to use light wheeled ambulances.

HQ:

During this period, the HQ of 147th Field Ambulance was chiefly engaged in evacuating the ADS of A Company, but did make some trips to B Company at Sandnes as well as collecting and evacuating casualties from the Navy.

The second phase covers the assault on Bjerkvik on 13 May. By this date, the Germans had been pushed out of Elvenes and their advance had stalled around Ankenes, so it was decided to attack Bjerkvik with a combined sea and land attack. The plan was to use the Poles and the French Foreign Legion to attack after a preliminary bombardment by the Royal Navy; no British troops except the Field Ambulances took an active part in this attack. In fact, 137th Field Ambulance comments that during the previous fortnight all their work had been with foreign troops. The medical arrangements were that A Company would follow in the Foreign Legion at Bjerkvik , two bearer squads from 137th Field Ambulance were attached to the Poles. The HQ Company from 147th Field Ambulance was to lie off Trondenes in two puffers ready to evacuate from the ADS. On the whole this worked well, the Poles encountering little opposition until they reached the outskirts of Bjerkvik. After a brief struggle the town was taken, and the casualties were evacuated by sea from the jetty there. The Germans had apparently mined the wooden jetty, but it had not been blown up and so was available for use, all casualties being evacuated by 2000. The report continues with a comment that the Germans fell back eastwards and the Allies reached Lake Hartvigvand and found nine or ten Heinkels which had been frozen to the ice, although "this loss seemed hardly to lessen the enemy's capacity for air attack".

The end of this phase found the Allies in possession of all former German positions except Narvik, Ankenes and the railway to the Swedish frontier. The stage was now set for the final assault on Narvik.

This was the third phase, the assault on Narvik on 26–27 May.

The plan was for a naval bombardment to be followed by simultaneous attacks towards Oijord and Ankenes.

Two Battalions of the Foreign Legion and two Battalions of Norwegian infantry crossed the fjord at Oijord in landing craft and soon came under fire from German artillery and machine gun fire, but still managed to land. The medical arrangements for this attack were as follows:

The French had what a British report calls a "*poste de secours*" (apparently a slightly smaller version of a RAP) on the reverse side of a hill to the north of Oijord. A Company from 137th Field Ambulance came down from Bjerkvik and evacuated from Oijord to Bjerkvik. Part of the HQ of 147th Field Ambulance cleared the ADS at Bjerkvik into puffers, some of the casualties sent direct to the CCS at Tarstad and some to the hospital ship *Trondenes*, manned by the remainder of the HQ in Bogen Bay. Wounded began to arrive in the *poste de secours* and the ADS in the early morning, and continued in a steady stream. The real danger was as usual the threat of air attack.

On the next day it was possible to evacuate from Narvik, but the French seemed happy to take their casualties to the civilian hospital in the town. Perhaps this was not such a wise decision, as the Germans targeted the town and it is reported that the Royal Navy evacuated large number of women and children from here; assistance was also given by the medical puffers. Meanwhile, three Royal Navy sailors were found in Narvik hospital, survivors from HMS *Hardy*, who were evacuated back to the UK.

The Ankenes attack was timed to coincide with the landing on the north side of Narvik, and was carried out by two Polish battalions advancing from Haakvik, one along the coastal road and the other over the mountains, to cut off any German retreat from Ankenes. The medical arrangements were as follows:

A Company of 147th Field Ambulance set up an ADS at Haakvik, later establishing a second one further round the bay at Emmenes. The Polish battalions had their own doctors, so there were two RAPs giving initial treatment to any casualties. Evacuation was by puffer from the ADS across the fjord to the *Trondenes* moored in Bogen Bay, and from here to the CCS. About 140 wounded were evacuated in the first 24 hours, and the ADSs were completely cleared.

The 137th Field Ambulance, like other medical units engaged in Norway, was split up, with its HQ, A and B Companies all operating separately. The HQ apparently had a somewhat trying time in Norway, and after spending about a week in billets in Harstad was sent to fit out the *Trondenes* so it was suitable for the evacuation of casualties. The ship sailed after about a week, but with some of the work still not finished, heading for Lilland on the north side of Ofoten Fjord, where it almost immediately opened up for business. They were advised within a day or so by locals that there were some naval personnel at Ballangen on the south side of the fjord, who had been on board HMS *Hardy*. These were visited at the hospital, which was about two miles inland, and brought to the shore on horse-drawn sledges borrowed from locals.

On their return to Lilland, the unit was ordered to Harstad, taking their patients with them. Once at Harstad, these were moved by ambulance to 22nd General Hospital. Their place on the *Trondenes* was taken by the HQ element from 147th Field Ambulance.

On 17 May, the unit embarked on HMS *Effingham* with the intention of going to Bodø, but the ship struck a rock on the way; and whilst there were no casualties amongst them, all the unit's medical equipment and the men's personal equipment was lost. However, some of the medical losses were made good by new issues from reserves held centrally. A few days later, on the 20th, the CO received an order to embark again on a destroyer for Bodø, and as the medical services report puts it: "This was received with a marked lack of enthusiasm. The CO entered a personal protest against the suggestion of sailing with incomplete equipment. Eventually the order was cancelled and the unit retired to billets near Harstad where it remained for the rest of the campaign." Norway was probably not the finest hour for the HQ of 137th Field Ambulance, but its A Company did fare slightly better. It operated for a time under the command of 147th Field Ambulance, and before this as an independent unit on the north side of Ofoten Fjord supporting first the 24th Guards Brigade, and later the Foreign Legion. They evacuated a total of around 500 casualties, with the most in one day being 86.

B Company, soon after disembarkation, was sent with the 2nd South Wales Borderers to Skaanland, but after about a week there they returned to Harstad. Then in response to a German threat coming from the Trondheim area, an infantry unit was moved to head them off at Mo, accompanied by B Company. An ADS was set up in a disused hospital about two miles north of the town. As there was no transport, all the stores that came by sea had to be manhandled from the quay to the ADS. Casualties during the first week were low, with just eight being admitted, including a German Luftwaffe officer, which is just as well as it was impossible to evacuate them.

A few days later, intermittent gunfire was heard from the south and it soon became clear that a withdrawal was in place. A passing Royal Engineers officer advised that they were planning to demolish the bridges on the road from Mo to Rognan. It therefore became necessary to evacuate the ADS, and luckily B Company was able to commandeer two lorries from an RASC section to move their 14 casualties, including four stretcher cases. The heavy stores were left behind, as most of the unit had to move by foot, with 28 miles being covered in the first two days. The wounded, escorted by an officer and two medics, reached the civilian hospital at Bodø after a tortuous journey of 56 hours. A week later, Bodø was heavily raided, the civilian hospital was demolished and the patients and medical staff were taken back by sea to Harstad, where the medics spent several days here before being evacuated back to the UK.

The HQ and B Company of 158th Field Ambulance, together with B Company of 146th Field Ambulance and four RAMC officers detailed for duty in the Base Sub-Area, arrived at Namsos on the SS *Chrobry* on 27 April. Of these, only the HQ of 158th Field Ambulance (six officers and 50 other ranks) actually disembarked. As this unit had no transport whatsoever and, for the first few days ashore at least, no equipment, they played no major role. A few did work with the French in the heavily bombed hospital in Namsos, but even then the only casualties they had the opportunity to evacuate were 11 walking wounded to a destroyer and six to a flying boat. On their last night ashore the unit evacuated 17 casualties to HMS *York*.

A Company took part in operations in the Åndalsnes area and set up an ADS in the church at Dombaas, but as they too had no transport, they could do little more than assist the local Norwegian medical services.

The 189th Field Ambulance (the HQ element only, without transport) and A Company of 146th Field Ambulance (without transport or equipment) were landed at Åndalsnes, but, except for a small party from the latter unit – who were attached to A Company of 158th Field Ambulance – did not operate in forward areas. The HQ of 189th Ambulance later opened a small hospital in a school in the town, but due to the 68 air raids during the unit's stay there they moved to Hen, a village some four miles away. They remained there and received some casualties from forward areas, and were later evacuated with the rest of the troops.

A Company of 146th Field Ambulance was sent to a ski-camp near the base, which was occupied by a detachment of Marines, and assisted the Royal Navy medical officer who was running a small dressing station there.

One report on the campaign states that the reasons for sending Number 9 Ambulance Train to the Narvik area, where the only railway line ran from Narvik inland to the Swedish frontier and was virtually entirely controlled by the Germans, were not very clear. The unit was never in a position to carry out its normal role, and so became a sort of general medical dogsbody, fitting out the coastal steamer *Salten* as a hospital ship and later worked on it as medical staff. When Bodø was bombed and the hospital damaged, in response to appeals the *Salten* was dispatched and managed to bring out all the casualties. They numbered 105 and were first moved to Harstad and eventually back to England. The personnel of 9 Ambulance Train worked on the *Salten* from 7 May to 7 June, during which time they evacuated 871 cases. These were distributed as follows: 193 to 22nd General Hospital, 463 to HS *Atlantis* and 215 to HS *Aba*.

Number 7 Casualty Clearing Station was established on the north shore of the Ofoten Fjord in early May at the village of Tarstad, located in numerous buildings as there was not one big enough. It was not an ideal location as water was only available from a river and local wells, and there was no electric power or light. Despite these difficulties, the unit worked all the way though to the evacuation.

The Advanced Depot Medical Stores was set up at Harstad with a small detachment of RAMC personnel led by a warrant officer, was located in a wooden building near the quay and apparently did excellent work. However, the medical services report complains that "its administration was not altogether satisfactory". The report continues by suggesting that in future expeditions an officer (QM RAMC) should be in charge of the detachment. It also mentions that many of the stores landed were superfluous and unsuited to the needs of the campaign, but a lot of them were got away and taken back to the UK in HS *Aba*.

Conclusions:
The medical services report for Norway has as one of its comments that lessons could undoubtedly be learnt from "the story of this campaign as of every campaign. Here, overshadowing all else in its far-reaching implications, is the lesson that good organisation is the first and essential factor working for ultimate success." Another point raised, perhaps unsurprisingly given how low down Norway was on the War Office's priority list, was:

> There is a necessity for RAMC personnel to be men of strong physique to meet the call of emergencies consequent upon the loss or absence of transport. Moreover it is noted that there was a great lack – apart from the TANS – of personnel who had practical training in nursing duties and that the absence of any reasonable opportunity of training in nursing and hospital work before going aboard was a serious handicap.

There were also unfavourable comments about the equipment, as it was felt that much of the kit taken was not of much use, either through duplication or by faulty selection in the first place. This can be summed up by the damning comment: "It is further suggested that hospital staffs in training should have the opportunity of knowing and handling their equipment before going abroad – a proceeding as desirable for a surgical unit as for an artillery unit."

Those in command positions back in London apparently had no real idea of the conditions in Norway, with little obvious planning to deal with its climate and terrain. It is doubtful whether anyone had really considered the practicalities of carrying a severely wounded man down a sleep slope covered in snow and ice. The time taken in evacuating casualties from the front-line medical facilities – while only a small proportion of the total casualties – averaged from 12–24 hours to the ADS and another 6–12 hours to the CCS. In an ideal world, the plan was for those needing urgent surgery to be on an operating table in about six hours. Those wounded in the rear areas – mainly as a result of bombing – seemed to be in the CCS within about two hours. Later, as the snow melted, transport became easier, but this seemed to go hand-in-hand with an increase in German aerial activity. Some of the puffers used for evacuating casualties were lost to air attacks, and it was decided not to risk the larger ships forward of the CCS unless the need was urgent.

On an administrative front, the chief difficulty was the splitting up of units and the delays and uncertainties regarding communication. The post-operation report stated that the 1,200-bed plan for the 22nd General Hospital was an anomaly, and recommended that such hospitals be set up as 200-bed facilities functioning as self-contained units. However, credit was given for the "high health level of the personnel of every unit of the Force. The credit for this lies primarily with those responsible for the selection, supply and distribution of rations and with those directly concerned in the organisation of the system of hygiene in all parts."
The report ends by giving a rose-tinted view of the campaign:

> Finally, in summing up the work of the Corps as a whole, three factors must be borne in mind:

1. Probably none of the personnel except a few senior officers and part of one field ambulance that had been operating in the campaign in France, had had experience of action in the field under modern conditions.
2. Almost complete lack of protection from air attack.
3. Lack of transport and heavy equipment, due partly to failures of organisation and partly due to enemy action.

> But they were not lacking many instances of individual courage in the field and under aerial bombardment; of resourcefulness in improvisation that solved suddenly arising and imperative problems; of devotion to duty that defied difficulties, danger and physical exhaustion. It was by force of such qualities that the work of the Corps was maintained in full keeping with its high traditions.

An idea of the experience of many of the men sent to Norway comes from Private Basil Keeble, who was a member of 189th Field Ambulance RAMC. Basil had joined the St John Ambulance in 1935, and after his initial medical for the Army he was sent to the RAMC. He gave the following recollections of his time before the war and in the Army:

> I was expecting war and knew I would have to serve in the forces, but I was not a fan of Chamberlain and felt he was giving way too much. I was called up on 15th December 1939 and I reported to the RAMC Depot at Church Crookham for 12 weeks basic training. I was not impressed with the training, to me it seemed well out-of-date to what I had done in the St John's [sic] Ambulance. Anyway I passed out and was posted to Barnet in north London helping to form 189th Field Ambulance. After about a week here mainly just putting up tents we were told we were going away and we travelled from Barnet to King's Cross station and here we got on a train to Scotland. Eventually after a lot of to and froing we got on a board a small ship called the *St Sinevar* which was not really big enough for us and our equipment went on the *Cedarbank*, which was sunk on the voyage across so we lost most of our supplies before we even got to Norway.
>
> Eventually we got to Åndalsnes where it was chaotic and we virtually waited around for two days for orders but in the interim we set up a small facility in a local school but we didn't have a lot of equipment. We did have a good relationship with the local cottage hospital but we were hampered by the lack of transport, but our RASC guys found a lorry dump and were able to get a lorry and a small bus which we used as ambulances. Then we were ordered to move to Dombaas but we did not start here long before moving back to the Åndalsnes area and set up in a Singer sewing machine factory, but got very few casualties to treat as most seemed to end up in Norwegian facilities. The deep snow certainly hampered our movements and then we got orders to evacuate. I went back on board the *Sheffield* and we got a tot of rum, a shower and decent meals on board. The locals understood what was going on with a bit of apathy about it due to the German superiority and no real hostility towards us. But all in all I felt the whole campaign was a fiasco.

7

15 Brigade and Major-General Paget

One of the main difficulties with the Norwegian campaign was the finding of suitable troops to go there. The Army high command gave permission for a unit to be withdrawn from the BEF in France and sent to Norway as part of Operation Hammer, and later Operation Sickle. The unit selected was 15 Infantry Brigade, which was part of the 5th Division and consisted of the 1st Green Howards, 1st King's Own Yorkshire Light Infantry (KOYLI) and 1st York and Lancaster. It had moved to France in the last few days of 1939, and early in January 1940 manned part of the defensive line in north-east France.

The units were warned on 16 April that they would be moving to Norway, and on the following day the CO of the 1st KOYLI, Lieutenant Colonel Herbert Edward Fitzroy Smyth, was told he was now the Brigade Commander, as Brigadier Berney-Ficklin had been appointed as Force Commander. His place as CO of the 1st KOYLI was taken by Major Cass. In the early hours of 18 April, the brigade left Boulogne and arrived a few hours later in Dover. The key commanders went up to London for a briefing at the War Office while the rest went by special trains to Dunfermline in Scotland. One of the saddest stories of this move to England is that of Private Thomas Poxon of the 1st York and Lancasters, who together with two other members of D Company was reported missing when the battalion was leaving Quesnoy in France. Private Poxon was later found drowned in a river near Quesnoy, but his death remains a mystery. He now lies in plot 11 row B grave number 2 of the Cite Bonjean Military Cemetery, Armentieres.

As further conformation of the confusion surrounding the whole operation in Norway, Major-General Bernard Paget was given command of Operation Hammer on 19 April, but immediately relieved of this command when the operation was cancelled on 20 April. He did not have long to think about a new job, as on 21 April he was given command of Operation Sickle. On that day he reported to the War Office together with his Chief of Staff, Lieutenant Colonel Nicholson, who later commented:

> Everything was in a state of improvisation. There were no maps; we had to tear them out of geography books and send the ADC out to the Norwegian travel agency to buy a Baedeker [travel guide]. From the Norwegian Embassy and a series of tourist agencies, we gathered an armful of travel advertisement folders. From amongst them we unearthed one showing a picture with a bit of Åndalsnes in the background and other photographs of the valley between Åndalsnes and Dombaas. These were our only clues as to what our prospective theatre of operations looked like.

Meanwhile, after being briefed at the War Office, the senior commanders left by the night train to Edinburgh, where the party split up. Brigadier Berney-Ficklin and his staff flew to Scapa Flow for a conference with the Commander of the Home Fleet, Admiral Sir Charles Forbes, while the others went to Dunfermline to catch up with their units. The 1st KOYLI war diary then records: "19th April 1400 Information received that Brigadier Berney-Ficklin and staff had been involved in an aeroplane crash in Orkney and were seriously injured. 1700 A message was received from DMO War Office, to the effect that no further action was to be taken about embarking Hammer Force. The operation to be considered in abeyance." On a more practical level, most of the day for the rest of the brigade was spent in being issued with arctic clothing and trying to bundle all equipment into one-man loads. At least for these units there was the realisation that it was going to be difficult on the other side of the North Sea. It would appear that the brigade had been told to leave all its transport behind in France, so everything they needed would have to be man-packed, which is not an easy task.

In view of the fact that it was likely an amphibious landing would have to be carried out, Smyth, the new Brigade Commander, visited HQ Scottish Command on the morning of 20 April, asking them to make contact with the Royal Navy and ask them if it would be possible to carry out a practice embarkation and disembarkation exercise. A meeting was arranged with the Chief of Staff of Rosyth Naval Base for 1400 that day, but it seems there was not time to carry out such an exercise, which would have been invaluable practice. The war diary of 15 Brigade records for 1200 that day: "Brigade Commander returned from HQ and found message to ring up DMO War Office. Rang up and received instructions to embark HQ and two Battalions with certain other details in HM Ships next day, 21st April. Liaison Officer from War Office to be expected morning 21st April with instructions, General Paget in command."

The 1st KOYLI records that on this day they were told that on landing in Norway their task would be to seize an aerodrome east of Trondheim. There is no indication that the York and Lancasters were given any instructions except that they were going to Norway. The third unit in the brigade, the 1st Green Howards, also do not seem to have been given a specific aim. It was very much a case of 'hurry up and wait' as the next few days were spent on order and counter-order, and trying to sort out newly issued kit. By 24 April everything was ready to go. Buses arrived at the camp at Dunfermline to take the men to Rosyth to board ships to take them to Norway.

The 1st KOYLI war diary records they left camp with a strength of 32 officers and 754 ORs at 2359 on 21 April, and by 0300 the next day had embarked on HMS *Glasgow*, HMS *Campbell*, HMS *Vansittart* and HMS *Witch*.

The 1st York and Lancasters left at 0245 on 22 April in 32-seater buses. Most of the battalion (510 all ranks) went onto HMS *Sheffield*, with the remainder dispersed as follows in parties of 60: two platoons of D Company on HMS *Impulsive*, two platoons of B Company on HMS *Ivanhoe*, andone platoon of D Company and one platoon of B Company on HMS *Icarus*. The total strength on embarking was 31 officers and 690, ORs giving a total of 721.

The 1st Green Howards left on the 24th in 27 buses, with 22 officers and 584 ORs going on HMS *Birmingham*, three officers and 57 ORs on HMS *Arrow*, three officers

German troops advancing towards Tretten, from one of their propaganda magazines. (Steve Foster)

and 57 ORs on HMS *Acheron* and three officers and 57 ORs on HMS *Griffin*. This gave a strength for the battalion on leaving the UK of 31 officers and 755 Ors, a grand total of 786.

As well as these three major units, various other elements went to Norway with 15 Brigade. The HQ and Signal Squadron, Anti-Tank Company, 55th Field Company RE, the 158th Field Ambulance RAMC and the 168th LAA Battery RA were all attached to the brigade. Meanwhile, just before sailing, the Brigade Commander received orders from General Paget to land at Åndalsnes and place himself under the orders of Brigadier Morgan of 148 Brigade. With most of the units at sea, Lieutenant Colonel Smyth (now temporary brigadier) went to see Rear Admiral Frederick Edwards-Collins, who was leading the group, on the bridge of HMS *Galatea* on the evening of 22 April to try to understand how and where his troops would be offloaded. The Navy's idea of things was as follows:

1. Expected hour of arrival at Åndalsnes – 2100.
2. Order of disembarkation; first HMS *Galatea* at Åndalsnes pier, second HMS *Glasgow* in stream, third HMS *Sheffield* at Molde. Troops and stores from HMS *Sheffield* could not be expected to arrive at Åndalsnes before 0500.
3. (a) Three destroyers to disembark troops and stores early and then be used as ferries for troops and stores in *Glasgow*. (b) Three destroyers to be used for anti-submarine patrols and to disembark their troops and stores last.

Brigadier Smyth wrote later about this plan:

> I asked that the KOYLI destroyers should be used for (3) (a), I would then have the whole of the KOYLI disembarked early. The Admiral was unable to agree to this as the KOYLI destroyers were small ones and not suitable for ferrying stores. In view of the fact that his orders were to sail at daylight whether the stores were unloaded or not, I did not press the point. It meant, however, that I could not have a complete battalion disembarked before 0500 at the earliest.

So yet another assault landing in this campaign was to be a rather makeshift affair, unrecognisable from what happened in June 1944 when the Allies went ashore in Normandy. But the latter campaign was planned in great detail, and in theory had learnt all the painful lessons from Norway and other previous landings.

Perhaps trying to cut his losses, Brigadier Smyth issued orders to his men in the early hours of 23 April, the main points of which are as follows:

a. Troops from *Galatea* (less Force HQ, AA detachments etc.) to assist RN personnel by moving stores from ship's side.
b. Other troops to be led to assembly positions recced by HQ 15 Infantry Brigade.
c. Stores to be dumped separately by ships.

The fleet seemed to have an uneventful crossing of the North Sea, and at about 1900 on 23 April the lead ship, HMS *Galatea*, entered Åndalsnes fjord and was tied up at the pier by 2145. Brigadier Smyth reported that even before landing, he received a message from Brigadier Morgan that "assistance was required as soon as possible at Tretten, 150 miles south east of Åndalsnes on the Dombaas-Lillehammer railway".

This message was backed up by Lieutenant Colonel Dudley Clarke when he came on board *Galatea* at Åndalsnes around 2200, and told Smyth the following information:

1. Confirmation that troops were urgently required at Tretten, because 148 Brigade was hard pressed.
2. Two trains, each capable of carrying 450, were available at Åndalsnes.
3. The railway line had been broken at Dombaas and it was not yet known if it was possible to get through.

So once again a senior commander was faced with a situation that seemed to be out of control, being asked to split his forces to react to a worsening situation. He was told it was best to move by night as the Luftwaffe tried to bomb the railway line or any trains moving on it in daylight. Smyth was faced with working out which of his troops would be ready to move in the next two or three hours. He decided that in order of availability this would be: Brigade HQ and A/T Company, 1st KOYLI (less two companies), two companies of the 1st York and Lancasters, part of 55th Field Company RE and adetachment from 158th Field Ambulance RAMC.

Smyth later made some comments about the readiness of these units to move and what he decided to do:

> 15th Infantry Brigade HQ had been allocated duties in connection with the organisation of the dock and assembly area. These were essential for the smooth running of the disembarkation.
>
> 15th Infantry Brigade A/T Company being the first unit to disembark, had been detailed to assist the Navy by clearing stores from the ship's side. I did not wish to alter the arrangement in view of the danger of the ships sailing at daylight with a large portion of the Brigade's stores still on board. Nor did any flats or ramps appear to be available for their guns.
>
> Two companies of the 1st York and Lancasters. It did not appear to me that it would be in the best interests of the Brigade or the Force to start splitting up the whole organisation of the Brigade at this stage of the operations.
>
> Part of 55th Field Company RE and detachment from 158th Field Ambulance RAMC for reasons that these units were very much split up and separated from their stores, they could not really be considered available at all.
>
> I therefore issued verbal orders, confirmed by a written order for:
>
> a. Advance Brigade HQ (Brigade Commander, Brigade Major, Norwegian Liaison Officer and W/T detachment)
>
> 1st KOYLI (less two companies) to entrain immediately with complete equipment and 7 days rations.
>
> b. Remainder of Brigade under command of Lieutenant Colonel Kent-Lemon, 1st York and Lancasters, to remain in Åndalsnes area and to be ready to move at two hours notice by road or rail. HQ 15th Infantry Brigade to arrange locations clear of port area.
>
> The 1st KOYLI reported this move in the following terms: "April 24th 0145 A, B, E and HQ Companies entrained for Otta and arrived at about 0415 without incident. Battalion was immediately ordered to take up a defensive position astride the road south of Otta. Except for continuous bombing of Otta during the day, no contact was made with the enemy forces. At 1530 CO's recce group moved forward to Kvam to reconnoitre a defensive position under orders of Brigadier, 15th Infantry Brigade. At 2200 the Battalion less C and D Companies entrained for Kvam."
>
> On my return to my Advanced HQ at Otta at 1300, I received information that 15th Infantry Brigade Anti-Tank Company and two Companies of the KOYLI were being despatched in accordance with my previous instructions. I then sent a message to Force HQ for the following to be sent forward to Otta during the night 24th/25th April:
>
> HQ 15th Infantry Brigade & Signals
>
> 1st York and Lancaster
>
> Section 55th Field Company RE
>
> During the afternoon Major Walters, 1st York and Lancaster reported to me that he was in command of three companies of his Battalion at Dombaas where

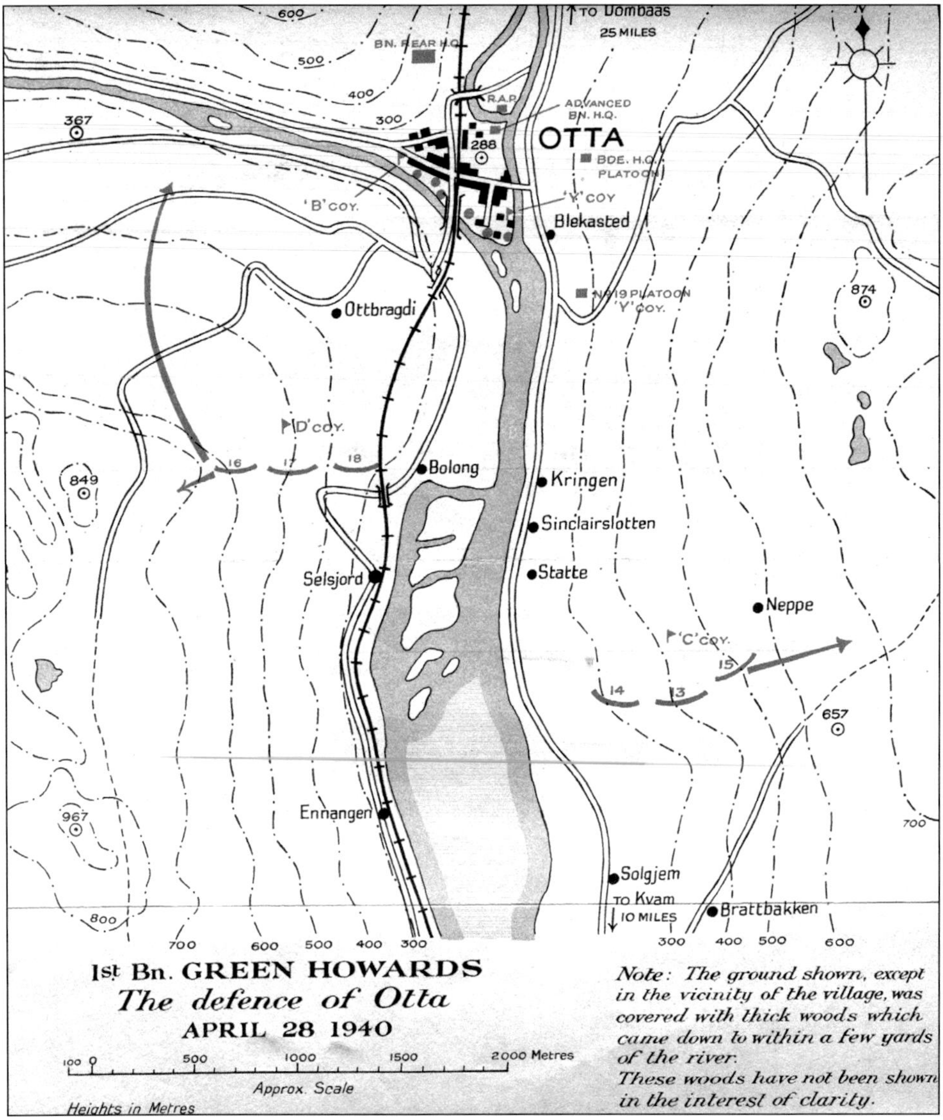

The Battle of Otta from the Green Howards Official History.

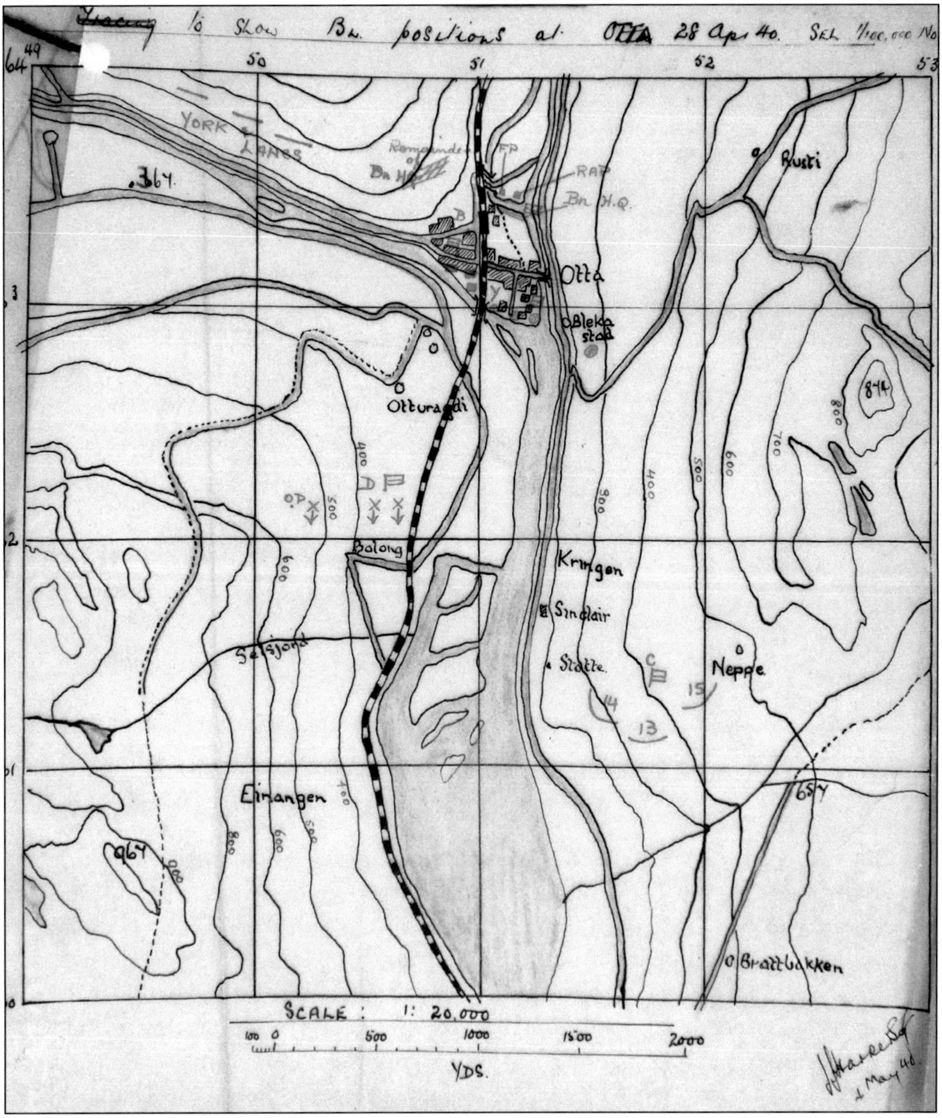

Otta battle map from Green Howards War Diary.

The Cross of Sacrifice in the Kvam Churchyard; 54 Allied servicemen are buried here, nearly all from the KOYLI and the York and Lancasters. (Steve Foster)

> they had been sent early that morning to clear the congestion at Åndalsnes. He asked for orders, but I told him that I had already sent orders for 1st York and Lancaster to be sent to Otta on night 24th/25th and that his Battalion would undoubtedly pick him and his companies up en route.
>
> During the day Otta was bombed fairly heavily from the air and considerable damage was done. I arranged for a train from Otta at 2100 to take 1st KOYLI forward to Kvam about 15 miles in order to give them more time to dig in. At 1700 at Kvam, just as I had finished making a recce of the position with my Brigade Major and Major Cass, CO 1st KOYLI, I met the General commanding the 2nd Division with his G1 on their way back from their old HQ. He told me that his troops at Faavang had abandoned their positions prematurely and were in retreat.

The Battle of Kvam took place on 25 April, coincidently exactly 25 years after the first landings of the Gallipoli campaign, which of course Winston Churchill also had a hand in. The train journey of the British troops to Kvam was not straightforward. There was a delay at Dombaas because the station there had been heavily bombed, but they eventually got through before suffering a further delay outside Otta station. Here Brigadier Smyth went forward to the station with his brigade major and the Norwegian Liaison Officer, and met Captain Tandy, the Supply Officer from 148 Infantry Brigade, who was asked for the latest position on his brigade. He replied that 148 Brigade had been heavily attacked by enemy tanks on the previous day and forced to withdraw to the Heidal valley, around six miles south of Otta. Smyth later commented, "I received the impression that the Heidal valley was now the Allied front line and that the situation was fluid."

Smyth was meant to be under the command of Brigadier Morgan, so he tried to find him for further instructions and recorded that he spent an hour or two searching the Heidal valley; all he found were several parties of men from 148 Infantry Brigade asleep in barns and other farm buildings. His report continues:

> I was unable to find anyone who could tell me the whereabouts of HQ 148th Infantry Brigade, the Norwegians or the Germans. I, therefore, decided to proceed south on the road to Ringebu in the hope of being able to discover the situation and, if possible, the location of the Norwegian HQ.
>
> I met several small parties of Norwegians by the roadside. None of them could tell me the whereabouts of any Norwegian HQ or of the front line. There was a certain amount of shooting going on, but this seemed to be entirely from or at German aircraft. Eventually I found someone who was able to direct me to HQ 2nd Norwegian Division and at about 1045 I found this HQ and I met the General commanding who stated:
>
> 1. That his troops were occupying a position astride the road at Faavang, 15 miles south of his HQ and that they would withdraw that night to a rest area in the Heidal valley.
> 2. That his HQ were [sic] moving that night north of Otta.
> 3. That one battalion was to occupy a position on the general line of the Vinstra river 5 miles south of Kvam and would hold this during 25th April, withdrawing during the night 25th/26th April.
> 4. That he would like me to occupy a position at Kvam and that I could occupy it either during the night 24th/25th or 25th/26th April.
> 5. That unless I agreed to do this and checked the German advance, allowing his troops to get some rest, he doubted whether they could continue the struggle.
>
> I replied that I was under the command of Brigadier Morgan, with whom I had not yet established contact, but that, if Brigadier Morgan approved, I was quite ready to do what he asked and that I would occupy the position during the night 24th/25th.
>
> About 1145 on the 24th, shortly after leaving the Norwegian HQ I met Brigadier Morgan and his Brigade Major. He approved of my carrying out the wishes of the Norwegian General and occupying the Kvam position. I suggested that he should withdraw the remnants of his Brigade on the night 24th/25th April from the Heidal valley to the Dombaas area with a view to protecting the L of C [lines of communication] and ensuring that no enemy forces from Trondheim could come in on the rear of 15th Infantry Brigade.

The first of the British units to arrive at Kvam was the advance party of the 1st KOYLI at about 0215, who commenced to dig in. About an hour later, C and D Companies arrived by train and also started to dig in. The KOYLIs were positioned as follows:

> Forward Companies:
> A Company on the right under Captain Gowans
> B Company on the left under Major Burr
> In reserve:
> C Company on the left under Captain Fox
> D Company on the left under Captain Vickers
> Then as the reserve E Company under Captain Riggs together with HQ Company under Major Jones.

The KOYLI war diary records:

> 0530 Battalion battle patrol was sent forward to reconnoitre south, down the road with a view to gaining touch with the enemy who were now advancing, owing to the premature withdrawal of the Norwegian forces. No information was received from this patrol before the enemy had made contact with the forward companies. The patrol eventually returned about noon and reported that the patrol commander – Lieutenant Oldman and two men had been severely wounded. It was not possible to recover these men.
> 1100 the enemy advanced along the road in column of route headed by three tanks and closely supported by artillery and infantry both on foot and motorised. Fire was opened by the forward companies and the guns of the Brigade A/T Company which inflicted casualties on the enemy and forced him to deploy. The tanks made no further advance but the enemy very rapidly deployed his artillery and commenced to shell all positions with great vigour. It was noted that houses were particularly selected for shelling and many were set on fire very rapidly.
> About noon Brigadier Smyth was wounded by a shell.

Meanwhile, the 1st Green Howards had left Åndalsnes at about 0400 by train for Dombaas, arriving there about 0800. The CO, Lieutenant Colonel Robinson, left B Company at the station to unload the baggage and positioned the rest of the unit in a wood to the west of the town. Later that day, B Company, under the command of Captain Lidwill, with the Carrier Platoon attached were ordered to move up to Lien to support the 1st York and Lancasters. There was considerable enemy air activity over Dombaas and a number of incendiary bombs were dropped on the Green Howards' positions, with the house in which the Battalion HQ was located being burned down. Later that day, most of the unit (excluding A and B Companies and the Carrier Platoon) left Dombaas about 2300 by train for Otta, arriving there early in the morning of 27 April, where they took up a defensive position astride the road to Dombaas. Most of the day was spent digging in and preparing positions for B Company, as the CO had been told they would be withdrawing to this area the following night. The area was intended to be occupied by the York and

Lancasters on the right, with the Green Howards on the left. The location was described by the Green Howards in their war diary as follows:

> The position was naturally very strong being a deep gorge running north and south through which the road passed but with the River Otta running from west to east down another gorge coming at right angles to the village, making a natural obstacle. To hold the location it was essential to go forward of the village across the obstacle to prevent the spurs at 508525 and 517618 astride the main stream, which had complete observation on the village and behind it, getting into enemy hands.

Things were quiet until the next day, B Company returning about 0600 and going straight into the defensive positions prepared for them. At around 0845, C Company reported that they could see German armoured cars and lorries advancing down the road from the south. For the next hour or so it is reported in their war diary that "there was continuous and intense bombing and machine gunning from the air of the two leading companies (D Company on the right hand spur and C on the left hand spur) and the hillsides on my flanks and rear. This was followed by artillery fire of some intensity combined with machine gun fire."

At 1020, German patrols reconnoitred below C Company's positions but were not fired on as orders had been given to refrain from opening fire until a "worthwhile target" presented itself, so as not to disclose their position. The opening exchanges really had to count. Around the same time, some German troops were observed crossing the river. Between 1030 and 1100, around 150 Germans, supported by tanks, armoured cars and artillery, were seen advancing along the track alongside the railway. The commander of C Company, Captain Armitage, felt this group was a worthwhile target and he waited until the Germans were about 400 yards from his men before giving the order to open fire. Many Germans were seen to fall to the ground before reaching cover. For a time at least, a stand-off developed until the Germans brought their air power into play and started bombing and machine gunning C and D Companies, to which they virtually had no answer. After this softening-up process, the Germans felt able to have another go with their ground troops, and around 1330, several light tanks were seen coming down the road from the direction of Kringen. The Green Howards' war diary records that the leading tank was fired on by Y Company, using their .55 calibre Boys anti-tank rifles, and it was put out of action and so blocked the road.

Other German efforts were made at the same time, including an attempt to cross to an island in collapsible boats; Y Company engaged them, and four Germans attempting to get into a boat were seen to fall and not move again. Fire was also directed towards another boat and only two men were seen to gain the safety of the island; their boat drifted off downstream and no further attempts were made to cross there. More meaningful efforts were made, and troops were seen moving in the woods above C Company's position, having made a wide detour. It seems a German O (Orders) Group was called for, attended by about 30 officers, and taking place in effective range of the Green Howards' C Company. It is recorded that a small party led by Lieutenant Rawson opened fire on them with a Bren gun and rifles, leaving very few if any survivors. D Company was also busy at this time, engaging German infantry at ranges of between 300–400 yards with positive effect.

At 1430, as the Germans were still moving above C Company, Captain Armitage sent his 15 Platoon higher up the hill to try to stop this outflanking movement. Only two men from this platoon returned. One of them, Lance Corporal White, later reported that when they were moving up the hillside they came under heavy machine gun fire from the Germans above them, and he and Private Bellis got separated from the remainder before managing to rejoin C Company. The rest of 15 Platoon were either killed or captured.

The Germans continued using their long-range weapons to fire at the Green Howards' positions for the next few hours, creeping forward under this support. Captain Armitage of C Company later wrote:

> By 1700 no less than four enemy groups were on the fringe of the position. I therefore sent Lieutenant Rawson with two sections on a fighting patrol northwards (a) to get into touch with the Battalion and (b) to find out what my role now was. I am afraid he cannot have gone very far though again I heard no fire from his direction. Lieutenant Rawson was to have asked for two platoons as reinforcements, if I was to hold out that night. At 1730 I further shortened my lines and took up position C as per the sketch map on page 173. This position had the advantage of being unassailable from the rear (a precipitous cliff). A most peculiar state of affairs now existed. Enemy posts of double my strength were entrenched on the verge of the position. They were entirely dominated by my sangars (small protected firing structures). If they showed themselves to move forward or fire, we shot them. They therefore waited for darkness. As the sangars had been unusually sited and skilfully built by Lieutenant McKenzie, I considered they could resist an attack if necessary after dark. I however, had decided to retire directly I had had a final look for Lieutenant McKenzie and it was dark enough to disengage. During this time a number of enemy had been hit, these included an officer (black uniformed) hit at point blank range, five men dressed as Norwegians and three or four other Germans. The enemy did not appear to realise why we were still in position or how he had got here. They also appeared uncertain what action to take and seemed to be awaiting orders.

While C Company appeared to have its hands full, at 1630 the other forward unit, D Company, could see large numbers of German infantry supported by two tanks moving forward along the road to the west of the river and stopped behind a house about 1,000 yards from the Green Howard positions. These were engaged at long range and the Germans suffered a number of casualties.

Meanwhile, orders were received that the position was to be abandoned, and so at around 1700 the CO issued orders for a withdrawal. It was intended that the two forward units, C and D Companies, would withdraw at 2100, the former by road and latter by railway. The next move was to be to a fall-back position astride the road and river at Kleber, just south of Sel. This position was to be held until 0100 on the 29th, when they would retire further. The two companies in support, B and Y, were to withdraw at 2300 using the railway, and Battalion HQ at 2345, again using the railway.

These orders were received by all units except C Company, as it was impossible to get through to them by runner; it appears there was no radio communication. Battalion HQ tried to contact them by visual signals on several occasions, apparently without success. Y Company was also unable to contact their No. 19 Platoon as they had moved position. In spite of these difficulties, the majority of troops did get the message and the transmission of these orders was probably helped by a slackening off of German interference.

However, around 2115, a small recce patrol of four Germans came towards a bridge in the B Company area, were spotted and fired upon, and disappeared from view. This was just the start. About 30 minutes later, the road-railway bridge in the B Company area was blown as a blocking action. Shortly after it was blown, a number of Germans were spotted trying to get on to the partially demolished bridge, but again they were fired on and suffered casualties. The time of the planned withdrawal was now approaching, and at the appointed time D Company slipped away, fording the River Otta about half a mile above the bridge.

To cover the withdrawal, the CO ordered the Mortar Platoon to move forward to the railway station and to put some bombs on the spur vacated by D Company. The short but intense bombardment, plus small-arms fire from B and Y Company positions, probably lulled the Germans into thinking a counter-attack might be imminent, so they did not follow up the retiring British troops. Most of the men got away safely, and were moved by a mixture of trains and motor transport to Dombaas, the majority arriving there in the morning of 29 April.

Captain Armitage of C Company said of these moves:

> At 2130 I had a final look for Lieutenant McKenzie with a section escort. I told Lieutenant Meldon to take command and to hang on till my arrival with or without 15 Platoon at about 2200. I failed to find 15 Platoon and arrived back late having missed my way in the dark. I arrived just as an action was drawing to an end in which the Germans were beaten off. They had fought for a quarter of an hour but failed (i) to penetrate the sangars and (ii) to get behind the posts. Many enemy bombs burst outside the sangar walls. This action was brought to a close by a Bren gun being brought out to the flank and enfilading the enemy. I can definitely say that the Germans employed double the strength of their opponents for this attack. I then broke off, retired the whole force, organised into four parties, across that part of the hill crest I had seen to be free of the enemy and keeping a course thirty to a hundred yards from the summit, moved back towards Otta. I gave strict orders that absolute quietness should be maintained. Only two enemy were encountered. They, after peering at us, moved away again, when we remained immobile.
>
> We arrived at the wooden bridge exactly seven hours later, complete in numbers and arms. This was a considerable feat for the troops in heavy equipment, since the reason I had struck such a course, was that it was much too steep for maintaining an enemy position, about half the way we travelled was on hands and knees or

> holding on to things, along ice or bare rock. On arrival in Otta the men were told to await orders. When however a German sentry opened fire on me I could not locate anyone except Lieutenant Meldon, who was with me, Sergeant Roche, Sergeant Bennett and Corporal Sheppard. We therefore proceeded at the run for the railway line; we finally got out of the line of fire some 500 yards further on.

The CO of the Green Howards summed up events on 28 April by saying:

> During the whole of this day, aerial bombing with heavy bombs in salvoes and machine gunning from the air was almost continuous. The most severe being from 1020 to 1100 but they did very little material damage and caused very few casualties. Everyone was well dug in, if they had not been so, the casualties would have been severe.

Meanwhile, after Brigadier Smyth had been wounded around noon on 25 April, both forward companies of the KOYLIs came under intense artillery and machine gun fire and were attacked by infantry, but maintained their positions until about 1400, when A Company, after suffering heavy casualties, gave ground on the right flank. The KOYLI war diary continues its account of the Battle of Kvam:

> The enemy failed to follow up this success and the line was again stabilised and pushed forward to within about 400 yards of the original line. This operation was carried out by C Company who took what was left of A Company with them.

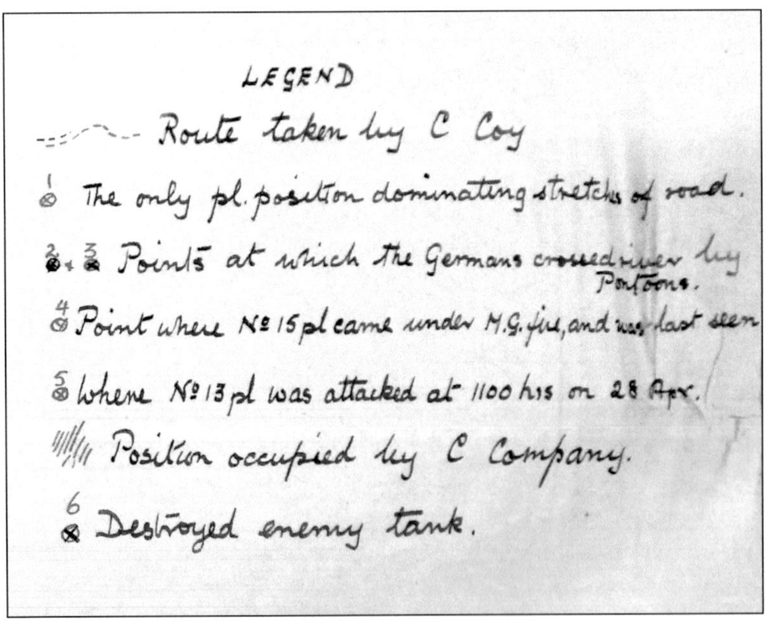

Key to map on following page.

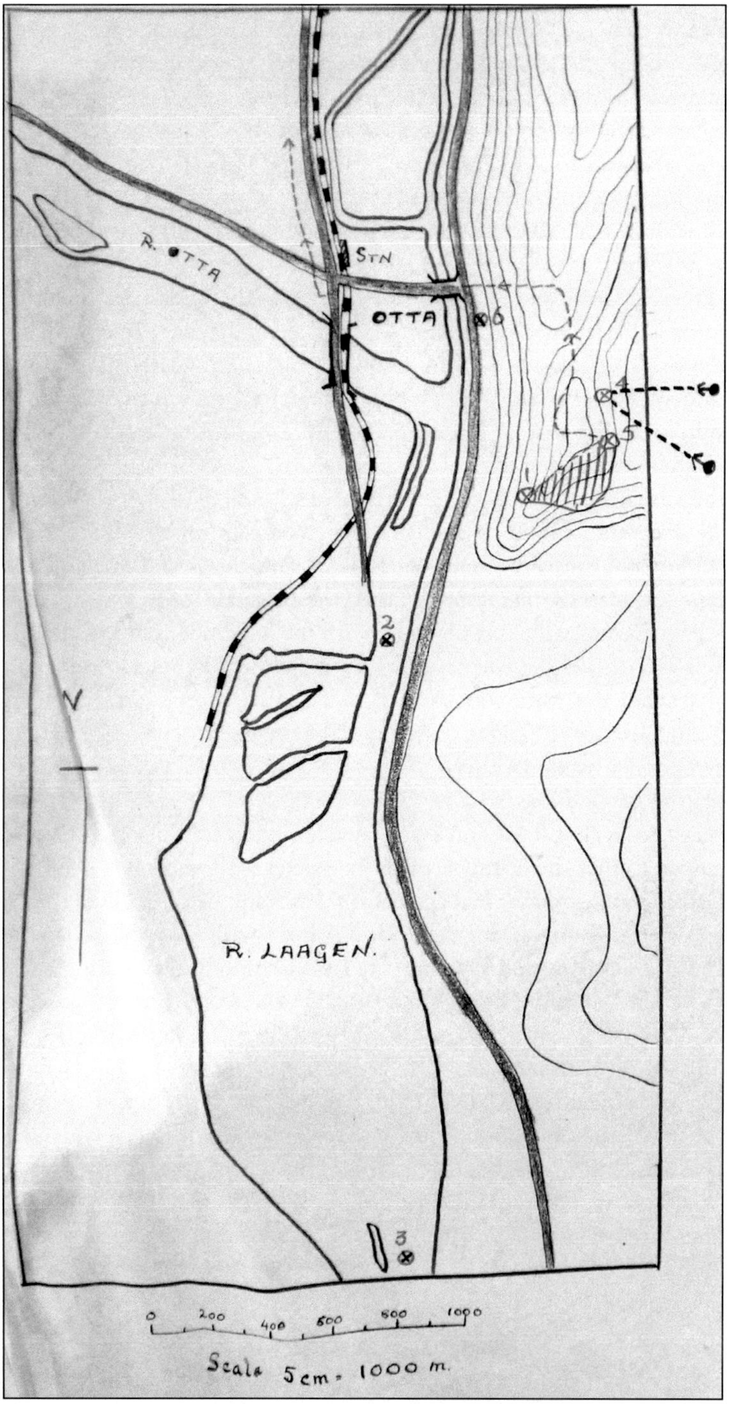

Otta battle map from Green Howards War Diary.

From this time A Company ceased to exist as an independent company, they had lost 4 officers and about 85 other ranks. The enemy also attacked B Company but was driven back with considerable loss.

1700 heavy artillery fire was directed against B Company and the enemy attempted to push forward MGs to close range against them. This operation failed as did further infantry attacks.

1830 a medium tank advanced down the road and was put out of action by the Brigade A/T guns, at the same time enemy infantry attempted to move round the right flank of C Company by way of the river bed. This attack was repulsed and E Company was placed in depth behind C Company to further strengthen this flank.

1900 the Brigadier placed C Company 1st York and Lancaster Regiment under command of CO 1st KOYLI. This Company was put into position up the hill towards the left rear of B Company to prevent a threatened movement to outflank them from their left.

2200 the situation was that the Battalion was holding all its original positions with the exception of the right flank, where the line had been forced back. This had left B Company somewhat isolated and exposed on both flanks. The Battalion Commander therefore obtained the Brigade Commander's permission to withdraw B Company in conformity with the remainder of the Battalion. This operation was carried out successfully but one of the platoons lost direction and was not available for some time.

The remainder of the night passed quietly, the enemy making no attempt to advance under cover of darkness.

April 26th Second Day.

0530 heavy artillery and MG fire was opened on the whole of the Battalion front. It was apparent that the enemy artillery had been reinforced.

0630 a strong attack developed against the left flank held by C Company, York and Lancaster, this attack was held off, but the enemy was able to work round between this Company and D Company KOYLI, and heavy fighting took place.

1130 the enemy attempted to advance astride the road against the junction of C and B Companies and get into the village, there was heavy fighting and the Battalion Mortar Platoon was able to assist in the defence.

From now onwards throughout the day fighting was continuous along the whole of the Battalion front and the enemy made use of tanks, which however were repulsed. Continuous artillery and MG fire was experienced and several low flying attacks were made by enemy aircraft.

Although the enemy were unable to make a definite advance he infiltrated into our position at several places and made it very difficult to keep touch with the various companies. This was especially the case with C Company York and Lancaster who were almost cut off. The enemy maintained intense artillery and MG fire up to the hours of darkness, his MGs were firing belt after belt of ammunition without a pause. It is difficult to understand this waste of ammunition, but it appeared that he was attempting to create an atmosphere of 'HATE' so as to effect our morale. If this was so, it was entirely unsuccessful.

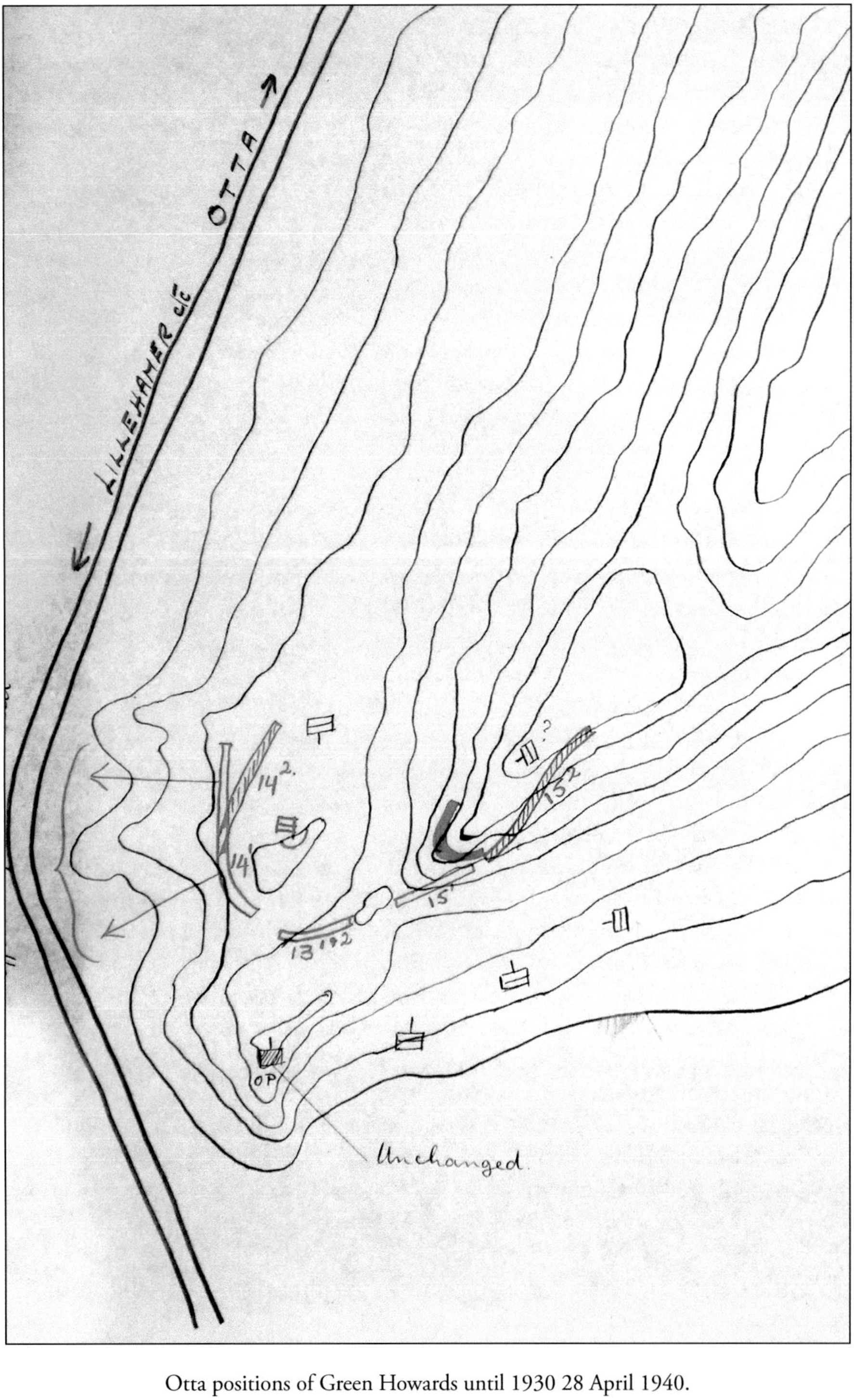

Otta positions of Green Howards until 1930 28 April 1940.

> 1730 CO was called to Brigade HQ and received orders to withdraw at 2300. 1900 the situation was difficult as the enemy had set fire to the woods along the Battalion front and appeared to be preparing to make an advance under cover of the smoke and confusion caused. CO informed Brigade HQ that he was preparing to withdraw at once and this was approved.
>
> The Battalion withdrew through 1st Battalion York and Lancaster Regiment to Sjoa and continued to Otta where they entrained to Dombaas. All the wounded were got away and although the enemy attempted to interfere, the withdrawal was carried out without loss.
>
> C Company 1st Battalion York and Lancaster Regiment were out of touch and failed to receive the orders to withdraw, but made a successful getaway later in the night after fighting a very gallant action throughout the day under the command of Major Jordan. D Company 1st KOYLI also on the left flank, were not able to rejoin until the next day.

A series of accounts were given of the experiences of the 1st York and Lancasters during the Battle of Kvam. During the morning the battalion was subjected to an aerial attack from German bombers who dropped a number of HE bombs, none of which caused much damage or many casualties. These were followed by machine gun attacks from the air and were repeated in the afternoon, but few or no casualties were caused. The following report of C Company's action on 25/26 April at Kvam was given by Major F. Jordan MC:

> At 1600 25th April I was ordered to occupy a large hill on the left (east) of 1st KOYLI and east of Kvam. My Company arrived by bus from Otta at 1830 and the hill was occupied by 1930. The line occupied by me was the forward edge of a pine wood along the crest of a hill to the east and south of the houses on the skyline. The position was occupied for all round defence. During the evening 25th April, the position was subjected to shelling and MG fire. Touch was established with the Platoons of D Company 1st KOYLI about 2030, later this Platoon retired having suffered casualties.
>
> At about 0530 26th April the enemy was observed assembling for an attack. At 0630 this attack was launched and my positions were subjected to heavy MG and artillery fire. On my front the enemy was held, but with the aid of good cover, he succeeded in working around my left flank, enfilading my position causing several casualties. I altered my position and held the enemy for some time, but by 1100 he had succeeded in crossing the valley between my position and D Company 1st KOYLI and obtained a position on the hill to the north east of my position. I was surrounded on three sides. I ordered Second Lieutenant French to establish a defensive position near the houses to enfilade the enemy and protect my rear. D Company 1st KOYLI blocked the enemy's advance along the crest. In this phase of the action the enemy lost about 20 men.
>
> At 1500 the enemy worked himself down a valley which separated my position from D Company 1st KOYLI. The enemy established a post near the wood mill

> and bridge over the river. This post cut off my communication with Battalion HQ 1st KOYLI.
>
> At 1600 I sent a Section under Second Lieutenant French to drive the enemy from this position. After very close fighting in which there were several casualties, Second Lieutenant French succeeded in obtaining possession of the mill and the bridge across the river, killing six Germans during the action. This bridge continued to be held by my Company until I withdrew. The battle now stabilised. I was holding my original position with a defensive locality covering the bridge and guarding my line of withdrawal.
>
> At 1830 I observed the enemy in the vicinity of Brigade HQ. I sent a recce patrol to discover the situation, as I had been out of touch with Battalion HQ 1st KOYLI since 1000. Receiving no orders and seeing the enemy advancing at 2100, I decided to withdraw after dark. The withdrawal was successfully accomplished by way of D Company 1st KOYLI's position. The enemy were in front and the rear of me, but no serious clash occurred. The withdrawal commenced at 2230. The Company sustained about 30 casualties during the action, including Second Lieutenant French and Second Lieutenant Kelso wounded.

A further account of the day's fighting on A and B Companies' front was given by Captain J. Oliver of 1st York and Lancasters:

> At about 0800 on 27th April enemy troops were observed advancing on the line of the road Kvam-Otta and the left platoon opened heavy fire upon the target presented. This fire was accurate and caused the enemy to scatter, leaving many casualties on the road. The enemy was seen to open fire on the right platoons of my position with MG fire and continued to fire at regular intervals throughout the morning. About half an hour later, it was observed that the enemy was assembling guns and AFVson the road some 2,000 yards away and opened fire on my right and on the position held by the company of the 1st Green Howards. Despite the violence of this fire, no casualties were suffered. At 1030 the enemy continued his advance with infantry and AFVs along the road and in the edge of the woods lining the road. We opened up with heavy LMG fire on these targets, causing the enemy numerous casualties. The enemy AFVs commenced firing incendiary bullets of a medium calibre at the log cabins held by one or two of my sections. Two of these huts were hit and set on fire, the garrisons being forced to abandon them and seek new positions outside. The AFV's MGs also commenced firing but caused no casualties.
>
> At 1100 the enemy was now firing with MGs from three points on to my position, and also shelling with mortar bombs. The latter were fairly accurate and caused some casualties to sections of A Company. After this there was a lull in the enemy ground action but enemy planes were active overhead with MG fire. These caused no casualties. When the planes had retired, it was seen that the enemy were advancing along the east bank of the river towards the position. They were fired on by LMG fire and forced to scatter. Battalion HQ were asked

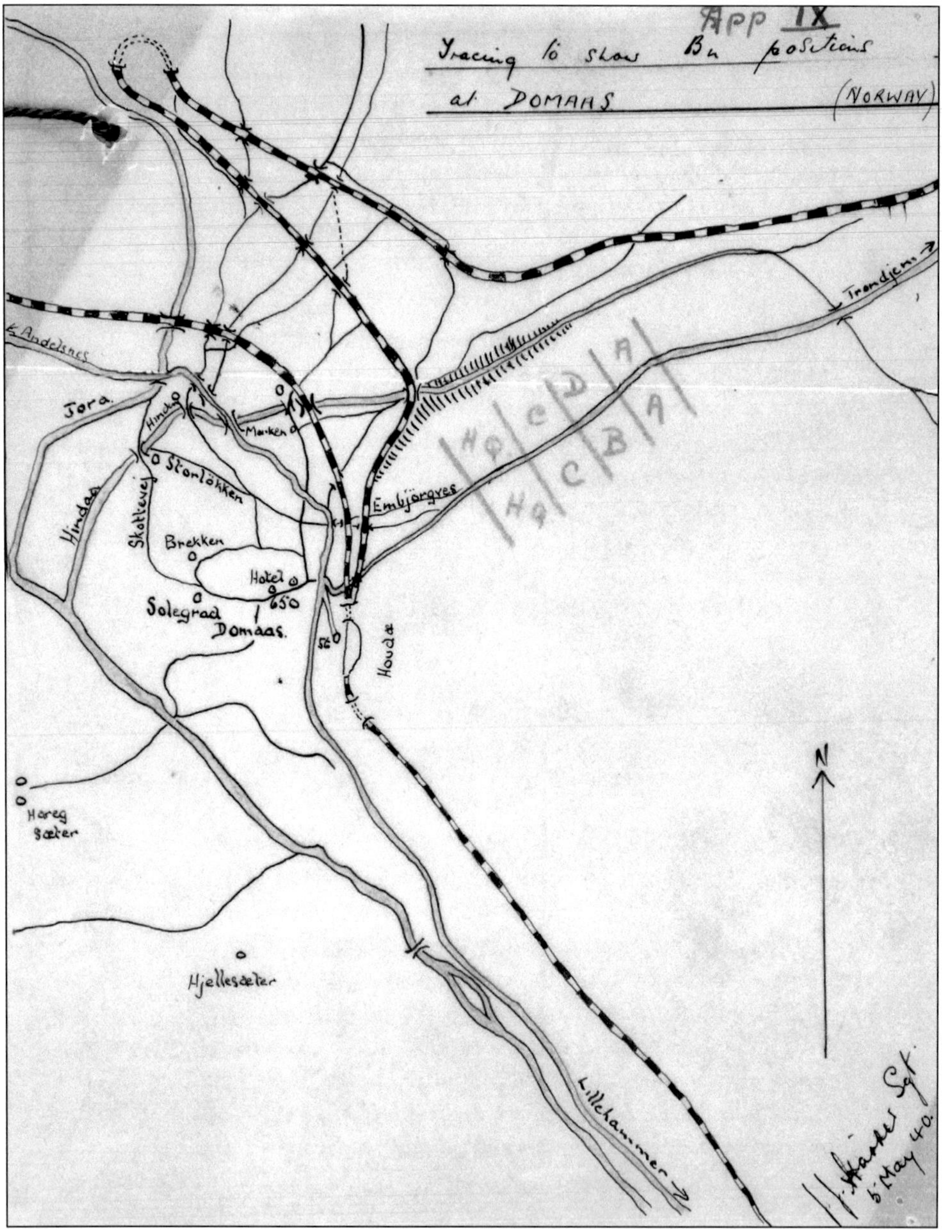

Positions of the Green Howards in Dombaas

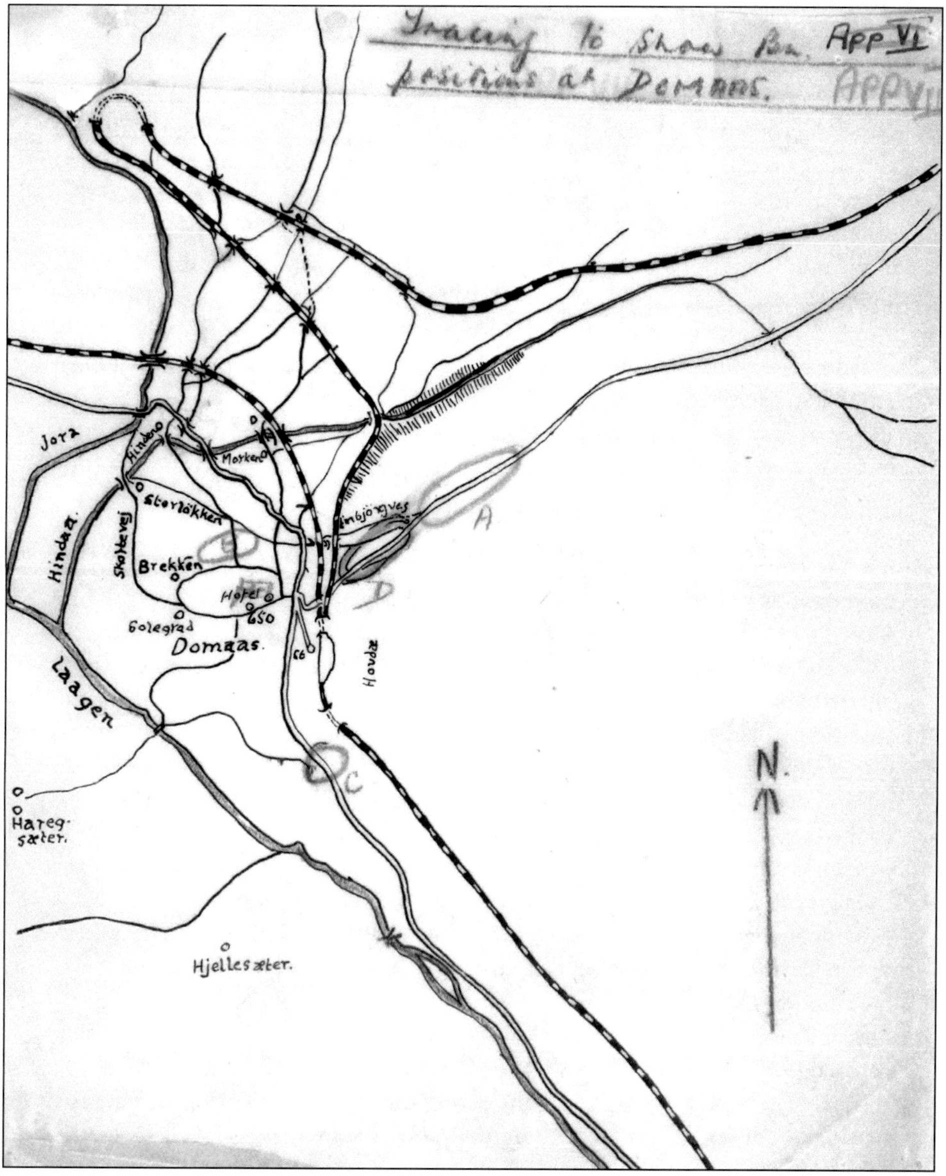

Later Positions of the Green Howards in Dombaas.

> to support me with 3" mortar fire on this advance by the enemy, but this was not immediately forthcoming, and when it did, the fire was inaccurate owing to short range and caused two or three casualties to my left sections. However, this action of small arms fire and the 3" mortar fire stopped the enemy advance temporarily on the east bank. The enemy was now seen to be concentrating on D Company's position on the west of the road Kvam-Otta, and it was reported that enemy patrols had been seen to the extreme right of my position near the crest of the hill. I sent out a patrol consisting of one section towards the top of the hill and at the same time asked Battalion HQ to assist with a patrol from 1st Green Howards. This latter patrol came down from the bank of the river and reported it had not seen any enemy movement, and was then sent up to search the high ground on the right. The enemy AFVs had by this time advanced along the road almost as close as the extreme right position held by D Company. At this time D Company's right was enveloped in smoke from fires caused in the wood by enemy incendiary shells and bullets.
>
> At 1600 the line communication with Battalion HQ became severed and was never re-connected again, so that all touch with Battalion HQ was lost from that moment onwards. My signallers had lost their signalling equipment in the fires started by enemy actions on my own positions.
>
> At about 1630–1700 the enemy was reported in the woods on the east bank of the river and threatening to enfilade my left positions. Also the AFVs had advanced still further down the road until they were firing with MGs into the rear of my positions. I could see that my left platoon was in danger of being cut off and decided to withdraw it to it's [sic] alternative position some 100 yards in the rear. This withdrawal was completed successfully. The AFV on the road was now enfilading my position with heavy and accurate MG fire, causing many casualties. I was out of touch with Battalion HQ and at 1800 I decided that it was impossible to hold the line any further and I gave the order to withdraw back to the line of the 1st Green Howards behind me. During the withdrawal MG fire from the AFV in the road was intensified and in consequence the Company suffered more casualties. At the Green Howards position in the rear I made contact with Battalion HQ and was ordered to continue my withdrawal to Sjoa and hold a position there to cover the eventual withdrawal of the Battalion. This would be at about 2200. Throughout the action I suffered some 70 casualties.

Captain Oliver also gave the following account of the actions of the remainder of B Company and A Company:

> During the morning of 26th April the Battalion moved from Otta by bus towards Kvam. Two platoons of B Company under the command of Second Lieutenant J. Cooke were ordered forward in support of 1st KOYLI. The remainder of the Company was ordered to take up a position on the right of A Company who were holding the right (east) bank of the river, on the middle slope of the high ground almost to the crest of the hill.

At 1100 A Company took up position and B Company less two platoons followed at 1300 (the right of the position was within 200 yards of the crest). All sections commenced to dig at once. At 1500 I was given command of this position consisting of A and B Companies less two platoons and informed by the CO that this position would become the front line after withdrawal of 1st KOYLI commencing at 2200 that evening and that the line was to be held until the night of 27th/28th April. Digging of position to afford all round defence continued throughout the night. A standing patrol consisting of one section was placed forward in the wood on the right near the crest of the hill. The night passed without incident. At 2000 the company of 1st Green Howards who were to come up with support behind my position, arrived and took up position.

On arrival of Battalion HQ – the fighting patrol under Second Lieutenant M. Willis were ordered to go forward as lightly dressed as possible and recce the high ground on the east side of the road in front of A and B Companies' position. This patrol, after being out most of the day – eventually arrived back at Battalion HQ during the early part of the evening.

During the afternoon line communication was established with D Company and visual with A and B. Battalion HQ was lightly shelled, but most of the shells were duds. Out of five shells which dropped only one exploded and without causing any casualties. Enemy aircraft attacked with MG fire but dropped no bombs. The A/A Platoon fought off the attack with courage and determination. Later, during the afternoon – the position of Battalion HQ was moved further back along the road to Otta and digging of position commenced. Line was ordered to be laid out to A and B Companies – this was accomplished in a very short space of time, considering the distance and the Carrier Platoon were connected into this line, so that by nightfall A, B and D Companies and the Carrier Platoon were in communication with Battalion HQ by line.

Communication with 1st Green Howards was by visual.

During the night, commencing at 2200 1st KOYLI fell back through our position on their way back to Dombaas. The two platoons of B Company and the remnant of C Company came back gradually and were fed and permitted to rest. Parties of C Company continued to arrive throughout the night. The fighting patrol and personnel of Battalion HQ continued to dig in relays all night. The signal office was securely dug in and continued its operations. The A/A Platoon were placed in position for ground defence of Battalion HQ.

The following account of D Company's action by is from Lieutenant D. Webster of the 1st York and Lancasters:

Throughout the evening the enemy shelled and machine gunned the position held by A and B Companies and the 1st Green Howards company on the right.

1200 – enemy reported massing 200 strong.

1300 – D Company positions were engaged by MG and mortar fire from across the valley to the right. Forward troops heard the enemy giving fire orders and corrections. Under cover of this MG fire an enemy tank (8 wheels and 612 painted on it) came down the road and off-loaded an MG. This was knocked out by our fire before it got into position. Another attempt was made to mount another MG in a building 150 yards in front of our forward positions – this also failed and the crew were all killed. A mortar was then mounted behind the building and engaged our position with HE and incendiary bombs – to some effect. The MG was re-manned by a crew brought forward by a tank and opened fire. The A/T rifles fire was seen to strike the tank several times without any apparent effect. No. 16 Platoon was pinned to the ground by MG fire from the front and right and during this time, the Company front was shelled with incendiary shells which set fire to the wood. All three platoons were compelled to withdraw to positions in the rear owing to flames and dense smoke. The Company was immediately reorganised and sent forward to cover the left flank of the Carrier Platoon, which was in danger of being enfiladed by fire. Reinforcements arrived from Battalion HQ. The front was then held and patrols were sent up the hillside to the left to investigate reports of enemy out flanking [sic] movements under cover of the fire. OC D Company (Major R. Walters) was reported missing after leading one of these patrols. The Company then withdrew 200 yards to some farm buildings in the rear where an all round defensive keep was formed – until a general withdrawal was ordered at 2300.

On orders received from Commander 15th Infantry Brigade the Battalion was ordered to withdraw from the Lien position at 2300. Five lorries arrived during the evening to load up with SAA and stores. These were loaded to capacity but were not nearly enough. Subsequently information was received that two enemy patrols, each about 60 strong, had already passed through our position and were now formed up in our rear with MGs in position prepared to dispute our withdrawal. Major Tennent commanding the Battalion gave orders for the withdrawal to be covered by the guns of the A/A Platoon used for ground defence while the Battalion withdrew with the fighting patrol being used as an advance guard. The order of march was HQ Company formed in two fighting groups, C Company, 2 Platoons B Company, D Company, covered by a rear guard under command of Captain S. Wilson.

The transport was to follow in front of the rear guard. The Battalion withdrew without any opposition from the enemy – for the first mile or so, when the advance guard encountered a road block covered by MG fire manned by the enemy. No information of this fact was communicated to the main body with the result that the main body blundered on to the block and was caught by MG fire. Sergeant Cully who was with the advance guard despatched one enemy MG post with grenades and another post was silenced by Private Ryan with LMG fire. Owing to the confusion caused by the enemy MG fire, there was a general scattering of the troops to both sides of the road. Some of the transport which had started from Lien made a rush at the road block which had partially been removed by Sergeant Cully and Private Ryan – got through safely. Scattered bodies of troops now began to make their way towards Otta. Some of these had encounters with enemy patrols.

This account is by Second Lieutenant J. Cooke, commander of the two platoons of B Company sent forward from Sjoa in support of 1st KOYLI:

> Soon after arrival at Sjoa, I was ordered to take my platoon and that of PSM Barker forward in support of 1st KOYLI near the village of Kvam. I reported to the CO 1st KOYLI at 0700 and was told to stand by. At about 0800 I was ordered to take up a platoon position on a hill on the east side of the road Kvam-Otta, to fill a gap in the reserve line. Platoons were in position by 0930. At about 1030 the enemy shelled my position, their fire became more violent later but no casualties were sustained. During the afternoon the shelling was accompanied by MG fire and I was ordered to withdraw to rear positions by the CO 1st KOYLI. My platoons eventually took up position near a bridge where 1st KOYLI Battalion HQ was situated at about 1900. After taking up this position which covered the bridge and the line, we came under heavy MG fire. This fire continued without slackening for the next hour. I was ordered by CO 1st KOYLI to remain in occupation of the position and to give fire for the covering of the withdrawal of his Battalion and to remain in position until 2359. This I did.

Brigadier Smyth's post-action report on this confusing period of combat around Kvam starts on Wednesday, 24 April:

> The roads at this time were congested with Norwegian troops in all sorts of motor vehicles heading north. The Norwegian General said that there was no alteration in the orders for the Battalion commanded by Captain Navelsaker, to take up a position 4–5 miles south of Kvam and that it was now getting into position. He told me that he was placing this Battalion under my orders and finished with the words; "I hand over the front to you."
>
> Before he left, I pointed out to him that my two Battalions were without any form of transport and asked him to arrange to supply twenty lorries per Battalion for the carriage of unit equipment and also to enable to form mobile reserves. He said he would endeavour to arrange this.
>
> At 1730 after the departure of commander 2nd Division I went south to gain contact with the Battalion that was taking up position in front of me and which had been placed under my orders. I saw a number of Norwegian troops in positions astride the road, but I was unable to discover Captain Navelsaker.
>
> At 2045 after my return to my HQ at Otta, I sent my Norwegian liaison officer to make contact with Captain Navelsaker and to tell him that I wished him to hold his position during daylight 25th April and to withdraw during the night 25th/26th April. As I understood from General Hauk that his troops were very frightened of the German tanks, I sent forward a 28 mm anti-tank gun and detachment with the liaison officer for Captain Navelsaker's protection. The liaison officer returned about 2300 and said that he had made contact with Captain Navelsaker, who understood his orders and appeared confident

of holding his position. I sent the liaison officer back to stay with Captain Navelsaker and keep me in touch with the situation in front.

At 2200 1st KOYLI (less two companies) arrived Kvam by train and moved into their positions and commenced preparing defences. In some cases these were dug, but where the ground was too rocky resort had to be made to sangars. Brigade Anti-Tank Company which moved forward by lorry was held up by the congestion on the roads. The five guns, for which positions had been selected, were in position by 0300. Time and tools were not available to dig these in before daylight. They were put in naturally concealed positions, built into wood stacks, etc. Three of the four reserve guns were ditched on the way forward owing to the spate of retiring Norwegians on the very narrow road.

Thursday 25th April

0430 My liaison officer with Captain Navelsaker returned to me and stated that his detachment (Navelsaker's) was withdrawing. Shortly afterwards, parties of Norwegians began passing through our position in retreat and an officer came up to me and said that his Battalion had been outflanked by German armoured cars during the night and had to withdraw. The last two companies of the KOYLI had not yet arrived and they were due to detrain at Kvam, which was now in the front line. I informed the CO KOYLI of the situation and ordered him to send his Battalion's fighting patrol southwards down the valley to give warning of any German advance.

0515 Two companies KOYLI arrived and detrained. They then took up their positions, which were, of course, not dug at all.

By 0600 all troops were in position and well concealed. Shortly after this German aircraft started to come over.

During the early morning, Brigadier Morgan arrived. He said that the Norwegian HQ had not agreed to his withdrawing his troops from the Heidal valley to Dombaas. Later he left for Åndalsnes to meet with General Paget.

About 0800 Lieutenant Colonel Kent-Lemon, 1st York and Lancaster reported to me. He had arrived at Otta with his Battalion less three companies. I was never able to discover how this occurred. In my message to Force HQ at midday 24th April I asked for 1st York and Lancaster to be sent forward to Otta on the night 24th/25th. Three companies had, however, been left at Dombaas.

My instructions to Lieutenant Colonel Kent-Lemon were:-

a. To remain with his Battalion at Otta. I told him that the commander 2nd Norwegian Division had promised me 40 lorries. With these he would be able to move rapidly either to Kvam or Sjoa as required.
b. On his way back to Otta, to recce a position at Sjoa in case his Battalion might be required to occupy this at any time.

About the same time, I sent Major Clinch, my Brigade Major, to HQ 2nd Norwegian Division to report my position to them and to press for the 40 lorries, which had been promised to me. All these lorries to be handed over in the first instance to 1st York and Lancaster at Otta to enable me to form a mobile reserve.

> Major Clinch returned later and said that 2nd Norwegian Division was arranging this.
>
> At about 0930 the fighting patrol of 1st KOYLI reported the German advance guard to be six miles away.
>
> At 1130 the German attack commenced and I went with Major Cass, commanding 1st KOYLI, to an OP (observation post) behind a stone wall on the hill to watch the battle. The Germans advanced with three tanks followed by sections of infantry moving along the road. As far as I could see, the three tanks were knocked out by our forward anti-tank guns with four rounds. German infantry then deployed on each side of the road and a battery of howitzers started to shell all houses, woods or other natural cover, which might be suspected of concealing troops or OPs.
>
> During this bombardment I was hit by a piece of shell in the left leg and was removed to the RAP [Regimental Aid Post]. While in the RAP I sent instructions to Major Cass to send a message ordering Lieutenant Colonel Kent-Lemon to bring up his Battalion to an area where it could act as a reserve to KOYLI, and for Lieutenant Colonel Kent-Lemon himself to take over command of the Brigade.

It can be said that the Battle of Kvam was no more than a holding action and the British troops were seriously outnumbered and outgunned, but it is usually easier to give a good account of oneself when in a defensive position and letting the enemy expose himself. The only real point to the action at Kvam seems to have been buying time for the evacuation. By around 28 April, 15th Infantry Brigade was withdrawing northwards towards an evacuation port. A and B Companies of the 1st York and Lancaster were providing a rearguard for the rest of the battalion at Sjoa while they withdrew to Otta. However, the idea of organised units of men in section, platoon and company groups probably does not paint a true picture of what was happening. The York and Lancasters' war diary records: "Small parties of the Battalion continued to arrive during the early hours of the morning at Otta where a general reorganisation of the Battalion took place under the command of Major Jordan." It then mentions nine officers who were either missing, wounded or known to have been killed, and that the RSM, Warrant Officer Haggerty, had been wounded and taken to the RAP.

But in spite of these losses, within a short space of time the York and Lancasters were ordered to take up a position on high ground to the south of the Otta-Lom road at the right rear of the brigade area. The 1st Green Howards had been allocated the main position at Otta, while Major A. Parry was ordered to bring A Company – who were in position astride the Hjerkinn road – and some elements of the HQ Company from Dombaas to defend the gorge in an area known as Laargaard. They were lucky enough to be moved here by motorised transport, and were in position by about 1900 on the 28th. The orders given to Major Parry were: (i) To cover a demolition party who were preparing the road and railway for demolition; (ii) To blow the bridge after the train and road parties from Otta had passed.

Meanwhile, the 1st KOYLI were around Dombaas and spent the early part of the day sorting themselves out as stragglers continued to arrive from Kvam. Then, at 1430, the CO reported to Sickle Force HQ and was ordered to take up a position to cover the withdrawal of the brigade. They moved off at 2030 to take up a defensive position astride the River Laagen about five miles south of Dombaas. The KOYLI were organised as follows:

> Forward Companies: Right, A Company, Lieutenant Maxsted; Centre, D Company, Captain Vickers; Left, C Company, Lieutenant Toplis.
> Reserve Companies: B Company, Major Burr HQ; HQ Company, Major Jones.

They did their best to dig themselves in and awaited the arrival of the Germans, who were expected at any time.

Orders were received for the Green Howards to retire at 2300, and it is reported that their withdrawal was carried out "in perfect order and without enemy pressure or casualties and was to take the line of the railway south of Dombaas; some 50 miles. Owing to lack of transport and the blowing up prematurely of the main road bridge no stores could be evacuated with the result that all the reserve SAA, rations and baggage was left intact to fall into enemy hands."

At 0545 on 29 April, after the bridge over the gorge at Laargaard was blown up, the elements of the 1st Green Howards located here returned to Dombaas and rejoined the remainder of their comrades. The York and Lancasters' war diary records: "The withdrawal continued down the railway line for about eight miles where two long trains were waiting to carry the force to Dombaas. After entraining, the force arrived at Dombaas at 0430 and laid up for the day in some neighbouring woods." The Green Howards also sheltered in these woods, and despite considerable German air activity, neither unit was spotted. Around 2000, the Green Howards left to take up a defensive position astride the Hjerkin road about a mile east of Dombaas, where they dug in and set up road blocks. The York and Lancasters moved at 2200 to Dombaas railway station, where they found a train waiting to take them to Åndalsnes: the strength of the unit there was recorded as 16 officers and 280 ORs.

For 30 April, the war diary of the 1st KOYLI records:

> Owing to the thaw the River Laagen became almost unfordable and it was decided to withdraw all troops west of the river. This was accomplished by 1400.
> A Company ordered away on anti-parachute duties.
> 1430 standing patrol of D Company on road was attacked.
> 1540 enemy made contact with D Company and suffered considerable loss. A considerable number of the enemy reported to be advancing north up the road with some transport.
> 1730 D Company withdrawn to Battalion reserve. Line now held by B and C Companies. HQ Company deployed in position in rear of forward companies. A Company returned and deployed in position in rear of HQ Company. C Company 1st Green Howards placed under command of KOYLI and deployed in position along river to protect right flank of A Company.
> 1900 C Company withdrew to Dombaas station.
> 2000 B Company withdrew to Dombaas station.

> 2115 HQ Company and C Company Green Howards withdrew to Dombaas station.
>
> 2145 A Company acting as rear party withdrew to Dombaas station closely followed by the enemy until they had passed through a company of the Green Howards who held a covering position in the southern exits of Dombaas.
>
> Battalion entrained at Dombaas and moved at 2230.

The other units had left earlier. The York and Lancasters got as far as Lesjaskog station by about 0330 on 30 April when the train ground to a halt and the CO, Major Jordan, was informed by a railway official that the line ahead had been damaged by German bombs and that it was not possible to proceed any further by train. The battalion was divided into company-sized groups and ordered to carry on by foot. To most men's relief, after trudging about a mile down the road towards Åndalsnes an RASC officer appeared with several lorries; he had instructions to convey any troops he found to an RV (rendezvous point) further down the road, but said his transport was limited. It also appears that there was at least one bus around, as this was commandeered, and a small recce group led by the QM (Major G. Tugwell) and the IO (Intelligence Oficer, Captain P. Edwards) were sent to the RV to ascertain any available information.

The first two groups to arrive were loaded onto the transport and taken to the Park Hotel, which was the RV. Force HQ and a supply depot were located around the hotel. As each group arrived here they were directed to various areas in the surrounding woods, but not before some probably very welcome rations had been issued. It is recorded that only half-rations were issued, even they went down well. By the late evening, the York and Lancasters had arrived virtually unscathed, although there had been several air attacks on the road, and towards evening hot cocoa and rum was issued. Some ineffective air raids were made against the Park Hotel, but the York and Lancasters camouflage and concealment in the woods was good and they were not seen or bombed by enemy aircraft. It is reported that during the evening large numbers of Norwegian troops passed along the road heading for the coast, and soon the York and Lancasters received orders to continue their withdrawal to Åndalsnes, starting at 2200. No transport was provided except the 'leather personnel carriers' (boots) of the men, but the march was completed successfully. At the port, the battalion was split up and detailed off to various ships – Battalion HQ and A Company being sent to *Galatea*, with the remainder to HMS *Sheffield*, HMS *Arethusa* and HMS *Glasgow*.

The Green Howards, meanwhile, had been acting as the rearguard, and during the night of 29/30 April they watched the Norwegian troops from Hjerkin passing through their positions in mototised transport and on skis. The Norwegian withdrawal was completed by noon on 30 April, shortly after which the Green Howards were also ordered to go to Åndalsnes by a train leaving at 2130 that night. Their CO recorded:

> But before I had issued any withdrawal orders firing was heard and news received that the Germans were in contact with the KOYLI astride the Dombaas-Otta road about 1½ miles south of Dombaas. Y Company were ordered to come under command of the KOYLI to prolong their right. A and D Companies took

> up a lay-back position astride the road and railway just north of Dombaas station under command of Major Chads. His role was to cover off the KOYLI and Y Company to the train. On departure of the train he was to proceed by MT to Åndalsnes as quick as possible.
>
> I brought back Battalion HQ, HQ Company and B Company to Dombaas in close reserve and then entrained about 2100. The withdrawal was successful and the train left about 2310, A and D Companies followed shortly afterwards in MT.
>
> [On] 1st May about 0100 the train ran into a bomb crater near Lesjaskog. The first two carriages were badly smashed. I got the Battalion out on the road as quickly as possible and got them fallen in by Companies.
>
> The Brigade marched off about 0145 to the tunnel at Verma, we arrived about 0800 having covered 17 or 18 miles, carrying all arms, Brens, A/T rifles etc. Here the Battalion spent the day.
>
> At about 1930 news was received that German motor cycle machine gun detachments were within four miles of the tunnel proceeding down the road from Dombaas. B Company were ordered to proceed up the road for not more than three miles to clear up the situation and cover the rest of the Brigade's entrainment. The troops although very tired indeed were on the move remarkably quickly and responded well.
>
> It was ascertained that the enemy were still some three to four miles down the road so orders were sent to B Company to take up a defensive position where they were and after the departure of the train to withdraw back to MT which was at the church at Verma and proceed direct in it to the jetty at Åndalsnes and embark.
>
> From B Company's position enemy fire could be heard and the bursts of mortar bombs seen about two miles further up the valley. Some time later Second Lieutenant Stroud RM and about four men came back through B Company. This officer with only two Lewis guns had remained forward when the remainder of the Marines had fallen back and had succeeded in making the enemy deploy and delaying them in their advance. The Company later withdrew and embarked without loss. In the meantime A and D Companies had arrived at Åndalsnes the previous night.
>
> The rest of the Battalion left Verma by train and embarked safely at Åndalsnes, the last party leaving at 0200.

After the train the 1st KOYLI were travelling on to Åndalsnes with other units of the brigade was derailed, they marched 17 miles to a tunnel, where they remained from 0800 until 1800, when the "enemy made contact with Royal Marine outposts".

The KOYLI, along with the other units, continued their withdrawal by train to the port, and within a few hours were on board Royal Navy ships for the journey back to the UK, sailing on board HMS *Birmingham*, HMS *Calcutta* and HMS *Manchester*.

The three units all record that they were well looked after by the Navy, and it seems that most servicemen took the opportunity to catch up on sleep. The ships first sailed to Scapa Flow, where they transferred to troop transports for the final leg of the voyage, most of the troops being on the *Lancastria*.

Private R. Brackenborough of the 1st KOYLI later related: "I was on HMS *Manchester* and the Navy looked after us well, they gave us tea, chocolates and sweets. Later we got fresh bread although most of the sailors said we looked like cavemen with our scruffy appearance and beards."

Upon their return to the UK, the units comprising 15 Brigade made some pertinent comments regarding their experiences in Norway.
The 1st KOYLI war diary made some general notes:

> Reluctance of enemy infantry to come to close quarters.
> Failure of enemy to press his tank attacks with boldness.
> Remarkable speed with which enemy artillery engaged vulnerable targets.
> Success of well camouflaged positions under stress in avoiding detection by aircraft.
> Serious effect on the holding of a defensive position in woods when they have been set on fire. This was deliberately done by the enemy.
> Necessity for great depth in defence to frustrate enemy flank attacks. He always went for our flanks.
> Difficulty in maintaining communication with forward companies.
> Co-operation of enemy artillery and machine guns.

The KOYLI also recorded some of their casualties. Lieutenant E. Higgins was reported as killed, with the following missing: 12 officers, four warrant officers and senior NCOs and 161 other ranks. There were another two officers wounded, along with two warrant officers and senior NCOs and 42 other ranks. This gave a total of 224 casualties of all types, from their recorded strength on 21 April of 32 officers and 754 other ranks.

The York and Lancasters recorded that after boarding the *Lancastria* at Scapa Flow and steaming down the west coast of Scotland, they started preparing casualty lists and reported that there was on board 18 officers and 375 other ranks. They recorded their losses as 10 officers killed and missing, with three wounded and sick, along with six other ranks killed, 180 missing and 21 wounded. This gave a total of 220 casualties.

The Green Howards reported five officers missing, with four other ranks killed, 11 wounded and 136 missing – a total of 156.

Even though the men at the front had done their best, they were hampered by the lack of reinforcements, heavy artillery or air support, which despite General Paget sending urgent signals asking for them, rarely materialised. The German bombing of Åndalsnes, which wrecked the port and its facilities, led the commander of the garrison there, Brigadier Hogg, to comment later:

> After seeing the extent of the damage and the obvious future prospects, I made a signal to the War Office to the effect that unless the air situation could be put right, the base would be unworkable, a fact which was rapidly demonstrated. Got in touch with Advanced HQ by telephone and informed General Paget who agreed, and wished emphasis to be laid on his precarious position. He was without

> guns and fighting an enemy who possessed field and medium artillery and having completely undisturbed mastery of the air. Discussed evacuation plans.

It is difficult to make any positive comments about 15 Infantry Brigade's time in Norway, except perhaps that they delayed the German advance. Ultimately, due to a lack of equipment and support, 15 Brigade's role was doomed before they even set foot there.

Lieutenant Colonel A. Robinson was awarded the Distinguished Service Order for his actions in Norway and part of his citation reads: "This officer showed exceptional ability in occupying a defensive position at Otta on April 27th 1940 and holding it throughout the 28th. He extricated his battalion on the night of April 28th/29th from very close contact, and succeeded in withdrawing it intact. He set a fine example of courage and devotion to duty which inspired his battalion."

Additional comments regarding the operations in Norway are of interest. The first is from one of the reports about the Green Howards at Otta from their Official History:

> Artillery was then employed on a most extensive scale, but none of these expedients could dislodge the Green Howards from their positions. Incendiary bombs set fire to houses behind the leading companies, aeroplanes dropped their bombs as near the defences as they could, artillery pounded them, but when the hostile infantry came on, they were met by controlled and accurate fire. Special emphasis is laid on this tenacious defence. Anything less good would have cracked.

The Anti-Tank Company of 15 Infantry Brigade, which had been formed from men of the three battalions, was commanded by Captain Paul Dessain of the Green Howards, who was destined to be the first Green Howard to be decorated for bravery in the Second World War with the award of a Military Cross. Part of his citation for his actions in Norway contained the following:

> Three of his gun detachments were situated in the front line; the approach to these was along the main road, on which the enemy had established heavy machine gun fire. Throughout the day Captain Dessain visited his detachments, and by his example and personal disregard for danger he encouraged his gun teams to hold on, and bar the way to any advance by hostile armoured fighting vehicles. In particular, in the afternoon, when the situation was becoming critical, the sight of this officer riding a lady's bicycle up the road under heavy machine gun fire and some shelling encouraged all who saw him.

Finally, Donald Creighton-Williamson had joined the Army in 1938 and went to Sandhurst, where he was commissioned into the 1st Battalion York and Lancaster Regiment and in late 1939 went to France as part of 15 Infantry Brigade before being shipped to Norway in 1940. He recalled:

Being sent to Norway never entered any of our thinking and the order with no notice to move to Boulogne came right out of the blue. At this time I was in command of the Signal Platoon and after a mad rush to collect our equipment we moved to Boulogne and then Dover and onto Scotland. I think it was in camp at Dunfermline where we were sort of let into the secret of knowing where we were going. I recall we were going to land at Trondheim in conjunction with two attacks from the south and north coupled with a naval bombardment of the area. But the Navy got cold feet. Then we were told we would go to Åndalsnes but in fact landed at Molde and cross-decked into those local ships called puffers and proceeded to the Gudbrandsdal area. My main recollection is moving into the valley and being amazed at the deep snow on both sides of the valley and how our movement was limited to either the road or railway. What transport we had was locally commandeered, I cannot recall seeing any Norwegian soldiers except drivers of the lorries we were using but my over-riding memory is how the whole scene was dominated by the Germans.

Then we come to the fighting around Otta on 26th April and this is my diary entry for this day: At about 0230 it was just about daylight when we got to Otta station and consequently easy to sort out the signal equipment and load it onto a small Norwegian lorry which was to take us to our positions at Sjoa, whilst the personnel followed in a crowded single decker bus which had some difficulty negotiating the cratered road.

I had many problems as SO (Signals Officer) in Norway and especially at Sjoa, [as] almost as soon as we had laid a line to a forward position, it either got broken or we had to move and so we often resorted to using signal lamps to send messages through in Morse code.

After we had settled in the KOYLI came through our position and the next day the full weight of the German attack came done on us. I felt they were using incendiary bullets as the woods soon caught alight. The Green Howards had set up a defensive position behind us and after a day or so we were to withdraw behind them but on the way we had to fight our way past a German road block. This caused some confusion and forced us off the road. The acting CO disappeared and a senior company commander took over and got us to Otta. Most of my signalling equipment however was lost and from now on I seem to recall that all communication was by word of mouth. We were now behind the Green Howards but there was no more fighting for us as the decision was taken to evacuate on 29th April and eventually we got taken off by the Navy and returned to England, I think we all felt somewhat frustrated at how badly things had gone in Norway and how under-prepared and equipped we were for a modern war.

8

Doomed Before They Started

As is abundantly clear from the preceding chapters, the Norwegian campaign of spring 1940 did not go well. Realistically, the NWEF was totally ill-prepared and ill-equipped to fight there, low down the pecking order for resources. It is difficult to pinpoint any major successes, apart from those obtained at sea against the German Navy. The Army and RAF came off particularly badly when in combat with the Germans. This was not so much the fault of the men, but more that they were fighting to a different set of rules from the Germans; what training the British had was geared towards what had happened in France and Belgium between 1914 and 1918. In that conflict, Winston Churchill came up with a grand plan to assist the fighting on the Western Front with an invasion of Turkey through Gallipoli, but it all ended in stalemate and eventual defeat. Churchill was also a prime mover behind the strategic initiative for Norway in 1939 and 1940, with a large amount of the political will for the campaign stemming from him, even though ultimately it was Prime Minister Neville Chamberlain who paid the price for Norway. On Thursday, 4 April 1940, just days before the invasion of Denmark and Norway, Chamberlain gave an optimistic speech to Conservative Party members, declaring that Hitler had "missed the bus". He was of the opinion that Hitler and Germany had squandered an opportunity to ratchet up the war in 1939 and the early part of 1940, and that the resultant delay had given the Allies the opportunity to build up their forces so that Germany would not be in a position to launch any decisive attacks.

A few days later, Chamberlain's ill-chosen words were probably half-forgotten with the German invasions of Norway and Denmark on 9 April. Over the weeks following the invasion of Norway, the British press and official briefings did much to 'big up' the campaign and how it would all be over in a matter of weeks. But within days, with victories scarce and defeats becoming all too commonplace, some members of the Government were expressing concerns at the consequences of a slump in the opinion polls. The Secretary of State for War, Oliver Stanley, is reported as saying on 22 April that "reports which had appeared in the press gave the impression that the Allies were sweeping victoriously forward after successful landings in considerable strength at various places in Norway. Unless the press could be persuaded to alter their tone, the public might suffer a severe shock if things went badly in Namsos." A few days later Chamberlain is said to have warned his Cabinet that "to admit failure in Norway would be a serious blow to the Government's prestige". It is also worth pointing out that General Carton de Wiart had been asked to delay evacuating his troops from Namsos for political reasons.

Public opinion was starting to go against the Government, and on 29 April a number of members of the Watching Committee of Peers and Members of Parliament, led by

Lord Salisbury, formally protested to Lord Halifax, the Foreign Secretary, about the "want of initiative shown by the Government" regarding its war policy. Another member of the Committee, MP Harold Nicolson, wrote in his diary: "The general impression is that we may lose the war." In Norway itself, evacuations were taking place and details of recent setbacks were becoming public knowledge, with reports of inadequacies in the equipment and organisation of the NWEF also leaking out. Rumours were going round Parliament of an increasing number of people becoming dissatisfied with the conduct of the war, and thus the leadership being shown by Chamberlain. An old friend and fellow MP, Sir Henry Channon, commented on 2 May that he was "beginning to realise that Neville's days, are, after all, numbered". On the following day, General Ironside, the Chief of the Imperial General Staff, heard that "there is a first-class row commencing in the House" and that "there is a strong movement to get rid of the PM".

In so small a 'village' as Westminster, these rumours would soon get to be heard by the Government, so steps had to taken to try to present some evidence that the Government had a grip on the situation. So on 4 May, in the Commons, Chamberlain, for reasons that are not clear, decided to announce the "evacuation of Åndalsnes" as a success – scarcely something to be proud of – and the rest of his speech was not much better. Nicolson commented:

> I find that there is grave suspicion of the Prime Minister. His speech about the Norwegian expedition has created disquiet. The House knows very well that it was a major defeat. But the PM said that "the balance of advantage rested with us" and that "Germany has not attained her objective". They know that this is simply not true. If Chamberlain believed it himself, then he was stupid. If he did not believe it, then he was trying to deceive. In either case he loses confidence.

In this speech, Chamberlain had promised a debate on Norway for 7 May, and it is clear that if the Prime Minister was going to survive, new arguments would have to be found. But that was no easy task when balanced against the growing amount of bad news coming out of Norway. The parliamentary session on 7 May opened in a highly charged atmosphere. It was known that the Government would have to face not only the traditional opposition on the Labour benches, but that many Conservative MPs were also expected to voice their (mainly negative) opinions about the conduct of the war so far.

Captain Martin Lindsay of the Military Intelligence Directorate had returned from Norway in the cruiser HMS *York* with Major-General Carton de Wiart, and when they reached Scotland, Lindsay travelled straight to the War Office in London with some papers. He was there on 7 May, and after finishing his military business he went to see Clement Attlee, the Leader of the Labour Party, at the Houses of Parliament. At this meeting, Lindsay – who had been an MP before the war – gave Attlee a memo about the appalling improvisations and deficiencies in Norway. Lindsay stated later that he did this because he was quite convinced that Britain would lose the war if they carried on like that. Attlee gave this to senior Labour MP Herbert Morrison to help him open the debate for the opposition that afternoon, while Lindsay sat in the gallery to watch and listen to the two-day debate.

A few of the *Luftwaffe* and German Mountain troops taken prisoner taken during the campaign. (Imperial War Museum N231)

At this time the Conservatives held a fairly large majority in the Commons, and there was in theory little chance of them being replaced by either Labour or the Liberals. The best that the opposition could probably hope for was the resignation of Chamberlain, which would hopefully lead to the formation of a coalition administration. But this would mean that the new Prime Minister would probably be a member of the Government that had just fallen, and there were realistically only two candidates to replace Chamberlain – Churchill and Halifax.

As soon as Chamberlain entered the Commons, he was greeted with calls of "Who missed the bus?". He started his speech with a tribute to the troops who had "carried out their task with magnificent gallantry". He then tried to 'spin' the somewhat desperate events of the previous weeks. Some of the following is taken from Hansard, the official account of Parliament:

> Chamberlain – I hope that we shall not exaggerate the extent or the importance of the check we have received. The withdrawal from southern Norway is not comparable to the withdrawal from Gallipoli. There were no large forces involved. Not much more than a single division. The German strike was made easy by treachery from inside Norway and had been prepared long beforehand by the concealment of troops and materials in apparently innocent-looking ships. The campaign is not finished.

Thirty-five men from the Leicesters, Sherwood Foresters, KOYLI and York and Lancasters are buried in Lillehammer Northern Civil Cemetery, of which 31 were killed in April 1940. (Steve Foster)

There were shouts of "Hitler missed the bus!" before Chamberlain continued:

> While I think the implications of the Norwegian campaign have been seriously exaggerated and while I retain my complete confidence in an ultimate victory, I do not think that the people yet realise the extent or the imminence of the threat which is impending against us.

So it continued until he said "A great many times, some Honourable Members have repeated the phrase 'Hitler missed the bus'," and he struggled on, calling for members to "close ranks" behind the Government and their policies. It probably fell on mainly deaf ears.

After a few comments from others, it was time for Attlee, the Labour Leader, to take the floor:

> The evacuation was a wonderful feat of arms, but after all, it is a retirement. It does represent a setback. We are paying the penalty now, because after great expectations, there is necessarily disappointment. It is no good trying to minimise the event. We were informed on 19th March that we had a force of 100,000 men ready to go to Finland. What I cannot understand is the rapid disposal of all these troops. I have heard stories of some boys being sent to Norway, quite young and having very little training. I want to know whether the right kind of troops were sent. I ask whether at any time, there was not delay and discussion where action was necessary? I am not in the least satisfied that the present War Cabinet is an efficient instrument for conducting the war. Norway comes at the culmination of many other discontents. In a life and death struggle, we cannot afford to leave our destinies in the hands of failures or men who need a rest.

Attlee was swiftly followed by the Liberal Leader, Sir Archibald Sinclair:

> In the field of propaganda, economically, above all diplomatically, and to a lesser extent militarily we have suffered a great reverse. So our force ought to have been prepared, organised and equipped beforehand. The Minister of Supply told journalists that he did not know of any force which had been so splendidly equipped in so short a time. I have seen men who have come back from the theatre of activity north and south of Trondheim and they told me a very different story. There is one thing they told me, and I should like to tell the House because I have heard so much in a different sense from other people. The men from both theatres paid a high tribute to the courage and determination with which the Norwegians fought alongside them. They paid a particular tribute to the Norwegian ski patrols. Norwegians at Lillehammer for seven days held up with rifles only a German force with tanks, armoured cars, bombing aeroplanes and all the paraphernalia of modern war. I want to tell the House what these men told me about the equipment of our troops. They criticised our assigning such a difficult task to Territorials instead of to seasoned troops. The French sent their

> best troops. Then there were serious deficiencies in equipment. The Minister of Supply appeared in a Press picture in a becoming white coat, but the troops at Namsos had no white coats at all. Apparently he had the only one. They had no snow shoes, and if this force were really prepared for Finland it seems incredible that they should have had no snow shoes, because without them soldiers cannot deploy in deep snow or scatter under air attack or send out patrols to guard their flanks. In the fighting which occurred at Namsos I understand that men were caught up to their waists in snow. Indeed, it makes me wonder whether the Finnish force really did exist, at any rate on the scale which I understood from the Prime Minister when he talked about the 100,000 men who would be available for Finland and for defending Norway and Sweden from a German counter stroke.
>
> These men gave me several examples of deficiencies of equipment, but there are two which I ought to tell the House, of the muddle, waste and confusion, because they ought really to be the subject of inquiry. At one place two anti-aircraft guns were landed. They had an unsuitable type of mounting, they were not provided with height finders, they had no means of testing sights, no trained men to work the guns, no fuse keys to set the fuses, no range tables and no trajectory charts. The House will not be surprised if I say that these men told me that the guns were utterly useless. The second example relates to a transport. This transport sailed without a chronometer or barometer. It had no international code book and, therefore, no means of communicating with other vessels. It had no arms – not even a rifle. It had no splinter-proof protection, not even a tin hat, and no escort on its return voyage. It had food for less than half the number of men on board and carried a small number of wounded soldiers for whom there was no medical attention or treatment of any kind. Only one in three of the lifeboats could be swung and held outboard – for these there were no water breakers, so that there would have been no supplies of fresh water if the men had had to take to the boats. They had some charts, but not for the particular Norwegian waters to which the ship was directed. They had no charts for the parts of the North Sea over which they returned on the way home. The greatest mystery about this ship is why she ever made the voyage. She carried a certain cargo, and I have worked out the proportions carefully to give the House a picture. The cargo represented an insignificant fraction of her capacity, and stores of this material which she carried existed at her destination amounting to just under 300 times the amount which she brought. Yet to convoy this absurdly insignificant cargo across the North Sea and to return she burned 350 tons of fuel.

So it continued, until his conclusion: "This breakdown in organisation occurred because there had been no foresight in the political direction of the war."

About 2000, Leo Amery, the veteran Conservative MP for Sparkbrook, got a chance to speak. He had been an MP for over 25 years and was held in great respect in the House. He later commented: "I knew that what I had to say mattered and, what was more, I was desperately anxious that it should have its intended effect. So I followed

An indication of how difficult the country can be in the Vardekampen area once you get off the valley roads. (Steve Foster)

impatiently the alternation between speakers who declared that all was well with the best of governments which had just won a successful campaign and those who dwelt on the military disaster which was the natural climax of years of incompetence." His speech ended with a damning sting in the tail:

> What I would say, however, is this: Just as our peace-time system is unsuitable for war conditions, so does it tend to breed peace-time statesmen who are not too well fitted for the conduct of war. Facility in debate, ability to state a case, caution in advancing an unpopular view, compromise and procrastination are the natural qualities – I might almost say, virtues – of a political leader in time of peace. They are fatal qualities in war. Vision, daring, swiftness and consistency of decision are the very essence of victory. In our normal politics, it is true, the conflict of party did encourage a certain combative spirit. In the last war we Tories found that the most perniciously aggressive of our opponents, the right hon. Member for Caernarvon Boroughs [David Lloyd George], was not only aggressive in

In the forest on the Vardekampen Heights. Imagine what it would have been like fighting here knee-deep in snow. (Steve Foster)

words, but was a man of action. In recent years the normal weakness of our political life has been accentuated by a coalition based upon no clear political principles. It was in fact begotten of a false alarm as to the disastrous results of going off the Gold Standard. It is a coalition which has been living ever since in a twilight atmosphere between Protection and Free Trade and between unprepared collective security and unprepared isolation. Surely, for the Government of the last ten years to have bred a band of warrior statesmen would have been little short of a miracle. We have waited for eight months, and the miracle has not come to pass. Can we afford to wait any longer?

Somehow or other we must get into the Government men who can match our enemies in fighting spirit, in daring, in resolution and in thirst for victory. Some 300 years ago, when this House found that its troops were being beaten again and again by the dash and daring of the Cavaliers, by Prince Rupert's Cavalry, Oliver Cromwell spoke to John Hampden. In one of his speeches he recounted what he said. It was this: "I said to him, 'Your troops are most of them old, decayed

> serving men and tapsters and such kind of fellows.' … You must get men of a spirit that are likely to go as far as they will go, or you will be beaten still." It may not be easy to find these men. They can be found only by trial and by ruthlessly discarding all who fail and have their failings discovered. We are fighting today for our life, for our liberty, for our all; we cannot go on being led as we are. I have quoted certain words of Oliver Cromwell. I will quote certain other words. I do it with great reluctance, because I am speaking of those who are old friends and associates of mine, but they are words which, I think, are applicable to the present situation. This is what Cromwell said to the Long Parliament when he thought it was no longer fit to conduct the affairs of the nation: "You have sat too long here for any good you have been doing. Depart, I say, and let us have done with you. In the name of God, go."

This speech had a dramatic effect on the House. Harold Nicolson wrote, "A terrific attack", while Winston Churchill commented, "Terrible words".

The debate continued until late at night and recommenced the following day. On the second morning, Herbert Morrison, on behalf of the Labour Opposition, asked for a vote of confidence to be taken at the end of the day's debate. After Morrison had sat down, Chamberlain was given the opportunity to respond, which he did, saying: "I say to my friends in the House – and I have friends in the House – I accept the challenge. I welcome it indeed. At least we shall see who is with us and who is against us, and I call on my friends to support us in the lobby tonight."

Commentators have said that was a "most unfortunate statement which caused consternation even on the Government benches". Chamberlain seemed to be treating the matter as a party political one rather than a matter of life and death for the country.

A telling contribution came from the ex-Prime Minister Lloyd George, who made probably his last telling contribution in his long Parliamentary career. He started with a response to Chamberlain's appeal to "my friends":

> It is not a question of who are the Prime Minister's friends. It is a far bigger issue. The Prime Minister must remember that he has met this formidable foe of ours in peace and in war. He has always been worsted. He is not in a position to appeal on the ground of friendship. He has appealed for sacrifice. The nation is prepared for every sacrifice so long as it has leadership, so long as the Government show clearly what they are aiming at and so long as the nation is confident that those who are leading it are doing their best. I say solemnly that the Prime Minister should give an example of sacrifice, because there is nothing which can contribute more to victory in this war than that he should sacrifice the seals of office.

Eventually the time for speaking was over and it was time for the vote of confidence. The number who voted for the Government was 281, with 200 against, so in theory it was a victory for Chamberlain. However, behind these bare numbers was the fact that those who voted against included 33 Conservative MPs, while another 60 had abstained. Churchill later commented:

> There was no doubt that in effect, though not in form, both the Debate and the Division were a violent manifestation of want of confidence in Mr Chamberlain and his Administration. After the debate was over he asked me to go to his room and I saw at once that he took the most serious view of the sentiment of the House towards himself. He felt that he could not go on. There ought to be a National Government. One party alone could not carry the burden. Someone must form a Government in which all parties would serve, or we could not get through.

Churchill tried to persuade Chamberlain to carry on, but later commented: "Chamberlain was neither convinced nor comforted and I left him about midnight with the feeling that he would persist in his resolve to sacrifice himself if there was no other way, rather than attempt to carry the war further with a one-party Government."

During 9 May, Chamberlain fretted and rumours abounded. Would Chamberlain step down? Who would come to power? Which person – Churchill or Halifax – was preferred? Some discussions went on as to whether Clement Attlee and his deputy, Arthur Greenwood, would serve with Chamberlain in a Government in which he was Prime Minister. They did not really answer this question, side-stepping it by saying they would put it to their Party Congress which was happening in Bournemouth, but added that in their opinions, the answer would almost certainly be a resounding "No".

On the afternoon of 9 May, Chamberlain invited Halifax and Churchill to Downing Street for one of the most decisive meetings in the history of the Second World War for Britain. After they had taken their seats, Chamberlain stated that he was now satisfied that it was beyond his powers to form a National Government, as the Labour Party felt they could no longer support him. He was going to see the king soon to tender his resignation, but the question was which of the two men he should suggest to the king to be his successor? In his mind his preferred candidate was Lord Halifax, but no member of the House of Lords had been Prime Minister since 1902 and so Chamberlain tried to set a trap for Churchill. According to one of Churchill's advisers, the conversation went along the lines of a question from Chamberlain: "Winston, do you see any problem with a modern day Prime Minister coming from the House of Lords?" This question had presumably come up beforehand in a briefing by his advisers, and Churchill apparently walked over to a window, kept looking out of it and did not reply.

Matters were not resolved until late the next day. In the early hours of 10 May, German troops attacked Belgium and Holland. Upon receiving the news of this, Chamberlain changed his mind again and was intending to soldier on. However, Sir Kingsley Wood (a close political friend of Chamberlain who in May 1940 was Chairman of the Home Policy Committee) was able to make him see sense and that this fresh crisis made the formation of a National Government all the more vital. Chamberlain finally agreed and went off to Buckingham Palace to see King George VI. At 1800 on 10 May, Churchill was invited by the king to form a new administration, a task he accepted, and Chamberlain thus became the highest profile casualty of the Norwegian campaign.

An interesting 'what if' question is what might have happened if the Norway debate had been a couple of days later; would Parliament have risked changing horses midstream in the middle of the Battle of France?

SECRET.

From:- Sickle.

Desp. 1740 25.4.40.
Recd. 1650 25.4.40.

To :- The War Office.

IMPORTANT.

cipher 25/4.

3 ton lorries entirely unsuitable roads in present area of operations 30 hundredweight largest suitable. 100 1 ton lorries and drivers urgently required. Railway constantly being broken Construction Company capable of dealing with 100 miles single track and equipment to deal with bombed rolling stock blocking the above required. Please liaise Admiralty regarding unloading facilities ex ship.

C.4. (Telegrams) M.O.8. (for action)

A message to the War Office that the transport sent to Norway was totally unsuitable.

A damning comment about the campaign comes from Brigadier Terence Clarke, who was a member of the HQ NWEF, the head of ordnance stores and responsible for the storing and distribution of all stores, ammunition and explosives. The main store was based at Harstad, where Clarke was quartered in a civilian bungalow. He said: "I felt we had enough explosives to blow up the whole of Norway but little was used and at the end of the campaign the unused explosives were placed in the bottom of the fjord and blown up."

In a campaign such as Norway with its climatic challenges, clothing was going to be a major factor, and in Clarke's words:

> The War Office had provided a specialist arctic winter outer garment called 'a stiffer' which looked a bit like a two sided white cloak. The problem was the garment only came in one standard size and so if the wearer was on the small side it looked like he was wearing a trailing wedding dress! Additionally the majority of the fur hats for the troops never made it to Norway before the campaign ended. I was amongst the first to receive one of the much prized fur hats which General Auchinleck saw me wearing and requested two for himself. I ensured he received the two fur hats requested!

With the withdrawal of the Army from Norway after a disastrous two-month campaign, it would be nearly five years before Norway was free from German occupation. The seizure of Norway allowed the German Navy, and in particular their U-boat fleet, better access to the North Atlantic. However, Norway also became a drain on *Wehrmacht*'s manpower, and in 1945 there were over 300,000 troops stationed in the country. In Britain, the chief political casualty was Neville Chamberlain, who remained in the Government as Lord President of the Council until ill-health soon forced him to resign and he died in November 1940. There were of course also those in the military who paid the price for the Norwegian fiasco.

At the top, it was decided that his time in front-line service was over for Admiral Lord Cork – the overall commander-in-chief in Norway – who was 66 at the time of his return to England. A position as flag officer commanding in Shetland began in July 1940. He was kept busy trying to put together some sort of defence against a not so unlikely German invasion, and remained there until November, when the danger of invasion had subsided. A brief mission to Gibraltar followed, and then service in the Home Guard. He retired on his 68th birthday. Some of the senior Army commanders also 'disappeared' without making their mark on the subsequent course of the war. One notable exception was Lieutenant-General Auchinleck, who became commander-in-chief of the Indian Army in 1941 before taking the same role in the Middle East. He was relieved of command before the Alamein campaign in 1942, returning to his position in India where he served with distinction until the end of the war.

Looking at the Norway campaign as a whole, it was felt that the losses on both sides had been roughly equal. British losses in the land campaign were reported as 1,869, which included killed, severely wounded and missing, with 1,335 Norwegian casualties and 530 for the French and Poles. Around 2,500 sailors were also lost in action at sea, making a total Allied loss of about 6,250 for the campaign. The Germans recorded a total of 5,296 killed and missing, but the majority of these would have been losses at sea. The RAF lost 112 aircraft in Norway, whilst the German *Luftwaffe* suffered more than double this amount, around 240, a large number being transport aircraft.

Perhaps most significant was the losses in ships. The Royal Navy lost three cruisers, seven destroyers, one aircraft carrier and four submarines, whilst the German *Kriegsmarine* had three cruisers, ten destroyers and six submarines sunk, with four cruisers and six destroyers heavily damaged. With the Royal Navy's huge resources, these losses were relatively insignificant, but for the German Navy's surface fleet it was virtually a crippling blow; never in the rest of the war did the Kriegsmarine venture out in any great numbers, and when they did make aggressive moves it did not go well. The only real success at sea for the Germans was the performance of their U-boat fleet in attacking Allied merchant shipping, but even that effort ended in failure. For the Germans, the real success was of course the securing of the vital iron ore traffic from Sweden and Norway through the port of Narvik – once it had been repaired. By 1943, 1.8 millions tons of the raw material was flowing through the port.

For the British, it is fair to say that the Norwegian campaign was an unmitigated disaster. However, it opened the eyes of the senior commanders that to try to carry out amphibious operations without the necessary landing craft, air superiority and proper equipment would be a recipe for disaster. These were lessons that would be slowly learnt and perfected, culminating in the invasion of Normandy in June 1944.

I hope that this book helps ensure that the efforts of the brave men who fought in Norway, who are often overlooked, are not forgotten, especially those who paid the ultimate sacrifice. At the going down of the sun and in the morning, we will remember them.

Appendix A

Instructions issued to Major-General Hotblack, April 1940

Object and Scope of Operations in Central Norway.

1. His Majesty's Government and the Government of the French Republic are agreed that the early capture of Trondheim is vital to the success of further operations in Scandinavia.
2. The immediate object of the Allied operations in Central Norway is therefore the capture of Trondheim. With this end in view, operations as follows are projected and in process of execution:-

    (a) Operation 'Maurice' – Commander, Lieutenant-General Carton de Wiart. This comprises an advance southwards on Trondheim from the Namsos area by 146th Infantry Brigade (Brigadier Phillips) which is probably to be reinforced by the first echelon of the leading French light division (three battalions and attached troops).

    (b) Operation 'Boots' – Commander, Major-General Hotblack. This comprises a combined operation by the Navy and Army, with an R.A.F. component to be added later, with the object of forcing the entry of Trondheim Fjord, capturing Trondheim, and destroying the German forces in that area.

    (c) Operation 'Sickle' – Commander, Brigadier Morgan. This comprises a landing by 148th Infantry Brigade (two battalions) at Åndalsnes, with the role of securing Dombas, preventing the Germans from using the railway to reinforce Trondheim, and possibly a subsequent demonstration northwards towards Trondheim.

3. You are appointed military commander of the land forces detailed for Operation 'Boots'.

    The forces placed under your command are as follows:-

    15th Infantry Brigade.

    Two Canadian battalions under Brigadier Samson (Princess Patricia's Canadian Light Infantry and another to be advised).

    147th Infantry Brigade (Brigadier Lammie).

4. The system of command of the combined operations to be carried out by force 'Boots' will be that of 'Joint Command' by the naval, military and air commanders as laid down in Chapter IV, paragraphs 2–5 of the 'Manual of Combined Operations, 1938'.

    The name of the naval commander appointed by the Admiralty is to be advised.

5. In view of the paramount need for speed, the plan of operations has been prepared by you in co-operation with the Staffs of the War Office and the Admiralty, and is being communicated by you to the naval commander.

Should you and the naval commander desire to depart from this plan, you will bear in mind that any appreciable delay may have the most serious consequences on the course of operations in Scandinavia.
6. The organisation of command of the Allied military forces in Scandinavia is given in Appendix A1.
7. Should you become a casualty or otherwise be prevented from exercising command of the force, command will pass to the next senior British officer, who will exercise command, and, in the event of a French General officer being with the force, assume the acting rank of Major-General until another British officer can be appointed.
8. When your forces have successfully landed, it is important that good relations with the Norwegians should be fostered.
9. You will be guided by Appendix A2 with regard to the conduct of all forms of bombardment.
10. You will be kept informed regularly by the War Office as to the latest situation.
11. You will keep a constant communication with the War Office, and report regularly as to the situation.

Appendix A1

Organisation of Command of the Allied Military Forces in Scandinavia.
1. First stage.

Major-General Carton de Wiart assumes rank of Lieutenant-General (local unpaid), and commands British forces now operating from Namsos and First Echelon (three battalions and attached troops) Chasseurs Alpins under General de Division Audet (Operation Maurice). Major-General Hotblack commands independently all land forces involved in seaborne Operation Boots for capture of Trondheim.
2. Second stage.

Major-General Hotblack's force (Boots) becomes subordinate command under Lieutenant-General Carton de Wiart at a time to be decided by the latter, which will not be before Major-General Hotblack has reported to Lieutenant-General Carton de Wiart that his force has been effectively established ashore.
3. Third stage.

When Lieutenant-General Carton de Wiart reports that he is in a position effectively to exercise direct command of components of Major-General Hotblack's force, Major-General Hotblack himself will be withdrawn under orders of the War Office.
4. Brigadier Morgan's force (Operation Sickle) remains independent under War Office until further orders. Lieutenant-General Carton de Wiart will report when communication has been established with Brigadier Morgan.
5. The movement of the Second Echelon Chasseurs Alpins (three battalions and attached troops) will be directed by the War Office in the first instance, but the intention is that as soon as the tactical situation permits, the whole French force should come under the command of General de Division Audet, subordinate to Lieutenant-General Carton de Wiart.
6. It is intended that once the Allies are in full control of the Trondheim area, a corps commander should be appointed to command all British, French and Norwegian forces in Scandinavia.

Appendix A2

Instructions by His Majesty's Government to Govern the Conduct of all Forms of Bombardment.

1. The following instruction will govern the conduct of all forms of bombardment until the restrictions therein contained are modified.

These restrictions, in the meantime, are not to be relaxed on any account pending further instructions, even in retaliation for indiscriminate action by an enemy.

2. The object of the instructions is not to define legitimate military objectives, but to lay down a course of action in accordance with the agreed policy, which it may be expedient to adopt at the outset of war. It will be observed that the effect will be to restrict bombardment more severely than is required by a reasonable interpretation of existing international law.

3. Only the following purely military objectives in the narrowest sense of the word may be bombarded from the sea or air. Army Commanders will conform generally to the spirit of these instructions.

(a) Naval forces, i.e. warships, auxiliaries actually attendant on the Fleet, naval dockyards, barracks, and other establishments manned by naval personnel.

(b) Army units, fortifications, coast defence works, barracks, camps, billets, depots, dumps, and other establishments manned by military personnel.

(c) Air units, military aerodromes, depots, storage units, bomb stores and other establishments manned by air personnel.

(d) Troop transports (whether at sea or in harbour), roads, canals, and railways used for military communications, military road and inland water transport. Trains, road and inland water transport are not to be attacked unless they can reasonably be presumed to be of a military character.

(e) Accumulations of Navy, Army or Air Force stores. (This does not authorise attacks on factories.)

(f) Naval, Army and Air Force fuel installations or dumps in the field or situated within the confines of the Naval, Army and Air Force establishments mentioned in sub-paragraphs (a) to (c) above.

(Note. – Bulk stocks of fuel not covered by the above definitions are not to be bombarded under these instructions.)

4. Action against objectives in paragraph 3 above will be subject to the following general principles:–

(a) The intentional bombardment of civil populations is illegal.

(b) It must be possible to distinguish and identify the objectives in question.

(c) Bombardment must be carried out in such a way that there is a reasonable expectation that damage will be confined to the objective and that civilian populations in the neighbourhood are not bombarded through negligence.

Thus it is clearly illegal to bombard a populated area in the hope of hitting a legitimate target which is known to be in the area, but which cannot be precisely located and identified.

5. Subject to the general policy set out above, Commanders must exercise their discretion,

and orders for bombardment should be framed according to the spirit of that policy and not necessarily to the letter. In particular it must be borne in mind that the fact of an objective being unquestionably military does not necessarily or invariably justify bombardment of it. Thus an anti-aircraft or coast defence gun situated in the centre of a populous area could not be bombarded with reasonable expectation that damage would be confined to it. A small detachment of troops in billets in, or a convoy of transport passing through a town, or a troop transport lying alongside a commercial wharf, are unquestionably military objectives, but the bombardment of such objectives in a town might involve risks to the civil population out of all proportion to the military importance of the target at the time and might thus be unjustifiable. Justification for bombardment even of unquestionably military objectives must therefore depend on circumstances and must be decided by Commanders acting in the spirit of these instructions.

6. The necessary action is being taken to secure the adherence of our prospective Allies to this policy, and the necessary communications are being made to the Governments of the Dominions and of India.

7. Later it may be desirable to extend the scope of these instructions to the full extent allowed for by the following:-

Naval Bombardment – Hague Convention No. IX Of 1907.

Air Force Bombardment – The Draft Hague Rules of AerialWarfare 1922/23 as interpreted in the Air Ministry instructions to be issued in the near future.

Until such times as further instructions are issued from London, however, the above will stand. They are, however, liable to be modified at the shortest notice.

8. The action of armies is well established by practice and is not in dispute. Commanders of military forces on the ground will use every reasonable precaution to avoid undue loss of civilian life by artillery bombardment.

Appendix B

Outline Plan for the Capture of Narvik, 23 May 1940

Record of a conference held by the GOC (General Officer Commanding) at 1215 23rd May to discuss plans for the capture of Narvik.

Present: General Béthouart, Group Captain Moore, Commander Hubback, Brigadier Gemmell.

1. It was decided, for reasons adduced by General Béthouart that the attack on Narvik must, in any case, be postponed until the night of 25th/26th May.

2. It was decided that the approximate timings of the operation would have to be as follows, taking Zero as the commencement of the operation:

Zero – Fleet to rendezvous at Tjelsundet.

Z plus 1 hour 30 minutes – Embarkation of troops starts about one mile north of the point on the peninsula at Oijordneset.

Z plus 2 hours 40 minutes – Fleet will be in position in Rombaks Fjord when the bombardment will start.

Z plus 3 hours – Landing starts.

Z plus 4 hours 30 minutes – Landing of the first battalion (1st Battalion Foreign Legion) should be completed.

Z plus 7 hours 30 minutes – Landing of the second battalion (Norwegians) should be completed.

Z plus 10 hours 30 minutes – Landing of the third battalion (Second Battalion Foreign Legion) should be completed.

3. It was decided that fighter protection against attack from the air would have to be provided from at least Z plus 1 hour 30 minutes (i.e. when the embarkation of the assaulting troops starts).

4. With the resources of the Gladiator Squadron at Bardufoss, Group Captain Moore said that he could provide a continuous patrol of ten hours during which two aircraft would be in the air, or any corresponding variations between the time and the number of machines.

5. General Béthouart was anxious to carry out the operation as early as possible and said that he was prepared to do so without the effective co-operation of fighter aircraft if the atmospheric conditions were suitable (i.e. if there were low clouds and mist over the hills).

6. Commander Hubback stated that it would be necessary to give six hours warning to the Fleet to enable the operations to be carried out, assuming that the plans had been previously prepared.

7. General Béthouart, however, stated that it would take at least nine hours to get the necessary orders to the assaulting troops. Assuming, therefore, that the operation was due to start at 2100 it would be necessary to decide by midday whether or not it was to be undertaken.
8. It was also pointed out by Commander Hubback that unless there was a calm sea the tanks would not be embarked in the MLCs.
9. The GOC stated that he hoped Hurricane aircraft would be available to assist in the operation if it were delayed until the night of 27th/28th May. This would enable five or six aircraft to be in the air for a period of ten hours to provide aerial protection for the operation. General Béthouart considered this to be a much more satisfactory degree of aerial protection.
10. It was decided therefore that:
(a) Plans should be prepared with the object of carrying out the operation on the night of 25th/26th May and that if the atmospheric conditions were favourable, both in the air and on the sea, the operation need not be delayed.
(b) Group Captain Moore agreed to provide air patrols on the 25th May and onwards to test the degree of immunity which might be expected from the air conditions and report the result to the French HQ.
(c) Similar reports would be provided by naval officers in the Narvik area regarding the conditions on the sea and in the air. This information also to be submitted to the French HQ.
(d) On this information it would be decided, on the recommendation of General Béthouart, by 1200 on the 25th or 26th May, whether or not the operation should be carried out the same night.
(e) Should the operation not be carried out either on the night of 25th/26th May or on the night of 26th/27th May it would be carried out on the night of 27th/28th May if fighter support from the Hurricane squadron was then available.

Appendix C

Report on Quays and Harbour at Narvik

The primary aim of the Norway expedition was always to either hold Narvik or deny its use to the Germans, and towards the end of the Allied occupation of the town the Chief Engineer, Brigadier H. Pyne, wrote a brief report on Narvik:

Report on quays and harbour at Narvik.

1. The iron ore industry in the Narvik area can be divided into the following:-
   The electric supply
   The railway
   The ore handling and crushing plant
   The quays and harbour

2. The electric supply.
   The main source is in Sweden but two power stations were in the vicinity. That at Nygaard (10,000 HP) has been totally destroyed but the one at Harvik (3,000 HP) is not seriously damaged. There are three large transformers, one 10 miles inside the Swedish border, one at Hundalen (in German hands) and one in Narvik which has been totally destroyed. The overhead transmission lines and the distribution system on the railway have been destroyed.

3. Railway.
   Of the ten electric locomotives, six have been destroyed, two were transferred to Oslo before the war, one is in German hands near Hundalen and one has not been traced. Four small shunting electric locomotives appear to be little damaged and there is one old steam locomotive. Some of the numerous ore wagons were run into the sea but many remain as the available area became full up. The bridge and viaduct above Hundalen are reported as seriously damaged; a 60 foot span bridge in Narvik has been destroyed; rails, points and crossings have been damaged. The tunnels seem more or less undamaged.
   Note: A considerable section of the cliff east of Narvik carrying the railway was blown up by the French prior to withdrawal.

4. Ore handling and crushing plant.

The crude ore from Kiruna was crushed and washed at Narvik before export, nearly doubling the iron content before shipment. These works, together with the workshops have been totally destroyed. The high level staging from which ore was loaded into ships by gravity has been destroyed and the access thereto.

5. The quays and harbour.

The ore quays and the quays at Fargenes, being mostly wood, have been destroyed by burning. The main city quay which is used for passenger traffic and has no facilities for handling heavy goods, has had a gap of 50 feet blown in it. There are a number of small quays south of the main quay which could be quickly repaired but the water is shallow here and unsuitable for ocean going ships.

There are supposed to be some 25 to 30 ships sunk in the harbour – a conservative estimate is 20. Several of these have been sunk close up to where the ore quays were. A ship has been sunk by the Fargenes quay and the 30 ton crane has been destroyed.

6. Conclusion.

In view of the work entailed in clearing the harbour and rebuilding the ore quays and railway in this climate it is clear that not less than one years work will be necessary before ore could be exported in appreciable quantities. This pre-supposes that work would not be interfered with from the air or the sea. The ore companies Norwegian engineers estimate the time at two years but it is considered that more energetic people could produce the result in a year under the conditions mentioned above.

Appendix D

Movement Order for the Evacuation of Narvik

NWEF Movement Order No. 1

Secrecy.
1. Secrecy is of paramount importance.
2. The contents of this order will NOT be divulged by recipients to anyone other than the next senior officer and only where this is considered necessary.
3. The recipient of this order is alone responsible for its safe custody.
4. To ensure secrecy amongst ORs only one clerk per HQ will be detailed for typing and reproduction where this is necessary. He will be sworn to secrecy.
5. The utmost care will be taken to see that drafts, carbon papers, waxes and spare copies are burnt.
6. No complete order will be issued by Areas or Units. Only applicable parts will be issued by each unit and then only at the last possible moment.
7. In no case will the method of final embarkation after leaving the shore be divulged by the recipient of this order.
8. Discussion of these orders on the telephone must be avoided and will be resorted to only in emergency and then by 'parable'.
9. It is essential that normal routine and work should be carried on as usual, in so far as it does not interfere with the execution of this order.
10. The utmost care will be used in conducting necessary discussions. It will be impressed on all those to whom even a small part of the order must be passed that secrecy is all important and that a thoughtless word may mean the loss of life.
11. The operation will be known as ALPHABET.
Embarkation.
12. The force will embark in accordance with the attached Embarkation Order. The embarkation will be carried out as a drill. To attain this, careful organisation and forethought is necessary. The date of Day 1 (D1) is being communicated separately.
Embarkation Places.
13. These are given below, together with alternative embarkation places to be used if required:

Area	Embarkation Places	Alternative Embarkation Places
Harstad	Harstad Borkenes	Kilbotn Lillengen Ferry
Skaanland	Skaanland	Fjeldal
Sorreisa	Sorreisa	
Sag Fjord	Salangsverket	
Ofotfjord	Ballangen Liland Skjomnes Vassvik Narvik Bjervik Lilleberget	Open beaches

Method of Embarkation.

14. By puffer to destroyer, thence to ships. The puffer link may not be necessary in the case of Harstad, but will be provided for.

Responsibility for carrying out Embarkation.

15. The Army is responsible for the embarkation of personnel into puffers (or destroyers if puffers are not required). The Royal Navy is responsible for the move of puffers to destroyers and for the transfer of personnel to destroyers and ships. The function of movement control for the embarkation in Ofotfjord is the responsibility of the French HQ.

Marshalling of Troops.

16. (a) Assembly areas, well away from places of embarkation and allowing for ample dispersion, will be arranged by the OC Troops concerned.

(b) OC Troops, as detailed below, will detail an officer to be in charge of each assembly area:

Base Commandant for Harstad.

OC Troops Skaanland for Skaanland.

Station Commander Bardufoss for Sorreisa.

Officers detailed by French QG (Quartermaster General) for Sag Fjord.

Officers detailed by French QG for Ofotfjord.

17. (a) OC Troops will ascertain from the Embarkation Staff Officer of Movement Control, the time troops will be required at the places of embarkation.

(b) OC Troops will be responsible for calling up troops to the Assembly Areas.

(c) Movement Control will be responsible for calling up troops from assembly areas, through OC Troops, to actual places of embarkation.

(d) OC Units are responsible that personnel under their command arrive at the assembly areas at the time ordered by OC Troops.

(e) OC Troops will arrange for a Report Centre, clearly indicated, to be in each assembly area.

(f) Troops should be held in the assembly areas the minimum possible time.

18. Each place of embarkation will have an Embarkation Staff Officer allotted to it. French QG will detail two Embarkation Staff Officers for use at alternative embarkation places at Ofotfjord.

19. In the case of British troops, each serial number of the Movement Table embarking will be under the command of an officer who will be accompanied by one NCO (Sergeant or above). This NCO will be provided with a nominal roll in quadruplicate. Two copies will be handed to the ESO in charge of the embarkation and one copy to the Ship's Adjutant on arrival on board ship. Units will keep an original copy.

20. Movement Control will be responsible for checking units embarking. One copy of the nominal roll will be sent to Force HQ at the first opportunity.

21. Movement Control will keep Force HQ informed of the progress of embarkation.

22. Each unit party will contain, as far as possible, cooks and medical orderlies.

Kit and Equipment.

23. (a) Personnel will embark in FS order with greatcoats and one blanket rolled round the pack.

(b) Bren guns and anti-tank rifles will also be taken unboxed.

(c) One kit bag only will be allowed in the case of personnel who have no web equipment.

(d) In no circumstances will any other kit or equipment be taken.

(e) Officers i/c assembly areas will see that this order is enforced.

24. (a) Officers will embark in FS order.

(b) Where practicable officers' kit will be sent to Neilsons Wharf, Harstad, by 1500 3rd June, where it will be handed in to Ordnance.

(c) Officers name, rank and original serial number of their units will be clearly marked on each package. No officers kit will be accepted after the stated time.

(d) Transport will be responsible for loading officers kit in the store ships.

Evacuation of Billets.

25. Before billets are evacuated all unit equipment and sleeping bags (packed in kit bags) will be removed from billets and will be stacked at some central point in the locality under cover if possible. Guards will NOT be left. OC units are responsible that billets are left scrupulously clean.

Disposal of Documents.

26. Secret and Security documents will be destroyed by fire prior to embarkation, except War Diaries. These will be forwarded to Force HQ by 3rd June in sealed envelopes clearly labelled with the designation of the originator. Separate instructions are being issued regarding ciphers.

27. Personal documents and records will be retained and carried by an officer or senior NCO in his pack or haversack.

28. All other documents, states and papers will be destroyed.

Materials Left Behind.

29. The policy for destruction will be:

(a) Guns will be rendered useless before last personnel of gun crews leave.

(b) All technical equipment, signal stores, instruments and the like will be rendered useless.

(c) Vehicles will be rendered useless.

(d) Food, clothing and non-military stores will NOT be destroyed.

The timing, place and allocation of responsibility for destruction will be issued later.

Action in case of Air Attack.

30. Embarkation will not be delayed by enemy air attack, except on orders of OC Troops in the area. This order will not be given unless the means of embarkation is destroyed. The ESO will indicate which alternative place of embarkation is then to be used.

Protection against Land Attack.

31. OC Troops in each area will be responsible for the protection against air-borne land attack of troops during embarkation and of the places of embarkation. In the case of Harstad, this will be co-ordinated by Force HQ. Each unit in its billeting area and in the assembly area is responsible for its own protection.

Prisoners of War.

32. All prisoners of war, other than officers and airmen, will continue to be handed over to the Norwegian Army. OC Troops will arrange to evacuate officers and airmen with fighting troops.

Transport.

33. OC Troops in each area will maintain a pool of transport to be available to move troops in case of emergency or change of place of embarkation. Force HQ will arrange for the provision of this transport.

Supplies.

34. Haversack rations and filled water bottles will be carried.

Medical.

35. Medical arrangements at Harstad, i.e. aid posts etc., will be made by ADMS Base and staffed by 147th Field Ambulance. Casualties too ill to be placed on boats will be conveyed to the Military Hospital or to the Slotteid Hospital if the former is not available.

36. OC Troops in other areas will arrange for an aid post to be in operation at all places of embarkation. The badly wounded will be evacuated to Harstad by such means as may be available.

Intercommunication.

37. Telephone. Should it be necessary for Force HQ or Base Commandant to evacuate their offices, the staff will move to the following new locations where a telephone will be connected in each cellar:

G Office B Mess

AQ Offices E Mess

Base Commandant's Office C Mess

Spare A and D Messes

38. Wireless. Wireless communication from Harstad will be established with the following localities by 1st June:

Narvik, Skaanland, Liland, Salangsverket and the UK.

39. Despatch Riders. A pool of DRs will be made from the pool as from 1800 1st June:

Base Commandant 10

OC Skaanland 4

Station Commander Bardufoss 2

The following officers are authorised to demand special DRs:

G1 and above.

AQMG and above.

Liaison Officers.

40. Staff officers for liaison between embarkation areas and Force HQ will be as follows:

Area	Officer	Transport
Sags Fjord and Sorreisa	Captain Rankin	Walrus seaplane
Skaanland	Captain Heaton	2 seater car
Narvik	Captain Bonfield	Walrus seaplane
Harstad Base sub-area	Major Sugden	2 seater car

These officers will make contact with the OC Troops in their respective areas by 2000 2nd June and will report to Force HQ at their discretion. In the case of the Narvik area, Captain Bonfield will report to Commander Hubback.

Communication at Embarkation Centres.

41. The officer i/c puffers at each embarkation centre will be responsible for obtaining all necessary orders from the ESO at his centre, especially in the eventuality of a change in the place of embarkation. A visual signal terminal has been provided by the Navy at each centre, where communication with destroyers is necessary.

HQs.

42. Force HQ, Base HQ and HQ of OC Troops in each area will remain open until the last troops embark.

Appendix E

Report on the Evacuation of Stores and Equipment from Narvik, by Lieutenant-General Claude Auchinleck, GOC-in-C, North Western Expeditionary Force

1. Five store ships were available, including a ship for the French mules. All ships were brought alongside for the loading of guns, vehicles and the heavier stores and then moved out into the harbour to complete loading of boxed stores and ammunition from puffers. A great deal more stores and equipment was loaded than originally anticipated due mainly to the earlier arrival of the ships and the departure being postponed 24 hours.

2. The priority of loading was arms and guns of all sorts, AFVs, ammunition, technical vehicles and equipment, tentage and supplies. Except for small reserves, ammunition and AA guns required for tactical purposes, this was carried out. The loading of vehicles, stores, etc., was apportioned as fairly as possible between the Army, RAF and French. Although four French store ships were loaded with vehicles and stores prior to the arrival of the British store ships, it however became necessary to load the following French guns, tanks and technical vehicles on British ships:-

6 tanks, 10 75mm guns and 20 vehicles.

3. (i) Vehicles (British). All technical vehicles and AFVs available in the Harstad and Skaanland area were loaded. 28 ambulances, a large number of lorries and motor cycles and approximately 20 cars were also loaded, making a total of 390 vehicles.

(ii) Vehicles (French). All AFVs available were loaded, also a large proportion of tractors and lorries, making a total of about 400 vehicles.

4. Mules. 340 were loaded on the SS *Theseus*.

5. Supplies. All reserve stocks were loaded, except 30,000 rations at Sorreisa.

6. Ordnance Stores. All technical equipment and such signal equipment as could be spared, plus over 95% of the remainder were loaded.

7. Ammunition. The following stocks were abandoned:-

25/18 pounder 4,000 rounds
3.7 AA 10,000 rounds
40 mm 8,000 rounds
3" mortar 1,600 rounds
2" mortar 5,000 rounds

All the remainder, except small stocks with men in action till the last moment, was loaded.
8. Unit G1098 equipment. A certain proportion was loaded, mainly in unit vehicles.
9. Rifles and LAAs. None were left.
10. Guns. The following were loaded:-
    6 25/18 pounders
    21 Bofors 40 mm guns
    5 3.7 AA guns
11. Accommodation stores. Practically none of the already limited stocks was loaded.
12. Petrol, oil and lubricants.
(a) One tank belonging to Standard Oil Company at Harstad, containing 200 tons of petrol was rendered unserviceable by the addition of sugar.
(b) 5,000 gallons of cased MT (Mechanical Transport) petrol at Harstad were also destroyed.
(c) The SS *Coxwold* did not unload 400 tons and was sent to Sorreisa to load as much MT and aviation petrol as possible, but amount is not known. All that had to be left was destroyed, but it is impossible to say how much as MT and aircraft were in operation up to the last moment.
(d) All stocks of oil and lubricant at Harstad were destroyed.
13. Approximately 400 British vehicles, consisting mainly of 15 cwt trucks were left behind. Of these, over 60% were destroyed or rendered useless by smashing cylinder blocks, carburettors, distributors, accumulators and back axle cases etc. Tyres were deflated and the walls pick-axed and slashed.
14. All explosives were sunk at sea.

Appendix F

Documents relating to the Hallamshires Voyage and Disembarkation, April 1940

7th April 1940
Ships Standing Orders by Lieutenant Colonel C. Robins Officer i/c *Chrobry*.
1. The following parts of the ship <u>are out of bounds</u> to all ranks except when on duty:
(a) Crews quarters
(b) Ship's bridge
(c) Boat deck
2. B deck is out of bounds to Other Ranks except when on duty.
3. Lights at Sea.

It is imperative for the safety of the ship, and all on it, that no lights are shown at night. The times of blackout will be given out on the loud speaker each day. No smoking or lighting of matches or interference with the methods employed to make the ship light-tight will be permitted. A carelessly smoked cigarette may mean the loss of the ship. All Officers and NCOs will see that this order is strictly enforced and anyone violating this order will be severely dealt with. After sunset, smoking is permitted in the shelter deck forward and aft.

4. Emergency Action.

In the event of emergency each unit will fall in the place assigned for parade in two ranks facing outwards. The Officer i/c will at once provide two armed sentries for each boat and double sentries on soldiers under arrest or detention. Men should double up to their places as quickly as possible in any dress. The CO with 2 i/c and Adjutant will go on deck to preserve discipline, immediately reporting to the Captain of the ship. Medical Officers on board will proceed to the hospital and prepare to remove the sick to such places as may be appointed. The Quartermaster will see all cabins are clear. All Officers to whom no duties are assigned are to proceed to the space allotted to them on the upper deck. Two armed sentries on fore part of bridge and two armed sentries aft.

5. Life belt regulations.

While at sea, life belts are to be worn constantly by all ranks except when the men are turned in, when the life belts will be kept in the berths. Life belt drill will be carried out every day so that all might become familiar with the manner of securing and wearing them. Gas masks will be left with the equipment, not worn.

6. Cleanliness of Quarters.

Troops must co-operate with the crew to keep quarters clean. Berths should be made up when Reveille is sounded and then the beds on lower berths rolled back exposing the deck underneath and so be left until the rooms are swept out and daily inspection completed.

7. Toilets.

Troops must avoid throwing any substances into toilets likely to choke pipes etc., thereby causing a stoppage of the sanitary outlets which cannot be repaired at sea.

8. Fresh water supply.

Troops must avoid any unnecessary waste. The fresh water supply is limited and with maximum numbers on board, strict economy is essential to avoid shortage.

9. Smoking on board.

Smoking is allowed on the upper deck only. To guard against fire only safety matches may be used on board.

10. Rubbish.

No rubbish may be thrown overboard at any time. Bins for it are by the Canteen.

11. Bugles.

No bugles will be blown on board ship.

12. The Orderly Officer will report to the Field Officer of the Day at 0900.

13. Appointments.

The following appointments are made:-

Officer i/c Troops – Lieutenant Colonel C. Robins
Ships Staff Officer – Major Potter
Ships Adjutant – Captain H. Marsh
Assistant Ships Adjutant – Second Lieutenant D. Bell
Ships QM – Captain J. Dobson
Ships Baggage Officer – Second Lieutenant G. Good
Senior Medical Officer – Lieutenant C. Wells
Ships Guard Commander – Second Lieutenant R. Longridge
Officer i/c Armoury – Second Lieutenant A. Somers

The Company on Duty will furnish guards and sentries by day and by night for about 30 posts.

14. Time Table.

0600 Reveille.
0630 Rations. Orderlies draw bread and butter.
0700 Breakfast – first sitting.
0730 Rations. Orderlies draw bread and butter.
0800 Breakfast – second sitting.
0800 Officers Mess.
0830 Dining Rooms clear.
0830 to 0930 Cleaning of Dining Rooms.
0900 Sick Parade.
1030 Inspection by ships Captain and Officer i/c Troops. All men standing by their berths.

1145. Orderlies draw rations.
1200 Dinner – first sitting.
1245. Orderlies draw rations.
1300 Dinner – second sitting.
1300 to 1400 Officers Mess.
1500 Battalion Orderly Room.
1730 Supper – first sitting.
1830 Supper – second sitting.
1900 to 2000 Officers Mess.
2000 Make beds.
2200 Lights out, stop smoking, everyone except guards and sentries go below.
2215 Rounds of Field Officer and Orderly Officer. Every man to be in bed.
2300 Lights out in Saloon.

15. Canteen.
The canteen will be open as follows: -
Wet canteen – 1100 to 1200. 1845 to 2145.
Dry canteen – all day.

The following instructions were then issued on 15 April:

Disembarkation – Warning Orders by Lieutenant Colonel C. Robins Officer i/c Troops MS *Chrobry*, issued at 1000.

The Battalion will be prepared to disembark at Namsos any time after 2100 onwards this evening. A landing will be effected by transferring to destroyers in the following order:-

1. A and B Company.
2. CO with the following HQ Company personnel:- Medical Officer (Lieutenant J. Wells), Medical Section, Intelligence Section, Signal Section, FS Police, Captain Currie and C Company.
3. Major C. Strong D Company, Cipher Personnel; attached signal personnel with wireless set.

Two signallers with lamps and four stretcher bearers will be attached to each rifle company.

The remainder of HQ Company personnel will remain on board and they will be responsible for:-

(a) Manning 10 AA guns from 1800.

(b) For unloading as may be required and disembarking with their respective stores, e.g., No. 3 Platoon with 3" mortars.

Transport Section will be detailed for unloading final baggage.

Administrative.
Dress:- As laid down in Preliminary Orders issued yesterday, except that water bottles will be filled and carried slung (not in haversack). Life belts will not be taken.

All Bren guns, tripods and spare barrels will be taken with loaded magazines in utility pouches. Each man will carry 50 rounds SAA.

A/T rifles, 2” mortars and Bren gun boxes will be left with Company baggage.
Each Company will leave the following personnel with the baggage:- CQMS, two store men and cooks.

Composite rations and cooking equipment will be with the baggage which will be carefully stacked as follows:-

HQ Company:- No. 5 Hatch D deck

A Company:- No. 1 Hatch D deck

B Company:- No. 5 Hatch C deck

C and D Companies:- No. 2 Hatch D deck

Haversack rations will be taken. Orders will be issued later regarding the time disembarkation is likely to take place and Companies will probably fall-in at their emergency stations.

Appendix G

Disembarkation Order for 4th KOYLI, 17 April 1940

Warning order for Disembarkation 17.4.40
1. SS *Chrobry* will be berthed at Namsos at H.1 hours, probably 2200.
2. At H-½ hours the following personnel will parade in the forward dining hall for unloading duties. Dress – fighting order. Equipment and arms will be left in the dining hall before work begins.

Three parties of one full rank and twelve men for unloading hatches 2, 3 and 4.

Reliefs will report as follows:

H.3 hours (i.e. after 2 hours)

Three parties of one L/Corporal and six men to relieve half the fatigue that started at H.1 hours.

H.4 hours (i.e. after 3 hours)

Three parties of one full rank and six men to relieve remainder of fatigue that started at H.1 hours.

H.6 (i.e. after 5 hours from start)

Three parties of one L/Corporal and six men i.e. those who were relieved at H.3 hours to relieve fatigue that started at H.3 hours.

H.7 (i.e. after 6 hours from start)

Three parties of one full rank and six men i.e. those who were relieved at H.4 hours to relieve fatigue that started at H.4 hours.

The above fatigues will be found by D Company 4th KOYLI. D Company will also find the following fatigues.

One officer, one Sergeant and twenty men to parade at forward dining hall at H-½ hour to assist in preparing ship for disembarkation.

Dress – fighting order. Equipment and arms will be left in the dining hall.

3. C Company will find the following fatigues:-
(a) Three parties each of one NCO and six men for taking baggage out of nets on the quayside from hatches 2, 3 and 4. Reliefs for these parties will be arranged by OC C Company as necessary.
(b) A fatigue party of one officer, three full ranks and 24 men for moving kit back from the quayside to unit dumps. Care must be taken to avoid congestion on the quayside. Reliefs for these parties will be arranged by OC C Company as necessary. The officer is responsible for selecting the site to which kit will be removed and for general supervision of quayside fatigues.

4. After disembarking C Company will march off to a suitable site selected by OC C Company where they can dump equipment and rifles before sending back fatigues ordered. This site must be sufficiently far away from the quayside.

OC Hallamshires will arrange for the unloading of all baggage from No. 1 hatch (i.e. Hallamshires baggage).

5. Troops will disembark in the following order:-

Brigade HQ and REs
C Company KOYLI
A Company
B Company
D Company
Battalion HQ KOYLI
HQ Company KOYLI
4th Lincolns
Hallamshires
Details

Dress – fighting order. No baggage of any description will be carried.

Appendix H

Report on Operations of the 4th Lincolns, 19–23 April 1940

Report on Operations 19th April to 23rd April 1940.
This report is divided into five phases.

1. The defence of Steinkjer.
2. The battle of Vist.
3. The withdrawal of B, D and HQ Companies (part).
4. The withdrawal of C and HQ Companies (part).
5. The action of A Company near Egge.

Phase 1.
The Battalion arrived by train in the early hours of 19th April at Steinkjer and was billeted in the school and barracks. I decided to take up defensive positions to repel a landing at Steinkjer as early as possible. Reasons:-

(a) The ice was starting to break up.
(b) Small boats were reported to be continually coming through the narrows at Vangshylla and returning after a time.
(c) Continuous air reconnaissance by enemy.
(d) The vulnerability of having my troops congested in the large buildings.

I accordingly made a reconnaissance and decided my dispositions as follows:-
A Company on propitious south of Egge to cover the landing stages there.
Carrier Platoon plus two detachments of AA Platoon in area timber yard. Main task to prevent enemy disembarking from a destroyer on the landing stage.
C Company in dock area.
B Company in station area.
D Company in Vist station area to prevent a landing from small boats in the bay there.
Remainder HQ Company in reserve at school.
Battalion HQ at school.

The position was occupied during the night 19th/20th April. At 0400 21st April a German gun boat was reported to be passing through the narrows, this was afterwards stated to be a destroyer. As the tide was out it was presumed that any attempted landing would be south of Egge, the only place where there was deep water and at 0545 21st April 1940, eight LMGs of the Carrier Platoon were sent there in lorries to come under command of OC A Company. At 0730 news came in that about 400 Germans had landed near Skjenstadaun, half of whom were proceeding north and half south. It was afterwards confirmed that they all proceeded north.

At 0747 I ordered B Company to be prepared to move in lorries to support D Company in Vist area.

B Company arrived at Vist station at 0900.

I sent up Major Black to take command of B and D Companies.

Phase 2.

The intention was that B Company should take up a position on the left of D Company along the line of the road towards Korsen but owing to the inefficiency and discrepancy of the available maps, Major Black advanced B Company down the road (not shown on any map) running west from Vist station.

Major Black followed the leading platoon of B Company. About two miles down the road the leading scouts were fired on from the high ground to the west. At 0945 by crawling and rolling in the snow the platoon got into position about the second 'k' in Krokshus. Captain Tweed came up and got his second platoon into a farm house on the right and the third platoon occupied a position in some houses slightly in the rear and covered the ground to the south. Major Black now went back and sent up Second Lieutenant Flint and a section of D Company to keep in touch with B Company. Major Black then went down to Sparbu and saw Colonel Hibbert (CO 4th KOYLI) and obtained his general dispositions. On hearing the position of B Company I sent Major Stokes and the reserve of HQ Company (55 men) with orders to advance with the reserve platoon of D Company and establish his forward post at Korsen cross roads. This was done without opposition.

B Company held their position till 1800 21st April when they were withdrawn to a position in woods astride the road about 700 yards west of Vist station. They had a hard day's fighting suffering about 20% casualties, chiefly from machine gun and mortar fire, but nevertheless gave a good account of themselves and accounted for quite a number of the enemy.

During the morning of 21st April Brigade rang up and told me to hold the line of the isthmus. I decided to take up a position from the crossroads at Korsen to the fjord near the 't' of Storeng. I saw OC C Company and explained the position to him and told him to extend the line northwards from HQ Company position and attempt to gain contact with B Company near the second 'k' in Krokshus.

C Company were in position by 2005 but patrols sent north failed to gain contact with B Company, who had withdrawn, as the farms had been set on fire by trench mortars, to their second position.

Steinkjer was heavily bombed from 1100 to 1200 and all communications on civil telephones were destroyed. No further communication was obtained with Brigade during the action except twice when Second Lieutenant R. Newsum managed to get through on a motor cycle. Signal communication with Vist was quickly obtained by connecting on to the railway wires. Steinkjer had now become anything but a health resort and Battalion HQ was moved to a house in woods 200 yards north of the school.

My dispositions on the night 21st/22nd April were:-
A Company plus eight LMGs south of Egge
D Company less one platoon Vist station area
B Company 700 yards west of Vist station
HQ Company plus one platoon D astride crossroads at Korsen
C Company on a line running north from this position
Battalion HQ in a house in woods 200 yards north of school Steinkjer
The night 21st/22nd April passed quietly, except for patrol activity on both sides.

22nd April 1940.
Major Black withdrew B Company to hills east of D Company about 0230.

1000 Mortar and machine gun fire on D Company from south west.

1030 German patrol appeared about the 'M' of Meieri and was dispersed by Bren gun fire.

1115 Mortar fire on D Company's posts.

1120 Major Black sent a message to C and HQ Companies saying that the KOYLI were withdrawing at 1215 and that they should follow and withdraw to Steinkjer. He also gave the route of the KOYLI's withdrawal. Note – this message did not reach destination till 1415.

1215 A bus came through to D Company with a CSM and three men of the KOYLI who reported that their two platoons had been captured while embussing. Captain Staniland actually saw a party of men with their hands in the air.

1240 Five enemy appeared on cycles from the south, one went back and the other four were shot.

1300 D Company sniped at from the south west.

1330 Enemy scouts appeared on the road through wood to west and were shot.

1400 Enemy reported to have crossed railway 800 yards south of Vist station.

1415 Major Black orders withdrawal of B and D Companies under cover of Bren gun post.

1430 I had previously instructed Major Black to hold on till dark and to withdraw through Steinkjer over railway bridge and along road near railway to Byafossen commencing from the left flank.

Phase 3.
On hearing that the withdrawal had commenced I gave an order to hold a line at Lod midway between Vist and Steinkjer. Steinkjer was again heavily bombed on the morning of 2nd April which necessitated the continual moving of HQ.

The withdrawal once commenced was impossible to check, but a Bren gun post was formed to give protection. Note – these personnel had to swim the river as the only means of getting out of Steinkjer during the evening 22nd April.

By 1530 part of B Company commenced to arrive in the town. I left the IO near the school to direct and moved my HQ to a small house 200 yards north of railway bridge. I sent the Adjutant with all personnel of HQ down road to Byafossen to collect the Battalion as they arrived there. I stayed to direct and guide men arriving over railway bridge.

They were continually bombed and machine gunned but suffered very few casualties. No men arrived after 1830 but I hung on with my RSM and batman till 2045 as I had not accounted for my C Company and the HQ detachment under Major Stokes. I then presumed they must have taken the other road out of Steinkjer. Before I left my position the enemy were shelling and machine gunning the town.

I followed the route picking up a few stragglers at the road block and more at Sunnan and eventually caught up Colonel Hibbert with the KOYLI at Folling at 1030 23rd April. After a fruitless trip to Kvam we got through to Brigade from Norwegian HQ. I moved with the KOYLI to HQ Hallamshires, where a lorry was provided to take me and my party of 22 to my Battalion near Rodhammer.

Phase 4.
22nd April. On receipt of message from Major Black regarding the withdrawal of KOYLI at 1215 and that C and HQ Companies (Major Stokes) were to withdraw after the KOYLI, Major Stokes decided to withdraw at once as the enemy were on his left flank and left rear. It was decided to withdraw quietly into the woods on the right and not to fire unless attacked and try to reach the wood west of Vist before dark where it was hoped to contact B Company. It was agreed to use no tracks.

1515 Heavy enemy machine gun fire in building just vacated by HQ Company near Kvitvang.

1530 – 1730 Sergeant Isaac and PSM Cannon lead the way through the woods under direction of Major Stokes and Captain Cragg. Rifle and LMG fire getting further away in the distance east of Vist station.

2000 Arrived in wood west of Vist station where civilians said that Steinkjer was in the hands of the Germans. Major Stokes decided to lie up till dark, then to cross the valley near Vist station and up the mountains to the east with the object of reaching Henning. He discarded steel helmets as a disguise, held hands in pairs and marched boldly across. Only protection two men in front with fixed bayonets. The snow was three to four feet deep and it took 4½ hours to do 1½ miles.

23rd April 0300 Arrived Holtaine.

0300 to 0800 Slept in barn.

0830 On the march to Henning via tracks.

1200 Arrived Henning, no food or water, found KOYLI stores and replenished.

1300 Left for Bruen and Ogndalen.

1930 Arrived Sunnan. Enemy approaching Sunnan along railway. Norwegians told them that I had passed through that morning, so they moved on.

2000 Norwegians blew up railway and stone bridge.

2015 Discarded respirators at Dal. Troops very tired.

24th April 0100 Rested for night at Five.

0830 Norwegian Battalion withdrew from Five towards Kvam. Marched south west across country via tracks to Meieri.

1600 Arrived Meieri intact. Opened half emergency rations at Rostad. Captain Cragg went forward by horse and dray and arrived at Hallamshires advanced post at Hiellosen to report situation.

The men were accommodated by the Hallamshires and gradually sent back to my Battalion. This was a most remarkable march under very trying conditions and everyone arrived fully armed with all rifles and Brens and carrying 100 rounds SAA each. No one was left on the road.

Up to reaching Meieri they marched 34½ hours out of 47 hours and covered 45 miles. I should like it to be put on record that Major Stokes made all decisions, gave all orders and by his calmness and encouragement kept absolute control and so brought his command to safety.

Captain Cragg acted as guide across very difficult country and always found his objective. Sergeant Isaac and PSM Cannon broke trail the whole way with fixed bayonets and showed stamina and determination.

Phase 5.

The position of A Company was strengthened by the addition of eight Bren guns early in the morning of 21st April. No communications with A Company was possible after 1630 21st April by civilian telephones. After which A Company was put under direct orders of 146th Brigade. Later in the evening a message was received from Brigade stating that the position would be held at all costs till darkness on night 22nd/23rd April and then proceed to new area about Jadoren. OC Company visited Brigade and ascertained that Jadoren should read Asp. 21st April was quiet on this front. 22nd April was also quiet till one platoon was trench mortared as it was withdrawing about 1945.

The Company withdrew at 1945 to Asp. OC Company was sent by Brigade Major with a message to the Brigadier and on his return he found that his Company had been put out in a screen by the Brigade Major about Asp and then were eventually withdrawn to rejoin the Battalion by transport.

Main reasons for failure of the operations.

1. Absolute air superiority by the Germans.
2. Lack of supporting weapons for the infantry.
3. Not properly equipped to cross the snow covered hills.
4. First time young soldiers were under fire.

My men showed no fear of rifle and machine gun fire, but the bombing, trench mortaring and shelling from the destroyer did have a demoralising effect on some of them.

In conclusion I should like to recommend that Second Lieutenant J. Flint and Private Roach be given awards and that the bravery of Captain Tweed, Second Lieutenant Pattin and Corporal Mallett should be set on record.

Appendix I

Report of 4th KOYLI for the period 20–24 April 1940

20th April.

B Company moved to Stiklestad on orders from Brigade.

1 officer and 55 other ranks RE moved to Stiklestad under orders of 4th KOYLI. Battalion now spread out on nearly 15 mile front with flanks open to attack by sea by Trondheimsfjord. Pointed out to Brigade Major when he came.

21st April.

A Company reported at 0445 that one German cruiser and one tanker steamed fast through Skarnsundet strait and that about 0645 approx 400 Germans had landed north of Strommen and were advancing north east and south east on Skjlevad and Strommen. 0700 A Company ordered to move north west to hold Germans advancing on Strommen and C Company ordered to move to Strommen in support of A Company. At about 0500 B Company reported 200 Germans advancing from Levanger on Verdalsonen. B Company sent section RE to bridge head to support Norwegian MG troops there. Just as the REs arrived the Germans opened fire; the Norwegians who had six machine guns retired, leaving the bridge open to German advance. REs forced to withdraw on Stiklestad. At about 0900 Adjutant sent by car to order A Company to return to and hold Strommen and C Company to move towards Verdal to stem German advance. C Company had two platoons in buses at Strommen and one platoon on foot at Röra. When the two embussed platoons reached Fleskhvs they were informed that approx one company Germans had landed west of Fleskhvs and were in position at Norberg. C Company left one platoon at crossroads south of Fleskhvs and moved with the other platoon about 1½ miles east to the high ground at Minsaas where he was joined by the platoon on foot. C Company gained contact with B Company at Stiklestad.

At about 1800 CO 4th KOYLI realising that withdrawal of B and C Companies and the REs via Röra was impossible sent a message ordering them to withdraw via the eastern shore of Lake Leskdals to Fiskness, where, in the event of the rest of the Battalion having to withdraw on 22.4.40 the Battalion would RV.

Major Black, 4th Lincolns, visited 4th KOYLI at Sparbu at 1100 and told us that two of his companies were on a line from Hegstad to the railway. During the afternoon CO 4th KOYLI sent an officer to 4th Lincolns to find out the situation.

At 1800 A Company withdrawn from Strommen to Roske.

At 2100 A Company withdrawn to Maere as CO KOYLI was doubtful of Lincoln's situation and consequently KOYLI's rear. D Company withdrawn at same hour to Roske.

2130 orders received from Brigade that companies at Röra, Strommen and Stiklestad to remain in position for the night and then to withdraw across country to Henning. In view of the situation and danger of carrying out this order CO decided to let his own orders stand.

German air activity had been continuous throughout the day. Owing to impossibility of moving off the roads owing to deep snow it was imperative to keep hidden by daylight. Any movement met with machine gun fire or bombs from the air. Owing to complete lack of any transport other than that requisitioned with great difficulty, CO ordered that all kit except fighting order to be abandoned.

22nd April.
German seaplane seen over Sparbu flying very low backwards and forwards. At about 0745 seaplane spotted D Company's position and dropped a flare. This started German attack. CO ordered HQ Company into woods just east of Sparbu and all transport ½ mile upward from Sparbu to Fiskness into dense forest.

First Germans sighted by D Company was a cycle patrol about twelve strong armed with LMGs. D Company opened fire and about six were seen to fall. Germans attacked frontally at first, supported by heavy mortar fire. Shortly afterwards both flanks were enveloped by ski troops with machine guns on sledges or carried.

At 1030 D Company were in a precarious position and were ordered to withdraw on Sparbu.

At about 0745 an officer was sent to 4th Lincolns and then to 146th Infantry Brigade to say that if and when we withdrew it would be to the east of Fiskness.

At about 1015 an officer was sent to 4th Lincolns to say that KOYLI were withdrawing east. At about 1030 CO went by car to A Company at Maere and ordered them to withdraw by bus and take up a covering position ½ mile east of Sparbu to cover D Company's withdrawal.

On his return CO ordered Battalion HQ and transport to withdraw east on Fiskness road.

OC A Company and two platoons A Company arrived by bus at Sparbu from Maere by which time enemy were in southern outskirts of Sparbu. Battalion was sent back with orders to remaining platoons of A Company to join 4th Lincolns as it was then too late for them to join us.

The Battalion withdrew to Fiskness where B Company and REs were already waiting and C Company arriving. Battalion less B and C Companies moved on to Henning.

The roads from Sparbu and Stiklestad to Fiskness were appalling and almost impassable. Transport continually went off the road and capsized. B and C Companies were compelled to organise sleigh transport which moved up the lake. Sleigh capsized and Bren guns and other equipment was lost. From Henning on to Stod there was no road but only forest tracks. Further sleigh transport was with great difficulty organised. The work done by our interpreter Matheson was magnificent and beyond all praise. Owing to impossibility of transporting anti-tank rifles CO ordered them to be left behind and destroyed. Battalion left Henning at 2130 and marched across country to Stod arriving there at 0430. Troops were very exhausted having marched continuously through snow and slush.

23rd April.
At 0700 CO was informed by a Norwegian officer that enemy were advancing from Byafossen on Sunnan and that they were four kilometres away. CO rang up General Wettera, commander Norwegian troops on telephone and asked for confirmation and proposed action by Norwegian troops and was informed that this was the case and that his troops were withdrawing to the north east.

Companies were ordered to get on the move immediately and to march via Sunnan bridge to the north in an attempt to rejoin the Brigade. All touch had been lost for 48 hours with Brigade whose position was unknown.

As the Battalion was very exhausted, having fought and marched continuously with scarcely any food for 48 hours, the CO decided to leave the Bren guns in the farms at Stod, as the choice lay between getting the men back without their guns or not getting them back at all.

The Battalion reached Sunnan bridge at 0900 and proceeded to Foling leaving half the REs and two platoons from C Company with orders to prepare the bridges for demolition. The REs and guard withdrew at 1500, having left the bridge intact at the request of the Norwegians. Contact was finally established by telephone with 146 Brigade and the CO informed them of our position and was ordered to withdraw at dusk to Beistad.

At about 1900 Norwegian troop at Foling informed us that the enemy were advancing north of Sunnan and north from Steinkjer. Companies were ordered to get on the move at dusk and march with a guide by forest tracks to main road Beistad-Namsos.

The Battalion reached Namdalseid at 0430 24.4.40 having marched approx 58 miles in 42 hours. The complete lack of any organised transport, the continued unopposed air activity by the enemy, the impossibility of moving anywhere off the roads and the lack of food made the march extremely hazardous and exhausting.

At Foling a barn occupied by some of the companies was destroyed by fire and many rifles and equipment lost.

Appendix J

Report by Brigadier Phillips, Commander, 146 Infantry Brigade relating to Operations 20–25 April 1940

Operations of 146th Infantry Brigade in the Steinkjer area 20th–25th April 1940.

20th April Dispositions.
Dispositions on the night of April 20th were as follows:
Hallamshires – on right.

One platoon Foldefoss
One company less one platoon Malme
One company Hjelle
Remainder of battalion about New Beitstad (situated north east corner of fjord)

4th Lincolns

One company Egge
One company Vist
Remainder of battalion Steinkjer area

4th KOYLI

HQ and battalion around Sparbu
One company Röra
One company Stiklestad with one section 55th Field Company RE in same area (Verdal)

Section 55th Field Company (Lieutenant McLeod) was sent to Verdal area to recce (under protection of 4th KOYLI) Verdal railway bridge which had been destroyed by the Norwegians and which we intended to repair.

Brigade HQ were between Egge and Steinkjer.

Brigadier Phillips was accompanied by a French officer in order to recce possible bivouac areas for French troops in this area. On 21st April a French officer accompanied by a British officer and an interpreter was sent to recce area around Verdalen and later the area Ogndal-Stod, as it was considered possible that each of these localities was capable of holding a battalion of Chasseurs Alpins.

21st April

0405 4th Lincolns report 300 ton ship sighted in Inderroy Narrows.

0445 German destroyer seen sailing full speed through narrows.

0606 Norwegian HQ report outposts at Vardolsora (Verdal bridge) attacked by force of approx 200 Germans. Two German armed trawlers passed Skarnsund (in fjord west of Verdal) sailing due north.

0610 Brigade intelligence report 200 Germans from Levanger were attacking Verdal bridge and RE Field Company were supporting Norwegians. Actually Norwegians left their position and retired as soon as the Germans advanced, leaving the matter in the hands of the Field Company.

0625 German cruiser (?) reported to have tied up north of narrows at Kirkenesvagen.

0710 Norwegian intelligence reported by telephone that 400 Germans had landed. 200 were proceeding to Sandvollan and 200 to Strommen.

0728 Landing from German trawler at Trone (200 men) was reported. Another trawler landed men at Hulla (on peninsula south west of Röra).

0740 Enemy marching on Strommen were reported by 4th KOYLI to have turned north in direction of Vist.

Later in the day the enemy were reported to have landed a further force on the quay at Vangshylla (south west end of Inderöy peninsula).

During the course of receipt of this information, Brigade ordered 4th KOYLI to send a second company to engage the enemy who had landed at Trone and to join up with the company of 4th KOYLI already at Stiklestad area and then retire in the direction of Röra.

The enemy at Trone appeared to have occupied a hill to the west of the main road and a few shots were exchanged with them. They otherwise remained impassive.

4th KOYLI were ordered forward from Röra to hold the causeway on the Inderroy peninsula. This movement apparently caused the Germans who were marching on Strommen to turn northwards to Vist. 4th Lincolns were ordered to send a second company to reinforce Vist and to take up positions from re-entrant of fjord west of Todnes to crossroads north of north end of Strommen Lake. Norwegian commander (Colonel Wetter) was asked and agreed to send two ski squadrons, one to watch the road Seli-Hofstad and the other to the road Sem-Viken.

0805 German warship reported by the Hallamshires to be moving slowly up the coast to Foldefoss.

0830 German warship reported moving north up fjord, apparently contemplating landing between Foldefoss and Malme.

0910 4th Lincolns were ordered to hold Vist peninsula at all costs and to move reserves in that direction in order to attack the Germans approaching in his direction.

1100 Local inhabitants report that 600 men have landed at Vangshylla.

Enemy air were active from early morning till late evening. During early part of day, enemy planes appeared to be on recce only.

1200 Enemy planes started bombing Steinkjer.

Several raids took place during the afternoon, each time carried out by four or more planes. By dusk, the whole town was in ruins, the road bridge destroyed, sawmills and houses burning, the railway line was reported broken about Summen and again a few miles south of Snasa. The water supply in the surrounding country was broken.

During the afternoon, the Germans machine gunned roads in the Steinkjer-Sparbu area and some bombs were dropped. During the day B Company 4th Lincolns advanced against the enemy on the Vist peninsula and tried to deploy off the road, which was impossible owing to the depth of snow – 3 to 4 feet. The enemy who possessed snow shoes were at a great advantage and B Company withdrew.

In the afternoon of 21st orders were sent to 4th KOYLI to hold the line Röra-Sparbu and during the night 21st/22nd to withdraw companies and section RE about Trone-Stiklestad to area Sem.

4th Lincolns were ordered to maintain their positions.

Hallamshires were ordered to send one company to Polling as Brigade reserve.

22nd April

On 22nd orders were given for a retirement for the night 22nd/23rd:-

4th KOYLI From Röra-Sparbu-Sem to Henning, thence northwards via Babuen-Ogndal-Stod-Sunen-Folling-Kvam road.

4th Lincolns To retire via railway bridge (if still standing) or bridge 3 miles north of Steinkjer-Asp fork roads -Folling, covered by company at Egge.

Hallamshires To maintain rear guard position Folling-New Beitstad-Hjelle with forward platoon at Malme. Platoon at Foldefoss to be withdrawn.

Brigade HQ Were to remain for night 22nd/23rd at Asp road junction.

During 22nd enemy to west and south of Röra took little action but enemy destroyers in fjord near Trones shelled Sparbu and Maere. 4th Lincolns position at Vist was heavily attacked by fire throughout the day, mortars and light artillery from the ground and from destroyers in the fjord south of Trones.

From 1400 to 1900 enemy machine gunned all the roads in the whole Brigade area.

Company Hallamshires at Folling was withdrawn to New Beitstad and platoon at Malme was withdrawn to watch road east of Hjelle.

1130 I was visited by GOC Lieutenant-General de Wiart, who instructed me to withdraw my Brigade along road Steinkjer-Namdalseid-Bangsund and not by road Folling-Kvam.

Orders to this effect were sent out to all units, but failed to reach one company, 4th Lincolns, who had become separated from their battalion during the fight.

1900 200 Germans on skis drawing some light artillery on sledges were seen coming at a good pace across the ice from the direction Todnes to Steinkjer, where they landed. These were engaged by the company from the 4th Lincolns at Egge who failed to stop them. Germans replied by firing at Egge with heavy machine guns and light artillery.

23rd April

During the night 22nd/23rd 300 men of 4th Lincolns came through outpost positions at Asp and were moved by the limited amount of MT to Elde, including company from Egge.

4th KOYLI bivouacked in area Stod.

At that time nothing was known or heard of the remainder of the 4th Lincolns but

Brigade got in touch with the 4th KOYLI at Sunnan.

During the night 23rd/24th 4th KOYLI marched from Stod to Namdalseid via Polling. It was only possible to assist a few of the personnel with the limited amount of MT available.

24th April

On the morning of 24th information was received from Folling that the missing part of 4th Lincolns had marched to Kvam. Orders were at once sent to them to return via Folling to Hjelle, where they arrived in the evening of 24th.

About 2030 on the evening of 23rd, reports were received from Norwegian forces that Germans were entering Sunnan from the south, along the line of the railway and their battalion at Folling was evacuating this position. There was no subsequent confirmation of this enemy move.

On the night 24th/25th fighting patrols from the Hallamshires were sent to (i) Malme, (ii) Asp cross roads and (iii) Folling. Three lorries and escort were sent to Kvam to pick up supplies and kit which had been placed at Kvam in anticipation of that being our line of retirement.

25th April

On the morning of 25th Brigade was situated as follows:-

Hallamshires Hjelle inclusive to Elde inclusive. Hospital, supplies, etc., Namdalseid

4th KOYLI from Namdalseid to Aargaard

4th Lincolns from Rodhammer to Reitin

This wide dispersion was necessary in order to find cover for the men at night. Enemy air activity on the 23rd was negligible and on 24th and 25th nil.

Appendix K

Documents relating to the re-embarkation of forces which had fought at Namsos

146th Infantry Brigade Admin Instructions Re-embarkation.

1. These instructions are to be read in conjunction with the 146th Infantry Brigade Operational Order issued under this heading.
2. Baggage.
Officers. What each can carry plus one bedding roll if in possession. Maximum weight 40 pounds.
Other Ranks. Rifle, personal equipment, pack (including greatcoat) one blanket per man. No kitbags will be carried.
3. Rations.
Preserved meat and biscuits will be issued to each man under unit arrangements.
4. Arms.
Rifles. It is possible that a proportion of rifles will be left behind to be handed over to the Norwegian Army. Men without rifles will be allotted to assisting in carrying valuable signal and other equipment and will be made available to this HQ.
Bren guns and A/T rifles. These will be embarked unboxed.
5. Ammunition.
All ammunition will be left except what is normally carried on the man.
6. Equipment (G1098).
Valuable signalling stores, etc., will, if possible, be taken, in particular W/T sets. Assistance in carrying these will, as far as possible, be arranged by this HQ.
7. Destruction.
No burning will take place in the open. Secret, confidential and security documents which are not essential will be burnt in stoves in houses. Any valuable equipment, etc., which at the last moment it is not found to embark, will be rendered useless by removing parts, depositing in the sea, or by being broken up by any means.
8. Reference paragraph 4, detailed orders regarding rifles to be left behind will be issued later.

Operation Order No. 2 dated 2nd May 1940 by Lieutenant Colonel C. Robins CO The Hallamshire Battalion, The York and Lancaster Regiment.

Orders for Withdrawal – 2nd May 1940.

1. Information.

Enemy cycle patrol in contact with French detachment at Hjelle. They were driven off and there has been no contact since.

2. Own Troops.

French detachment withdrew to South Aargaard late last night. They will withdraw tonight through KOYLI and Hallamshires to Klingen at 2030. They will be clear of Skdle by 2130.

They will blow the bridge at Aargaard before leaving. On arrival at Klingen they will protect the left flank. The KOYLI will withdraw through the Hallamshires to Namsos bridge area after 2000.

Two French A/T guns will withdraw with the French detachment as far as Bangsund bridge where they will come under command of Hallamshires.

3. Intention.

Hallamshires will cover withdrawal of KOYLI and will deny the Bangsund bridge area to the enemy until further notice.

4. Method.

Phase 1. C Company will form rear guard and will move through B Company to Kling area by march route as soon as rear of KOYLI have passed them.

Phase 2. B Company less one platoon will form rear guard and will move through A Company to Bangsund as soon as C Company are through them.

Phase 3. One platoon of B Company will remain south of tunnel to protect the preparation of the tunnel for demolition and blocking by French engineers. This platoon will not withdraw until ordered to do so by CO Hallamshires.

Movement during daylight.

It is possible that the movement of B Company will have to be carried out after dawn tomorrow, in which case they will move at not more and not thicker density of one section every 200 yards. In the event of aircraft coming over, they will immediately hide in the trees by the road and will not move until all is clear.

Demolition of tunnel.

The tunnel will be prepared for demolition by French engineers and will also be blocked by all their available material by the platoon. The tunnel will only be blown by orders of the CO Hallamshires. The bridge at Bangsund will only be blown by orders from the GOC or, in the event of an attack, by CO Hallamshires.

5. Administrative.
(i) The reserve SAA will be sent to Rear Brigade HQ at Skage tonight under arrangements to be made by the QM.
(ii) Two 15 cwt trucks will report to C Company at 1800 to move their baggage. This is all the transport they will receive.
(iii) Two 15 cwt trucks will report to B Company after the KOYLI have passed through. This is all the transport B Company will receive to move their baggage.

6. Intercommunication.
(i) By cable to Adjutant and QM Stores. By runner to remainder.
(ii) Captain W. Cave will act as Liaison Officer with the French detachment and will inform KOYLI, C Company and B Company when the French detachment has passed.

1st May 1940. The Hallamshire Battalion. The York and Lancaster Regiment.

Orders by Lieutenant Colonel C. Robins.

Information.

Enemy. Not in contact.

Own Troops. 4th KOYLI will withdraw from their recent position tonight to area north of Namsos bridge by MT. A French detachment will come under command from midnight tonight and will act as our rear guard.

Intention.

To hold Bangsund bridge area until 2100 tomorrow 2nd May 1940 when the Battalion will withdraw to Namsos.

Method.
(1) Two sections Chasseurs Alpins will occupy rear guard position about Gryten and will remain there until about 2030 tomorrow.
(2) B Company will occupy an outpost position in vicinity of their present billets at Fjor until about 1800 tomorrow.
(3) C Company will move tonight by march route to area Klingen; they will not move until the rear of 4th KOYLI have passed through.
(4) A Company will occupy the French positions on the north side of the Bangsund bridge as soon as 13th Regiment Chasseurs Alpins leave. Time of their withdrawal and that of the other companies will be issued later.
(5) Two French anti-tank guns will move tonight to a position covering the Bangsund bridge.
(6) Battalion's withdrawal tomorrow will be by MT which will report to companies late tonight. It will be carefully hidden by them during the daylight tomorrow.
(7) No movement more than is absolutely necessary will be made by day.

Administrative.
(1) All fighting equipment i.e. Bren guns, anti-tank rifles, mortars etc. and dixies (iron cooking pots) will be moved and every man may take with him his sea kitbag if in possession. The pack containing groundsheet will be worn on the back.
(2) Reserve ammunition and any spare rifles etc. in the QM stores will be moved tonight to Namsos. This movement must not interfere with that of other troops.

Intercommunication.

Signals Officer will cut all telephone communication on the north side of the Bangsund bridge from midnight tonight.

Communication forward to B Company and Chasseurs Alpins will be by DR. Captain W. Cave will act as LO with the French.

Brigadier Phillips, 146th Brigade commander, issued an order to his troops on the return journey as follows:

146th Infantry Brigade Order of the Day.
At Sea.
6th May1940.

I wish the following appreciation of their services to be brought to the notice of all ranks who served under my command during the recent operations in Norway.

To Officers, Warrant Officers, NCOs and Men of the 146th Infantry Brigade and attached troops.

The Brigade and attached troops were called upon to fulfil a difficult and arduous task in the Namsos area in Norway. I am sure that the part played by the Brigade and attached troops, in an entirely novel sphere of operations, was not an unimportant one and that the Brigade successfully fulfilled the task allotted to it. The fact that the Brigade was faced with difficulties of deep snow, indifferent roads, improvised transport, subjected to enemy attack from land and sea and intensive attack from the air, to which it possessed no effective counter beyond the normal infantry weapons, and yet was able to fight a two day engagement and then to withdraw successfully under very adverse conditions, will surely be remembered with pride by all who took part.

The loss of personnel and material that was necessarily entailed I deplore, but am quite confident that they were not incurred in vain.

The experiences that have been gained by this initiation into modern warfare will stand us in good stead in whatever role we may be called upon to perform in the future.

I wish to record my appreciation of the cheerfulness and courage shown by all ranks under the difficult and trying conditions to which they have been subjected.

I further wish to express my thanks for the wholehearted and loyal co-operation I have received from all members of the staff and units under my command throughout the operations in Norway.

Appendix L

Accounts from the War Diary of the Sherwood Foresters, 16–23 April 1940

The Left Wing account 16th to 23rd April 1940 by Major Dowson.

17th April Left port of embarkation.

18th April Left Wing arrived at Åndalsnes at 2000 and disembarkation was completed by 2100. Some marines, who had already arrived acted as guides and took A Company and ½ HQ Company to the local schools and D Company to billets in the near vicinity of the landing stage. A party of A Company was kept on the quay to sort and load ammunition and stores on to a train.

OC Left Wing received verbal orders from Commander 148th Brigade, who with Brigade Staff had accompanied Left Wing to move to Dombaas with one company by train leaving at midnight. D Company were warned for this duty and entrained at 2345. Sufficient stores for D Company's immediate needs had by this hour been placed aboard the train by A Company's working party. The train left shortly after midnight and arrived at Dombaas without incident at 0400 on 19th April. The Brigade Commander accompanied us.

19th April On arrival at Dombaas D Company was at once detrained and suitably dispersed. OC D Company allotted platoon areas, AA defence posts and detailed a party to offload stores from the train and arranged for his men's meal.

The enemy were reported to have cut the railway eight kilometres to the south east. The Brigade Commander, using a locomotive and one coach, proceeded to reconnoitre the situation. He returned to Dombaas at 0730. The following was the situation as received from the Brigade Commander:

1. The enemy, estimated at 500 strong, consisted of parachute troops. They were in two groups, covering the railway which they had cut.

2. Two groups of Norwegians were attacking these two groups, one operating from the north west and the other from the south east.

OC Left Wing received instructions from Brigade Commander to prepare for and carry out a dawn attack on the following day if the Norwegians had not, by then, been successful in their attacks.

Brigade Commander returned to Åndalsnes, stating that he would send up A Company and ½ HQ Company as soon as possible. At 0830 OC Left Wing went with the Assistant Adjutant (Lieutenant Bradley) to reconnoitre the position, taking one Bren gun section for local protection. This reconnaissance group used the locomotive and coach to within 3,000 yards of the enemy's position, where the train was left standing in a convenient tunnel. Soon after leaving the train a naval detachment with a 3.7 inch howitzer was found in position on the railway embankment. Also close by was the HQ of the Norwegian force operating from the north west.

Reconnaissance group remained here until 1200, during which time the enemy was constantly being flown over by his own planes, from which supplies of food and ammunition had been dropped. The enemy was now concentrated in a large farm building overlooking the railway and was being subjected to heavy concentrations of mortar and MG fire.

At 1200 the enemy surrendered and a number were made prisoners. Approximately seventy passed through Dombaas station in the first party. The train was used to take them from the scene of the battle to Åndalsnes. Returning to Dombaas, OC Left Wing rang up Brigade HQ at Åndalsnes and reported the capture of the position and the opening up of the railway by the Norwegians. The Brigade Commander said that A Company and ½ HQ Company were on their way up to Dombaas and ordered that they should not detrain. Instead OC Left Wing was to join their train on arrival and proceed southwards, where the Left Wing would come under command of HQ Norwegian Forces.

A and ½ HQ Companies remained in billets at Åndalsnes for the night of 18th/19th and left by train at 1125, arriving at Dombaas at 1430. OC Left Wing and A/Adjutant joined A and ½ HQ Companies train at Dombaas station, which left at 1500 for the south. Also present were Captain James RN, two Norwegians and a liaison officer. Before leaving, D Company was ordered to follow by train as quickly as another train could be commandeered. OC A Company reported that enemy planes had flown over Åndalsnes at 0800 that morning, but no bombs had been dropped.

At 1700 the air alarm was sounded and everyone had to leave the train. There were, however, no bombs and the men rejoined the train which reached Farborg at 1845. A and ½ HQ Companies detrained and boarded a number of lorries which were waiting. The baggage and stores were offloaded and placed also in lorries. This convoy of MT left Farborg at 1930 and arrived at Biri, on the west bank of Lake Mjösa at 2130. OC Left Wing reported to Norwegian HQ at Biri for orders. This force was known as 'Dahl Force'.

The following was the situation as given to OC Left Wing. Information (i) The Norwegian force on the west of Lake Mjösa consisted of one brigade infantry of three battalions, one battery field artillery, engineers and a supply column. (ii) This force was holding Gjövik and the river to the south of it. (iii) Colonel Dahl, who commanded the force, stressed the danger of his right flank being outflanked by the enemy. The left flank was secured by the lake, on which it rested.

In view of this threat, Colonel Dahl ordered that Left Wing should move to Nykirke, approximately thirty kilometres away, where it was to cover the right flank of Dahl Force. OC Left Wing requested to be given one company of ski troops to protect flanks of own force. This was considered very necessary owing to the snow, which lay to a depth of two to three feet. These ski troops were duly promised.

On receiving the above instructions, orders were issued to A and ½ HQ Companies, to divest themselves of all unnecessary baggage and take only the minimum stores, in the form of food and ammunition, which would be required for the next twenty-four hours.

A suitable barn was taken over as a dump and a guard of one NCO and four men were placed over it. Due to D Company's late arrival they did not receive this order and they took their baggage and stores forward with them.

20th April The force, once more comprising the whole of Left Wing, arrived at Nykirke by 0200, the 20th, having driven through a blizzard, the road being at least one foot deep in fresh snow. On arrival at Nykirke our transport was required elsewhere and it therefore had to be released. The troops were fed in the church by kindly inhabitants, during which time OC Left Wing made his reconnaissance of the position. It proved entirely unsuitable, being overlooked from the front and the fields of fire were not good. A kilometre in front, however, the ground sloped steeply to a stream and gave the defence good fields of fire, some of which were completely enfiladed from the front. It was decided, therefore, to occupy this position in front of Nykirke. Left Wing was in occupation of this position by 0500. Dispositions taken up were as shown by accompanying sketch map number 2 on page 93.

A road block was constructed just above a sharp bend in the road and on the steepest gradient, marked x in the sketch. The snow was an average of three feet deep. It's [sic] surface became soft after some sunshine and anyone attempting to cross it frequently went up to his middle in the snow. It thus proved a valuable obstacle, during the day, to all except those on skis or using the road.

At 0700 a report was received from a civilian, stating that the enemy was pressing round the right flank of the Norwegian position. A patrol consisting of one officer and one section was immediately sent forward to verify this information and, on their return, confirmed that a small party of the enemy, approximately a platoon in strength, had passed along the road which ran parallel to our position, in pursuit of some Norwegians who had withdrawn in a north westerly direction.

At 1100 a Norwegian officer came in and reported that Gjövik had fallen. OC Left Wing immediately rang up HQ Dahl Force and asked for confirmation. No such information, however, had reached that HQ. Note:- If the enemy captured Gjövik it would cause a serious threat to Left Wing, situated as they were twenty three kilometres out on the extreme right. No communications existed other than the road up which the force had come to Nykirke. This road ran parallel to and only a few kilometres north of the front line. See map 1.

At 1300 Colonel Dahl rang up to say that the information in respect of Gjövik was correct. Realising the situation of his small British force he issued instructions for its withdrawal, after first handing over to the company of ski troops, which had previously been promised but had not yet arrived. The orders were for Left Wing to withdraw to Biri, using the transport which brought the ski company. They arrived at 1330 and the position was handed over to them. Their transport, which consisted of commandeered vehicles, was totally inadequate for half a battalion. D Company was ordered to take the transport and proceed to Redallan, at the end of the road and take up a position astride the lakeside road facing south. They were to send back the transport for A and ½ HQ Companies. OC Left Wing then went to Biri for further instructions and to arrange for adequate transport.

D Company left Nykirke at 1430 reaching Redallan by 1530 and sent back the transport for A and ½ HQ Companies. A Company taking what they could of ½ HQ Company, left Nykirke at 1630 and having reached Redallan, sent back the transport for the remainder of ½ HQ Company, who reached Redallan at 1800.

A Company with a part of ½ HQ Company reached Helverun, where they were eventually directed at 1900. Helverun was ten kilometres north of Biri. The transport returned to Redallan for D and the remainder of ½ HQ Company who arrived at Helverun at 2300.

At HQ Dahl Force OC Left Wing was given the following information and instructions.

Information. The enemy had succeeded in taking Gjövik and had crossed to the north bank of the river.

Intention. It was the intention to withdraw Dahl Force northwards.

Method. Left Wing was to become the rear guard to Dahl Force and was to take up it's [sic] first position at Helverun. This position was to be held until the last element of Dahl Force had passed through and for a further number of hours. These timings would be issued later.

OC Left Wing immediately requested that:-

(1) He should be supplied with adequate transport which was to be under his command.
(2) A company of ski troops to be placed under command for the purpose of guarding the right flank of the rear guard. The left was protected by the lake.
(3) A detachment of engineers, complete with demolitions for mining and blowing selected bridges.

Requests (1) and (3) materialised and proved to be of great advantage to the rear guard, both from its mobility point of view and the delaying of the enemy's advance. On leaving Biri OC Left Wing went to Helverun, reaching it at 1630 and spent until 1850 reconnoitring positions down to and including platoon and section posts, so that valuable time might be saved and work continued on the positions at daybreak next day.

At 2000 he again visited Biri where he was informed of the plan of withdrawal. Colonel Dahl intimated that he might require one company to hold the River Stokeröen, one kilometre in front of Redallan on the 21st. In the event of this taking place the Stokeröen would become the first rear guard position.

On return to Helverun it was found that D Company had arrived with the remainder of ½ HQ Company. As D Company had already held a position in the vicinity of Stokeröen and A Company had been allotted their sector on the Helverun position, D Company was selected for the forward position and duly warned as liable to go to the Stokeröen next day to occupy the position.

21st April The night of the 20th/21st was the first rest that D Company had had since the night of 15th/16th and the second for A and ½ HQ Companies, who had secured a very disturbed nights [sic] rest at Åndalsnes on the night of the 18th/19th owing to having had to supply working parties up to midnight.

Reveille on the 21st was at 0500. A Norwegian liaison officer had been sent to collect a load of wire and tools from Biri the previous evening and digging and wiring of the position commenced at 0630. During the night, the transport, a collection of commandeered vehicles, arrived in charge of a Norwegian officer.

Colonel Dahl had rung up during the night and confirmed that one company was required to occupy a rear guard position on the Stokeröen in the morning and that it was to be [in] position by 1200 on the 21st.

At 0900 D Company left Helverun for the Stokeröen arriving in the vicinity at 1000, where they were met by OC Left Wing who had gone to the Stokeröen in advance to make a reconnaissance. Owing to enemy aerial activities D Company were made to debus at Redallan village and moved up on foot to their position on the Stokeröen, where they were in occupation by 1200. Dispositions on the Stokeröen were as shown in sketch map number 3 on page 96.

Up to date the enemy had not bombed or machine gunned Left Wing's positions, although he had been very active with reconnaissance planes. In view of this instructions were issued to all Officers and ORs to the effect that they were on no account to open fire on enemy planes unless bombing or MG fire had first been opened on them. It was considered that the enemy were endeavouring to locate the various movements and positions of the force and had so far not actually done so. As an additional precaution to prevent being spotted and as camouflage for men in section and platoon posts, a number of rolls of white americano cloth was procured, with which smocks were made and issued to the men.

At 1200 Brigade Commander and Lieutenant Colonel Clarke arrived at Stokeröen and inspected the position and the bridge over the river, which had been mined and was ready for demolition. Brigade Commander informed OC Left Wing that up to date the enemy had not used tanks but was liberally supplied with tracked vehicles used as troop carriers. The enemy had made considerable progress on the east bank of the lake and was approximately on a line with Helverun, fifteen kilometres north of the Stokeröen. As the lake hereabouts was only between 3,000 and 4,000 yards wide, the enemy's advance threatened our communications along the lakeside road, which was the only practicable one.

Lieutenant Bradley (Assistant Adjutant) was sent down to Helverun in the Brigade Commander's car with instructions to OC A Company to complete the digging and wiring of D Company's area, which they commenced at 1600, after completing their own tasks.

At 1400, OC Left Wing got in touch with Major Brock, commanding the left forward battalion of the Norwegian forces and together they went to Biri for a conference with Colonel Dahl, to coordinate the plan of withdrawal. En-route they were heavily shelled by enemy field artillery, firing from the east bank of the lake and one of their cars was put out of action. Colonel Dahl informed them that the withdrawal of his force was to commence as soon as darkness fell that evening, the 21st, and it was considered that the rearmost battalion under Major Brock would be clear of the Stokeröen bridge by 0500 on the 22nd. Major Brock was instructed to inform OC D Company when his last element had passed over the bridge, whereupon OC D Company was to order the bridge to be blown. Colonel Dahl instructed that D Company should hold the Stokeröen position for two hours after the bridge had been blown and then withdraw northwards through the Helverun positions, which was now to be held by A Company and ½ HQ Company, to a new position at 'Escarpment Hill', eleven kilometres north of Helverun. He stated that engineers were already preparing bridges for demolition along the route of withdrawal, which would be blown successively after D Company had passed over next day.

Whilst this conference was taking place the enemy bombed and machine gunned HQ Dahl Force and the village of Biri. During this bombardment, the C-in-C Norwegian Army arrived together with Lieutenant Colonel King-Salter, the British Military Attaché.

At 1600 Major Brock and OC Left Wing returned to Stokeröen by a mountain track, thus avoiding the lakeside road which was still under artillery fire and aerial bombardment. They arrived at the Stokeröen at 1700. OC D Company was acquainted with the situation and given his instructions which entailed the blowing of the bridge; the holding of the position for two hours afterwards and his withdrawal to Escarpment Hill behind Helverun. D Company was self-contained with its own transport, which had been concealed in the woods surrounding Redallan village. OC Left Wing left the Stokeröen position at 1830 and arrived at Helverun at 1930 and informed the force there of the proposed leap-frogging of D Company next day to the new position in their rear. OC A Company was instructed to (1) To take over the Helverun position with A and ½ HQ Companies. (2) To drop the road block when the last of D Company was clear next day. (3) To hold the position for one hour after the road block has been let down. (4) Then withdraw his force to the new position on Escarpment Hill.

OC A Company reported that during the day an enemy plane had flown over the position at 1500 and again at 1630, during both times it had machine gunned the position. During the second visit at 1630 the AA section and three Bren guns of the company had opened fire on the low flying plane, which was hit. An enemy plane was seen to have fallen, one mile to the south of the position, by the OC Left Wing on his return journey to Helverun that evening which had not been there previously. Dispositions at Helverun were as shown in sketch map number 4 on page 102.

On completion of the orders to OC A Company OC Left Wing proceeded to make a reconnaissance of the new position on Escarpment Hill. It was a bright moon-lit night. Leaving with a liaison officer at 2130, he returned to Helverun at 0200 on the 22nd and rang up HQ Dahl Force to make arrangements for the despatch of tools and wire to Escarpment Hill, also for the bridge there to be prepared for demolition. This bridge had been prepared and the tools and wire dumped by 1100 on the 22nd.

During the 21st the A/QM (Lieutenant Sketchley) had been engaged in recovering all Left Wing's surplus baggage, from the dumps at Biri and Helverun, to the railway station at Farborg, so that the force would not be unduly hindered with baggage and stores. This arduous task, on a road completely covered for fifteen kilometres by enemy artillery, was completed by 2000 that night without mishap.

On arrival at Åndalsnes OC Left Wing had requested the Brigade Commander for a medical officer and Captain Stoker RAMC was attached. Regimental Aid Posts had been set up at convenient sites behind the positions at Nykirke and Helverun. At the latter place Left Wing was supplied with additional staff including a Norwegian doctor, who was placed under Captain Stoker.

At 2030 on the 21st the Norwegian withdrawal, through D Company's position on Stokeröen commenced.

22nd April Throughout the whole of the night 21st/22nd Dahl Force was passing through the Helverun position. Their rear guard party passed through the Stokeröen position at 0500, when orders were given by OC D Company to blow the bridge. D Company maintained their position until 0700 and their leading platoon passed through the Helverun position at 0800. OC D Company arrived at 1030 with the last platoon and reported having been heavily shelled on the road between Stokeröen and Biri. One truck had received a direct hit, five ORs being killed and one officer (Second Lieutenant Dowson) and two ORs wounded. The Norwegian engineers blew a number of bridges behind the withdrawal of D Company, thus retarding the advance of the enemy. D Company were collected at Escarpment Hill by 1100, where they were allotted the right sector of the position. OC A Company let down the road block at 1030 and after holding his position for one hour, withdrew A and ½ HQ Companies to Escarpment Hill, arriving there at 1200. They were allotted the left sector.

Due to the position having previously been partially dug by the Norwegians, first tasks were devoted to the siting of Bren guns, A/T rifles, wiring and the forming of a road block on the short causeway leading from the bridge to the high ground. The bridge was blown at 1400 after the Norwegian engineers and some mule transport had passed through the position.

This position was a strong one but lacked the deep snow of the other positions. It was believed that a stand would be made here. This was welcomed as everyone was extremely tired, due to the continual movements and the taking up of successive positions day and night. Dispositions on Escarpment Hill were as shown in sketch map number 5 on page 103. Fresh meat having been procured, a hot meal was arranged for that evening.

At 1800 instructions were received, ordering Left Wing to withdraw from Escarpment Hill and go to Gausal via the mountain road which, here, joined the lakeside road.

As the meal was due to be served at 1900 it was decided to give the troops this meal as arranged and, in view of the new orders, move at 2000. Instructions were accordingly given to this effect. Such however, was not to be the case. At 1815 further instructions were received, ordering the rear guard to evacuate their position at once, as the enemy had crossed the lake on the ice, above Lillehammer. The bridge at Lillehammer over the lake had been blown at 0400 that morning. This meant that the enemy were now seven kilometres in our rear and had cut our communications to the north via the lakeside road.

The darkness of the night, together with a heavy snowstorm and the overcrowding of the transport, which was on the very short side, all added to the difficulties of starting and it was not until 2200 before the convoy was ready. All arrangements were in the hands of the Norwegians, but to ensure the arrival of the column, the Norwegian officer i/c transport was ordered to bring up the rear and collect vehicles which might break down and the OC Left wing, together with the Norwegian liaison officer, led the way.

23rd April D Company who were in the lead, arrived at Gausal at 0200. Unfortunately, however, the column became separated when one of A Company's trucks broke down and the rear of the column did not appear at Gausal until 0600. It had been hoped that a rest could be obtained at this secluded place in the mountains. The local priest had most kindly placed his church, which was well warmed at our disposal. D Company was actually 'bedded down' for the remainder of the night, when fresh orders were received at

0400. These directed that Left Wing was to rejoin it's own Brigade, on the east bank of the lake at Tretten, where it was directed to proceed at once. Furthermore it was intimated that the outskirts of this village were already in the hands of the enemy. D Company was roused and loading of vehicles was complete just before A and 1/2 HQ Companies arrived at 0600.

The column left Gausal at 0600 in groups, to prevent the whole being surprised. Bren guns and A/T rifles were placed on each vehicle, ready to deal with ambushes. No enemy, however, were met and Left Wing reached Tretten at 0700 without incident. At Tretten enquiries were made for Brigade HQ. Rear HQ of 5th Leicesters was found, whose Adjutant reported that Brigade HQ was three kilometres south of the village and was then engaged with the enemy, together with the remnants of 5th Leicesters and Right Wing (8th Foresters).

As the enemy had crossed the lake just north of Lillehammer, it meant that our right flank was exposed. OC Left Wing, therefore, placed D Company on the west bank of the river flowing into the north end of Lake Mjösa. By this measure the approaches to the Tretten bridge were guarded. A and ½ HQ Companies were sent to the creamery, where they were told to feed themselves and prepare and send out food to D Company. They were also to hold themselves in immediate readiness for further orders.

At 0730, after seeing to the above, OC Left Wing went south with his A/Adjutant to get in touch with Brigade HQ. After going three kilometres he found HQ Right Wing and reported to Lieutenant Colonel T. Ford, informing him of events since separation, at the port of embarkation, on the night 16th/17th April. These included the withdrawal of Dahl Force, the employment of Left Wing throughout as the rear guard; the few casualties suffered and the extremely exhausted state of the officers and men from lack of rest and meals.

Having reported to Lieutenant Colonel T. Ford, OC Left Wing relinquished his independent command and resumed his appointment as Second-in-Command 8th Sherwood Foresters.

Appendix M

Account from Major B. Dowson on the Activities of the 8th Sherwood Foresters, 6 April–7 May 1940

The Battalion was finally ordered to entrain for an unknown destination on Saturday, 6th April, in two trains at 10.45 and 11.45 p.m. respectively. The first train, under the command of Lieutenant Colonel T. Ford, contained C and D Companies and half HQ Company, while the second train, under the command of Major J. Roberts, contained A and B Companies and half HQ Company, the writer travelling in the second train. The second train was considerably delayed owing to a railway accident on the main line and we were over two hours late arriving at Waverley station, Edinburgh, where tea was provided. The Movement Control Officers still being unable or unwilling to inform us of our destination, the writer went forward to the engine and asked the engine driver where we were going to and immediately received the answer "Rosyth". Rosyth was duly reached at about 9.30 a.m. The troops detrained on the dockyard station in slight rain and endeavoured to fit each other with the impedimenta entailed in full marching order. This operation was hurried on by a party of Naval Officers who immediately arrived on the scene, took charge of the troops and separated the Warrant Officers and Sergeants who were put in charge of a Petty Officer. To the amazement of the troops, these two parties were immediately marched on to the jetty and embarked in HMS *Glasgow*, where the party which had come in the first train were already installed. Nothing of any particular note occurred during the remainder of the day except sleep and the enjoyment by both Officers and Men of excellent Navy rations. All our motley collection of stores, amounting to something under 50 tons, was duly conveyed aboard ship by baggage parties with the assistance of naval ratings.

Word had been received that the ship should be ready to sail at 8 a.m. next morning. Then at 11.30 news came that several ships including HMS *Glasgow* were to sail without troops at 12.45 at 10 minute intervals. On receipt of these orders the Navy acted methodically and swiftly. The troops were told that a meal would be served to them immediately and the Navy would put all our stores ashore. This was duly done and the confusion and mixture of stores on the dock side is quite indescribable. The troops marched off the ship laden with their equipment, Officers mainly carrying their own, between 12.30 and 12.40 and promptly at 12.45 hawsers were slackened off and HMS *Glasgow* slipped away from the quay. As well as ourselves the 5th Leicesters, 4th Lincolns and 4th KOYLI were on the quayside and we were faced with the above mentioned indescribable confusion of stores and the necessity of conveying ourselves and stores to some place for the night. We had already been in touch with Scottish Command and it appeared that there was a camp which could easily hold four battalions unoccupied three miles north of Dunfermline. Lorries were only available for such baggage as it was estimated we should need during the next day or two and A Company were put on to sort out such immediate requirements from the mass of stores on the quay. The remainder of the troops had to march the eleven miles from Rosyth to the camp. A guard of one platoon was left to look after the stores on the dock for the night and it should be mentioned that this party had a busy time. The Admiral in charge of the dockyard refused to allow all the small arms ammunition, mortar bombs and other demolition explosives to remain in the vicinity of the dockyard in case of an air raid, and this platoon, in company with the guard left behind by the 5th Leicesters, worked all night placing this ammunition and explosives in barges for taking out of the way up the river.

During the Battalion's stay in Dunfermline camp a party had been sent down to Rosyth dockyard to load the bulk of our stores into railway wagons and a guard was set over them. One morning this guard reported that the Railway Company had removed the wagons during the night to an unknown destination and it was not until much later on that we discovered where they had been taken. On Saturday afternoon, 13th April, we received the order to march out of camp at 7 o'clock on Sunday morning and proceed to Rosyth dockyard, where we would be taken by boat to a liner which was lying off Leith. We were informed that the baggage wagons mentioned above had been sent to Leith and that the contents had been placed in the hold of this liner. This was very unfortunate because B and D Companies were told that they would not travel in the liner with the rest of the Battalion, but would travel in HMS *Arethusa* and HMS *Galatea* respectively from Rosyth. Captain Branston and Major Kirkland spent the whole of the night of Saturday April 13th in RMS *Orion*, sorting out as far as possible the ammunition and stores etc. which would probably be required by these two companies should they be separated from the Battalion on arrival on the other side. The ammunition and stores were eventually loaded on to trucks and brought by road to Rosyth, from which they had originally been removed and arrived at about 11.30 a.m. on Sunday morning. B and D Companies and a portion of the 148th Brigade staff remained in these two cruisers tied up at Rosyth dock for the nights of Sunday, 14th and Monday, 15th, without any particular incident and there this history must leave them while the activities of the rest of the Battalion, which the writer accompanied, are explored.

RMS *Orion* was another revelation to the troops, practically all of whom had never seen the inside of a liner except in films. Each man was accommodated in a bunk and the Officers were provided with very pleasant cabins and everyone thought they had fallen on their feet.

Monday, 15th April was spent in boat drill, mustering, issue of lifebelts and in general routine activities such as practising abandoning ship etc. Tuesday, 16th April, inspections of arms were carried out and physical training. Letters home, duly censored, were also permitted on this day. At 5 p.m. the order for a further move was received and HMS *Galatea*, HMS *Arethusa*, HMS *Carlyle*, HMS *Curacao* and two destroyers appeared. We and the 5th Leicesters were told that we must all be on board the respective vessels allotted to us by 6.30 p.m., but owing to the crowded gangways in *Orion* and the quantity of arms and equipment which it was necessary to transfer this proved to be quite impossible and it was not until well after 7 p.m. that the troops and their arms and kit bags were transferred. Several of the latter were dropped into the sea as the only possible method of putting them aboard the cruisers was to throw them on the deck, and it can hardly be expected that even with so large a target a hit would be registered each time. The Battalion was now sorted out as follows for the night of Tuesday, April 16th:-

HMS *Galatea* – D Company (already aboard) A Company about one-third of HQ Company

HMS *Arethusa* – B Company (already aboard) C Company the majority of HQ Company

Half the 5th Leicesters were distributed among the four smaller vessels and the other half returned temporarily to Dunfermline camp. It may be mentioned at this juncture that the reasons for this entraining, detraining, embarking and disembarking were never given to us and we could only exercise our imagination as to what the next move was likely to be. While in HMS *Glasgow* we were issued with maps of Stavanger and while in RMS *Orion* these were withdrawn and we were issued with maps of Namsos. These were withdrawn in *Arethusa* and it was then indicated to us that we were bound for Åndalsnes, the only map available being in the possession of the CO and this was only a tourist road map.

During the first night we spent on *Galatea* and *Arethusa*, an attempt was made by two overworked and perspiring parties commanded by the Quartermaster and that of the 5th Leicesters to sort out the Battalion stores in the holds of *Orion* and somehow or other during the night the bulk of these were conveyed from *Orion* to the cruisers. In case it should be forgotten later, it may be mentioned here that of the stores which were not transferred from Orion, the principal and most important items were all the 2" mortar HE bombs, almost all the 3" mortar HE bombs and practically all the Officers' Mess stores. [Author's note: the latter probably on purpose by the sweating fatigue parties!] Also during the night two AA Bofors guns were shipped to each of the larger cruisers *Galatea* and *Arethusa*.

The convoy sailed at 7 a.m. on the morning of Wednesday, April 17th, in the following order:-

The two destroyers leading, followed by *Galatea*, *Curacao*, *Arethusa* and *Carlyle*. Norway was reached at 8 p.m. on Thursday, April 18th, without any more incident or catastrophe than that about 90% of the Officers and Men were more or less violently seasick. It had been arranged that the two destroyers, *Galatea* and *Curacao* should discharge their troops and stores at Åndalsnes itself and *Arethusa* and *Carlyle* should disembark their parties at Molde. The writer being with the party that disembarked at the latter place, the story of this period will have to be confined to them. Action by hostile aircraft was expected at any moment and at 8 p.m. there was still three hours of daylight. On tying up at the jetty at Molde the troops immediately disembarked and dispersed into the nearby woods and roads and among the ruins of the town, which had been bombed during the day. The troops from Carlyle crossed *Arethusa* and so on to the jetty and the Navy made themselves responsible for putting all our stores ashore. This was duly done by 9 p.m. and both vessels then slipped away.

The cruisers having departed, five local coastal vessels came alongside the jetty and we proceeded for the next three hours to load ourselves and our stores into them. During this time there was an air raid alarm but no hostile aircraft appeared. Lieutenant Colonel Ford and Major German, commanding a company of the Leicesters from *Carlyle*, were very anxious to get the party over to Åndalsnes as soon as possible so that they had a chance of disembarking there before daylight.

The five coastal vessels left Molde about midnight and arrived at Åndalsnes at 2.30 a.m. By this time nothing was to be seen of any troops but large quantities of stores were still lying about on the jetty. The party from Molde was then ordered to unload the stores on to the jetty, which naturally added to the quantity of same and the general confusion very considerably and having done this, this party was then ordered to proceed by lorry to an improvised camp about five miles from the town.

It should be mentioned at this point that of the Foresters who had arrived at Åndalsnes from *Galatea*, D Company under the command of Major Kirkland had immediately proceeded by train to Dombaas and A Company under the command of Captain Beckwith, followed them at 11 a.m. and the two companies were under the general command of Major J. Roberts. Until they rejoined the Battalion at Tretten their story must be the subject of a separate narrative by another narrator.

Returning to the story of HQ and B and C Companies, instead of settling down to rest after their midday meal, orders were received about 2.30 p.m. for all stores which had been conveyed to the camp to be reloaded on to lorries and returned to the station and the troops were to march back in time to entrain at 6 p.m. This came as a considerable surprise to everyone, as it had been originally intended that our force should establish a base ready for the arrival of fully trained troops of all arms. It was subsequently learnt that the reason for the change of plan was as follows. On his arrival in Norway, Brigadier Morgan was met by the British Military Attaché and was informed that if the British force did not immediately proceed to the front line some 160 miles away in front of Lillehammer, the Norwegian Government would throw up the sponge and give in to Germany. Brigadier Morgan explained that his orders from the War Office were to occupy Dombaas and then to demonstrate towards Trondheim, and that the requirements of the Norwegians were contrary to these instructions. The C-in-C Norwegian Army stated that unless the British forces arriving in Norway were to come under his command and act according to his plan, he would resign. Brigadier Morgan consequently was forced to comply in order to avoid a major political catastrophe. The 5th Leicesters were to follow us two hours later.

It was therefore a very tired party which entrained and left Åndalsnes at about 6.15 p.m., as our troops had had no sleep since disembarking from the cruisers and no period of rest to recover from their seasickness. The troops, however, were in good heart and appeared to take the keenest interest in the country through which we were travelling. This same country, however, was the cause of some considerable anxiety on the part of the officers. For the first 60 miles from Åndalsnes to Dombaas the line wound slowly up a narrow valley, which was in places narrow enough to be described as a gorge. Alongside this single line was a road and there were one or two vital bridges and tunnels. It was obvious to the officers at the start that these lines of communication were extremely vulnerable to attack from the air, and there were many places where the road and railway ran so close together that one well aimed heavy HE bomb would put both road and railway out of action for some considerable time. We arrived at Dombaas just as it was about to get dark about 9 o'clock, when a pause was made to issue blankets and bully beef to the troops. On proceeding again, darkness had now fallen completely and all ranks took the chance of getting an hour or two's sleep. There were only two coaches on the train, one occupied by officers and the other by sergeants and the men were forced to travel in closed goods wagons for the most part. We arrived at Lillehammer at about 2.30 in the morning, where we were glad to meet the Brigadier and to receive his definite instructions. The troops were immediately set to work unloading the train and the platform and station yard were soon strewn with stores and ammunition of every description. By this time it was getting light and the troops were removed from the vicinity of the station which it was estimated was not a safe place in daylight and were put in barns and similar accommodation just outside the town. The stores were left to a party of about 60 men under the command of the writer with Lieutenant Ellis and were duly conveyed to a warehouse nearby. This party worked throughout the whole of this day with frequent interruptions to conceal themselves from hostile aircraft. No bombs were dropped, but occasionally if anyone was seen or was late in hiding, bursts of machine gun fire from the enemy bombers were turned on. No casualties were suffered. Battalion HQ and Brigade HQ were established in the principal hotel in the town.

Next day, Sunday, April 21st, a reconnaissance of the position held by the Norwegians was made by the CO and it was agreed that a portion of the line should be taken over at dusk with the 8th Foresters on the right bordering Lake Mjösa with the Leicesters further to the left. This plan was nullified by the fact that arrival of British troops appeared to be the starting gun for the Germans to launch their attacks in earnest and during the day the Norwegians were driven back so that the Battalions were compelled to take up a position just in front of Lillehammer. It must be understood that the general plan for the 148th Infantry Brigade at this time was to send forward the troops as rapidly as possible, as they arrived by train loads, in order to stiffen the resistance of the Norwegian troops in that area. Consequently they were divided into three groups – two companies of Foresters under Major Roberts on the western side of Lake Mjösa, under direct command of Colonel Dahl, the other two groups under Lieutenant Colonel German and Lieutenant Colonel Ford were directly under General Haug. A conference was held at HQ 2nd Norwegian Division and a time programme for a general withdrawal to a line north of Lillehammer was agreed. It was mutually agreed between the two COs that the Leicesters should retire down one road and the Foresters down another, and the Norwegians promised to provide lorries at a point on each road for the use of the troops in this retirement. (It may be mentioned here that the transport, carriers and predictors for the Bofors AA guns all went to the bottom of the sea when SS *Cedarbank* was torpedoed on the way across and we were entirely dependent on the Norwegians for supplying transport.)

B Company, who were in touch with the Leicesters, duly saw them march back at 11.30 p.m. to their rendezvous for the lorries, and then retired themselves, covered by C Company, and as far as the Foresters were concerned this retirement went without a hitch. A considerable quantity of the stores that had been placed in a warehouse in

Lillehammer, had to be left behind, although the writer, the Quartermaster, Lieutenant Ellis and a party of men worked all night to remove as much as possible. Shortage of lorries hampered these activities considerably, as the only lorries available were those which could be commandeered or seized in the streets of the town.

When the Foresters arrived at the rendezvous they were surprised to find no trace of the Leicesters and although it was unknown how far the Germans had actually approached towards Lillehammer, Second Lieutenant Dixon volunteered to go back with the lorries and see whether the Leicesters could be found. This he did successfully and picked up practically all of them, the majority of whom had already marched some 15 miles and brought them back to the rendezvous.

The late arrival of the Leicesters had, however, a very serious effect upon the defensive position which was now in process of occupation, as the same had to be occupied after daylight and the troops were pushed off into positions by the Brigadier as they arrived down the road. Both Battalions were completely intermingled. This subsequently prevented the joint Battalion HQ of the two units knowing where anyone was, and as all the signalling equipment had had to be abandoned in Lillehammer owing to the lack of transport, it was not possible to run a line out to any of the forward troops. The configuration of the country made visual signalling an impossibility. The last vehicle to arrive was a small two seater car, pushed along the road by Lieutenant Ellis, which had run out of petrol some 400/500 yards down the road. As means of conveyance were so scarce, he was determined to save this valuable asset if possible. It may be mentioned here that during the whole of the retirement, cars and lorries were found abandoned by the roadside and the few with petrol and keys were quickly acquired. Altogether four cars and three lorries were appropriated in this manner.

The position was occupied as described above by about 4.30 a.m. on Monday, April 22nd, and the morning was spent by the Germans in reconnaissance by low flying aircraft about which we could do nothing. It was hoped that by not firing at the aircraft we could conceal our positions and the men were ordered not to use their Bren guns unless actually attacked, as the probability of hitting them with Brens seemed rather remote. About midday the Germans dropped several incendiary bombs on various houses, which it is to be assumed that they thought might contain HQ, but in actual fact the house used for the HQ of both Battalions was a very small and insignificant one and escaped these unwelcome attentions. Shortly after noon the Germans began dropping quantities of 4" mortar bombs on the position and on the only open road which there was in the area and which ran north and south up and down the valley. This made it impossible to bring up the food which had been prepared by the cooks in a small wood yard some three miles to the rear. Under the command of the Quartermaster at this time were about ten lorries which were piled high with (1) ammunition, (2) boxes of composite rations, (3) Officers' mess and Officers' personal baggage and (4) a number, but by no means all, of the men's kit bags.

At about 2 p.m. in the absence of the CO who had gone to Brigade HQ, the writer ordered Second Lieutenant Dolphin to take all the personnel at that time at Battalion HQ (about 20 in all) to try and check an enveloping movement by the enemy on our left flank, and as far as reports can be obtained, it is believed that this party were so successful in their efforts that this movement was checked sufficiently long to enable at least some of the Battalion to retire from this position later in the day. It was obvious, however, that the Germans were in sufficient numbers to turn the position before nightfall and bombs from aircraft and 4" mortar bombs were very harassing and made communication in the Battalion, even by runner, very difficult. On the return of the CO together with Lieutenant Colonel German from Brigade HQ about 4 o'clock, by which time the Brigade had reverted to the control of the Brigadier, the order was given for retirement, as it had become obvious that if this force was completely surrounded there would be nothing between the Germans and the base 150 miles away except two companies of the Leicesters who had followed the main body out three days later, and it was thought that if at least some of the force could escape they might possibly put up some resistance further back. The only means of evacuating the Battalion, which was in close touch with the enemy, was by lorry, and the only lorries available were those under the command of the Quartermaster. The writer, riding on the carrier of a motor cycle which had been acquired by Second Lieutenant Crane, was ordered to proceed at once, obtain these lorries and have them backed up the road towards the troops which were now retiring under the command of the two COs. In due course all the troops that were anywhere near the road were picked up and piled on the lorries and all the stores, ammunition, Officers' baggage etc. was dropped on to the roadside to make room for the troops. Second Lieutenant Crane undertook to stay behind with his motor cycle and blow up the road at a place prepared by the engineers in order to delay as far as possible the German advance. How far this was successful history does not relate, but the fact remains that the convoy of lorries was not actually molested by ground troops. The convoy was, however, caught up by German aircraft some 5 miles back and suffered considerably from bombing, although the troops temporarily retired into the adjoining woods.

Shortly after 6 p.m. this convoy of lorries met one company of the 5th Leicesters proceeding in the opposite direction in buses. This was one of the two companies above referred to, and it was then considered that it might be possible to hold a line for the rest of that day, about three hours and make a further retirement during the night. This company of Leicesters therefore took up a position around Öyer, with a composite party of Leicesters and Foresters from the lorries, under the command of Lieutenant Colonel German in support.

This plan was to some extent successful, although the leading company of Leicesters suffered considerable looses [sic] and the remainder of the Foresters, mostly HQ Company not actually in position, found it necessary to make a further retirement. By this time the only Officers of the Foresters whose whereabouts were known were the CO, the writer, Captain Renwick and Second Lieutenants Fitzherbert and Dolphin. All of the Officers of B and C Companies, who had been holding the front line just in rear of Lillehammer, were missing and it is to be feared that the original order for retirement can never have reached them.

The position was considered too critical to allow anyone to sleep on this night and while Lieutenant Colonel German's party hung on during the night in spite of the fact that by 9 p.m. the Germans had brought up their big mortars and some of their AFVs a line was established some five miles further back by daybreak on Tuesday, the 23rd, as follows. On the right, one Company of Foresters composed of the remainder of the two rifle companies plus a small portion of HQ Company, on the left the last and intact Company of Leicesters, who had spent the night in Tretten under the command of Major Atkins. As soon as it got light Lieutenant Colonel German's party retired through this line to a position just in front of Tretten village and the remainder of the HQ Companies of both Battalions were in the village itself. At this point about 8 a.m., there arrived in the front line from the rear Major Roberts, who, together with his party of two companies, had not been heard of for some days. He reported that these two companies were at Tretten station and were practically intact, having retired on a road on the other side of the river parallel to the one used by the party on the east side. These two companies were therefore not nearly so tired as the other troops and in fact had had a meal that morning, whereas the troops on the other side had now been practically 48 hours without either food or sleep.

The CO immediately asked Major Roberts to inspect the positions that had been taken up and the writer returned to Tretten village to send up A Company under Captain Beckwith to strengthen the front line, and to see whether anything could be done with regard to food, without which it was obvious the troops could not go much further. Lieutenant Sketchley, who had been with A Company, had already busied himself with preparing food to put into hot containers to send up to the troops and things looked a little brighter. A request had come down for more ammunition at about 11 o'clock and this had been duly loaded onto a lorry, and it was thought that the lorry could take up both ammunition and the food containers. It was very distressing, therefore, to learn from the party of Leicesters holding Tretten bridge that two enemy medium tanks had appeared on the road between them and the forward troops, making it impossible for the supplies of food and ammunition to be sent up for the troops in the front line. We had nothing with us which could deal with these two tanks as the troops reported that the bullets of our anti-tank rifles bounced off them, and we had no anti-tank guns of any kind with us. It became obvious that the German plan was to prevent communication up and down this road between Tretten village and the forward troops, and very shortly after the appearance of these two tanks at this point, Tretten village and the surrounding woods came under a considerable bombardment from a battery of enemy 5.9s which they had previously not brought into action. This bombardment was preparatory to another encircling movement on our left flank by their Austrian ski troops and it became quite clear to those in Tretten village that nothing could save the forward troops under the command of Lieutenant Colonel Ford from being completely cut off. For some considerable time Lieutenant Colonel German and such troops as he could collect in Tretten hung on to the bridgehead in the hope that the forward troops would realise the position and some of them filter through, but it subsequently turned out that the number which actually did escape was very few indeed. At this juncture, D Company under Major Kirkland, were engaging the enemy from the west side of the river, and it had become obvious from the very fact that they could engage the enemy at all that the forward troops on the east side must have been overrun. A portion of this Company under Second Lieutenant Kirk eventually made their escape across the river bridge before its demolition and came under the command of Lieutenant Colonel German. Such lorries as were available were collected and headed north about 7 o'clock in the evening, closely attended by enemy aircraft with bombs and machine guns. There were in consequence some further casualties, and subsequently Lieutenant McConnell, the Foresters Medical Officer, who had been attending to the wounded with the utmost heroism at the roadside amidst constant shelling, was probably cut off with a small party of wounded and exhausted men and was probably captured.

By the time some eight or nine lorries reached Ringebu there were very few Officers left and Lieutenant Colonel German was now missing. No one knew whether the promised reinforcements had yet arrived in the country and the prospect of saving the remainder of the force with over 100 miles to go to the base seemed extremely remote. On our arrival at Otta during the night of Tuesday, April 23rd, however, with petrol tanks practically or entirely exhausted, it was that a Company of the KOYLI from the 15th Regular Brigade had actually reached this point and were preparing to take up a position in front of it. The remainder of the Foresters and Leicesters had now ceased to be a fighting force. There were very few Bren guns or anti-tank rifles left and little ammunition for them in any case, and the men were quite exhausted. We were therefore ordered to rest for the day in a side valley known as the Hydalen valley, spread out over a distance of some four miles and were quartered in huts and houses.

Instructions were issued that we should on no account expose ourselves to view from enemy aircraft, and so might escape any unwelcome attention. All movement, even that of issuing a meal, the stores for which had been acquired in Otta, was carried on with the greatest regard for concealment from view. A check was made and it was discovered that the 5th Leicesters had five Officers and we had the writer, Lieutenant Hallam, Lieutenant Sketchley and Second Lieutenant Kirk only, and both Battalions had approximately 300 Other Ranks left. During the two days we remained in this valley, stragglers continued to come in, but it is to be regretted not nearly as many as had been hoped. On the night of Thursday, April 25th, as soon as it was dark, we secured some buses and proceeded to Otta Station and there entrained to go to Dombaas. Owing to delays the second train only reached Dovre by the time dawn arrived and the troops had to remain in that area in the woods for that day. Those that arrived in Dombaas were sent to out-lying houses and told to remain hidden for the rest of the day. Practically the whole town had been demolished by air action except the big hotel which appeared to be intact and it must be assumed that the Germans were carefully preserving this for their own use. During the three days [we] remained in Dombaas, we were subjected to periodic aerial attack with both HE and incendiary bombs. We suffered no casualties killed, but a few were injured. The days for all ranks were very boring and somewhat demoralising. The hours of darkness were spent in feeding ourselves and in sorting out stores, in the tunnel near the station, which had been brought up by a supply train which was unable to proceed further owing to the almost complete demolition of the railway tracks in Dombaas station.

At this stage all were beginning to wonder what would finally happen to us. Officers had no kit since it was jettisoned to assist in the evacuation of the troops from the battle behind Lillehammer, and the men had neither packs nor kit bags. At the end of our third day in Dombaas the order for the evacuation of all forces in this part of Norway came through. It should be mentioned that the front line for the last few days since we ceased to be a fighting force had been held successively at various points by the 15th

Brigade Battalion by Battalion, and the last position just in front of Dombaas was held very gallantly by the remnants of the Green Howards and KOYLI while the remainder proceeded by any means at their disposal to the base for embarkation. Demolition on a considerable scale had been carried out on the road and railway between Otta and Dombaas, and as a result of this, in the last position the Battalions above mentioned were not troubled with AFVs or artillery which the Germans had not been able to bring up. The railway from Dombaas to the base (60 miles) was by this time completely out of action and the road required constant repair and the filling in of enormous shell craters. Driving a car without lights at night down this road was a nightmare, especially when it must be realised that there were vehicles going in the other direction ready for the final evacuation of the Green Howards and KOYLI.

For proceeding from Dombaas to the base the composite Battalion of Leicesters and Foresters under the command of the writer was divided into four groups which by day were to watch for possible landings by enemy parachutists on the lines of communications at four selected points, and to reach Åndalsnes by daylight on the morning of Tuesday, April 30th.This journey was undertaken in part by lorries, but many were full with Norwegians. Incredible distances were marched and a small portion of the journey was accomplished by train. Each of these groups was commanded by an Officer and the last to arrive, under Lieutenant Sketchley, did not reach Åndalsnes before the afternoon of Tuesday, April 30th.

Orders were received for the embarkation at 6 p.m. and the troops had been in the woods all day some three miles outside the town, and constant air activity and bombing again with HE and incendiary bombs had made movement almost impossible, although during the day most of the men received some sort of a meal. Rations at the base by this time were very short and it may be mentioned here that the Norwegian supply service, which was supposed to feed us, never once functioned, and if it had not been for the 14 days composite rations taken out by all troops, it is most probable that the force would have starved altogether.

At 10 o'clock a column was formed composed as under:- 5th Leicesters, 8th Foresters, York and Lancs, RASC, RAMC and a party of Royal Marines and this column marched down to the jetty under their Unit Commanders. A number of fires had been started in the woods around the jetty lighting up the whole place, so that it boded ill for the embarkation as it was assumed that the bombers would arrive at any minute. Luckily for us no bombers were seen that night. A cruiser and destroyer came alongside the jetty punctually at 11 p.m. and the 1,800 Officers and Men were embarked in 40 minutes. The writer was aboard HMS *Sheffield* and the Commander met the Officers in the Ward Room with the following words: "Boys, there is hot soup, bacon and eggs, whisky, buckets of beer and baths available below. Get on with it!" These were the most acceptable orders we had received in Norway. (Author's note: one hopes the men got similar treatment.)

As soon as we were all on board, the cruisers set sail from the fjord at 32 knots and an uneventful voyage was made to Scapa, where we arrived on the morning of Thursday, May 2nd. Two days were spent at Scapa on board a transport vessel, after which we set sail for the Clyde and dropped anchor at Gourock on Sunday morning, May 5th, but it was not until the morning of Tuesday, May 7th, that we actually disembarked and all the Men were completely re-issued with clothing and necessities by the RAOC in King George V Dock, Clydebank.

It only remains to touch on one other aspect of this expedition. All the time we were in Norway we had about 20 hours of sunshine each day and the lack of cloud at this time of the year was said to be exceptional. Be that as it may, we prayed for cloudy weather which would have seriously hampered the activities of the German aircraft in mountainous country. The complete supremacy of the German aircraft was really a vital factor throughout, as there was no possible base for our fighters anywhere in the area. Without air support the lines of communication containing only one single-line railway and one road were hopelessly vulnerable. The weather which, was so unkindly good during our stay in Norway, remained equally good for our voyage home from the time of leaving Åndalsnes to the Clyde, and the troops arrived at the latter port looking extremely healthy after a week's rest lying on the decks in the sun. The writer personally has never seen such a change in mind and body of all concerned in so short a period.

Appendix N

Accounts by Lieutenant F. Sketchley and Second Lieutenant M. Kirk, Sherwood Foresters, April 1940

The following is an account by Lieutenant F. Sketchley and Second Lieutenant M. Kirk on the activities of one half of the Sherwood Foresters battalion consisting of A and D Companies and a detachment from HQ Company, between embarking on HMS *Galatea* on 16 April and joining up with the other half of the battalion at Tretten on 23 April.

HMS *Galatea* in company with HMS *Curacao* arrived at Åndalsnes about 9 o'clock on the evening of Thursday, 18 April. The writers were on board the *Galatea* where the majority had been seasick nearly all the way across the North Sea, and unfortunately for D Company, CSM *Ryde* collapsed just before we landed and had to remain on board ship and return to England. On the quay we found lorries waiting to deal with our baggage and guides to lead us to the school [where] A and HQ Companies were to spend the night. We finally got settled in there about midnight and managed to get some blankets up, also rations for breakfast. D Company were to leave for Dombaas with Major Roberts and the Brigadier at 1 a.m. and working parties were very busy sorting out the stores, ammunition, rations etc. on the quay and loading up their train. D Company's task was to secure Dombaas, an important railway junction, which had not been occupied by the Germans but there was said to be a band of about fifty parachute troops causing trouble in the neighbourhood particularly on the railway line and these had to be rounded up. The train arrived at Dombaas about 4.30 a.m. on Friday, [the] 19th, where the baggage, stores and ammunition were unloaded on the platform. The men were then put into billets, consisting chiefly of outlying farm buildings. During the morning the baggage etc. was brought down from the station and camouflaged in a wood near the hotel. Work was frequently interrupted by air-raid alarms, but only once did we see an enemy plane – a very old biplane which was trying to make contact with the parachutists who had fortified themselves in a farm about five miles south of Dombaas. About 10 a.m. Major Roberts went out with a patrol consisting of two sections to reconnoitre the area held by the Germans. Meanwhile a Naval howitzer manned by a crew from HMS *Hood* arrived and took up a position and opened fire on the Germans. After a dozen or so rounds had been fired the remaining Germans surrendered, thus opening the way to the south.

About 1 p.m. orders came through that D Company was to pack up and move south with A Company and the detachment of HQ Company and Major Roberts and

Lieutenant Bradley immediately went off to the station to move south on a train which had arrived bearing A Company and the HQ Company detachment, leaving Major Kirkland and D Company to follow by another train. A Company and the detachment of HQ Company had left Åndalsnes shortly before midday, after being up and about by about 5 a.m. We had had our first experience of an air raid at about 7.30 when we were eating a hastily prepared breakfast of tea, bully beef and biscuits in the open under a brilliant sun shining down from a cloudless sky. Two German planes suddenly appeared over the mountains and guns on the ships opened fire.

There were also guns of which we were not aware, in the woods behind the school, and everyone had a distinct surprise when these guns opened fire from positions quite near to us. However, the planes soon moved off and we proceeded to the quay to sort out baggage and load up the train on which we were to leave for Dombaas about 11 a.m. This was no easy task as, in addition to our own baggage and stores, the baggage of the other half of the Battalion who had arrived in the early hours of the morning was also on the quay. The Brigadier arrived back from Dombaas about 10 o'clock and our train finally left about 11.30 a.m. We had been very nervous of air activity while loading baggage at Åndalsnes and we were equally nervous when in the train. Sentries were posted at the end of each coach and LMGs and ammunition were in the corridors ready for us to take with us should we have to leave the train, orders having been given that if enemy aircraft appeared, the train would stop immediately and give four or five shrill blasts of the whistles and everyone was to leave the train and make for cover in the woods as quickly as possible. This did actually happen once, but not until later in the day about 6 o'clock when we had passed through Dombaas and were nearly at Farborg. The train reached Dombaas between 1.30 and 2, and there was a wait of at least an hour before Major Roberts joined the train. A company then heard to their surprise that they were proceeding south and that D Company were to follow in another train an hour or two later. It had been previously understood that we should remain at Dombaas to protect the line, road and bridges etc.

The train finally reached Farborg, about six miles north of Lillehammer, about 7 in the evening, and there we found trucks and lorries (mostly open), which we were told would take us up to the front line about 35 miles away. We finally got away in the trucks into which we had loaded baggage and stores about 9 o'clock and proceeded south through very snowy country. The train carrying D Company arrived at Farborg about 9.30 p.m., having left Dombaas about 5.30 and D company having loaded up their trucks and lorries set over the mountain road about two hours in the rear of A Company. It was very cold and after about two hours there was a halt at a place called Biri to brew some tea and dump our heavy baggage. At this point Major Roberts met Officers of the Norwegian HQ and we learnt that we were going up into the hills to a village called Nykirke, which was on the only other road in the district on the west side of Lake Mjösa, apart from the road which ran north up the valley from Lake Mjösa along the railway line.

It was apparently thought that the Germans might try and surround the Norwegian forces by advancing up this road which ultimately joined the road in the valley at Rosendal about eight miles south of Biri. Lieutenant Sketchley remained at Biri with a party to offload heavy baggage such as kit bags, bales of blankets and sheepskin coats and rations and to then take up to the front line stores which would be required there. They were accompanied by a young Norwegian guide, certainly not more than fourteen years old, who couldn't speak a word of English, and [during] a nightmare drive in a snowstorm they met a continuous stream of Red Cross ambulances, cars and lorries, which were mostly evacuating the civil population. They finally caught up with the rest of the convoy at Nykirke about 3 a.m. when the whole convoy, extending nearly a mile, was stationary in deep snow on a hill leading into the village. While the trucks were being sorted out and offloaded, most of the stores being dumped in the snow at the side of the road, some of the troops were able to take advantage of the hot drinks and food which locals kindly provided in the church. We then endeavoured to take up and occupy a defensive position on and near the road on which it was thought the Germans might advance. In the deep snow this was no easy job, and in positions off the road one often saw people well up to the waist in snow as they tried to move about. We managed to get our own cookers going and provide some sort of a meal during the morning and about 12.30 p.m. orders were received to load up the trucks as we should be moving not later than 3 p.m. There had been no sign of the enemy, but there had been considerable activity on the part of reconnaissance aircraft throughout the morning. We got away soon after 2 o'clock and moved to some farmhouses and huts about eight miles north of Biri. Some anxiety was felt over D Company who had not arrived but they eventually arrived about 8 p.m.

It was decided that the heavy baggage must be moved from Biri to a position further north, and after consulting the map it was finally decided that it should be dumped at the railway station at Farborg, about 8 miles north of Lillehammer, the above mentioned party spending all the night of Saturday, 20th April, and part of the Sunday evening transferring this baggage with a convoy of trucks and lorries. The decision to dump the baggage at Farborg was made in the complete absence of any information from, or communication with, the Norwegian HQ as to what was happening on the other side of the lake, although on Sunday a visit was received from Major Dowson who arrived in the Brigadier's car. It will be seen from what is said elsewhere that the other half of the Battalion withdrew through Lillehammer in the early hours of Monday, 22nd April, and the enemy must have reached Farborg by Monday evening. At any rate it was later reported that a big fire was burning at the railway station and it seems probable that this [was] our baggage dump. It is regretted that nothing more was seen of Corporal Perrons or any member of the guard of six men left over the baggage. A Company and the HQ Company detachment remained in their position north of Biri all Sunday, the time being spent in occupying a defensive position with some digging and wiring. About midday D Company moved south in trucks and arrived at Sveern about 2 p.m. where they came under fire for the first time.

They were actually attacked by a German Army co-operation aircraft of the same type as our Lysander, which spotted them as they were debussing. After the second MG attack, the enthusiasm of the troops broke loose and they rushed into the road firing LMGs and rifles at the enemy plane, which beat a rapid retreat home. They then moved forward about a quarter of a mile south of Sveern to the forward edge of a dense wood, where two platoons under Second Lieutenants Parry and Kirk were put in position covering a bridge. The third platoon under Second Lieutenant Dowson took up a position about a quarter of a mile to the right flank on an adjoining road, while Company HQ was in Sveern.

Digging in started about 3.30 p.m. but this was not a success owing to the hardness of the ground, and the numerous roots from neighbouring trees, luckily though, there were a great number of large stones which were used as parapets to the shallow weapon pits, to the width of 4 to 6 feet. A hot meal was provided about 4.30 and they were visited by the Brigadier and Major Dowson. The completion of the position went on till dusk when the Norwegian Army began to withdraw through us. The withdrawal continued all through the night and was completed about 5 a.m. next morning. Luckily there were no air attacks which had been so prominent during the previous afternoon, bombing the road behind us. At 5.15 a.m. the Norwegian engineers blew up the bridge in front of the position and felled prepared trees across the road all the way back to the village. Our orders were to remain in position for one hour after the bridge had been blown and then to withdraw through A Company to a position about 23 miles away at Rendau. At 6.15 a.m. the withdrawal began and was completed by 6.45, no Germans being seen. Buses were waiting for us on the outskirts of Sveern, where the Company embussed as follows:- Second Lieutenant Kirk and 17 Platoon in the first bus, Second Lieutenant Parry and 16 Platoon in the second bus, CQMS Cleary third with the ammunition, Major Kirkland and Lieutenant Esam in a car, and Second Lieutenant Dowson with 18 Platoon last. The first seven miles were uneventful, when suddenly turning a sharp corner in the road, heavy mortar fire was encountered coming from the other side of the lake. Immediately all the drivers put their foot down hard and shot out of the danger area. The first two Platoons and the ammunition truck got through without suffering any casualties, but Second Lieutenant Dowson and his men in an open cattle truck suffered casualties when the driver, a Norwegian, ran off into the woods leaving the truck a stationary target and a shell burst overhead. Second Lieutenant Dowson himself receiving slight facial wounds from splinters. Major Kirkland immediately went back to his assistance and with the help of some Norwegians managed to get the wounded safely to a hospital. The journey continued uneventfully and the Company arrived at their new position about 8 a.m. where they again dug in.

All through the night of Sunday, April 21st, the Norwegian soldiers and civil population were streaming along the road leading north through the valley. Captain Beckwith OC A Company was in conference with A and HQ Company officers and sergeants from 1.30 a.m. to 3.00 a.m. on the Monday morning, giving orders for the defensive position to be held by the Company to cover the withdrawal of D who were to pass through A as soon as the Norwegians had passed through. It should be mentioned that this conference was disturbed by a terrific explosion at about 2.30 a.m. when the bridge across the lake at Lillehammer was blown up by the Norwegians. A Company were to hold their position for one hour after the last truck of D Company had passed. A Company and the part of HQ Company were then to withdraw and join D Company at Rendal about eight miles north of the position they were then holding. Road blocks had been made at three points and engineers from the Norwegian Army were expected to blow up a bridge just in front of the position but they never appeared. D Company arrived about 7.30 a.m. having been out in the open all night. They moved on to Rendal and were followed an hour later by A and HQ Companies and as soon as they got to Rendal both were ordered to occupy a defensive position.

D Company had had no food since 4.30 p.m. on the previous day and they were immediately given the hot meal which had been prepared for them the previous evening but which could not be sent to them, as we were told that they were in sight of the enemy.

We were troubled a lot by aircraft and were almost unceasingly running for shelter, but no bombs were dropped and we eventually moved off in the trucks about 8.30 p.m. by a side road through the mountains. The night drive in the trucks was even more of a nightmare than the drive on the previous Friday night. It was a bitterly cold night and most of the trucks were open and the majority of the men had no greatcoats. At about 11.30 p.m. the front half of the convoy came across the transport belonging to the other half of the Battalion which was parked in the middle of the road over a distance of about a mile. A valuable hour was wasted trying to find the drivers for these buses who had gone off to rest, carrying with them the ignition keys, but eventually the column moved about a mile further on where the road broadened out so that the tedious journey could be continued. About 1 a.m. there was a halt at a church near Ganadal, the men who had travelled without food or greatcoats through ice cold mountains in open trucks were assisted by Lieutenant Stoker (RAMC), who found that one or two men were suffering from exposure and he wrapped them in blankets and set to work to revive them. After not more than an hour's halt, a message was received that the convoy had been cut off by the Germans who had advanced more rapidly than anticipated (this was afterwards confirmed as a false report), so we again embussed in the open trucks, mounting Bren guns on the roofs of the cabs and in the rear while men with fixed bayonets sat on each side, for we fully thought that we should have to run the gauntlet.

The front half of the convoy moved off about 2.30 a.m. arriving unmolested at Tretten about 4 a.m. The rear half of the convoy of trucks was cut off from the front half owing to one of the trucks turning over on a bend in the road. This truck fortunately only contained baggage and stores, including two petrol cookers, petrol and a few boxes of rations which we managed to hang on to, and no one was injured. The stores ended up in deep snow down the bank at the side of the road and it took nearly two hours to get the convoy going again. No sooner had this rear half of the convoy been re-started than we met the convoy of empty trucks (which the first half of the convoy had met) going in the opposite direction, and there were scenes of complete confusion and chaos in the deep snow in the narrow mountain road while we tried to get the convoys past each other. Operations were hampered by the Norwegian drivers, only one of whom could speak a few words of English, and who nearly always did the wrong thing at the wrong moment. The road was so narrow that the only way of getting the trucks in the convoy moving in the opposite direction past our own convoy was to shove them partly off the road and through the snow which was several feet deep in places. This caused a further delay of between one and two hours, and it was about 7 o'clock on the Tuesday morning before this rear part of the convoy reached Tretten. By this time the men were nearly starved through having been 11 hours in the open trucks, and D Company in particular must have been very nearly exhausted as they had been out in the open all the previous night. Everyone in Major Roberts' half of the Battalion was in fact very tired indeed, as the only rest they had had was a few hours on Thursday and Saturday nights. Major Roberts himself worked throughout without respite and was in considerable pain through a box of ammunition being dropped on his foot on the quay at Åndalsnes.

Captain Athorpe and fifty ORs of the transport personnel also reached Tretten in the early hours of Tuesday morning, having travelled by train from Åndalsnes, where they arrived shortly before midnight on Sunday. They had rations and ammunition with them, and these were taken off the train and dumped at the rear of Tretten village. Major Roberts and Lieutenant Bradley acting as his Adjutant went up to the position south of Tretten, which was being held by the Colonel with the remnants of his half of the Battalion and the Leicesters. A and D Companies went forward to assist these remnants and later in the morning a party consisting of approximately 60 ORs were sent up under Second Lieutenant Laing to try and hold the flank on the east side.

The fighting on the left side of the lake began in the early morning and by 10 a.m. had intensified to such an extent that an order was received for A and half HQ Companies to move up to the left to support the remainder of the Battalion, and the Leicesters, who were by now badly battered about, leaving D Company to hold the right. At 1 p.m. Lieutenant Colonel King-Salter arrived and ordered Major Kirkland to move his Company five miles south to take up a position on the extreme right flank to (a) try and enfilade the German advance and (b) to stop any possible filtration of Germans across the lake at that point which might endanger our left. A guide was to meet D Company at the debussing point and would lead them to the position on the flank. It is perhaps very lucky that a counter order came through just as the Company were about to move off, as looking back now it seems that no one would have returned to tell the tale, as the Company would have been hopelessly cut off and captured. The counter order instructed Major Kirkland to take two Platoons to support the left as the Germans were making a flanking movement and endeavouring to cut off our forward troops. The position was now that the right was only held by Lieutenant Esam, Second Lieutenant Kirk and 30 men. About 5 p.m. the order to withdraw was received as the Germans had got through on the left flank, and was duly being carried out when a strong platoon of Germans was seen advancing towards our position on the flank, firing as they came with sub machine guns using incendiary and tracer bullets. Luckily the fire was high and very inaccurate and a number of the enemy were accounted for before the withdrawal was complete with the loss of only two men. Trucks were waiting at Tretten and this party crossed the bridge to join with the remnants of the Battalion and Leicesters. The other two Platoons of D Company suffered a considerable number of casualties as did A Company and the part of HQ Company under Second Lieutenant Laing, who were also on the left.

Appendix O

Statement by Captain J. Thompson, 8th Sherwood Foresters, Intelligence Officer, HQ 148th Infantry Brigade

During the late afternoon of Tuesday April 23rd 1940, Brigade HQ was established at the north end of the village of Tretten. Forward elements of 5th Leicesters and 8th Foresters were holding positions some miles to the south of Tretten and a road block was held by 5th Leicesters at the south end of the village. About 1700 hours the Germans penetrated the left flank of the position, and commenced an attack upon Tretten itself, supported by artillery and mortar fire. Small bodies of troops who began to filter back were collected by members of Brigade Staff and were put into positions astride the main road, in and immediately north of Tretten village, in an effort to hold the position until 2100 hours, when a general withdrawal had been ordered. I took charge of a position to the NE of the main road some 400 yards north of the village. Between 1700 hours and 1900 hours the attack developed to its greatest intensity and all positions were subjected to heavy fire from artillery and mortars and by aerial bombardment. At about 2045 hours the firing had subsided and as I had received no orders to withdraw, I worked my way back into Tretten village through the woods in order to try and find Brigade HQ and ascertain the position. I made my way into the village without incident, but on arrival found that the Germans were in possession of it and had in fact passed beyond it down both the main road and a side road running parallel to it. I observed an AFV on the road which I approached to within 50 yards. I was able to identify this vehicle as a medium tank.

Realising that I was now well behind the enemy lines, I lay low till dusk among the buildings and at about 2200 hours approached the road where I had observed a stationary lorry. I got into this vehicle and attempted to start it, but was unable to do so. I therefore worked my way out of the village through the woods and up the hillside on the NE side of the main road. About half an hour later I came across Captain Coleman 5th Leicesters in the woods and we proceeded together to a farm house high up on the hillside some 2 miles north of Tretten. We there obtained some food and rested. Early next morning we reviewed the situation together and came to the conclusion that we were probably the only people left behind the enemy lines. We therefore decided to attempt to get through to our own forces in civilian clothes which we were able to obtain at the farm house. We set out in a northerly direction over the hills and about midday fell in with three Norwegians who helped us on our way and advised us to go to a place called Rollsetrer where they said there were other British troops. We thereupon pressed ahead and after a long march through the snow we reached Rollsetrer about 2200 hours. There we found the Brigade Major, Lieutenant Colonel King-Salter, certain officers of 5th Leicesters and about 40 other ranks both 5th Leicesters and 8th Foresters.

After a few hours rest the whole party left about 0400 hours next morning, April 25th with the object of rejoining our own troops at Ringebu. In the late afternoon after an arduous journey over the hills through deep snow we came to Speilen where we learned from Norwegians that the Germans were in Ringebu and had a patrol up the road at Brekkum. It therefore became necessary to push on to Stottestrer which was reached about 2130 hours that evening. By that time the party had picked up more stragglers and totalled about 80, including Lieutenant Colonel G. German, CO 5th Leicesters. After a few hours rest the situation was considered in detail and it was decided that it was essential to pass Ringebu and get into the Frya valley, if possible up as far as Venoisen. This involved a long move early next day (26th) to a position SE of Ringebu, to be followed by a night march in order to get round the German position at Ringebu. The day move was accomplished without incident and the whole party (which was joined during the day by Second Lieutenant Butler of 148th Brigade Signal Section) lay up till dark in the prearranged assembly position.

The night march started at 2130 hours, the order of march being – Colonel King-Salter and myself with six men and a Bren gun to act as point section, followed at 200 paces by the main body under Colonel German, the rear being brought up by another section with the remaining Bren gun. At about 0100 hours it was realised that the point section had lost their way in the dark and that the main body had lost touch. The point section thereupon retraced its steps and regained the correct route but without making contact with the main body. About 0300 hours [on the] 27th the point section emerged from the woods into the road running up the Frya valley and proceeded as rapidly as possible towards Venoisen. About 0500 hours when approaching the village of Wenebygd, a body of German troops observed the point section and opened fire with rifles and an MG. The section immediately scattered into the fields, but I being in civilian clothes remained standing in the roadway. The bluff succeeded and the patrol rushed past me in pursuit of the point section and as soon as the German attention was sufficiently diverted I slipped down between some houses and got into the valley and round the patrol. I was however able to establish that the troops who had been taken prisoner were the main body who had got ahead of the front section during the night march.

As soon as the coast was clear I pressed on to Venoisen where I obtained food and got some sleep. Early next morning I moved on to Venasete and Eldersete where I arrived about midday. By that time the snow was too soft to allow further progress and I was forced to wait until 1930 hours before moving on. At 1930 hours I moved on and at 2100 hours had reached Frypollan where I found about 40 Norwegians and five ORs of 8th Foresters. I consulted with the Norwegian Officer in command who stated that he was going to make a night march and endeavour to regain his lines at Sel. The night march commenced at 0300 hours on the 29th and passing by way of the Frya river we came to Mysuseter about 0830 hours, only to find that the Germans had passed Sel some four hours earlier. At this point the Norwegian forces were ordered by their Commander to disperse into the hills, but he and I together with a Norwegian NCO and 5 other ranks 8th Foresters decided to push on [to] Peergymthytta that morning with the object of making a night march during the hours of darkness and to rejoin the line at Dovre. After an exhausting climb through deep snow Peergymthytta was reached about 1230 hours. We rested here and obtained some food. At 0200 hours, [on the] 30th the night march to Dovre began. This path led over the mountain passes and was carried out at an average height of about 3,500 feet. When daylight came it was necessary to move at 200 yards intervals in order to avoid detection by aircraft. The party had also obtained white overalls from the Norwegians. About 0900 hours, [on the] 30th we arrived on the hillside overlooking Dovre and to our relief the place was reported clear of Germans. We sat down to eat some food when to our dismay the head of the German column appeared in the valley moving up towards Dombaas. By this time the party was very exhausted but it was decided to make an immediate effort to pass along the hills as far as Dombaas, in the hope of being able to get through. In order to accomplish this it was necessary to climb back up the mountains and the going was so difficult that it was not until 2300 hours that the valley running from Dombaas to Trondheim was reached, a distance of some six miles only, as the crow flies. We emerged onto the road Dombaas-Trondheim about 2330 hours and moved down in single file towards Dombaas with the object of crossing the railway and working into the valley leading to the base. About half a mile down this road however, a wire road block was encountered and I did not deem it wise to proceed in the dark for fear the road had been mined. We therefore lay in the woods till first light, 1st May and then succeeded in passing through the German lines and gaining the railway about 2 miles NW of Dombaas. By this time the party was very exhausted and were unable to stand the pace with the exception of the Norwegian Officer and myself and it was decided to proceed independently. He and I, after marching up the railway found a workmen's pedal trolley which we placed on the lines. On this conveyance we were able to make good progress and we travelled up the line until about 0800 hours when we came up behind a wrecked train in the neighbourhood of Lesjaskog and had to take to the road. After proceeding for about one mile up the road I found a RM picket holding a road block and identified myself to the officer in charge. At this point the Norwegian Officer left me and continued on towards Åndalsnes on a bicycle which was found by the roadside. I remained with the Marine picket and moved back with them at 1000 hours, eventually reporting to General Paget's HQ at Verma. I remained with him till nightfall and went aboard HMS *Birmingham* about 2345 hours, 1st May.

The journey took in all eight days during which I estimate that I covered on foot 100 to 110 miles much of it through snow. I covered 20 to 25 miles on the railway trolley and the remainder of the journey in a lorry and a car.

Appendix P

The Experiences of Captain Roger Barratt, 5th Battalion Leicestershire Regiment, Norway 1940

The following is an account of his experiences written in his diary by Captain Roger Barratt while interned at Mora in Sweden. Captain Barratt had been Assistant Adjutant of the 5th Battalion, the Leicestershire Regiment, in Norway:

St Magnus came alongside the little wooden pier at Åndalsnes just in time to be seen by an enemy reconnaissance plane. Disembarkation was carried out as rapidly as possible in case the aircraft above was a bomber and the companies were loaded onto a waiting train. One of the destroyers fired her guns at the aircraft, which very quickly disappeared.

Major Garner and myself joined Major Atkins at a hotel where the Royal Marines had made their Headquarters. The Marine Colonel informed us of the latest situation and all events as he knew them, since the landing of the first part of 148th Brigade during the night of 19th April. It would appear that the original intention had been for the force to proceed to Dombaas, some 60 miles away; organise a base there and then proceed northwards to Trondheim and join issue with the German forces there. But now, reports had been received that a company of German paratroops was causing trouble just south of the town. The Colonel then informed us that Brigadier H. de R. Morgan, the force commander, had decided to deal with these before anything else. Later and from another source, I heard that the Brigadier had met General Ruge the Norwegian Commander-in-Chief, probably at Öyer, [who] had constrained on him to send his force south to assist and relieve the exhausted Norwegian troops somewhere in the region just north of Hamar, just over 100 miles south of Dombaas. These Norwegian forces had met the full force of the German invasion from the start. The Colonel was able to inform us that the German parachutists had been overcome and Brigadier Morgan and his force had gone south.

Communication between the base at Åndalsnes and the forward force was almost non existent and had in fact been cut off since early that morning but by about 9 a.m., telephonic communication was again restored and Major Atkins received his orders to bring the fighting part of his force south to Otta, at which place further instructions would be received. By this time the two companies of the Leicesters and the other part of HQ Company together with stores from the two coasters, departed about 9.45 a.m. for Otta. Personnel of all other sub-units were to remain at the base.

Monday 22nd April

The train from Åndalsnes arrived at Otta about 11 a.m. Troops were detrained and AA mountings set up. Some of 148th Brigade personnel were stationed here. Soon after our arrival at Otta, a message was received that we were to proceed further south to a place called Tretten some 45 miles away. B Company personnel were left at Otta, while the remainder of the Leicesters only, proceeded south by train. These last 45 miles were covered in just over an hour but not without harassment from roving fighters which machine gunned anything that moved on the road or railway. The train didn't stop but carried on regardless. These attacks were very frustrating for we couldn't hit back.

Eventually, the train pulled into Tretten about 1.45 p.m. to the sound of an air raid siren. This caused a hurried detrainment and dispersal among the trees and huge boulders at the side of the track. In a few minutes a huge aircraft appeared above the station flying low. Someone shouted, "Don't fire at it for it will give our positions away." But the train standing in the station had already given our position away. The plane circled Tretten station twice and disappeared back down the gorge the way he had come.

A Norwegian Captain then arrived from Norwegian Headquarters who informed Colonel German and the Adjutant that we now came under Norwegian Command. His only orders to us were that we should remain dispersed for protection against enemy aircraft until night-time, when we would receive orders to go forward into the line.

There were six or seven men from A Company of the Leicesters who had landed in Norway some three days previously. They told a strange tale of an action with the Germans and how they had got lost in the dense forest of conifers and separated from the rest of their company and had eventually found their way back to Tretten.

Not long afterwards, Brigadier Morgan arrived, and it was confirmed that the British force was functioning under the Norwegian High Command, but that any orders received from them were to be confirmed from 148th Brigade HQ before being acted upon. The Brigadier gave orders that we were to take up a defensive position on each side of the River Laagen with a weather eye on the right bank, where it was possible that some enemy tanks or armoured cars might be encountered having circumvented the British troops in front.

There were then two possibilities; either the British forces would withdraw through these positions and leave them as the outposts of a new position – or B and C Companies would move forward to strengthen the present positions being held by the Sherwood Foresters and A and D Companies of the Leicesters. Accordingly, B Company took up a position to the east of the Laagen, astride a road leading south from Tretten while C Company took up a position on the Vardekampen heights on the east bank of the river. Fighting personnel of HQ Company consisted of parts of the MT platoon and the Carrier Platoon under the command of Lieutenant A Speak in the old cheese factory at Tretten.

Several Norwegian troops in lorries were seen about this time retiring through Tretten and within a few minutes the sound of aircraft engines was heard approaching the gorge. The Norwegian soldiers fled from the truck and took to the trees while the inexperienced British troops were hypnotised by the sight of three German fighters roaring towards them up the gorge, all guns firing. In seconds, not a soldier was to be seen; they had flattened themselves on the ground as the bullets pinged off the rocks. In a few moments it was over and the aircraft thundered on up the gorge.

Brigadier Morgan arrived again and gave orders that C Company of the Leicesters was to proceed forward in buses to a position just north of Öyer. These buses were then to return and transport B Company to another position at Tolstadt some six miles south of Tretten.

B Company was then to take up a position some distance to the east of the road right up in the hills. Twice before the British position astride the road had been held, but the Germans had worked round the left flank along the side of the hills: a thing the Norwegian High Command had said was not feasible. Hence B Company was being dispatched to this position in the hills to prevent a reoccurrence of these German tactics when held up in the valley.

C Company got away about an hour later, by which time the retirement of the Norwegian forces was in full swing and caused some considerable congestion on the narrow roads. It was considerably more difficult to get B Company away as the transport never returned. Lorries were commandeered and eventually the first of these got away. Both B and C Companies went forward on the east side of the river and it was now that planes continually swooped to machine gun the retiring Norwegians along the road. As there was considerable congestion in the Tretten area, it was not surprising that the Germans concentrated their fire power in this area.

Rather foolishly, Bren gun fire was opened [on] the offending planes. Which of course gave the position away. It was very fortunate that both sides of the road were heavily wooded, which meant that it was fairly easy to obtain visible protection and often protection from fire. At last, all B Company were collected together and sufficient transport to take them, but every time there was heard the drone of an aircraft engine, the Norwegian drivers would disappear and would not emerge for at least a quarter of an hour. The last of B Company was taken forward in transport some three-quarters of an hour after the first lot had departed. Meanwhile, the endless stream of retiring Norwegian lorries full of troops continued, making progress against oncoming traffic very difficult.

By this time, the remainder of HQ Company of the Leicesters had crossed Tretten bridge onto the east side of the River Laagen. Food and ammunition from the train which still remained in Tretten were also brought across the river and dumped in the cheese factory. An HQ was opened in a quarry about a hundred yards forward from the bridge. Round this area small defensive posts were placed. These posts consisted of men from the intelligence section and the Signal Platoon with one or two from the MT and Bren Carrier Platoons. No orders were received at all as to what this remaining part of HQ Company of the Leicesters were supposed to do and whether we were to remain an isolated and detached sub-unit. B and C Companies had now been sent forward without any means of communication with Tretten. By mid afternoon a few British stragglers began to arrive back having got lifts on lorries with the Norwegians. They were taken to the first aid posts in the cheese factory.

It appeared that these stragglers had got lost in the trees in various actions with the enemy, who were expert in setting the trees on fire with incendiary bombs, causing as much confusion as possible, and when they saw the Norwegians retiring they thought a general retirement was taking place and joined with them. Gradually, more and more started to arrive and at about 5 p.m. or soon after, a large party of C Company (40 to 50) men arrived back in considerable disorder under the leadership of the CSM. They told of chaotic encounters with the enemy and swore that many were dressed up in Norwegian uniforms and fired their weapons at them regardless. Then there were the rumours that the Germans were behind them, causing more confusion and panic amongst the troops making them withdraw needlessly. They said that the whole British force was in retreat some miles further forward and that the CO Colonel German was coming back with them.

It was at about this time that two German Stukas appeared over the gorge and dived on the train in the station. The bombs left the engine intact but derailed one of the carriages. About 300–400 yards north of Tretten bridge, on the east side of the river, there was a large hotel in front of which was an open space. Here, a reorganisation centre was set up, where various stragglers could be organised into their original and proper companies. Some hot tea and rum were also prepared here.

A culvert over a stream some 150 yards south of Tretten bridge and just forward of the quarry caused the road to narrow and a road block was prepared. It could not of course be closed until all British troops had retired through that point. Bren guns and those useless anti-tank rifles were withdrawn now that it was becoming dark, as they were too widely separated to be able to function at all.

At about midnight, over 100 Foresters personnel with their commanding officer, Colonel Ford, arrived in buses having, it was said, received orders to retire. By this time only B Company of the Leicesters was forward intact, personnel of all other sub-units having retired to Tretten.

Tuesday 23rd April

Monday passed into Tuesday unnoticed. About 1 a.m., Major Jones (attached to 148th Brigade HQ) came forward to Tretten by car, with orders from the brigade commander that the forward position was to be held at all costs. It thus became clear that Colonel Guy German must be informed of this at once and of the present whereabouts of all the troops, as there was no sign of him coming back yet. Major John German was back in Tretten at this time. He knew where the CO had last been at Battalion HQ and so, with persuasion, Major Jones loaned his car for the purpose of taking me forward with Major German to find the Colonel.

We drove about four or five miles and then stopped for fear of running straight into the enemy. Jones remained with the driver of the car, while German and I worked our way forward on the road for twenty minutes or so and came to some large buildings and a garage where the Colonel had last been seen. It was now nearly 3 a.m. There was a sentry at this point who hadn't seen the Colonel for about half an hour and had no idea where he might be at the moment. At last we found him in one of the buildings with the Adjutant Captain J. Ford-Smith and Captain Ramsden, OC C Company, where they were snatching a few minutes sleep.

The Colonel was completely unaware of the true situation and was under the impression that all companies of the Leicesters and two of the Foresters were in forward positions. In fact the whole of B Company and about fourteen men of A Company and thirty of C Company were forward. All B Company officers and all A Company officers still alive were forward. The situation was serious indeed as it was a foregone conclusion that the enemy would continue his advance that day. The exact position in the hills of B Company was not quite clear to the Colonel and so Captain Ramsden and myself were sent out to search for them, while the Adjutant and Captain Coleman, the battalion intelligence officer, were sent back to Tretten to get as many troops as possible sent forward again and to find out from Brigadier Morgan exactly what was to be done. After a search in the hills on the east for nearly an hour, we returned without having seen a trace of B Company, but we did come across a lost party of eighteen or so of C Company that Captain Ramsden sent down to report to the Colonel at the garage buildings. When we returned, the Colonel had organised a defensive position just behind the wooden buildings astride the road and was constructing a road block.

After distributing some food which we found there, we settled down patiently to wait and observe. Presently, Major Garner came forward up the road followed by B Company. He had been unable to get to his position up in the hills owing to the ravines and steep gradients between the road and his would-be position. At the same time Lieutenant Colonel King-Salter came forward and gave his report as to what was happening in the rear. A position (Tolstadt) was to be held half-way between Tretten and the present forward position where we now were, with B Company on the left in the hills in the original position allotted to them. The most satisfactory route to this position was to retire three miles or so before starting up into the hills. King-Salter promised to take Major Garner back and show him exactly where this position was and how to get to it. Also, all other available troops were to be sent forward. Meanwhile the forward position had to be held.

At about 9 a.m. the CO sent me back to Tretten on a bicycle which I had obtained to discover when more troops would arrive forward. I had barely gone three miles when I met Captain Coleman and a Forester MO walking forward. The former had a written message from the Adjutant to the CO and having obtained as much information as possible, I returned to the CO with the message. Some troops had been sent forward and a meal was also being sent forward. A secondary position was being prepared at Tretten; as many of the dispersed troops of the Leicesters were being collected together for a final stand against the Germans. Colonel Ford and some Foresters had gone forward to the next defensive position to place themselves on the right of B Company of the Leicesters. Such were the main contents of the message.

The CO then sent me back again to Tretten to find Brigade HQ and discover when and if this forward position was to be vacated; also any other information available. I proceeded some two miles on my bicycle and then with the help of two people who were carrying rations forward, took a motorcycle from the back of a derelict lorry and by good fortune managed to get the thing started. It was not long before the remaining five miles or so were covered and I was in Tretten where I immediately saw the Adjutant, who told me all he knew. He had apparently sent a previous message up to the CO via Second Lieutenant Speak and it later transpired that he and all the men with him were placed on the right flank of B Company by King-Salter while on their way forward to the CO's Position, with the exception of a section of the Bren Carrier Platoon who were detailed to climb the hill on the east bank to guard against ski troops who might outflank the Tretten defences. The Adjutant was unable to put me in touch with Brigade HQ. He informed me that besides B Company of the Leicesters, the worn-out remnants of B and C Companies of the Foresters and Second Lieutenant Speak, with a fair number of HQ personnel of the Leicesters and all available miscellaneous personnel, were in a secondary position at Tretten under Major Atkins. A Company of the Foresters was also to be sent forward to the intermediate position at Rindheim on the east bank of the Laagen and just south of Tretten bridge. The west side of the bridge was to be held by D Company of the Foresters only.

On going forward to inform the CO of this, I met King-Salter. He showed me the exact dispositions of the troops on his map. I asked him if he knew when the CO was going to retire from his forward position, and his reply was that it was up to Colonel German to decide, but presumably when it was no longer feasible to hold it. I then proceeded forward again and met the CO about a mile behind his original forward position. It appeared that he withdrew some three hundred yards away from the original position in case of shelling, and within minutes of having done so, the forward position and the garage buildings were heavily shelled by 100mm mortar bombs. Thereafter, the CO and some thirty men of C Company and three officers with another fourteen men were gradually retiring. I took up my position with rifle beside the CO and told him all I knew but I realised this was where our lost field telephone equipment would have been invaluable to all concerned.

It was not long before the advance guard of enemy infantry appeared round the corner into the straight road about three hundred yards away. When they were properly into the straight the CO gave the order to open fire and a Bren gun and several riflemen scattered the enemy. The CO then ordered me to go back to Tretten and inform them there that he was retiring to the intermediate position in face of the enemy advance. This I did, taking Major German with me on the back of the motorcycle. I then collected nine volunteers with three Bren guns as a patrol to go forward and to relieve the CO. I took the motorcycle forward with a lorry load of the troops following up as far as where the intermediate place of Rindheim came down to the road. Here we debussed and advanced forward on each side of the road; two Bren guns in front and one behind, in case the enemy should have got through the forest on the east side of the road and should attack us from the rear. There was always the possibility that the CO and his party might be completely cut off in a similar way.

After advancing for quarter of an hour or so we passed Second Lieutenant Musson and about 120 personnel of A Company with an anti-tank rifle, who informed us that the CO was some way further forward but still retiring. After advancing for over half an hour, we came across the CO and his party. Captain Ramsden had been killed and one or two others wounded. He explained he was retiring as slowly as possible in order to delay the enemy as much as he could. He then left me in charge and made his way back to Rindheim to see what was happening there and to see if he could find Colonel Ford, CO of the Foresters.

After remaining there for some time, one or two of the enemy started shouting words of command or information, from one side of the river to the other. Eventually, when one of the enemy [was] not far away, and almost parallel to us on the other side, he started shouting to some others who were in front of our position but below the road and in the trees between the river and the road. It looked as if it was about time to be moving again, for we had little option; our rifle ammunition was running low with no prospects of obtaining any more.

Second Lieutenants Kirk and Adcock and their C Company followers therefore withdrew and went right back to the intermediate position at Rindheim, leaving only a volunteer patrol. Having given them sufficient time to get well on their way the patrol party started to withdraw in two sections, one covering the withdrawal of the other. After going about a quarter of a mile all personnel were sent straight back to the intermediate position except four people to man two Bren guns, one crew to cover the retreat of the other. The possibility of the enemy getting through the forest above the road and cutting the whole party off seemed to me to make it advisable to get as many men back to the next properly defended position where the enemy could not break through on the left, and to leave only a minimum to cover their withdrawal.

The two Bren gun crews withdrew steadily and after about twenty minutes or so, we came across Sergeant Millington of the Carrier Platoon, the Leicesters, who had backed a lorry up the road in order to get us back. In a few more minutes we were at the intermediate position, where Captain Coleman placed all available personnel into the right flank of this position. The CO and Coleman on a lorry and myself [on] the motorcycle then returned to Tretten to discover any available news. I was never quite clear whether or not the CO had managed to contact Colonel Ford. It was about this time, around 3 p.m., that the enemy started shelling from behind the hills to the west of the River Laagen. The forest to the west of Tretten was heavily shelled. This was thought to be a 150mm howitzer. We arrived in Tretten in the vicinity of the hotel, some 400 yards north of the bridge. Captain Coleman and I then set off to find a telephone to ring up the Staff Captain on receipt of a message from the latter requiring an immediate call to be put through. On the way we passed the Norwegian High Command Staff in a house and while we were having a word with them, Brigadier Morgan drove up in a car. We took him to where Colonel German was having a bite to eat.

A conference was to be held at 148th Brigade HQ, some half a mile north of Tretten at 4 p.m. and I accompanied the CO and the Brigade Commander up to the house. The Norwegian staff and Colonel Jensen, CO of the Norwegian staff were there also and Colonel Jensen, CO of the Norwegian Dragoons, whose troops were operating on the left flank of the intermediate position. By 5 p.m., high level bombers began to give the Tretten area a pounding and a plan was formulated for a general withdrawal to take place as soon as it was safe to do so without the continual threat of air attack. Fresh and experienced troops were to hold a position at Ringebu some sixteen miles north of Tretten, and the remnants of the two British battalions were to withdraw through them and take up a new position a further five miles north up a valley at right angles to the main Gudbrandsdal. The withdrawal was to commence at 9 p.m.; troops under the command of Colonel Ford in the intermediate position were to come out first, followed by D Company of the Foresters from the west of Tretten bridge at 10 p.m.

Only one platoon of D Company was left here, as the remaining two platoons were taken out and sent forward to the intermediate position on the east bank of the river. But they never got there, owing to the enemy break through and so the platoon left on the west side of the bridge were cut off by the enemy. Finally, the troops under Major Atkins in the Tretten position were to come out at 10.20 p.m. Transport was to be provided by the Norwegians and assembled at a place still to be agreed and notified to OC's troops. The Norwegian Dragoons with their own transport higher up in the hills were to start withdrawing about 7 p.m.

After all arrangements had been made, I was detailed to go forward and pass these withdrawal instructions to Colonel Ford about 4.30 p.m. I found Captain Ford-Smith, the Adjutant, and gave him all the details and asked him to notify D Company of the Foresters and Major Atkins. I then procured my motorcycle which had been refilled with petrol and went forward. I passed Major Atkins and told him briefly the plan; I also came across the RSM who had come on the patrol earlier in the day and I asked him what was happening. He said that German tanks had appeared on the road and as no further orders had been received he decided to get back to Tretten. Three-quarters of a mile forward of the Tretten position a road block was being prepared by a mixed party under the direction of King-Salter. It was impossible to proceed further on the motorcycle and from all accounts this would have been most unwise. German tanks had come well forward to recce and had then retired again.

I proceeded to walk forward, with a Forester officer, Brian Bradley and King-Salter who wanted to see the front line. We each had a rifle and proceeded cautiously in single file down the road. All was well for the first ten minutes or so when suddenly we were machine gunned from the west side of the river. We took cover amongst the trees and proceeded forward. Firing was heard in front of us for some time. Coming into sight of the road again after rounding a little knoll, there down in the road not forty yards away were lorry loads of the enemy. Three tanks had gone forward and could be seen 200–300 yards behind us on the way to Tretten. The enemy had now got well behind us and the road to the right of us was swarming with them. We lay absolutely flat for ten minutes or so wondering what to do, when a 100mm mortar started firing not fifty yards in front of us. After it had been firing for a bit, we decided to stalk it and see if we could put as many of its crew as possible out of action. King-Salter was the first to move and he was immediately spotted by a German from the road, who raised the hue and cry; bullets and hand grenades came hurling at us and we withdrew further up into the forest returning rifle fire. The Forester officer, Brian Bradley, who had gone rather further forward was hit, but King-Salter and myself got well up into the wood. We decided it was useless to go further forward as the intermediate position at Rindheim must by now have been broken completely and so we decided to get back to Tretten. From the sound of it a very fierce battle was going on at Tretten. When we eventually got out, the firing seemed to be coming from a little further north, suggesting that the enemy had got through the Tretten defences. After about 6 p.m., the firing had diminished considerably and was only spasmodic, but air attack still continued. The few shots that were exchanged could be heard coming from well north of Tretten and in the dusk several houses and part of the forest round the village were seen to be well ablaze. A heavy smoke hung over the valley. The Battle of Tretten was over.

After the Battle of Tretten, I became completely separated from the rest of the troops.

Suffice to say that I owe my life to two people – King-Salter, (is mentioned several times in *The Naked Soldiers* [by Joseph Kynoch]) and it was he who extricated me from the Germans at the time that Lieutenant Bradley of the Foresters was killed. The other person was Second Lieutenant Parry of the Foresters who subsequently piloted me across country and mountains to the Swedish/Norwegian frontier. After a few days there being well looked after by the Swedes, we were sent to the internment camp at Falun. Eventually, there were collected about two hundred and thirty members of all arms, including the Merchant Navy. The Swedes were very hospitable and through contact with the British Legation in Stockholm, we were supplied with English books and other reading material.

In the autumn of 1940 we were repatriated in two sections back to the UK. I was with the first section of about a hundred and twenty and we travelled north by train and coach from Falun to Petsamo in the very north of Finland. There we embarked on a Finnish ship with a Swedish captain and sailed around North Cape and eventually made landfall at Lerwick in the Shetlands. We were all subjected to the severest security restrictions of the events of early 1940 given that the Norwegian Government was not willing to jeopardise its neutrality until it was too late. At the same time, the Allies were desperate to do whatever was possible to prevent King Haakon from falling into enemy hands. This might explain much of the chaos prevailing over embarkation problems with our troops at the various northern ports. But even the rescuing of King Haakon and his country's gold bullion didn't justify the gross mistreatment of Britain's young soldiers in sending them to a strange frozen country with inadequate clothing and grossly inadequate equipment to protect them from the enemy. Then of course came the cover up; the shambles of Norway was pushed into the background in view of the much greater shambles to come in a few days time – that of Dunkirk.

Appendix Q

The Early Recollections of Captain Martin Lindsay

Prior to the war, Martin Lindsay had been a polar explorer and had led a 1,100-mile sledging expedition across Greenland. He had joined the Army in 1925 and been commissioned in the Royal Scots Fusiliers, but by 1939 was Member of Parliament for Brigg in Lincolnshire. He was then recalled to the Army and resigned his seat. He recalls:

The Norwegian campaign had just started and I had been summoned to the War Office to give some advice upon Arctic clothing. After the conference there was more than enough time to take me back to the officer cadet unit where I was teaching military law. As I sat with a paper in Brigadier Holland's room I heard his secretary put through a call and say: "The Brigadier asked me to let you know that he can't get home tonight." I remembered that I used to play tennis with his wife so, for old times sake I took over the telephone. We both agreed that the war was very dull. It could scarcely have been duller. As I put down the receiver Brigadier Holland came into the room.

"I want you to fly to Norway with Peter Fleming at once," he said. "You must start in three hours [sic] time. You are to find out if the Norwegians still hold Namsos, as we want to land there. You will have two officers as interpreters and two signal sergeants with W/T sets. You'll get the full story from Peter."'

All that afternoon we flew north and spent the night at a small naval station in Scotland. On arrival we [were] told that an air raid was expected and as there were no spare beds available, we slept on stretchers. At first light next morning, we climbed aboard a Sunderland flying boat. We flew very low over the sea, at only about 100 feet. Eventually we arrived in the right area and had to climb to look for our fjord. Then we recognised its outline and saw far away below us, the tiny port of Namsos. We did not fly in at once, since we did not know whether it was in German hands.

Round and round we circled gradually losing height and peering down through field glasses. We landed and, with our gunners at the alert, taxied towards a wharf. We were the first troops to land and were greeted by a ragged cheer and Peter made a short speech.

After wirelessing to the War Office that Namsos was clear our first action was to blanket the town, so as to prevent news of our arrival from reaching the enemy. The mayor placed pickets on the roads leading inland. For several days we worked hard, collecting information, selecting a headquarters and tactical features for the covering force which would land at night, inquiring about rolling stock and road transport, arranging for an air raid warning system and for accommodation in neighbouring hamlets for the troops we were expecting.

Two or three days later General Carton de Wiart, VC, the force commander arrived in another Sunderland. By this time air attacks were a common occurrence. Though no bombs had as yet been dropped upon the port, raids upon shipping occurred whenever a worthwhile target was presented.

The small Norwegian inter-fjord schooners and timber-boats had now stopped altogether. Our sloops and destroyers were dive bombed repeatedly. Unfortunately the General's plane chose such a moment to arrive; though he himself was untouched, his ADC was shot through the knee in a low-flying attack as they came in.

The General decided to visit the nearest Norwegian formations, taking Peter Fleming with him. The transports, escorted by cruisers and destroyers, were to arrive at the mouth of the fjord some twenty miles from Namsos port, at dusk next day. My job was to collect three or four Norwegian pilots and meet the fleet. With the help of a splendid harbour master the details were arranged.

We met on the afternoon of the next day in the saloon of a small schooner owned by one of the volunteers. It had already been a bad morning and unhappily my arrival on board coincided with an even more noisy raid than usual. Bomb after bomb could be heard detonating on the water.

The pilots looked self-conscious as I walked in. They nodded to and nudged one of their number – their spokesman whom I will call Ohlsen said; "We cannot go down the fjord today. It is too dangerous." I thought it best to treat this as a joke – to pull their legs and jolly them along. We sat down to a drink and skolled each other several times. Everyone was very witty at the expense of the Germans. There was no lack of jovial good-fellowship but it soon became clear that they had no intention whatever of putting to sea. I was appalled.

In a few hours the fleet would be at the mouth of the fjord, but there would be no pilots. The warships and crowded transports would be faced with the alternative of trying to come through in darkness, with considerable navigational hazards, or of withdrawing for 24 hours with all the dislocation this would mean to our plans, to say nothing of the risk of their being bombed next day. All because Lindsay had failed to carry out his orders. There are no adjectives to describe my agony of mind.

I argued and cajoled. I tried to appeal to their sense of patriotism and adventure. It was all in vain. The atmosphere in that stuffy little overcrowded saloon changed to one of acrimony. We had reached a deadlock and time was getting on. Faced with this ghastly predicament I decided that there was only one thing for me to do. I would draw my revolver and present them with an ultimatum. I would say; "Unless we sail at once I will shoot first Ohlsen. Then, if you others will not come. I will next shoot YOU, then YOU, then YOU."'

I was perfectly clear in my mind that this was no bluff. The stakes were altogether too high. If it came to it, I was certainly going to shoot – yet it seemed such a florid, theatrical flourish that I was about to make. Before saying anything I unbuttoned my revolver holster. I am not suggesting that this in any way affected what followed. They may have thought that I was reaching for a flask or tobacco pouch, but at that moment Ohlsen got up, threw away the stub of his strong black cigar and said; "Now we go."

When we were halfway down the fjord German aircraft started to bomb another ship. I was watching this with such interest that it was something of a shock when I heard the crack of bullets passing overhead. We ourselves were being machine gunned.

I dived under cover, grovelling in the scuppers like any coward. But Captain Ohlsen, whose courage I had evidently so greatly misjudged, stood at the wheel a rock. During repeated attacks from diving aircraft during the next twenty minutes, he never flinched. As soon as the last one was over he shook my hand, beaming all over. "You see I was right! I have been at sea for more than twenty years and I always know when it is dangerous."

Martin Lindsay survived the fighting in Norway. Perhaps as a result of seeing first-hand the power of the German Army, and the old-fashioned way that the British were fighting, he was encouraged to volunteer for 'special service' in the middle of 1940. He found himself in No. 2 Commando, which was converted into a parachute unit – the first in the British Army. He was later sent to India to raise a parachute battalion, which started out as the 151 (British) Parachute Battalion and later changed its number to 156. It was under this number, and under a new CO, that the battalion virtually fought itself to extinction at Arnhem in September 1944. By this time Lindsay was no longer with the airborne troops; he had taken part in the Normandy campaign with the Gordon Highlanders as part of the 51st Highland Division.

Appendix R

Report by Lieutenant Colonel Edward King-Salter, Military Attaché to Norway

King-Salter was appointed on 11 April 1940, then wounded and captured on 27 April.

11th April 1940. On 1st March 1940, I took up my duties as Military Attaché at Helsinki, during the first Finnish-Russian War. On the 11th April at about 4.25 p.m. I received the translation of a cypher telegram from the War Office appointing me as Military Attaché to Norway. The telegram also instructed me to find the French Military Attaché to Norway, to go the Norwegian GHQ and keep the War Office informed of the situation, reporting via Stockholm. Having handed over my duties to the Assistant Military Attaché and obtained the necessary visas for my passport, I left Helsinki in a special plane at 6.45 p.m., 2½ hours after receiving my orders. The plane had been obtained from the Finnish Air Force by our Air Attaché. I arrived at Stockholm soon after dark and at once got in touch with our Military Attaché, Lieutenant Colonel Pratt, who gave me every possible assistance.

12th April 1940. The next day, he bought me a Ford V8 car and issued me with the necessary cash. I obtained diplomatic papers from the Norwegian Legation and also collected a small staff consisting of a young British-Norwegian, Mr F. Olsen, who had been at the British Legation at Oslo and who volunteered to come with me, bringing his own car. Also a returning British-Finland volunteer, Mr H. Boddam-Whetham. It was of particularly value to have Mr Olsen with his perfect knowledge of Norwegian and the additional car. During the 12th; while these arrangements were being made at Stockholm, Major-General Lewin arrived from England and told me that he thought the British Government intended to land troops only or primarily at Narvik.

13th April 1940. In company with some members of the British Legation at Oslo who were rejoining their Minister, I started from Stockholm after dark on the 12th and travelling all night found the British Minister to Norway about midday 13th in a hotel just inside the Swedish frontier, where he had moved to keep in touch with the Norwegian Government. With him I found also the French Minister and the French Naval and Military Attachés. The two latter came on with me the same evening after a few hours unavoidable delay to report to the Norwegian Foreign Minister who was also in Sweden some 30 miles to the south. We found him at about 9.00 p.m., and I obtained from him the necessary papers showing that I was a Military Attaché. We were told that it would be impossible to join the Norwegian GHQ by road and an effort was made to obtain an aeroplane.

14th April 1940. During the night about 3 a.m., I telephone to Stockholm a message in a special code (suggested and given to me by Lieutenant Colonel Pratt). The message was for the War Office stating that the morale of the Norwegian Government was very low and suggesting landings at several places as well as Narvik and in particular proposing Namsos. The next morning we heard that it should be possible to get through to Norwegian GHQ and as no aeroplane could be obtained we started by road; intending to feel our way. In the frontier region we had to negotiate mountainous snow-covered roads. Then, travelling via Elverum, we reached Lillehammer at about 10.00 p.m. We had no trouble coming through Norway and were very favourably impressed by the arrangements for internal security which had already in such a short time been organised. We frequently had to show our papers and there were numerous road blocks already formed. We eventually found Norwegian GHQ about 1.30 a.m. and decided that as we were the first Allied Service representatives to arrive and as there seemed to be imminent danger that the Norwegians would surrender we would ask to see the Norwegian C-in-C, General Ruge at once, even though we had no particular message for him. He got out of bed to meet us and made us very welcome. He put us up in his HQ for the night and arranged a conference for the morning.

At this conference he explained to us the situation in Norway and we assured him that Allied assistance would not be long in coming. After the conference, billets were found for us and I was very relived [sic] to find a Major Foley (retired), a secretary at the British Legation, assisted by his secretary, Miss Reid and later by two other ladies. He had joined the Norwegian GHQ, a day or two previously and with a special code of his own was in touch with London via a Norwegian broadcasting station. For some days this was the only channel of communication and the code being a very laborious one there was a limit to the messages that could be received and sent. Major Foley and his staff were working continuously day and night. Major Foley had in addition, entirely on his own, been fulfilling admirably the functions of an Allied Mission!

From my arrival until I was cut off on the 23rd I was the senior British officer with the Norwegian GHQ – for the first few days the only serving British officer – and took a liberal interpretation of my functions. I worked in closest co-operation with the French Military Attaché during this period and we were agreed on every step taken and on every telegram sent.

15th April 1940. Norwegian GHQ was well dispersed and well concealed; in fact, as I was told later by a member of GHQ, it was never bombed during the whole campaign up to the end in June. It had only a very small staff. General Ruge had only been in command for about three days, the original C-in-C having resigned. General Ruge impressed us most favourably. He was a man of strong personality and with all the strain of responsibility that had just been thrown on him remained absolutely calm. About the time of our arrival he obtained a reply from the British Prime Minister to his appeal for help, promising every assistance. During the next few days my time was fully occupied in carrying on liaison with the Norwegian GHQ and sending messages home to report the situation and to ask for various forms of assistance.

General Ruge was not in touch with all the Norwegian forces holding out in various parts of Norway; but was in direct contact with his forces north of Oslo. The latter were weak in numbers and seriously lacking in equipment and were to a large degree improvised. I do not think that even General Ruge realised how weak they were. The withdrawal of German forces about this time from Kongswinger aroused perhaps a false sense of optimism. We expected, however, that the German northward advance to link with Trondheim would begin any day. We were all convinced that the successful prosecution of the war in Norway demanded the recapture of Trondheim – but that this would not be possible if the Germans from Oslo were allowed to effect junction with their forces at Trondheim. General Ruge's views were sent to the War Office. He was very distressed at the fact that no information as to future plans was being communicated to him, which made it extremely difficult for him to conduct his operations. This difficulty was explained to Admiral Evans who paid a fleeting visit to GHQ about the 17th.

17th April 1940. I was asked to visit a member of the Norwegian Government at Lillehammer. He wished me to get a message of his to the Norwegian people broadcast from London. On this day an Air Ministry message indicated that troops might be arriving at Åndalsnes. We had previously heard of the landing of troops at Narvik which had pleased General Ruge in showing that help was really coming, but had also disappointed him because he would have preferred the troops on the Oslo-Trondheim area. So he was now much encouraged at the prospect of a landing at Åndalsnes.

18th April 1940. I together with the French Military Attaché visited our Minister on the question of who should be in supreme command in the area Trondheim-Oslo. We felt strongly that it was impossible to have two commanders acting independently in that area and that General Ruge must have the command. The Minister agreed and promised to wire home to that effect. We had already wired our recommendation.

On the evening of the 18th we were overjoyed to learn that British troops were landing at Åndalsnes. These proved to be 148th Infantry Brigade. By this time the Norwegian troops north of Oslo were being driven rapidly northwards by the Germans and the situation looked most critical. British help, both from the morale as well as the actual point of view, was urgently required. Telegrams from home indicating that the reinforcements we had requested were coming left us in no doubt that General Ruge could call on the troops landing at Åndalsnes. Consequently a message was sent to Brigadier Morgan, commanding 148th Infantry Brigade to bring his Brigade south. I gave this message personally over the telephone to Brigadier Morgan soon after he landed. These instructions conflicted with his previous orders; but he agreed, eventually, that he must come south.

19th April 1940. I realised however that the situation must be explained personally to Brigadier Morgan; and General Ruge welcomed my offer to go to Dombaas to meet him. The French Military Attaché asked to accompany me. At this time the communications from Åndalsnes to Lillehammer had been interrupted by German parachute troops near Dombaas. But it was hoped that the parachutists would soon be dealt with and we decided to feel our way through. We started on the morning of the 19th, and the parachutists were cleaned up just before our arrival. We met Brigadier Morgan and discussed with him the problem of the conflicting orders. He agreed that he must come south; and late that night he reported to General Ruge at his HQ. The ensuing conference began badly because

General Ruge was evidently very displeased with some orders Brigadier Morgan had given to the Norwegian railway officials earlier in the day. General Ruge made it clear that he himself must be in supreme command. Either at this time, or next day, General Ruge also made it clear that the continuance of Norway in the war was entirely dependent on himself. Brigadier Morgan made a reply satisfactory to General Ruge and cordial relations were fully restored. Brigadier Morgan only had two weak battalions, which had to be provided with Norwegian transport. Though it must have been very painful for him he agreed that it was best for his troops to be distributed under the orders of the Norwegian commanders on each side of the Lillehammer Lake, where they were urgently required.

20th April 1940. We all met a troop train which arrived at about 1.00 a.m. The Norwegian motor transport was assembled ready for them. Later that night however after I was in bed I was rung up by General Ruge who complained most strongly because Brigadier Morgan had withheld two of his companies a long way up the valley. Neither he nor I had understood that he meant to do this and he asked me to speak to Brigadier Morgan at once on the telephone. I was put through to Brigadier Morgan and in the ensuing conversation some sharp words passed between us. He eventually agreed to send on the two companies. I can understand that he wished to keep some troops back because of instructions he had from the War Office; but he had not given any indication that he was going to do so and I pointed out to him how disastrous it would be if the battle was lost because of the absence of these companies which I maintained could achieve nothing where they were.

21st April 1940. I accompanied General Ruge on a visit to Colonel Dahl commanding the forces on the west of the lake. We also saw some of the Sherwood Foresters occupying a reserve position. On the same day the Norwegian troops on the east side of the lake met with a severe reverse and had to be withdrawn through our troops during the afternoon and night.

22nd April 1940. Early on the 22nd our troops on that side consisting of half a battalion Sherwood Foresters and half a battalion Leicesters had to occupy a position which they had not had the opportunity to reconnoitre. They had been [the] rear guard the evening before and had had a most difficult night move (the Leicesters on foot); and the Germans arrived almost immediately they had got to their new position. Meanwhile, on the west of the lake the German pressure had relaxed. In the early afternoon, I happened to be visiting the HQ of the Norwegian General Hvinden-Haugh commanding the forces on the east of the lake when a report came in that the British were falling back from their new position. At the time and not knowing the circumstances in which the position had been occupied and as the position was an important one, being the entrance to the defile immediately north of Lillehammer, this report caused considerable consternation, particularly as no Norwegian troops were in position in the rear. The Norwegian troops, utterly exhausted, had been withdrawn to rest and reorganise. It seemed clear that I must offer to help in this situation and General Hvinden-Haugh gladly accepted my offer. Brigadier Morgan's Brigade Major came with me.

General Hvinden-Haugh's HQ was at Öyer, some seven miles north of the British position. We had only proceeded about half a mile southwards when we met the first lorry load of British troops. I stopped these and the two that followed and intended to send them forward again; but more and more arrived and the Brigade Major suggested that it would be better to take up a position at Öyer, half a mile behind us, where there was a good field of fire. I agreed with this suggestion; and Lieutenant Colonel German (commanding the Leicesters), who had now arrived, put the troops into position at Öyer. The Foresters half battalion was under the command of Lieutenant Colonel Ford. While debussing the troops were heavily bombed from the air. Two sticks of four bombs fell right amongst us; although there were not many casualties to men or vehicles, the effect on the already tired men was very serious. Fortunately the remaining half battalion of the Leicesters arrived from Åndalsnes and joined Lieutenant Colonel German at Öyer. Meanwhile I had disposed a platoon to cover the occupation of the position and later I helped to get back a quantity of our transport from which the Norwegian drivers had disappeared and was now lying in front of our position. I then found General Hvinden-Haugh still in Öyer, waiting for the German aircraft to go home before he moved back to his new HQ. He asked me to give Lieutenant Colonel German his further orders, i.e. to hold the present position until 2000 and then to hold the edge of a forest 2½ miles further north, during the next day. I found Lieutenant Colonel German and gave him these orders. I then went back with his second-in-command to the edge of the forest; but while there a Norwegian staff officer arrived with a change of orders – to hold the edge of the forest as outposts during the night and to hold a prepared position on which work had been done in the middle of the forest during the next day. A company of Norwegians was to help occupy this position.

22nd April 1940.I passed these orders on and a little after dark was on my way back to General Ruge when I passed Lieutenant Colonel Ford commanding the Sherwood Foresters moving to the position at the head of some of his Battalion. He spoke to me and asked me urgently to represent at HQ that our troops were not capable of holding the position on the next day. It should be pointed out here that most of our troops had had several nights without sleep and many of them had apparently not received any rations. They had come across from England in a rough sea, had travelled straight down by night a distance of some 200 miles and some of them had to go straight into action, being harassed by the German air force on the way. Many also had had a terrible night's march through the mountains. They were simply rifle companies with no artillery, tanks or aircraft to support them. Consequently I agreed to take this message. I found General Ruge at his new HQ near Ringebu about midnight and told him that our troops could not hold the position next day. He replied at once that they must hold it, because otherwise the whole of the Norwegian forces on the west of the lake would be cut off. Their only way back was across a bridge at Tretten two miles behind the position that he had ordered must be held. He then made me an urgent appeal (though obviously I was absolutely ready to do what he asked) to go forward again at once and ensure that the troops did hold the position. I said that I would and he shook hands with me.

23rd April 1940. I stopped a short time at his HQ to get some food and then Brigadier Morgan appeared possibly about 1 a.m. on the 23rd. It will be remembered that he was not in operational command of his troops but he had been visiting them and he came back with exactly the same comment as I had brought that they were too exhausted to hold the position the next day. General Ruge held a conference and Brigadier Morgan agreed, as I had, that our troops must try to hold it. Brigadier Morgan wanted to go forward to Lieutenant Colonel German himself but General Ruge wished me to do this as I knew the position which it was required to hold, having taken the orders from the Norwegian staff officer the previous evening. Brigadier Morgan was to go and see General Hvinden-Haugh and urge him to collect Norwegian troops to help. General Ruge was also very anxious that Brigadier Morgan should meet the fresh British troops reported to be landing on the 23rd at Åndalsnes, under Brigadier Morgan's command until General Paget arrived, and bring them south.

I accordingly went forward again almost immediately after the conclusion of the conference, I found a number of the British troops at Tretten and gave orders for all fit to fight – including personnel of Brigade HQ – to move south again into the forests. I was told that Lieutenant Colonel German was with the outposts on the south edge of the forest. It was now perhaps 0500. I then went on to see and found him in the front line of the outposts. He had had some fighting in the night. It was decided he should remain where he was as long as he could while I went back and reconnoitred the position in the forest and helped our troops to occupy it.

Lieutenant Colonel German gave orders for a company he had in reserve to move back to the position and I went back and began to reconnoitre it. Its strength lay in a high spur jutting out from the main ridge and precipitous on the side facing the enemy's advance. Apart from the main road at the foot of the spur and its immediate vicinity, there were only two passes over the spur. Its weakness was that it was closely wooded, except on the actual slopes and except for a very narrow open stretch up the re-entrant at its foot, giving a field of fire sometimes of less than 100 yards.

Seeing that some of the troops had arrived, I went down again so as to start as soon as possible getting some into position. There was a little delay, however, as units and sub-units were mixed and had to be re-organised. As each sub-unit was ready it was sent up the re-entrant to me and I allotted it its area.

I addressed the men of some of these sub-units and told them how important it was for them to hold this position. I had not yet reconnoitred further up the re-entrant where there appeared to be no open ground at all. The company commander who was to be on the left (i.e. east flank high up the re-entrant) now came with me to reconnoitre. We had to go further and further trying to find a suitable position to cover the left flank; the ground had now flattened and we were on a wooded plateau. There had been no time to get a covering party and I momentarily expected to meet German ski patrols. At last the forest came to an end and we got a fairly good field of fire over the plateau covering the left flank. Returning down the mountain we met his company on its way up. Going on down, I met Major Roberts, 2 i/c of the Sherwood Foresters. He had been commanding the half battalion Sherwood Foresters, operating on the west side of the lake. During the night his two companies had been brought back to Tretten (two or three miles north of the position where we now were). He told me that he had left one company holding the bridgehead at Tretten facing west and the other company was spare. I said I would send it up. Major Roberts told me also that he had persuaded his CO to take a rest and that he was temporarily in command. He seemed to have a good grip of the situation and I left him and went back to Tretten.

I was thankful that we had got the troops on the ground in time; but I was worried because there was no wire and they had no tools even if it had been possible to dig in this frozen rocky ground. With the short field of fire, in places there being no open ground at all, the danger of infiltration was great. The steeply rising ground in the rear made movement of reserves within the position extremely difficult. It was a case of having 'everything in the shop window'. The position however, seemed absolutely tank-proof, the road being the only possible route. The Norwegians had promised a company to help in this position but it had not arrived. A Norwegian motor machine gun unit was sent up, however, and occupied the two passes high up on the precipitous slope.

I went back to Tretten – at perhaps about 1000 – intending to send forward the other company to Major Roberts, to inform General Ruge that the position was occupied and to try and arrange for protection of the left, or east, flank from the Tretten side of the high spur. I was still not satisfied that that flank was adequately protected and an approach through the deep snow over the plateau was more direct than the line of the road, which went round two sides of a triangle. I sent forward Major Roberts' spare company telling them, as Major Roberts had asked me to do, to drop one platoon to give depth to the defences on the road itself.

I motored up a mountain road above Tretten to reconnoitre; but found that owing to the forest it was very difficult to do anything to protect that flank adequately. Eventually, I decided to post a small party of troops on the eastern outskirts of Tretten where they could oppose across some open snow-covered fields any attempt to attack Tretten from over the mountains. While this party was being organised from some of the HQ Company troops still in Tretten, I had some food which they offered me.

Shortly afterwards I again met the Norwegian staff officer and with him the commander of the Norwegian motor machine gun unit. They were both extremely anxious lest the enemy should be working up the west bank of the valley and asked if I could send some troops southwards on that side. I was surprised, as I had assumed the forces on the west bank were responsible on that side. When receiving this request, I was uncertain whether to take action, not knowing if Lieutenant Colonel German was back yet or if Brigadier Morgan was perhaps functioning again (I had heard of him in Tretten); and I felt that I had accomplished the special task with which I had been entrusted. But the Norwegians were very insistent and I agreed to act. They sent a Norwegian officer with me to find a local guide and we motored to the west side of Tretten bridge, where I found Major Kirkland at perhaps about 1400 holding a bridgehead with his company (one of the two which had been under Major Roberts on the west side of the lake). I explained to him what was required and he agreed to take his company one or two miles south down that side of the valley. Dinners were to be served soon and I told him to wait until the men were fed; a difficult decision because it seemed of great urgency for him to move without any delay.

I then decided to revisit the defensive position. I had heard no firing whatsoever and as it was by now about 3 o'clock I was feeling very hopeful; and the shock was very great when about half a mile south of Tretten at the entrance to the forest I met some stragglers, utterly exhausted, who told me that German tanks had just broken through their position. An RE officer – Major M. Jefferies, was with me, who had earlier been carrying out demolitions on his own. I sent him back in my car to warn the troops at Tretten of what had happened and I stopped where I had met the stragglers.

More and more stragglers appeared all with the same story and I was at a loss what action to take. There were some felled trees at that point and I ordered the men to make a road block. Many of them would not assist and some of them even refused to stop and continued to retreat. I even considered whether I ought to fire on these men – but they seemed to have no reasoning powers left and I thought it better not to! All this time – about 15 minutes – I felt that I ought perhaps to go forward to see what the situation really was and to help if I could. I always remembered that it was vitally important to hold the position all day if the forces on the west bank were to be saved. Then an officer, I think an IO, called Barratt, arrived with a message for the commander of the forward troops to hold their position until 2000. I felt that he must go on with his message and decided to go with him. An officer called Bradley who appeared at that moment volunteered to come with us. None of the men would come. We three then walked up the road, each carrying a rifle. We had gone about ¾ mile through the forest when on approaching a bend we heard shots, some of which passed over us. As we had been prepared to meet tanks at any moment we immediately ran into the forest and lay down in a slight depression about 20 yards from the road but unavoidably in full view of it. A few seconds later we could hear tanks; and we then lay motionless, momentarily expecting to be discovered and watched the German tanks and infantry go by.

From now until the 27th I was behind the German lines, but before describing what happened to me during this time, I will give a short account of the general events that followed that afternoon. When I sent Major Jefferies back to Tretten I told him to try and get hold of Major Kirkland's company if it had not already started off. I have subsequently met Major Kirkland who tells me that he did receive fresh orders and these were to take 1½ platoons to the east bank and go forward and 'deal with a tank that had broken through and broken down!' He came up the road with his 1½ platoons shortly after us and encountered the German advance just inside the forest. The Germans were halted and Major Kirkland saw them first and deployed an A/T rifle and a Bren to engage the leading German tank and the infantry section immediately behind it. He opened fire but the German tank came on and Major Kirkland's troops were overrun. He himself was wounded and captured and lost a leg. The Germans then proceeded to bombard Tretten heavily both with 6" guns and from the air, also with machine guns which had worked their way forward on the other side of the water. Eventually they advanced on Tretten and captured it. The garrison of Tretten can only have consisted of those men who had been too exhausted to be put into the defensive position earlier in the day, and of the remainder of Major Kirkland's company and of various HQ details. After capturing Tretten the Germans pushed on some miles before being checked by Norwegian troops at Faavang. As a result of the failure to hold the forest position the whole of the Norwegian force on the west bank was cut off. I have heard from a member of that force, subsequently, that their commander, Colonel Dahl, tried to get his troops back into the main valley over the snow-covered mountains. He was, however, unable to succeed unless he abandoned his transport, which he did not wish to do. He accordingly returned towards the main valley but was kept away from it by German troops including tanks. Colonel Dahl's force remained bottled up in the mountains in this area until it received orders from General Ruge to surrender about the 3rd or 4th May, i.e. after our troops had left Åndalsnes.

I am not clear as to exactly how the breakthrough in the forest position occurred. It would appear that the German tanks were not stopped by our A/T rifles and that they succeeded in forcing an entry into the position down the road. Infantry followed and the troops higher up the re-entrant had their position turned and were cut off. Many of them got away into the mountains. Most of these were eventually captured but some reached Sweden. At the end of the day there was virtually nothing left of the two battalions of the 148th Infantry Brigade as a fighting force. They tried to carry out a vital task which we thought was beyond their powers, exhausted as they were, and completely lacking in artillery, tanks or aircraft the enemy in fact proved too strong for them.

Back now to what happened during my three days behind the lines. Barratt, Bradley and myself were lying watching the Germans' advance guard of tanks and infantry going by. At last there was a lull. Barratt wanted to rush out and shoot as many Germans as we could and get killed ourselves. This was the right spirit; but as our position was overrun and as I personally belonged at GHQ I dissuaded him. Later he suggested we should attack a 6" gun we could hear in the vicinity. I felt perhaps we ought to but was unwilling! He got up on his knees and I followed suit; and I was seen. A few moments later a German soldier crept up and fired at me from 10 yards range. He then threw a hand grenade which just missed me. I took a snap shot at him. We then decided to run for it, through the forest and snow, up the mountain. We did so, ignoring the challenges to stop and were fired on. Bradley was killed but Barratt and I got away. (Lieutenant R. Bradley's date of death according to the Commonwealth War Graves Commission is 26th April 1940; he was a member of the 8th Sherwood Foresters and was aged 31. He now lies in grave IC1 of Lillehammer North Civil Cemetery.)

Laboriously working our way through the deep snow up the mountain we made our way round the crest line while the Battle for Tretten was going on. We found a car in a farm in the mountains above Tretten and hoped to get ahead of the Germans. Barratt stopped, however, as a party of his own men appeared and he felt he must walk with them. I picked up two or three of his men who were lame and started in the car. We had, however, only gone about a mile when we ran into a German column that had passed through Tretten. The car stopped a few yards from the enemy and we tumbled out and scattered into the forest. For the second time that day I was challenged and under heavy fire at point blank range, but again got away. I tried to work round to head off Barratt to warn him but could not find him. By now it was dark and I moved very cautiously so as not to run into German patrols. Eventually I got some food in a farm and pushed on in a northerly direction along the mountain top through the forest, following a sleigh track.

24th April 1940. About 2.00 a.m. I found a little shed and in it were about 10 British troops with 2 officers. I decided to remain with them and during the next two days our party grew and grew. The following evening we were about 10 officers, including Lieutenant Colonel German and about 80 other ranks. Two thirds of the men had lost their rifles and all were utterly exhausted from lack of food and sleep. Two stout-hearted men however still carried their Brens. We could only move very slowly, stopping everywhere we found an inhabited dwelling to try and get food. Often all we could get, if anything, was some milk. The bigger our party became, the more difficult was our task.

25th April 1940. On the second day we had to make a wide detour over the mountains away from the valley to avoid an impassable peak. On the night of the 25th/26th we billeted ourselves in an empty mountain hotel, together with some Norwegian troops. Our object during this time was to get the men fit again and to work along the mountain tops and regain our own lines further up the valley. We could hear the battle going on all the time but always many miles ahead of us. I felt sometimes that we ought perhaps to attack the German L of C for which we were favourably placed; but with scarcely any ammunition and only 2 Brens and 20 rifles and with the men utterly exhausted it did not seem practicable. The efforts of climbing up and down these mountains in the deep snow was very great.

25th/26th April 1940. On the night in question we had reached the edge of our map and were in doubt as to the best route to follow the next day. However a young Norwegian civilian who had been carrying despatches and who knew the district arrived during the night, on skis, and he offered to guide us the next day. I may mention here that if there had been any other officer who could ski and if we could have got two pairs of skis, I would have perhaps left the party, seeing that Lieutenant Colonel German was with it and that they were many of his own troops. All the time I was anxious to get back to my post at GHQ.

We now had an awkward decision to make. Some high open mountains blocked our line of advance a few miles ahead. We would either have to go over the mountains through the deep snow, with no tracks to help us and with little prospect of getting food, or we could keep to the line of the upper farms on the main valley and at one point practically go down to within ¼ mile of Ringebu where the Germans were sure to have troops. The latter course, though very risky, had the advantage of saving much time as the valley at this point bent away to the west. We were on the east side. Also, to have gone over the open mountains referred to might lead to many men collapsing from exhaustion or to being caught out in the open in deep snow by some of the enemy aircraft which were continually passing. We accordingly decided to take the more immediately risky course and pass close to Ringebu.

26th April 1940. The men were now to some extent refreshed and we decided to do a continuous movement during the next day and the following night to reach another lie-up beyond Ringebu. We hoped to reach it before daylight. Everything went well and we succeeded in getting a little food from the upper farms. We reached a point beyond which we could not move unseen, above Ringebu, and so we rested for two or three hours in the snow and forest waiting for darkness to fall. We were able to issue a small but hot meal before starting the night march. Our guide was to lead us part of the way. We had to make a big detour up a gorge to cross a mountain torrent and all this took time. We formed a small advance guard of about eight men with one of the Brens (with two or three magazines which were all we had). Just outside Ringebu we had to cross some fields and hit a mountain road. Lieutenant Colonel German and I reconnoitred ahead and thought he [sic] had found this road. I then started up it with the advance guard. We soon came to a gate barring our way, but a road at right angles led thirty yards to the right and then left again and so we followed it thinking it was the right road. Looking through glasses in the afternoon I had seen a similar kink in what I took to be our road. But after a time I became anxious as to whether I was on the right one as we were climbing too steeply. The main body we found was no longer behind us. The road we had followed after meeting the gate was evidently not the right one and the main body had missed us but managed to get on to the right one and during the night they got ahead of us. I heard afterwards that they passed a small post of men whom they thought were Germans near Ringebu but who took no notice of them. Eventually I regained by a track through the forest the right road without having to lose height. It was now light and I did not know whether the main body was in front of me or behind me. We were a long way out of sight from Ringebu. I decided to push on up the mountain road to our selected lie-up. I was feeling cheerful as we appeared to have passed the danger point. We had walked about a mile up the road and I and the Brigade IO who had got into plain clothes on the 23rd, were some way in front of the rest of our little party. The country on both sides of the road was open. Suddenly I saw on the road about 100 yards in front of me a small party of soldiers in grey and beside them a party in khaki. On second thoughts it occurred to me that they might be Norwegians not Germans. But the men in grey then began to wave their arms and shout "Hallo". I suddenly became certain they were German. The officer with me, being in plain cloths, slipped away and was obviously taken by the Germans to be a civilian. I felt I was in a desperate situation and thought for a moment about firing with my rifle but there was no cover except a small stone in front of me. So I turned and ran at full speed about 40 yards to a farm building behind me. I received a bullet through the elbow but carried on running between the farm buildings to the far side where I paused to get my breath. A few seconds later a German who must have been in the farm appeared 15 yards away but somehow did not see me. 100 yards up over the snow was the edge of the forest. I appeared to be in a hopeless position but thought it might be worth trying to run to the forest. I had only gone a few yards however, when I came under heavy rifle fire and a little later under machine gun fire as well. I was about 20 yards from the forest when I was brought down feeling I had been shot through the back. As I fell I threw my rifle away as a sign that I was finished. As I lay on the ground I looked round and saw that my right foot was nearly shot off. Later it was found that I had received eight hits. Within two or three minutes four German soldiers arrived. One of them put his rifle on my chest and called me "*Verbrecher*" (criminal) and I thought he was going to shoot me. I argued with him in German. An hour or two later this man came back and apologised for what he had done! The other men bandaged me most considerably using their own dressings and [took] me to a farm. This was about 5 a.m.

Lieutenant Stoker RAMC was brought in to see me. It appeared, as I had already guessed, that Lieutenant Colonel German's party had been captured by this enemy outpost perhaps half an hour before I met them. Five men had been killed. Lieutenant Stoker gave me a morphine injection and I was later taken in a lorry to Ringebu where a German doctor looked at me; and then by ambulance to the Norwegian Civilian Hospital in Lillehammer where I remained for about six months. The Germans had taken over the hospital, but the doctoring and nursing was carried out by the Norwegians, who looked after me admirably. The Germans also allowed visitors without restriction. The local Norwegians visited the British wounded every day and brought us frequent gifts. We were in fact as well off as if we had been in hospital in England. In November 1940 with the last six of our men in the hospital, I was transferred to Germany. An artificial leg, which the Norwegians made for me and was given as a gift to me, reached me just before the hospital ship left Oslo.

For a long time, while in hospital, I wondered why we had so unexpectedly run into the German outpost up the mountain road. It was at a hamlet called Venalygd. We had used a 1/100,000 black and white Norwegian map of Ringebu and from it the road we were following ended in the mountains and there seemed no reason to expect an outpost so far up it. Some weeks later a motoring map came into my possession and I found that on it a major road coloured red leading over the mountains from the next main valley – the Osterdal, joined our mountain road at Venalygd. Seeing this map I realised at once that Venalygd was an obvious place for an outpost force. I then found that this connecting road was quite new and so probably not shown on the 1/100,000 map we were using and since my return I find it is not shown on the War Office copy of this map. In any case in winter it was snowed up; which would account for the fact that our guide never mentioned it when we were discussing our plans. This explanation accounts for our being to some extent surprised – on the other hand, of course, the whole time we were in the mountains we were liable to run into the enemy, because if we were ever to rejoin our own forces we had to move parallel and not far from the main L of C of the Germans. I estimate that in the 3½ days from when I was cut off until I was captured I covered 35 miles through the mountains.

Lieutenant Colonel King-Salter remained a prisoner until it was realised he had been the Military Attaché in Finland and Norway, and he was returned to England via a diplomatic exchange in Lisbon in November 1942.

Appendix S

Post-Operation Report on Maurice Force

Lieutenant-General Carton de Wiart, Maurice Force commander, made the following lengthy post-operation comments:

25th April. About 2000 HMS *Manchester* put in to Molde. The remainder of the convoy with its escorts of destroyers went on to Åndalsnes. Some three quarters of an hour later HQ Staff Sickle Force was transferred to the Norwegian destroyer *Sleipner* for passage to Åndalsnes. On boarding the *Sleipner* I was met by Brigadier Morgan, commanding 148th Infantry Brigade, Captain Denny, SNO Molde and Åndalsnes and Wing Commander Keene, RAF Liaison Officer.

During the voyage to Åndalsnes I held a conference in the wardroom of the *Sleipner*. Opinion was universal. The expedition was ill-founded. Lack of air support, AA defence, facilities for base expansion, artillery support and alternative means of communication were already apparent. In spite of this somewhat discouraging welcome, the promise of 60 Gladiator fighters, the prospect of extending the base organisation to Sondal and Geiranger, and the anticipated Allied offensive at Trondheim, all made me confident that we might achieve our objective of stopping the German advance from the south for the required period.

I wired to the War Office giving the situation stressing the need for acceleration of the above projects and ordered Lieutenant Colonel Festing GSO1 to return to London by the quickest method in order to report on the general situation. I landed at Åndalsnes about 2230.

After a short call at HQ Sickle Force and the Royal Marines HQ, I started off about 2330 with Brigadier Morgan for the front to assume command in the forward areas and to get in touch with the Norwegian GHQ as soon as possible. On my way up I called at the Park Hotel just outside Åndalsnes to see Sir Cecil Dormer, the British Minister. Our support was badly needed and unless the effects of it were soon apparent, he doubted the will of the Norwegian people to resist. The troops were of good material but needed direction and time to reorganise or re-equip.

After this I went to the Norwegian C-in-C's HQ near Dovre about 0500. I met General Ruge who handed over the fighting in the Gudbrandsdal valley to me, at the same time saying that the remnants of the Norwegian 2nd Division would help as much as they could. I called on General Haug, commander Norwegian 2nd Division at Sel and it was soon apparent that all the help I could hope for would be from ski troops – the rest of the Division was spent and in no mood to fight. After leaving General Haug I went to Advanced HQ 15th Infantry Brigade near Kvam to find out the situation.

26th April. 1st KOYLI were holding a position across the valley at Kvam with 1st Y&L (York & Lancaster) in a supporting position some two miles in the rear. 1st Green Howards moved up from Åndalsnes to Dombaas by train joining the remnants of 148th Infantry Brigade in that place.

By 1600 it was obvious that 1st KOYLI could not maintain their front much longer. They had held the Kvam position for nearly 48 hours, in spite of repeated enemy attacks and constantly subjected to enemy artillery fire, air bombing and low flying MG fire. I therefore ordered Brigadier Kent-Lemon to withdraw 1st KOYLI by MT to Dombaas night 26th/27th through 1st Y&L who were to maintain their present position reinforced by one company Green Howards (sent up in MT from Dombaas) in order to cover preparation of a strong position just south of Otta.

The situation on my left flank was causing some anxiety, as the enemy were reported to have reached Alydal in the Osterdalen valley. There were only small detachments of Norwegian troops at Foldal and Hjerkin. Hence it was possible for the enemy to develop a threat against my L of C by way of Foldal, Hjerkin and Dombaas. I therefore placed Brigadier Morgan in command of the troops in Dombaas to organise the defence of the village with his own force (400 strong but short of officers and weapons) and one company Green Howards, who were given the task of blocking the Hjerkin road.

I then moved the remainder of the Green Howards by train at night to Otta to occupy a position south of the village as a firm base in rear of 1st Y&L north of Sjoa. During the withdrawal of 1st KOYLI several minor demolitions were successfully carried out. My object at this stage was still to stop the enemy. I judged that I could not expect my forward troops to withstand the enemy for more than 48 hours in any one position without any form of artillery and air support, yet opposed by an enemy well supplied with both. My planning was therefore directed to delaying the enemy as much as possible so as to give time for the arrival of my artillery and air support. Thus equipped I anticipated little difficulty in stopping the enemy.

27th April. The withdrawal of 1st KOYLI was successfully carried out and 1st Y&L held the Sjoa position throughout the day. The enemy had been slow in following up and did not press his attack for the time being, contenting himself with air and ground bombardment. 1st Green Howards organised the Otta position for defence and the preparation of the Dombaas defences was continued. Owing to the rocky nature of the ground it was seldom possible to dig and concealment from the air was essential.

During the morning a report from the French Military Attaché again indicated enemy action from the direction Foldal-Hjerkin. General Ruge was confident in the ability of his detachment to hold off any such threats; but I judged that a recce was desirable in case it became necessary to reinforce the Norwegian troops. Unfortunately the inability of the car at my disposal to negotiate a steep hill, limited my recce to the vicinity of Dombaas. Throughout the day the need for recce aircraft was acute not only for normal tasks but also to confirm or deny the many alarmist reports received.

I had conferred with General Ruge earlier in the day and we had agreed that the Otta position was a strong one, on which we should have a good chance of holding the enemy until I could get up my guns from the base. General Ruge asked me to hold on to the Otta position until a Norwegian detachment under Colonel Dahl which had been isolated in the hills west of Tretten, could be withdrawn by the roads leading into the Gudbrandsdal in the area Otta-Sel. I assured him that I would be prepared, with the situation as it then was, to hold the Otta position for two or three days, and that we would do our best to cover Colonel Dahl's withdrawal. The Otta position required two battalions to hold it and as the Y&L would have found difficulty in hanging on to the Sjoa position I ordered them to withdraw on the night 27th/28th to reinforce the Green Howards on the Otta position.

The withdrawal was not as successful as on the previous night. The enemy had anticipated it and made every effort to work round the flank. Parties of the enemy (dressed as Norwegian troops) succeeded in cutting off some of the forward companies and eventually only some 12 officers and 300 ORs were available to assist the Green Howards on the Otta position.

Note. Many of the 1st Y&L who had been cut off rejoined subsequently after an adventurous passage of the hills on the flanks of the valley.

28th April. At about 0500 the liaison officer who had taken up the MT for the withdrawal of the 1st Y&L returned to Force HQ with the news of the difficulties experienced by this Battalion. In his opinion the Y&L were not in a fit state to hold their sector of the Otta position, which would thus be held solely by the Green Howards.

The situation was thus indefinite but necessitated some precautionary measures. Movement of troops in the open or on the L of C by daylight could only be justified as a last resort; but there was still some 2½ hours left before the usual time of arrival of the German early air recce. Throughout the operations the enemy was methodical in his air action and his probable active hours could be forecast with accuracy.

I therefore ordered CO 1st KOYLI from Dombaas to report to Force HQ forthwith and move the Dombaas company of the Green Howards some two miles south of Dombaas into a concealment area with MT immediately available to move forward if necessary. 1st KOYLI were put at one hours [sic] notice to move.

While these moves were taking place the first news of the intended evacuation reached me. The War Office telegram requested my acceptance of a plan or a suggested alternative. I would not answer this without reference to General Ruge as the evacuation was not possible without his co-operation. I therefore went to his HQ and told him frankly the situation which at first he was unable to accept. Finally he did so on my assurance that I would in all circumstances cover the withdrawal of the Norwegian Army and not relinquish Dombaas until this had been affected.

Meanwhile the situation of Green Howards and Y&L was causing commander 15th Infantry Brigade anxiety. Y&L had not recovered from the severe handling they had received during the previous nights [sic] withdrawal and though the Green Howards were in good heart they were all too few to cover an extensive position. The enemy had gained contact at 1030 and quickly began a methodical bombardment of the forward troops with artillery and trench mortars. The bombing and machine gun fire on the forward troops were the heaviest experienced up to that time. It was apparent that to hold the position until dark and then extricate the forward Battalions might be a matter of considerable difficulty. The time and space problem of the withdrawal had now to be considered. The major factors were:-

(a) My obligation to cover the withdrawal of all Norwegian troops to this area.

(b) Shipping available night 29th/30th, 30th/1st and 1st/2nd.

(c) Withdrawal dependent on one single railway line and road over a distance of 100 miles.

(d) The physical endurance of my troops.

It was obvious from the start that demolition must play a large part in the plan. A vital point was the bridge over the Rosta gorge between Dovre and Otta. If this was successfully blown the enemy would be unlikely to be able to get wheels (including tanks and guns) forward of the gorge for at least 48 hours.

I withdrew one section 55th Field Company at once from the forward area to prepare the Rosta demolitions and sent up the company of Green Howards (then lying up south of Dombaas) by MT to cover their preparations.

During the afternoon and early evening the Green Howards on the Otta position fought splendidly. One medium and two light tanks were destroyed by the 25 mm Anti-Tank Company. Other targets included recce parties and groups of enemy in buildings. There is no doubt that the enemy suffered many casualties in this battle and his subsequent actions showed little desire or ability to press home an attack. It was, however, irritating in the extreme, owing to the lack of artillery to be unable to deal with the German close support guns, which came into action in the open, outside the range of the LMG and 3" mortar.

At about 1800 I ordered the KOYLI to occupy the position south of Dombaas, which had been recced in the morning. The plan for the night withdrawal is worth considering in some detail, because it was the first of a serious of precarious operations, where the balance between success and disaster was extremely slender. Otta is some 25 miles from Dombaas where lay the next secure base, the KOYLI. The only means of transport available were the trains and a very limited amount of MT, both of which had to be wheedled out of the Norwegians. There was only a limited amount of MT available which was allotted to the rear parties. The train was assembled at Dombaas and the transport at Dovre with a staff officer in charge of each. Both started about 2000. The train ran forward to Ruditj and the MT to Forma, both of which were close behind the front line. At about 2030 the fighting slackened on the whole front and the withdrawal started about 2300, the troops falling steadily back on the train and MT column.

The train left Ruditj about 0230 and the troops detrained into assembly areas at Dombaas between 0500 and 0600, where they were covered by 1st KOYLI in position, south of Dombaas. Demolitions at Rosta and Dovre were blown after the rear parties had crossed the bridges. The breakaway was clean and the fact that the enemy made no immediate attempt to follow it up was undoubtedly due to the reverse he had suffered during the afternoon.

I should here mention the value of the Norwegian ski troops operating on my flanks. They were my only means of flank protection and were of great value in guarding against surprise. During the night 28th/29th many Norwegian troops were withdrawn from my L of C and I found myself faced with the possibility of having no troops between Dombaas and the base of Åndalsnes some 60 miles away. The obvious danger was the possible use by the enemy of parachute detachments, which might land on my L of C. I therefore disposed Brigadier Morgan's force in detachments at Lesje, Lesjeverk, Lesjeskogen and Verma, with as much MT per detachment as he could raise.

29th April. During the night 28th/29th April Force HQ moved to Botheim. I made an early recce of the Dombaas position and found the KOYLI well established, with the Green Howards and Y&L just assembling in the woods after their train withdrawal. On my return to my HQ I met General Ruge and a staff officer who breakfasted with us. The former was as helpful as usual, but pointed out that he could not withdraw his Poidal detachment until the night 29th/30th. There could thus be no question of our withdrawal from Dombaas until 30th/1st. This meant that the enemy had 48 hours to follow us up Otta and that therefore we might have to fight on the Dombaas position. General Ruge offered me the support of a Norwegian field battery of four guns which I gratefully accepted. These guns were later to prove most useful.

A representative from the War Office was due to arrive at my HQ during the day with a complete plan for evacuation. I arranged with General Ruge that I should visit his HQ later to explain this plan. The enemy was very active all day in the air, bombing and machine gunning all movement on the L of C. It was the habit of his bombers to fly direct to their objective, drop their bombs at the most convenient height and then pass the time of day on their way home by low flying MG attacks on the road traffic. About noon Lieutenant Colonel Clarke arrived with the plan from the War Office. Briefly it was:–

Night 29th/30th ship capacity 1,000 – 1,500
30th/1st ship capacity 2,200
1st/2nd ship capacity remainder

I accordingly planned to withdraw 1st Y&L from Dombaas and send them with base details 29th/30th. All the forward troops night 30th/1st and any remaining night 1st/2nd. I took this plan over to the Norwegian GHQ where the necessary details were arranged. I ordered a conference of unit commanders at 15th Infantry Brigade HQ at 0600 tomorrow 30th April.

During night 29th/30th April the Norwegian detachment at Hjerkin and Foldal withdrew through our forces at Dombaas. These were the last Norwegian troops in my area for the covering of whose withdrawal I was responsible.

30th April. 0600 conference HQ 15th Infantry Brigade Dombaas. The following outline plan for withdrawal night 30th/1st was settled:-

(a) Night 30th April/1st May 15th Infantry Brigade and all troops (less 1st Y&L) will withdraw from present positions through Royal Marines (covering Åndalsnes) and embark.

(b) The following are approximate strengths:-

HQ Sickle Force 40
1st KOYLI 500
1st Green Howards 500
Anti-Tank Company 80
Sections 55th Field Company RE 100
168th LAA Battery RA 65

HQ 15th Infantry Brigade 60
Signals 15th Infantry Brigade 40
Morgan's Force 400
Total 1,775
(c) Transport by MT

Leave Dombaas 2030 55th Field Company RE, HQ 15th Infantry Brigade and Signal Section and rear parties KOYLI and Green Howards.

By train. Leave Dombaas 2130 KOYLI and Green Howards (less rear parties), Anti-Tank Company and details RA and RE.

There was a generally quiet air of confidence about this conference and it was evident that the day's rest at Dombaas had allowed the troops to recover and the morale was good. The train conveying the Y&L to Åndalsnes night 29th/30th only reached Lesjeskogen owing to a break in the line. There was no train available to take them on from the other side of the break to Åndalsnes, so they marched on.

Enemy recce aircraft and bombers were active, but no other special incident occurred during the day until 1530 when 15th Infantry Brigade reported that the enemy could be seen advancing up the valley from Dovre. The early reports were conflicting, one mentioned four battalions, another parachute troops and a third transport. The force was probably the usual recce detachment, possibly reinforced by MG and mortar detachments landed by parachute. This contact, though not unexpected, was undesirably early. There were some 5 to 6 hours of daylight left and it seemed possible for the enemy to stage an attack on the KOYLI from which it might be difficult to extricate them.

It was interesting to watch the situation develop. The KOYLI were extremely well driven; it is probable that the Germans were surprised to find them there at all and they must have been even more surprised when the Norwegian guns opened fire on their forward positions. Lieutenant Colonel Cass commanding 1st KOYLI had made a very wise decision earlier in the day to withdraw his right hand company across the river, as the water level had risen considerably making the river unfordable for the withdrawal. When later the Germans made contact, they were forced to use rubber boats to attempt the crossing. These were all destroyed and their crews knocked out.

The enemy's forward troops were supported by a close recce aircraft, which dropped bombs and flares on likely targets. Fortunately this aircraft was shot down by our troops early in the engagement and thus the Norwegian battery was able to fire unmolested. About 1800 Brigadier Kent-Lemon sent a most reassuring message to the effect that he was confident he could hold the enemy and that he was adopting an aggressive attitude. The train was assembled in the Dombaas tunnel, wherein it lay all day. This tunnel was indeed providential throughout the operations. It housed trains, rations, ammunition, stores and was a secure refuge for the Norwegian station staff without whose loyal help the system could not have been maintained. During the afternoon it was discovered that owing to a misunderstanding Brigadier Morgan had withdrawn his anti-parachute detachments. This might have had serious results as all Norwegian troops had also been withdrawn from this area. I therefore withdrew the Anti-Tank Company (now minus their guns) to occupy Lesje against parachute attack and for a possible attack and for a possible threat by German ski troops using the Vagano-Lesje road. Throughout the day there had been considerable doubt as to whether the line was clear to Åndalsnes, but by 1700 it was reported in working order and the withdrawal started according to plan. The train started a little late, but both it and the rear parties in MT got away well and the road and railway demolitions west of Dombaas were blown. The train stopped at Lesje to pick up the Anti-Tank Company and 300 Norwegian infantry – the last Norwegian troops to be withdrawn.

I moved my HQ back by MT and tried en route by telephone to find out the progress of the train. This I was unable to do until I reached Verma some 19 miles from Åndalsnes. This meant that the troops would have a 17 mile march to the nearest shelter which was in the tunnel at Verma.

I sent a staff officer to get the Marines up from Romsdalshorn to cover the Verma gorge and to get as much transport forward as he could to help the troops in their journey from Lesjeskogen to Verma. On my return to Lesjeskogen I found that the train had been wrecked by a bomb crater. Both engines had overturned, the front coach had telescoped and there were a good many casualties.

1st May. At 0100 the troops set out on their long march – rather a desperate effort after the Dombaas battle, train journey and crash. It was, of course, too much to hope that they would gain the security of the Verma tunnel before the early enemy air patrols were active; but I was anxious that as many as possible should have crossed the open Lesjeskogen plateau and have reached the comparative security of the Verma gorge. The Marines came up about 0530 and established a road block near the scene of the train wreck which they held till 1000, subsequently withdrawing to cover the first of a series of demolitions arranged in the Verma gorge. With the aid of some MT all the troops were in the tunnel by 0900 but their destination had been spotted by the enemy aircraft and many parties had been subjected to low flying attacks on their way back.

The tunnel merits description. In it was a loaded ammunition train; the train which was our only means of reaching Åndalsnes, and our 1,500 troops who were packed like sardines and filled the tunnel completely. The tunnel itself ran through the side of a hill and was bomb proof.

Throughout the morning the men slept, disturbed occasionally by bombing and low flying MG attacks on the entrance to the tunnel. In the afternoon they began to recover and their spirits were remarkably high. Apart from any wishful thinking I consider that this was a remarkable recovery proving once again the high powers of endurance of the British soldier.

I held a conference at 1600 and issued my orders for withdrawal to Åndalsnes. The train was to start at 2230 and the rear parties by MT at 2300. At about 1730 the engine in the tunnel began to get up steam and the tunnel filled with an impenetrable and choky smoke. I was forced to get the men out of the tunnel and accept the risk of their detection. They behaved very steadily and went quickly outside to disperse.

At about 1800 a message came in reporting that the Marines at the head of the gorge had broken and the enemy had made contact in some strength.

Both the KOYLI and the Green Howards deployed immediately and the former sent forward one company 2,000 yards up the gorge to reinforce the platoon of the Green Howards. I asked the Norwegian station master to get the train ready as soon as possible.

He estimated that it would be ready by 2000. Success or failure now depended on the loyalty and goodwill of the Norwegian railwaymen. As a precaution the engine driver was placed under an armed guard. There was no doubt that the troops, tired as they were, could hold off the enemy; but I did not want the withdrawal to be interfered with as the train ran forward up the valley for about half a mile before turning north to Åndalsnes.

At 2030 the train was ready and the troops started to entrain. They were very steady and the whole entraining was quickly carried out covered once more by the rear parties whose MT was waiting on the road below. Just before we left Colonel Beichmann, our Norwegian liaison officer came up from Åndalsnes to say goodbye. This action was typical of him; he had proved wholly loyal and reliable throughout. My only remaining anxiety was the security of the 300 Norwegian infantry who had entrained at Lesje. Transport had gone up to Lesjeskogen to evacuate them early in the morning but their subsequent return was not confirmed. The train journey was without further incident and the troops arrived on the quay at Åndalsnes about 2300 to embark. They were taken on board HMS *Birmingham*, HMS *Manchester* and HMS *Calcutta*, while HMS *Auckland* remained for the rear parties who were all on board by 0200.

Åndalsnes had been bombed earlier in the evening, but the actual embarkation was carried out unmolested and once again we have to thank the Royal Navy for rescuing us from a precarious situation as they did 25 years ago.

Conclusion.

That it was possible to withdraw my force over a distance of 100 miles under the conditions which I have described, to fight five rear guard actions and finally to re-embark without enemy interference was due primarily to the skilled and determined leadership of subordinate commanders, notably Brigadier Kent-Lemon, commanding 15th Infantry Brigade, Lieutenant Colonel Cass commanding 1st KOYLI and Lieutenant Colonel Robinson, commanding 1st Green Howards, and to the endurance, discipline and fighting qualities of the troops engaged; also to the fine work of the Royal Engineers in the destruction of communications which successfully delayed the enemy for the required period.

Appendix T

Sickle Force in the Norwegian Campaign

Major-General Paget, who had overall command of British forces in central Norway, made the following comments, now retained in the National Archives, on Sickle Force's role in the Norwegian campaign:

I am not in a position to pass judgement on recent operations in Norway as a whole and I do not presume to do so. My conclusions are therefore based only on the operations of Sickle Force:

(a) The first point I have to make is one which is constantly emphasised in our peace time training, namely the importance of adhering to normal organisation and method as far as possible, and to the system of training which we have practised in peace. Sickle Force was far from being a normal organisation, presumably this arose from the urgency for sending speedy reinforcements to Norway. But I suggest that there might have been more foresight in appreciating the situation at the War Office as a result of which it would have been anticipated that intervention in Scandinavia at short notice might be necessary and plans made accordingly.

As regards applying in war the lessons we learn in peace, the conclusion reached at every exercise in combined operations is that this type of operation is only practicable given some measure of air superiority. This lesson seems to have been ignored. The same applies to preliminary reconnaissance of the base area and to careful appreciation of the administrative problem. In the War Office on the Saturday before I left for Norway, the Deputy Quartermaster General, Thomas Riddell-Webster, stated that he was prepared to take a chance that three infantry brigades could be sustained through the port of Åndalsnes. I do not know the assumptions on which he made this statement but the facts proved that there was no such chance, and these facts should have been ascertained before Sickle Force was disembarked. Similarly there should have been preliminary reconnaissance for AA [anti-aircraft] protection, the importance of which is always emphasised in our peacetime training. Such reconnaissance would have shown that the configuration of the base area rendered effective AA defence practicably impossible.

(b) My next point concerns air action, and in this respect I consider that though the operations in Norway were in many ways abnormal, they give us a clear indication of the decisive effect of the air arm in relation to land operations. I feel strongly that unless this fact is appreciated we may not win the war. The effect of enemy air action on the base area, L of C (Lines of Communication) and in the forward area was tremendous. The morale effect of heavy bombing which is cumulative, is a serious factor and produces a deadening effect on the mental processes. Troops in the forward areas did not suffer so much as the personnel at the base, but even so the former were at times considerably shaken especially as they were prevented on occasions from digging in owing to repeated attacks from the air to which there was no adequate reply. The counter bombing of enemy aerodromes is not enough and, if the morale of the troops is to be maintained and they are to be given a fair chance, there must be close co-operation between the ground and the air, as practised so efficiently by the Germans.

Air action also very much affects the organisation of HQ and the exercise of command. Concealment of HQ by every possible means, is of course, of primary importance and the discipline for this required to be strictly applied as a skill. Concealment is also a matter of the cover available; this will often be limited, as it was in Norway, to a few farm buildings, and the size of the HQ must be adjusted accordingly. Also an alternative site for HQ should always be reconnoitred and prepared. As regards the size of HQ it is not possible to lay any definite rules but the number of clerks and orderlies can be much reduced, if staff trained liaison officers are available; and I found that under the conditions of Sickle Force operations such liaison officers were by far the best and most economical means of exercising command when events are moving rapidly.

(c) Finally as the result of my experience in these operations I would say that our peace time training has been broadly speaking on sound lines, and in particular I have no qualms of conscience about the work of the Staff College. An outstanding lesson is the need to apply in the field what we have practised in peace, to foresee events by means of careful appreciation of possibilities and probabilities and thus to go a long way towards the avoidance of 'ad hoc' plans and improvisations.

Summary.

My considered view in the light of experience remains that which I expressed to the DQMG before I embarked. It is that the possibility of maintaining any force through the single port of Åndalsnes depended primarily upon whether or not local air superiority could be established and maintained. To that view I would add that, since the necessary degree of air superiority could scarcely be expected to exist throughout the whole length of the line of communication, and since that line was particularly vulnerable to both air action and to seasonal changes, the Åndalsnes project was not administratively practicable. Operationally, therefore, it was doomed to failure.

In conclusion I would suggest that, if in the future a similar military gamble becomes politically necessary, the task should be entrusted to a complete regular formation the composition of which has not been subject to recent changes. This is particularly important for headquarter units. The force I have had the honour to command has done magnificently. It contained a highly trained and admirably led regular infantry brigade, but the force as a whole was extemporised. Work of this type is difficult and arduous calling for a standard of team work which is not to be expected in a hastily assembled formation.

Appendix U

Report from Hansard – Debate in the House of Commons on 28 January 1999 regarding the Sinking of HMS *Glorious*

Mr. A.J. Beith (Berwick-upon-Tweed)
On the afternoon of 8th June 1940, two German battle cruisers, *Scharnhorst* and *Gneisenau*, sighted a wisp of smoke on the arctic horizon. Two hours later, the carrier HMS *Glorious* and her two escorting destroyers, *Ardent* and *Acasta*, had been sunk. More than 1,500 lives were lost, qualifying the incident as one of the worst naval disasters of the Second World War.

I have no direct personal link with the tragedy, but some of my constituents do. A cousin of mine was close by, serving as a rating in the escort party to the Norwegian royal family and the diplomatic corps as they embarked for evacuation on HMS *Devonshire*, which features in the story that I am about to unfold. He was never able to tell me about these events, because he was lost with almost the entire complement of HMS *Hood* a year later, another tragedy with a similarly massive loss of life.

My constituent Mr. Sam Farrington lost his brother, who was only 17 when he went down with the *Glorious*. Another constituent of mine was Captain Nick Barker, who died not long after retiring to Northumberland. He famously commanded HMS *Endurance* at the time of the Falklands war. He lost his father, Lieutenant-Commander Ben Barker, who was in command of HMS *Ardent*. Nick's son produced a television programme about the event, which appeared in the 'Secret History' series on Channel 4.

Those family members, and others, have written to me from all over the country, and they have convinced me that the official history of the tragedy needs to be revised to take account of what has subsequently come to light.

For many years, those people have been deeply troubled by the belief that the loss of their loved ones has not been properly explained. No one is looking, after all these years, for blame or retribution, but where a supreme sacrifice has been made on such a scale, the record should surely be as accurate as possible. An unconvincing explanation produced in conditions of war should no longer be given unchallenged official approval.

The families have aroused the interest of several hon. Members. The hon. Member for Linlithgow (Mr Dalyell), who is here, my hon. Friend the Member for Winchester (Mr Oaten) and the hon. Member for East Londonderry (Mr Ross) have all spoken or written to me. The Admiralty, and now the Ministry of Defence, always maintained that the sinkings were merely an unfortunate accident of war. A significant number of naval historians continue to suggest what the few survivors and the relatives have long suspected – that a catalogue of errors and misjudgements culminated in the tragic events of that afternoon.

On 8th June, HMS *Glorious* and its two escorting destroyers were heading for Scapa Flow, having left the coast of northern Norway that morning. At about 4 o'clock, two German battle cruisers were spotted on the starboard horizon. Unable to launch its protective aircraft into the wind without turning straight towards the enemy, *Glorious* sent out her first radio signal at 1615, fired up the boilers, which had been shut down, and slowly increased to full speed in an attempt to run to the south east.

Shortly afterwards, one of the battle cruisers opened fire with terrifying accuracy. Following several direct hits, the order to abandon ship was eventually given at about 1720. *Ardent* was sunk at 1728, and at 1808 *Acasta* joined her. The bravery of the men of the doomed destroyers was later vividly praised by German crew members from the *Scharnhorst*. In the programme, one was quoted as saying: "Our flags flew at half mast and the whole bridge stood to attention because of the courage of the English sailors." Only 41 survivors were picked up after two days in the icy waters.

Two Members of Parliament who suspected that the sinkings might not have been only another tragic accident of war first expressed disquiet about the explanation for what had happened in this House in the summer of 1940. In 1946, when morale and security were no longer paramount with the war over, Labour MP Richard Stokes asked the First Lord of the Admiralty "when the promised report on the loss of HMS Glorious and her attendant destroyers will be published (Official Report, 8th May 1946; Vol. 422, c. 1050)." Pressure was growing in the Admiralty for a full inquiry into the sinking, but in a memorandum that came to light many years later, R. Powell, head of the military branch, advised strongly against a detailed investigation. He wrote: "A full report at this date would make very dismal reading and would invite Mr. Stokes or other MPs to ask why this or that was not done." We are still asking those questions 60 years later.

The official account given by the Admiralty in Hansard on 8th May 1946 has remained almost unaltered to this day. It has frequently been criticised by naval historians and some naval officers for raising opinion and conjecture to the level of fact and for failing to give an adequate explanation of the main areas of controversy.

Why was *Glorious* returning home independently of the main convoy? Why was she so badly prepared? Why was her air power not used even for reconnaissance? Was there not sufficient intelligence about German activity in the region to suggest that *Glorious* should have been in a much greater state of readiness? Could HMS *Devonshire* have helped the stricken vessel or did its commander have no idea of what was happening?

Mr. Tam Dalyell (Linlithgow)
I welcome profoundly the fact that the right hon. Gentleman has raised this matter. If they still exist, should not the orders of the Commander-in-Chief of the Home Fleet be made available? That would be important, because the film put the captain in a bad light. I wonder whether that is fair.

Mr. Beith
Those are among the records that should be readily available to the naval historical branch. The point can be pursued after the debate.

The list of those who cast doubt on the explanation of the Admiralty and the MOD is distinguished. It is headed by the First Sea Lord of the day, Admiral of the Fleet Sir Dudley Pound, who in 1940 questioned whether *Glorious* was suitably prepared for such an encounter. Aware from survivors that she had no reconnaissance aircraft aloft, no aircraft ready on deck, and no proper lookouts, and that her crew were at only the fourth level of readiness, he wrote in an Admiralty file: "Glorious seems to have forgotten that she was a Man o' War" – a comment that hardly sits comfortably with the official explanation that the disaster was due to a series of misfortunes rather than errors. A naval historian later wrote: "An aircraft carrier not operating her aircraft is one of the most helpless things afloat." In 1948, in his history of the Second World War, Winston Churchill expressed his doubts about the reason given for HMS *Glorious* leaving the relative safety of a convoy of ships to head home independently. The official reason, still expressed today, is that the ship needed to return to Britain because she was running low on fuel. Churchill wrote: "This explanation is not convincing. The *Glorious* presumably had enough fuel to steam at the speed of the convoy." In 1970, Captain Roskill, who had earlier written the Navy's official and authoritative war history, expressed his view about why *Glorious* left the convoy. Following preliminary research, he wrote a letter to a senior member of the staff at the Royal Naval Staff College at Greenwich and said: "the shortage of fuel theory is bunkum." Ten years later and after much more detailed work, he took the debate further in a long article that appeared in *The Times*. He stated: "The answer is distressing. The Admiralty has tried to suppress the truth for 40 years, but it looks as though 1,515 men were killed partly as a result of a whole chain of Admiralty errors."

The MOD's naval historical branch, apparently unaware that Roskill had changed his mind about what happened, used his official war history as recently as 1997 to support its theory that a lack of fuel was fundamental to *Glorious*'s decision to depart from Norway. There has never been supporting evidence that fuel was the reason for *Glorious*'s independent return from Norway. The arithmetic of *Glorious*'s ton-mile figures would seem to torpedo the MOD's certainty. Furthermore, if a ship is low on fuel – as *Glorious* was, with up to a third of her boilers shut down – she cannot raise full power and speed in an emergency. She was a lightly armed and thinly armoured Second World War carrier, but she should not have proceeded independently. Had she remained under the protection of other warships, she would have been steaming at convoy speed, which would have consumed less fuel.

The truth may lie in a different direction. HMS *Glorious* may well have become detached from the greater safety of the convoy because of a serious breakdown in relations among her senior officers. She was an unhappy ship. Her commander, D'Oyly-Hughes, was a brave and distinguished veteran of submarine warfare in the 1914–18 war, but he seems to have been unsuited to commanding a carrier. He was ill at ease with the role of air power at sea and seemed unable to work with officers experienced in, and responsible for, air operations from his ship. Tensions ran high. After a major dispute he put ashore his Commander, Flying, J.B. Heath, and was preparing to court martial both Heath and

Lieutenant-Commander Slessor. Lieutenant-Commander Slessor had written a despairing letter to his wife saying, "JB and I are in great trouble. I can't tell you the story but you'll guess the cause of it. It was bound to come sooner or later I suppose, and perhaps it's a good thing. I needn't tell where right lies, nor that my conscience is absolutely clear, but we do need your thoughts and prayers very much." That was a message from a man serving on a very unhappy ship.

Lieutenant-Commander Slessor perished in the sinking. Commander Heath was cleared of all charges and continued his distinguished service in other sectors, finishing as Commanding Officer of HMS *Heron* at Yeovilton.

In 1968, Commander Le Geyt, one-time captain of the destroyer *Diana*, wrote in an Admiralty file that he had seen *Glorious* send a long signal by lamp to her Admiral in *Ark Royal* asking permission "to part company and proceed ahead to Scapa Flow for the purposes of making preparations for the impending courts martial." Why would that signal have been sent if fuel was really the reason for *Glorious* to leave the convoy? D'Oyly-Hughes' known state of mind and the implausibility of the fuel theory lend credibility to the alternative explanation.

In 1978, Sir Harry Hinsley, an historian and vice-chancellor of Cambridge University, wrote the official story of British intelligence in World War Two. He states that, during the 10 days prior to the *Glorious* sinking, Bletchley Park – where, as a young man, he analysed German naval wireless traffic – repeatedly informed the Admiralty that analysis of the traffic indicated that German "main units" were likely to emerge from the Baltic and proceed to Norwegian waters. He tells how that intelligence was ignored and consequently, in his words: "The *Glorious* was caught unprepared." In attempting to counter Sir Harry, the MOD's naval historical branch drew attention to what it felt was an inconsistency between his more recent comments and those found in his official history. The NHB pointed to a sentence in that history which reads: "It is not difficult to understand the Admiralty's scepticism. Traffic Analysis was an untested technique and one that yielded only broad and inferential clues." What the MOD did not draw attention to was Sir Harry's very next sentence, which reads: "But … although the evidence of Traffic Analysis was unsupported by other indications, the (Navy's) Operational Intelligence Office had no good reason for resisting Bletchley Park's suggestion that it should at least issue a qualified warning to the Fleet." That differs sharply from the MOD's 1997 comment paper, called 'Points of Controversy', which asserts: "There was no indication from any source that a powerful German squadron was preparing for a sortie." That statement is wrong. At this point, we are not arguing about alternative theories; it is a matter of fact, and the comment paper should be corrected on that point. In a letter written shortly before he died last year, Sir Harry wrote: "The Admiralty later realised that it had made a mistake." Indeed, it was his view that lessons were learnt from the mistake and that much greater attention was given to the results of traffic analysis thereafter, with considerable benefit gained.

What of events surrounding the incident itself? *Glorious* sent several signals during the engagement, but the MOD has claimed that, although the nearby HMS *Devonshire* did pick up one of those signals, it was "garbled", "corrupt" and "almost unintelligible". The *Devonshire* was under instructions to maintain radio silence. On board were the King of Norway and the Norwegian Cabinet, so there are legitimate questions as to what she could have done to help the stricken vessel. However, that radio silence was broken 12 hours later, when *Devonshire* checked on an expected escort. More important is that five members of *Devonshire*'s crew have testified that the signals from *Glorious* were far from unintelligible. Despite differing in the detail, all five were adamant that the signal was sufficiently clear to cause considerable consternation on *Devonshire*'s bridge.

At 1625, *Devonshire*'s log states, "Exercised main armament" – the first time that all her 8 inch turrets had been exercised in more than a month, and at almost the same time as a petty officer on *Devonshire* claims that he received an audible signal from *Glorious*. To man all one's 8 inch guns is indicative of a perceived surface threat, as they are not much use against aeroplanes. The official explanation for the exercising of the main armaments has been that it was coincidental to the time of *Glorious* signals. That seems too much of a coincidence.

Similarly odd is that, during her passage of 1,300 miles, *Devonshire* travelled at almost top speed only once. That occurred within four minutes of *Glorious* last signal at 1719, just before she was sunk, when *Devonshire*'s log states "Increased to 30 knots", which was probably her maximum speed, and for seven minutes "Negative zig-zag". That speed was held for two hours, until she reduced to 26 knots. Why did she accelerate if she found the signal "unintelligible" and – according to the Admiralty – did not even know where *Glorious* was? Would she not have feared that, by doing so, she was accelerating into danger? The MOD has suggested that the unusual behaviour demonstrated by *Devonshire* that afternoon was coincidental to *Glorious* signals, but it seems more likely that she gleaned sufficient information from a supposedly "almost unintelligible" signal to be worried about something.

Those who inquire of the MOD what actually happened that afternoon will be sent a paper called 'Points of Controversy'. The covering letter states that there is "sufficient collateral evidence received by this department from key participants to permit reasonable conclusions to be drawn and convincing explanations to be given for the sequence of events." I suggest that there are reasonable conclusions and convincing explanations – long advanced by respected naval historians – that are different from those advanced to this day by the MOD.

Two of the key participants in the covering letter were Fleet Air Arm squadron commanding officers in *Ark Royal*. One of them, Commander Casson, denies that he was involved in any way in any of the decisions or actions surrounding *Glorious*'s early departure for home or in the subsequent circumstances of her sinking. He was not even asked by the MOD if he could be cited as a key participant, and he expressed surprise when he found out that the MOD was using him as a supporting witness. Commander Casson's colleague was no closer to the seat of decision making that day. In short, while both may have valid contributions to make on Fleet Air Arm practice and procedures of the 1940s, neither was involved, directly or indirectly, in what happened.

One of the other key participants was Stanley Rogers, a telegraphist on *Devonshire*, who testifies that he heard nearly all of *Glorious*'s enemy report. The MOD, by contrast, claims that the signalman supports its contention that the signal was almost unintelligible. He wrote to the MOD in an effort to set the record straight. The recollections of another key participant, who was also a signalman, are also at variance with the MOD's account.

The covering letter sent by the MOD also states that official conclusions have been reached following "exhaustive analysis of all available records." It has subsequently become clear that that really means analysis of all official records – those held by the Admiralty. For example, it does not include the Roskill papers in the Churchill archives in Cambridge, which are a good source of information containing all of Roskill's research into the controversy.

As well as the First Sea Lord of the day, Winston Churchill, and later, the Navy's official war historian, there are other well-known naval historians such as John Winton, Julian Thompson and Correlli Barnett, who maintain that the official version lacks credibility.

Mr. John Burnett (Torridge and West Devon)
Is there any evidence, other than the hearsay evidence provided by the MOD connected with receipts of signals by *Devonshire*, that the signalling equipment in HMS *Glorious* was defective?

Mr. Beith
I know of no such evidence, although there is testimony as to the difficulty of reading some of the signals. However, there is strong evidence that they were far from unintelligible, both in the recollections that I have quoted and the fact that there appears to have been a response by *Devonshire* to what must have been worrying indications in those signals.

As I was saying, several well-known naval historians have cast doubt on the official version. They ask other questions that are too numerous to raise in a short debate. I cannot believe that the Ministry of Defence would suggest that it has, in its in-house naval historical branch, a monopoly of competent or credible naval historians, or that they are uniquely qualified to arrive at the true version of what happened.

I have great respect for the knowledge and diligence of those in the naval historical branch and the care that they have taken in responding to letters from me and in assisting Ministers to do so in the two years that I have been involved in the matter. However, they can be wrong or, as in this case, too zealous in defending conclusions reached in more difficult times with less information than we have now.

The sinking of HMS *Glorious* and her escort ships took place almost 60 years ago. Definitive conclusions may never be reached. All the surviving evidence is freely available, yet respected naval historians have consistently come to conclusions different from those of the MOD. The few remaining survivors and the relatives of those who were lost, many of whom have written to me, are entitled to an open and public recognition in the official account that there are other viable explanations for what happened.

It is perverse and harmful to go on defending an explanation in which hardly a knowledgeable person outside the Ministry of Defence believes. I hope that the Minister will tonight recognise the need to put the record straight as far as possible and, in doing so, to give the naval historical branch the brief to consider all relevant records, not just official records.

Mr. Tam Dalyell (Linlithgow)
The House owes a debt to the right hon. Member for Berwick-upon-Tweed (Mr. Beith) for raising this subject.

I shall explain my own locus in this matter, such as it is. As a child, I repeatedly saw *Glorious* in the Firth of Forth, because she was often based at Rosyth. My parents had friends on the ship. I recollect their extreme distress when it was sunk, since many of the crew who had been with the ship since 1938 or 1939 were on board.

I ought to declare two other loci. I was taught by the late and wonderful Sir Harry Hinsley, who talked about this matter. I used to go to see him, especially during the Falklands War and afterwards, in the master's lodge of St. John's College, Cambridge. That relationship lasted until he died. I was also a student friend of Tim Slessor who, along with Mr. Harrison, has done so much work on the film. I was very sorry for Captain D'Oyly-Hughes's daughter, who was obviously put in a very difficult position over the film, and naturally came to her father's defence.

I should like to put gently – it is very difficult to be wise after the event – a point made by Tim Slessor, which I have given in writing to the Minister and his advisers: "The MOD tries to have it both ways. In the Under Secretary's letters, it claims to have nothing stronger than 'reasonable conclusions' and 'convincing explanations'. In the MOD's 7-page paper 'HMS *Glorious* – Points of Controversy' it goes much further; it is firm and quite unequivocal in its assertions. For example, on the matter of intelligence available about likely German warship movements into Norwegian waters, the MOD paper claims: 'there was no indication from any source that a powerful German squadron was preparing to sortie, let alone that one had been at sea since 4th June'. This is in direct contradiction to the Official History of British Intelligence (HMSO 1978 – page 141) by Sir Harry Hinsley: 'A fortnight before the German battle cruisers made their sortie, Bletchley Park began to report to the Admiralty that German main units were preparing to move from the Baltic northwards up the Norwegian coast ... The Admiralty had no good reason for resisting the suggestion that it should at least issue a qualified warning to the fleet ... *Glorious* was caught unprepared'. This is many miles from the MOD claim that 'There was no indication from any source'." I ought to add that I was also taught by the late Sir Frank Adcock, who was also a decryptor at Bletchley, and who had perfect knowledge of German, which he had studied in Berlin under Williamwitz Nöllendorf. Sir Frank later edited the 'Cambridge Ancient History'. In his discussions about Bletchley, Adcock again referred to hindsight. I never put Hinsley's and Adcock's accounts together, although Hinsley was sometimes given to exaggeration. I suspect that we cannot regard him as an absolute, definitive source in his recollection of what he did in his youth. If we are to talk of the distant past, we ought to be a little careful.

Slessor says: "Given that John Spellar's letter to Alan Beith (August 1997) specifically says 'I agree that if any one of these contentions (of which the above is just one) to which the Admiralty and the MOD have consistently adhered could be disproved, then [it] would justify public concern over the handling of the matter [the whole of the official account] from 1946 to the present day'." In a sense, there is a balance between Sir Harry Hinsley's work and that of the naval historical branch. I do not come to the conclusion that the naval historical branch is necessarily wrong, although the Minister's reply will be of very great interest.

The Parliamentary Under-Secretary of State for Defence (Mr. John Spellar)
I apologise to you, Mr. Deputy Speaker, and to hon. Members who have spoken and the rest of the House – although one term almost encapsulates the other – for the state of my voice. I hope that it lasts until the end of my speech.

I agree with my hon. Friend the Member for Linlithgow (Mr Dalyell) that we are grateful to the right hon. Member for Berwick-upon-Tweed (Mr Beith) for raising the issue of the loss of HMS *Glorious*, HMS *Ardent* and HMS *Acasta* off the coast of Norway on 8th June 1940. Several issues were raised on which I shall need to write to the right hon. Gentleman, but I hope to reply to him on other issues during the debate.

As we all agree, the tragic loss of the *Glorious* was one of the greatest disasters suffered by the Royal Navy during the Second World War. I am sure that hon. Members would wish to join me in expressing sympathy to the families and loved ones of those lost.

Over the years since the loss of the *Glorious* and her escorts, Members of the House have understandably expressed concern over the circumstances surrounding their loss. It is a sensitive issue. It is of genuine interest to the House, and interest has been revived by the recent showing and repeat of the Channel 4 documentary 'Secret History' – mentioned by the right hon. Member for Berwick-upon-Tweed – about this episode. It may help if I expand further on the background that the right hon. Gentleman has provided.

The evacuation from Norway, in May 1940, took place at one of the blackest and most confused periods of the war. At that time, the German Army had invaded France. British forces, including the Royal Navy, were heavily involved in these operations, which culminated in the fall of France and the evacuation of the British Expeditionary Force from mainland Europe. Moreover, Italy had just entered the war on the side of the Axis powers and, understandably, the risk of a German invasion was regarded as a serious threat.

The aircraft carriers *Ark Royal* and *Glorious* had sailed from Scapa Flow for Narvik, in Norway, on 31st May. *Ark Royal* was tasked with providing fighter cover during the withdrawal from Norway. *Glorious* was tasked with the evacuation of RAF aircraft from Bardufoss in the north of Norway; those aircraft would be urgently required for the defence of the United Kingdom.

At 0300 on 8th June, having embarked the RAF Hurricanes and Gladiators, the *Glorious*, together with the destroyers *Ardent* and *Acasta* as anti-submarine escorts, set sail for Scapa Flow.

At about 16.00, *Glorious* sighted the mastheads of what we now know were the battle cruisers *Scharnhorst* and *Gneisenau*, which were on course to close on the *Glorious*. *Ardent* was ordered to investigate, and the *Glorious* altered course to the south. At the same time, orders were given to prepare a Swordfish reconnaissance aircraft, but it was too late, and none were airborne before the *Scharnhorst* opened fire at 1631, followed shortly after by the *Gneisenau*. As the right hon. Member for Berwick-upon-Tweed said, the order to abandon *Glorious* was given at 1720. At 1740 *Glorious* sank. The *Ardent* sank at about 1730. The *Acasta*, with great gallantry, continued to close with the enemy and succeeded in damaging the *Scharnhorst*, which was forced to return to Trondheim.

Understandably, and regrettably, no report of proceedings, or deck logs for May and June 1940 survived the loss of the *Glorious* – nor, tragically, did any officer or senior rating who was in a position to comment on navigation, operations or command decision making. Any reconstruction or analysis – I believe this would be common ground – is therefore wholly dependent on evidence given to the board of inquiry by relatively junior personnel, and external sources such as signals received during the period under review, the reports of other ships and naval authorities, and recollections of participants. In addition, we now have the unambiguous German records. Nevertheless, the picture is not complete. Inevitably, there are gaps, which cannot be filled, and that has understandably allowed room for speculation to grow about the circumstances of the loss of the vessels.

Over the years, several points of contention have been raised. I should like to make it clear that we believe that many of those arise entirely from genuine differences of interpretation. What is clear is that, when *Glorious* detached to return to Scapa Flow, she had already carried out the mission for which she had been despatched – the retrieval of the RAF fighters. She could make no further contribution to the safety of the evacuation convoys, which were the fleet's next main concern. It is also assumed that, after five days at sea off Norway, she had only sufficient fuel to return to base, allowing for the obligatory requirement to maintain a reserve of 33 per cent. The House may be interested to know that that figure has been increased to 60 per cent for today's royal naval vessels. That is not just because of problems with sludge at the bottom of fuel tanks, although that is a serious consideration.

[…]The need to maintain stability is another consideration. I asked exactly the questions that the right hon. Gentleman raised. Those are relevant technical matters, and I am satisfied with the answers.

The assumption has been challenged in recent years but there is no documentary evidence to support the attack on it. What is known is that *Glorious* had been at sea at considerable distance from base for six full days, and that her normal routine would have allowed her to remain at sea for only five days.

The right hon. Gentleman said that *Glorious* had to leave the convoy. At the time of her departure, the convoy had not formed, and if she had remained off the coast of Norway waiting for the convoy to form, fuel would certainly have been consumed and could have become an issue. In that event *Glorious* might not have had enough fuel to reach the United Kingdom and also to retain a prudent margin for emergencies.

Mr. Beith
Does the Minister know anyone outside the current MOD who believes that part of the theory, bearing in mind that the amount of fuel used on convoy passage at convoy speed would have been less than that required for the vessel to proceed with any hope of safety at a faster speed to make for home with only the destroyer escort?

Mr. Spellar
As I said, that would also have meant waiting for the convoy, and the possibilities had to be balanced. The question is whether the decisions were honestly made. We have to work on that assumption. There seem to be reasonable grounds for doing so. It is difficult at

this distance and with the lack of records, but the assumption seems reasonable, given standard working practice in the Navy at that time, so we should not lightly discard it.

For reasons that I have explained, it is still considered likely that lack of fuel was a consideration in the decision that *Glorious* should return to the UK, but it is not possible to state that as a definitive fact. We have agreed that. What I can say is that even if *Glorious* was low on fuel, she would have been capable of raising full power and speed in an emergency.

I shall deal with the question whether the Admiralty ignored intelligence warnings about naval activity in the area. Although the right hon. Gentleman draws from the late Professor Sir Harry Hinsley, he does not make it clear that the last warning to be circulated within the Admiralty related to German ships in Norwegian waters being associated with operations in the North Sea. A day later, the *Glorious* and the destroyers were sunk nearly 1,000 miles to the north of the North Sea.

In the letter that Sir Harry wrote shortly before he died last year, to which the right hon. Gentleman referred, Sir Harry speculated: "I think that the best evidence that the Admiralty later realised it had made a mistake in ignoring my warning lies in the fact that its relations with the Naval Section at Bletchley Park changed significantly after the disaster." That is an example of conjecture, but it may also have been selectively quoted fact.

My hon. Friend the Member for Linlithgow [Mr Dalyell] advised me that he had urgent travel arrangements and apologised to the House for the fact that he could not stay until the end of the debate. The quote from Sir Harry Hinsley's 'Official History of British Intelligence' compressed quotations that were expanded by the right hon. Member for Berwick-upon-Tweed – a page of text is compressed into a few lines. Among those phrases, into which comes a warning of a move from the Baltic into the Skagerrak, is a warning that ships in Norwegian waters may be associated with operations in the North sea.

I draw the attention of the House to the section which, as we heard, gives a balanced view. Sir Harry Hinsley stated that it was not difficult to understand the operational intelligence centre's scepticism that traffic analysis was an untested technique. However, as the right hon. Gentleman commented, Sir Harry stated later in the paragraph that the OIC had no good reason for resisting Bletchley's suggestion that it would issue a qualified warning. I would say to my hon. Friend the Member for Linlithgow that there is therefore a balance of judgment to be struck. We have to look at both sides, as did the official history.

Another main issue of speculation, which has been raised in the debate, has been the signals dispatched by *Glorious* and the role played by HMS *Devonshire*. It is known that *Glorious* sent two signals before it sank: the first, 'enemy report', at 1615 hours; the second, an 'amplifying report' at 1640 hours. There are no British records which record the receipt of the first signal. Receipt of the second signal is recorded. It is difficult to conceive that *Devonshire* would record receipt of the second signal and not the first. It is known that the first signal sent by *Glorious* was not received by any British vessel, although subsequent records have shown that the full text was recorded by the *Gneisenau*.

The text of the second 'amplifying signal' was recorded by *Devonshire* in the admiral's record as "My 16.15. 2P/B". The time of the signal was also given. Unlike the first signal, this signal did not give the position of *Glorious*, nor was it stated whether the sighting was made from the ship, or if it resulted from an air sortie.

That signal did not state that the ship was under attack. Records show that the quality of the signal was poor. I suggest that the content, which was discussed on the bridge, may have puzzled the hierarchy on *Devonshire*, but did not provide information which would give cause for *Devonshire* to break radio silence.

The right hon. Member for Berwick-upon-Tweed also raised the question of Captain D'Oyly-Hughes and the early departure. The official documentation on that subject consists of one note – by the Commander-in-Chief, Home Fleet – instructing the *Glorious* to proceed to Scapa Flow to conduct the court martial.

That does not automatically lead to the conclusion that Captain D'Oyly-Hughes was responsible for that decision, which had to be approved by Vice Admiral Wells. I was slightly concerned when the right hon. Gentleman questioned whether all the records were available. As far as I am aware – he should write to me if he has any information to the contrary – all the official records are available, including records from the Commander-in-Chief, Home Fleet.

The right hon. Gentleman also asked whether it was coincidence that the *Devonshire* exercised its main armament as *Glorious* was transmitting the 'enemy report'. I have looked into that as well, and I am advised that that would appear to be so. I understand that, traditionally, the Navy uses the period between 1600 and 1800 for what is known as evening quarters, to exercise the gun crews. It might also be worth noting that the cruiser was already at defence watches, with three out of four turrets manned.

The right hon. Gentleman also asked whether *Devonshire* would have manned its main armament, because of the prospect of an attack from the air rather than an attack from the sea. I am advised that the 8 inch guns of the County class cruisers were designed as dual-purpose weapons, for long-range use against aircraft as well as surface ships. The turrets enabled a 70-deg angle of elevation, and rapid rates of slew and elevation, for anti-aircraft use. In the absence of surface ships, German long-range reconnaissance aircraft were the expected threat to the west of Norway.

There are a number of alternative theories, and we could discuss them and their merits, but I am not sure that that would serve any great purpose. Many of these issues are inevitably matters of interpretation. We believe that there is a sound basis for the interpretation that the Ministry of Defence has put forward, drawn quite properly from departmental records, and supplemented, where appropriate, from personal recollections. The severe loss of life and lack of documentation means that there is no definitive record, and no one is qualified to arrive at a true version. I am satisfied, however, that all Admiralty records relating to the incident are in the public domain.

Mr. Beith

I think the Minister took to be from me a comment made by the hon. Member for Linlithgow (Mr Dalyell) about the availability of records. I have not questioned the availability of records.

May I discourage the Minister from going wholly into defensive mode? He has suggested that there is a considerable area for speculation and disagreement.

The nub of my case is this. The paper 'Points of Controversy' suggests that is so, but the text of the official report – which has, however, been slightly revised since it first appeared in Hansard in 1946 – does not.

It would greatly help the families concerned if the area of disagreement, or the potential alternative explanation, were aired more clearly in the document.

Mr. Spellar

We are satisfied that there has been no cover-up of these tragic events, and that the MOD's interpretation is soundly based. We are satisfied that it is the most likely explanation. As I have said, however, it is a question of interpretation – as we accept, honest interpretation – of different views. The problem is that there is no new evidence on which we can draw to resolve the differences.

I feel that those who criticise the MOD's interpretation of events should themselves accept that our conclusions have been honestly drawn and rigorously researched. We argued it all through, and also looked at new information, which, in some instances, led to a slight modification of our conclusions.

We provided the right hon. Gentleman with a detailed and, perhaps, complicated account of the incident in July 1997, which we believe will interest other Members. I shall arrange for it to be placed in the Library. Members who read the record of the debate will gain an impression of its nature, and of the reasons for the position taken by the MOD and the Naval Historical Branch: an honest position that has, I think, stood the test of time.

Appendix V

Lessons from the Campaign in Central Norway by Lieutenant-General Claude Auchinleck

Anti-aircraft defence.

AA defence cannot be provided from warships for any length of time owing to:-

(a) The strain on the crew.

(b) The high consumption of ammunition.

(c) The vulnerability of vessels as targets.

Consequently AA equipment must be among the first stores landed and must accompany the leading troops and not be landed afterwards.

Air Attacks.

These were carried out by the German Air Force at heights as low as 50 feet with both bombs and machine guns. Reconnaissance machines also used smoke flares to indicate our positions to the enemy artillery.

Casualties were not actually heavy though the morale effect was considerable.

Any movement on roads and railways was heavily attacked, even motorcycle despatch riders. Roads suffered considerably from cratering.

All bombs were continually attacked during daylight hours. Bombs of all sizes up to 1,000 kgs were used but though considerable material damage was done (including craters up to eight feet diameter) not many casualties were caused. Incendiary bombs (aluminium cylinders about one foot in length) caused considerable damage as in many places the water had failed and the earth was too hard to be used.

Raids varied in intensity and at their peak were carried out about fifteen to the hour. Raids were regular in timing, starting at about 0900 and finishing at 2030. Later raids by single planes took place with the assistance of fires started by incendiary bombs. It must be realised that German air operations were almost entirely unopposed. When opposed, bombing was carried out at a high altitude. Further, all roads were virtual bottlenecks. No movement is possible off the roads and yet, in spite of this, traffic was kept going. It is evident therefore that attacks on actual roads and railways are ineffective as compared with attacks on the troops and transports using those communications.

It is emphasised that the morale effect on the troops was far greater than the physical casualties incurred. The solution lies in the rapid construction of entrenchments for all personnel everywhere. Once these are in being, immunity from casualties will immediately have its effect and morale will be restored.

Enemy bombers appeared to be armoured against small arms fire but in certain cases Bofors guns inflicted casualties. Fighter opposition to enemy bombers could only be provided from aircraft carriers. These caused considerable damage to enemy formations and prevented them pressing home their attacks. Fighter support given by carrier-borne aircraft can never take the place of land-based aircraft. They can be invaluable during the initial landing but a land base must be established as early as possible, together with AA protection.

German AFVs.

The following AFVs were used by the Germans – medium and light tanks and armoured cars. Light tanks and armoured cars could in no sense stand against the Boys anti-tank rifle, but the medium tank was proof against it. The medium tank was not proof against the 25 mm anti-tank gun. Medium tanks worked in close co-operation with infantry who employed hand grenades freely. 148th Infantry Brigade was without its Anti-Tank Company and morale consequently suffered. Troops must never be divorced from their anti-tank weapons if there is any possibility of AFV attack.

Security Personnel.

Germany devotes great attention to Fifth Column activities. Consequently security personnel must be early in a theatre of operations to deal with spies, saboteurs etc. This is especially necessary in a country where the civil administration has largely broken down. As the civil telephone system was used, security personnel were particularly necessary to secure its unhampered working.

Concealment of HQs.

Owing to the shortage of personnel, all HQs were small and thus not easily identifiable. Where movement was seen, instant attacks were made. The lessons to be learnt are that HQs must be widely dispersed and that protection of some sort must be found for all branches of an HQ.

German parachute troops.

The roles of German parachute troops appear to be:-

(a) Seize and hold landing grounds for the arrival and disembarkation of airborne troops.
(b) To effect sabotage of vulnerable points and destruction of vital communications.

The normal height for dropping is 240–300 feet. Parachute troops were not used to such an extent in Norway as in Poland because of:

(a) Difficultly of finding suitable landing grounds.
(b) Lack of German settlements which could be used as rallying points.
(c) Difficulties of maintenance.

Communication.

Our forces were equipped with the following wireless sets – No. 11, No. 9 and 'Mission'. The 'Mission' set was lost early owing to a lack of transport. The other sets were very little used because:-

(a) Commanders were loath to give away their positions to German D/F sets.
(b) Climatic conditions and bombardment caused considerable interference.

Signals were also passed through HM ships and though this caused great delay, there is no record of a message failing to get through. The civil telephone system was considerably used and in spite of operating in a friendly country, the following lessons were learnt:-
(a) Operators and linesmen under a senior Signal Officer must be available among the first troops landed to keep an existing signal system in order.
(b) There is no security in conversation and great care must be exercised. Owing to difficulties of unloading ships, cable and telephones were not available, consequently the few DRs available were badly overworked.

Liaison Officers did valuable work in replacing signal communications and were largely used both in the field and in carrying messages to and from England. It is stressed that Liaison Officers should be trained staff officers in the higher formations and should be specially trained in the lower formations to appreciate and interpret the picture to Commanders.

The main signal lessons are:-
(a) That full preparation must be made before hand including appointment of staffs and allotment of signal units.
(b) All units and formations must be accompanied by their signal equipment.
(c) Advance parties must be accompanied by their signal officers and a proportion of signallers.

Administrative Policy.
Lines of Communication parties must accompany the leading formations to investigate and organise the bases and Lines of Communication. Such personnel must be separate from the leading formations and must not be responsible for their maintenance.

Far too little consideration was given to the effects on administration by changes in operational plans. This led to considerable confusion in shipping programmes and resulted in units landing without their MT or MT being landed without their drivers. For instance at Åndalsnes there were no sandbags or shovels and at one time only 48 hours rations. Again at Namsos the only transport was 15 cwt trucks for which there were no drivers, so that unreliable Norwegians had to be employed.

Many administrative units never left the UK but were transferred to various ships and ports as operational plans were changed. No previous liaison with local authorities had taken place with the result that local facilities were late in being exploited and were never fully effective. A liaison organisation must in future be established in advance of disembarkation.

Second Echelon.
This operated from Margate and was too far from the scene of operations to function adequately. Consequently no accurate figure of strengths could ever be complied.

Miscellaneous.
The standard 3 ton lorry was unsuitable for use in Norway. The local truck is the light 1 or 2 ton American low-sided lorry.

Appendix W

Causes of the Failure in Norway, comments by Major-General Carton de Wiart

The following comments were made by Major-General Carton de Wiart in a summary of the causes of the operation in Norway's failure:

It is I think only fair to give a summary of the numerous other errors and omissions which contributed to the failure of the expedition apart from any question of enemy action:-
1. Apparently no appreciation or plan had ever been made in advance.
2. Plans as such were concocted from hour to hour without any first hand knowledge of the situation and without keeping the local commander on the spot informed. The commander was in fact committed to the course of an advance southwards from Namsos and left with the impression that a direct attack was to be made on Trondheim and then the troops for this operation were diverted elsewhere without any reference to the commander.
3. No situation reports of the progress of events on other fronts or of the general intentions of the commander at home were ever sent to this force or to the staff before joining up with the commander.
4. The troops selected for the operation were totally unfitted for such a campaign:-
(a) Battalions in 146th Brigade had not even completed any training.
(b) Many had hardly fired a rifle and very few really knew the Bren.
(c) Only a few demonstration rounds had been fired with the 3" mortar and their own mortars were only received a day or two before sailing.
(d) An excessive issue of clothing, three kit bags per man, which made the force virtually immobile unless a great deal of the clothing or a proportion of the arms and equipment was abandoned.
(e) None of our men could use or were equipped with snow shoes or skis and movement off the road was impossible.
5. 147th Infantry Brigade was loaded as for France, with only a small proportion of arms and equipment with units and the remainder loaded in the MT ships, while MT drivers were in a third ship.
6. Divisional HQ on the other hand had complete G1098 with it but no MT and no personnel to carry the very bulky cases etc.

7. The Light AA Battery were invaluable but were landed much too late, had no predictors with them and did not know identification signals of our aircraft and were never told that our planes were coming over on 1st May.
8. The Royal Marines 3.7" Howitzer Battery was quite untrained and had never fired a shot. Four howitzers were eventually landed, without any ammunition and except for drag ropes had no means of transportation.
9. For considerable periods the only means of communication between the Army and Navy was via the Admiralty – this was a very severe handicap and at one time rapid communication was vital.
10. Maps were very out of date, most difficult to read and only received when it [was] almost impossible to make a proper distribution.
11. Liaison Officer from the War Office arrived knowing nothing of the situation either in London or Norway. Only had a 1/1,000,000 map and did not know anything. Was definitely a hindrance and not a help.
12. If the GOC had not been an excellent French scholar, difficulty of working with the French forces would have been greatly increased. As detachments of French troops were often under British command at least one interpreter per battalion was required.
13. Only infantry brigade signals on a slightly increased establishment. Four despatch riders only available and two motor cycles soon broke down and could not be repaired. Units were many miles apart and considerable use had to be made of civil telephones without any real security measures.
14. The French had no WT and made extensive use of our signals and many of their messages had also to be put into our cypher.
15. It has always been considered a definite principle that during the early stages of a combined operation air superiority is desirable and that air parity is essential if there is to be any hope of continuing the campaign with success.
16. Our bombing of enemy airfields may have been very accurate and may have inflicted local losses but in actual fact had little or no effect on enemy activity. Trondheim may have been put out of action for a short time but 800 local labour workers very soon put it in order again.
17. On the other hand the arrival of our Fleet Air Arm fighters had a very considerable effect but all too short. On the first occasion we were warned of their arrival but on the second this was not done, the result being that our Bofors opened fire and very nearly shot one down.
18. In spite of our most urgent and pressing request no air assistance was given to us for the morning of the evacuation – it must have been perfectly clear after the PM's speech that the enemy would put in a big effort. In fact he put in the biggest effort of the war, 39 to 50 machines taking part and we can consider ourselves very lucky that our losses were only two destroyers.
19. It was most strange to us that the enemy made no late recce over Namsos or that his first recce on the morning of 3rd May was not earlier – as if caught in the fjord destruction of the convoy seemed certain. In this respect the enemy kept true to type, a fact we rather banked on, for his first recce was never earlier than 0330 and his latest 2030.

20. The enormous amount of trouble caused by the proposed Grong detachment and the withdrawal to Mosjöen, once again showing complete lack of appreciation of local conditions. The recce by Captain Lindsay proved the futility of the suggestion.
21. Lack of confidence in the Norwegians. They were of very little fighting value. They were continually sending in erroneous reports and wild rumours. Our difficulty in not being able to keep our promises or even to warn them of impending evacuation. The 7,000 rifles and SAA were never landed but we gave them 200 rifles and some 20,000 rounds of SAA just before we left.
22. We had no means of dealing with the local inhabitants, many of whom were most unreliable. We would very shortly have been faced with the problem of feeding those in the area.
23. Lack of suitable landing craft – we were told that any amount of small craft would be available, in actual fact there was none as the Norwegians removed practically all their small boats as soon as we appeared. Nothing could have been more unsuitable than setting out in a series of luxury liners. We wanted ships not exceeding 3 to 4,000 tons and lots of small craft and MLCs [Motor Landing Craft].
24. This was a campaign for which the book does not cater. Big frontages, great distances, a mixture of the North West Frontier, Palestine and Gallipoli with air the dominant feature.
25. French equipment was infinitely superior to ours – we cannot expect to have a Division or even a Brigade of mountain trained troops but any regular Battalions would have had a number of officers and men with experience of Palestine or NWF and would have been invaluable.
26. We should I think have a definite war establishment drawn up on a pack basis or a very reduced scale of MT, at present we are mechanised to immobility.

Finally I am forced to the sad conclusion that not only had the lessons we had learnt so dearly in Gallipoli, Salonika and Mesopotamia been forgotten but we now make even more mistakes of a most elementary nature.

Appendix X

Lessons and Deductions on Operations at Åndalsnes from 25 April to 2 May 1940 by Brigadier D. Hogg

Hogg commanded the garrison at Åndalsnes.

1. The Air Situation and its Consequences.
The Germans enjoyed marked – virtually undisputed – air superiority and were thus able to make our base unworkable. This made maintenance of the forward troops difficult, and their reinforcement impossible.

Had our base and L of C been comparatively secure from serious interference, we could have got ashore guns; transport, etc. and Paget could in all probability have given the Boche a good hiding.

2. Our Air Defences.
In the base area, the most we disposed of at any time was:-

1 3" HAA (+1 out of action)
5 Bofors LAA (40 mm)
6 Oerlikon LAA (20 mm)
2 Naval Vickers 2 pounder

To this the Royal Navy further contributed an AA ship, usually a sloop; but this invariably ran out of ammunition in half a day, so that more often than not we were without help. In addition, we had occasional sorties by Skuas of the Fleet Air Arm, but they usually arrived when the sky was empty – perhaps the Boche got wind of them and kept clear. The entry of the Gladiators – followed by their rapid destruction – was unfortunate.

It is a matter of conjecture what might have been the outcome had it been possible to operate a squadron of Hurricanes from a landing ground from the start. It is however clear that sea-based air defences (AA sloops and carrier aircraft) can only be a stop gap during the opening phase of a land operation, before the surprise element has completely disappeared, pending the organisation of land-based air defences, which alone can give security. The Germans had a system of land aerodromes within range. We had not. They won.

3. German Air Attack on the Base.
During the first three days the Boche only worried us between about 9 a.m. and 6 p.m. Later he extended these hours and towards the end he attacked about 10 p.m. and on one

night at intervals throughout the night. At first he seemed to direct his attack on the port area with very accurate high level bombing from as high as 17,000 feet at times. Later, he destroyed the greater part of the village of Åndalsnes which overlooks the quays and railway station, working gradually inland. On one morning, he set about the landing ground at Veblungsnes, bombing it from 6.30 a.m. to 1.30 p.m., the last three hours being practically continuous without a let-up. Towards the end he began to destroy the village of Veblungsnes, possibly with the idea that we might have moved across to there from Åndalsnes. Towards the end, also, when most of us had taken to the woods, he amused himself with ground strafing with machine guns, bombs and incendiary bombs. This is rather irritating.

I am not an expert in bombing techniques, but I append my views, as a layman, on what seemed to be his policy.

4. Heavy HE bombs.

Used for cratering communications; road and rail, cutting bridges, cratering aerodrome surface and attacking the quays and small craft alongside. He did not score a direct hit on a bridge, but one of his near misses completely blocked the road some two miles north of the port. The RE [Royal Engineers] restored a one-way crossing over the crater with a sleeper crib-pier.

He scored several craters on the railway, including a considerable number in the sidings of the station yard, two or three of which derailed railway wagons.

5. Light HE bombs.

Man-killing, overlapping with the uses in paragraph 4 above. I believe we had very few casualties from HE bombs, chiefly because it was rapidly found to be impracticable to work 'en masse', e.g. working parties in the port area, by day, and because everyone learned to take cover or at least to lie down whenever bombing was on.

6. Incendiary bombs.

These were most efficient, especially against the timber houses that are the rule. He seemed to favour laying a stick across the objective. In addition to destroying a vast number of houses, he burnt an important wooden jetty and a small steamer together with some ammunition and other stores which it had not been possible to clear from the port area. Certain dumps of stores which we had camouflaged among trees remained undetected and unharmed.

He also put incendiary bombs down on many of the woods where the dead leaves and wood caught fire and burned or smouldered. This was probably meant to deny us of their friendly shelter, but actually he got the wrong woods. On two occasions he fired houses near the port area in the evening in such a manner as to suggest that he was lighting a beacon for night bombing, but this did not materialise.

7. Ground Strafing.

As matters were, this was no more than a nuisance, but it might have got worse had our stay been much prolonged.

8. Main Effects of Bombing.

(a) Stoppage of port working and of the running of trains by day.

(b) Similar threat by night, if night bombing had been maintained.

(c) Interruption of rail and road communications by physical obstacles.

(d) Evacuation of civil population and consequent removal of all local labour. Deterrent to small local shipping craft.
(e) Destruction of accommodation for personnel and stores.
(f) Destruction of store dumps.
(g) Damage to personnel.
(h) Morale effect.
9. Morale and Discipline.
Whilst it is natural – and no cause for shame – for the ordinary man to admit to some fear when bombs are dropping, some degree of control of one's feelings is essential. I formed the impression that some of the very young men present (not only Army) were inclined to get out of hand. Quite a number disappeared into the hills – not unnaturally. But they failed to return when the party was over.

Similarly, men detailed for duty during the rather anxious period of embarkation disappeared. I have no doubt that they slipped into the queues of troops embarking in the dark. I fully appreciate their feelings.

But these things ought not to happen; and the answer is discipline, a discipline that can survive some of the trials of nerves that are inevitable in war.
10. The Assembling of the HQ of New Formations.
I think it needs to be borne in mind that the mere publication of an establishment, followed by the arrival of various bodies, does not constitute the formation of an efficient HQ. It takes time for them all to get to know each other, for the machinery to start to turn over, for standing orders and procedure to be got going.

Therefore, all these new HQs should be assembled well in advance of the contingencies for which they may be required. There is far too much delay in the production of these establishments. Minute financial arguments about a Staff Captain or a clerk may be a harmless diversion in peacetime, but they are out of place in war. The whole procedure of committees now in force is a positive menace. Any competent AAG [Assistant Adjutant General] can produce an establishment roughly adequate to the proposed functions. Adjustments can be made later.
11. Compo Ration Packs.
These are good and useful. On the other hand, more variety is needed. There are many excellent varieties of M&V (meat and vegetables) and there is no need to put all of one variety in one pack. Each pack should contain an assortment.
12. Security.
There was a strong feeling among most of us that the country was riddled with Boche agents. No proof – merely a feeling. I discount yarns of signalling lamps on hillsides. These were mostly due to smouldering vegetation set alight by incendiary bombs. On the other hand there were curious happenings. The day after I heard that it was mooted to send a Hurricane squadron to Veblungsnes, the Germans set out to destroy the landing ground. On the Tuesday evening, directly the first ship berthed to take off troops, a beacon went up on a peak above the port. Next night we put a piquet up on the peak. Was it a chance coincidence?

Among foreigners it is easy to camouflage Boche agents. There are to many of us only two races, namely Englishmen and foreigners. The latter can be recognised as they either do not speak English or speak it with an accent. What can we do to tighten this up, and to accelerate the retribution of the firing squad on the agent?

13. General Conclusions.

(a) The Boche has developed an excellent technique for giving the maximum air support to his land operations. We must do the same and better. I suggest that it is one of the possibilities that we may have to bomb our way into Germany in co-operation with an Army advance. Anyhow, our major offensives must be backed 100% by land-based aircraft, used ruthlessly.

(b) The Boche operations against Åndalsnes violated (I think) the rules of international law about danger to non-combatants. Nevertheless, common sense suggests that their operations were military justifiable. We have got to fight with the gloves off and the knuckle-dusters on. It is not Queensberry rules – it is 'all in'. Let us burn their crops before harvest, let us spread Colorado beetle on their potatoes, let us give them every form of hell we can devise. We are fighting for our lives and for the victory of right.

(c) The incendiary bomb needs exploiting and watching. How does the BEF protect its store depots? Are they safe?

(d) We have got to learn to wage 100% war. Among other things we must stimulate training and discipline and eliminate the hearsay that we can win this war without hard ruthless fighting.

Bibliography

The National Archives

War Diaries:

WO168/53 1st Battalion The King's Own Yorkshire Light Infantry
WO168/54 1st Battalion The York and Lancaster Regiment
WO168/55 1st Battalion The Green Howards
WO168/56 1st Battalion Scots Guards
WO168/57 1st Battalion Irish Guards
WO168/58 2nd Battalion The South Wales Borderers
WO168/59 4th Battalion The Royal Lincolnshire Regiment
WO168/60 The Hallamshire Battalion, The York and Lancaster Regiment
WO168/61 4th Battalion The King's Own Yorkshire Light Infantry
WO168/62 8th Battalion The Sherwood Foresters
WO168/63 5th Battalion The Royal Leicestershire Regiment
WO168/86 229th Field Company Royal Engineers

Other Reports at the National Archives:

CAB106/1168 Report from Major-General Mackesy
DEFE2/675 Report from Lieutenant-General Auchinleck
WO222/1480 Medical Services Norway report
ADM1/11658 Loss of HMS Glorious
ADM199/280 Interception and Boarding of German Auxiliary *Altmark*
CAB106/1161 Report by Lieutenant Colonel King-Salter
WO106/1904 Major-General Paget's report on Sickle Force
WO106/1938 Maurice Force Historical Statements
WO106/1889 Independent Companies in Norway
WO106/1905 Reports on Sickle Force

Imperial War Museum
Interviews at the Sound Archive Imperial War Museum:

Robert Brackenborough
Charles Cheshire
Charles Cox
Donald Creighton-Williams

Vernon Day
Albert Harris
Basil Keeble
Alistair Mackenzie
Ronald Mills
Frank North
Richard Partridge

Printed sources

T. Derry, *The Campaign in Norway*, HMSO, London 1952.
G. Haarr, *The German invasion of Norway: April 1940*, Seaforth, Barnsley 2009.
W. Hingston, *Never Give Up, a History of the KOYLI* volume 5, Lund-Humphries, London 1950
J. Kynoch, *Norway 1940: The Forgotten Fiasco*, Crowood Press, Marlborough 2002
F. Kersaudy, *Norway 1940*, Arrow Books, London 1990.
N. Macmillan, *The Royal Air Force in the World War. Volume 1, 1939-1940*, Harrap, London 1942.
W. Synge, *Story of the Green Howards 1939-1945*, Green Howards, Richmond 1952.

Internet sources

The HMS Cossack Association
Hansard
Uboat.net
WW2 talk

Index

Index of People

Index of Places

Index of Military Formations & Units

Index of Ships

Index of Miscellaneous & General Terms